Chris Notes!

A Set of Notes for Differential Calculus

Dr. Chris O'Neal

ISBN: 978-1-7346347-0-9

Table of Contents

Prologue

Welcome, and may I personally thank you for being so kind as to purchase these differential calculus notes. My main goal of writing them was to make the material in differential calculus classes easier to understand, as it can most certainly be a little confusing at times. Many students in high school and university need to take this class as a requirement for their future studies, and so I wanted to help make this leg of their journey a little easier.

I have written these notes with clear definitions and formulas, along with plenty of helpful examples illustrating how everything works. As much as possible, I have explained everything in simple terms so that the reader can easily follow along. If you are like me and learn best from examples and graphs and even mnemonics, then you will love this book. I don't focus on theoretical proofs in this book, although I will show you how certain formulas are derived. Instead, get ready for plenty of helpful examples that hopefully will be of great use for you.

The material in this book covers hopefully most or all of what you are expected to know in your differential calculus (sometimes called Calculus I) class. Of course, your instructor might add or remove certain topics, so please remember to use your own assigned textbook as required, and treat my notes as a helpful supplement. I am also currently working on my next book, which will focus on the next class, integral calculus. Since there's a lot of important material in both subjects, I thought it would be best to split it into two books.

Calculus is the sort of subject that not only has a lot of formulas to learn, but also at times requires a dose of creativity to set up and solve a problem. The best way to learn these procedures is to work plenty of examples and exercises. You will be amazed at how many times you'll need to draw upon some result from algebra, geometry, trigonometry, or pre-calculus to set up a calculus problem. In fact, it can truly be said that the majority of a calculus class isn't calculus but instead results from other math classes. To say that mathematics builds upon itself would be an understatement!

Depending on the nature of your class or the exam you will be taking, you may or may not be allowed to use a graphing calculator. I have structured most examples in this book to be worked out by hand since this is the best way to learn the material. However, I will occasionally show you some useful features of graphing calculators if you choose to use one. The calculator I used as a reference was a TI-84 (specifically the TI-84 Plus Silver Edition). Most graphing calculators have the same functions we'll discuss, although they might be in different locations.

The topics in this book are generally the ones you most likely will come across in your course. One section contains material that is not always taught in a calculus class, and that section contains an asterisk (*) next to the section name. Also, Chapter 4 contains material that is sometimes taught in differential calculus and sometimes is saved for integral calculus. You can either skip these sections, or you can read them anyway if you are up to the challenge! The appendices include a list of all the important formulas, TI-84 commands, the very important unit circle, and even the complete Greek alphabet (so it's all Greek to you!). There is even a Chapter 0 at the very beginning that covers basic material from other math classes that you need to know to do well in a calculus class. After all, should a Chapter 0 be surprising here, especially since this math book also has a prologue (and an epilogue!)? Textbooks sometimes contain an introduction, so why not call it a prologue instead?

A little bit about me – I have a PhD in statistics from the University of Georgia, and I work as a statistician for my main job. I am from England, and one of my favorite non-academic interests is nature photography (the book cover is one of my photos, and somewhere in this book you'll find a reference to it!) And I really hope you enjoy using these "Chris Notes!" as much as I enjoyed writing them, and that you find them very helpful and, dare I say, enjoyable, to completing this required class. If you bought this book on Amazon, please leave a review for me, and you can also follow me on Instagram (chris.notes.math) and on YouTube (ChrisNotesMath).

Cheers!

Chris O'Neal

Chapter 0 – Topics You Need to Know

Yes, Chapter 0! When is the last time you encountered a book with a Chapter 0? I am including this introductory chapter to remind you of some basic concepts that you have learned in earlier math classes, particularly algebra and pre-calculus. More results are in Appendices A – H in the back of this book, but the concepts that are most important for learning differential calculus are in this opening chapter. I'll also tell you a few useful calculator commands for the TI-84 graphing calculator.

Section 0.1 – Topics from Algebra

The following concepts are usually presented in algebra classes, so let's review them.

EQUATION OF A LINE THROUGH TWO POINTS

The formula for a line is $y = mx + b$ where m is the slope and b is the y-intercept. Given two points (x_1, y_1) and (x_2, y_2), the slope is computed as

$$m = \frac{y_2 - y_1}{x_2 - x_1}$$

The equation of the line is found using one of two techniques. Using the **point-slope formula**, pick one of the two points (say (x_1, y_1)) and solve the following formula for y:

$$y - y_1 = m(x - x_1)$$

Using the **slope-intercept formula**, pick one of the two points (say (x_1, y_1)) and solve for b in the following formula:

$$y_1 = mx_1 + b$$

Having found m and b, you can write down the equation of the line $y = mx + b$. The following graph illustrates what the line and two points might look like.

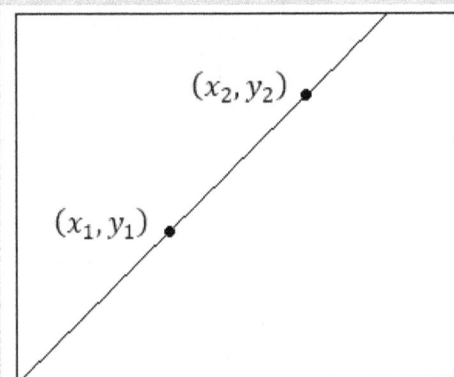

Either method is acceptable, but I personally find point-slope a lot easier to use.

EXAMPLE

Find the equation of the line passing through the points $(1, -2)$ and $(4, 7)$.

Solution: The slope is

$$m = \frac{y_2 - y_1}{x_2 - x_1} = \frac{7 - (-2)}{4 - 1} = \frac{9}{3} = 3$$

Using the point-slope method and choosing $(1, -2)$,

$$y - y_1 = m(x - x_1) \Rightarrow y - 2 = 3(x - 1)$$
$$\Rightarrow y + 2 = 3x - 3$$
$$\Rightarrow y = 3x - 5$$

Δ

QUADRATIC FORMULA
Given the quadratic equation $ax^2 + bx + c = 0$, the two roots are found by

$$x = \frac{-b \pm \sqrt{b^2 - 4ac}}{2a}$$

If $b^2 - 4ac > 0$, there are two real roots. If $b^2 - 4ac = 0$, there is one real root. If $b^2 - 4ac < 0$, there are no real roots (they are complex).

EXAMPLE
Find the roots of $x^2 + 8x + 1 = 0$ and $2x^2 - x + 1 = 0$.

Solution: The first quadratic has $a = 1$, $b = 8$, and $c = 1$, so

$$x = \frac{-b \pm \sqrt{b^2 - 4ac}}{2a} = \frac{-8 \pm \sqrt{8^2 - 4(1)(1)}}{2(1)} = \frac{-8 \pm \sqrt{64 - 4}}{2} = \frac{-8 \pm \sqrt{60}}{2}$$
$$x = \frac{-8 \pm \sqrt{4 \cdot 15}}{2} = \frac{-8 \pm 2\sqrt{15}}{2} = -4 \pm \sqrt{15}$$

The two roots are real and equal to $-4 - \sqrt{15}$ and $-4 + \sqrt{15}$. Next, the second quadratic has $a = 2$, $b = -1$, and $c = 1$, so

$$x = \frac{-b \pm \sqrt{b^2 - 4ac}}{2a} = \frac{-(-1) \pm \sqrt{(-1)^2 - 4(2)(1)}}{2(2)} = \frac{1 \pm \sqrt{1 - 8}}{4} = \frac{1 \pm \sqrt{-7}}{4}$$

Since $b^2 - 4ac = -7$ is under the square root, there are no real roots. They are complex numbers, which thankfully we won't be dealing with in a calculus class.

Δ

DOMAIN AND RANGE
The **domain** of a function $f(x)$ is the set of x-values over which the function exists, and the **range** is the set of y-values over which the function exists. In particular, suppose $f(x)$'s domain goes from a to b, the endpoints.

We write brackets [ ] to indicate that the domain includes the endpoints, or in other words the interval is inclusive. This is called a **closed interval**.

DOMAIN AND RANGE (CONTINUED)
We write parentheses ( ) to indicate that the domain does *not* include the endpoints, or in other words the interval is exclusive. This is called an **open interval**.

If the domain includes one endpoint but not the other, then we write [ ) or ( ]. This is called a **half-closed interval**.

If the domain includes all possible real numbers, then the correct way to write the domain is $(-\infty, \infty)$, not including the endpoints (because it's impossible to actually get to infinity). Another way to write the domain is $\mathbb{R}$ (read as "all reals").

EXAMPLE
Find the domains of $f(x) = \sqrt{1 - x^2}$, $g(x) = \sqrt{x + 2}$, $h(x) = \frac{1}{x-4}$, and $j(x) = 2x^4$.

Solution: Note that $f(x)$ is only defined when x is between -1 and 1, including the endpoints. This is because the contents under the square root cannot be negative, so we require

$$1 - x^2 \geq 0 \Rightarrow x^2 \leq 1 \Rightarrow -1 \leq x \leq 1$$

The domain of $f(x)$ is $[-1, 1]$, or equivalently $-1 \leq x \leq 1$.

Similarly, for $g(x)$ we need $x + 2 \geq 0$, which means $-2 \leq x$. That means that the domain of $g(x)$ is $[-2, \infty)$, or equivalently $-2 \leq x < \infty$.

Next, for $h(x)$ we can't have 0 in the denominator, and the only time that happens is at $x = 4$. The domain therefore includes all real numbers except for $x = 4$. The following are all acceptable ways of writing the domain for this function:

$$(-\infty, 4) \cup (4, \infty) \qquad x \neq 4 \qquad -\infty < x < 4 \text{ and } 4 < x < \infty \qquad \mathbb{R} \backslash \{4\}$$

Lastly, for $j(x)$ any real numbers work in the domain; there aren't any at which the function fails to exist. The following are all ways of writing the domain for this function:

$$(-\infty, \infty) \qquad -\infty < x < \infty \qquad \mathbb{R}$$

Δ

VERTICAL ASYMPTOTES
Suppose $y = f(x)/g(x)$. Then y has a **vertical asymptote** at any x-values where $g(x) = 0$ and $f(x) \neq 0$. Of course, these x-values are not in y's domain. If a vertical asymptote occurs at the x-value a, it has equation $x = a$.

EXAMPLE
Find the vertical asymptotes, if any, of $f(x) = \frac{3}{x-3}$, $g(x) = \frac{x-1}{x^2+x-2}$, and $h(x) = \frac{2}{x^2+4}$.

Solution: These can be found by setting the denominator equal to 0 and then verifying that the numerator isn't also 0 at those spots. For $f(x)$, the denominator is 0 at $x = 3$, so the vertical asymptote is $x = 3$.

Next, note that $g(x)$ can be written as

$$g(x) = \frac{x-1}{(x-1)(x+2)} = \frac{1}{x+2}.$$

The simplified equation cannot be equal to $x = -2$, so there is a vertical asymptote at $x = -2$. What about at $x = -1$? The $(x-1)$ pieces cancel out, which means that $g(x)$ does not have a vertical asymptote at $x = -1$; instead, there is a hole there.

As for $h(x)$, notice that the denominator $x^2 + 4$ is never 0 because the sum of a squared number and a positive number is always positive. That means that $h(x)$ has no vertical asymptotes.

Δ

Speaking of holes, let's go to the next concept.

HOLES
Suppose that $f(x)$ is in the form $f(x) = N/D$ where N and D are the numerator and denominator, respectively, and if we substitute in $x = a$, we get the indeterminate form $0/0$ (which is not a proper number). Now suppose that by using manipulation, we manage to reduce the function to a simpler function $g(x)$, and $g(a)$ is now a real number. Then we say that the original function $f(x)$ has a **hole** at $x = a$.

EXAMPLE

Find the vertical asymptotes and holes, if any, of $f(x) = \frac{x}{x(x-1)}$ and $g(x) = \frac{x^2+4x}{x^2-16}$.

Solution: Notice that $f(x)$ reduces to

$$f(x) = \frac{x}{x(x-1)} = \frac{1}{x-1}.$$

The simplified function still has $(x-1)$ in the denominator, and so $f(x)$ has a vertical asymptote at $x = 1$. Since the x's canceled out, that means there is a hole at $x = 0$. Next,

$$g(x) = \frac{x^2+4x}{x^2-16} = \frac{x(x+4)}{(x-4)(x+4)} = \frac{x}{x-4}.$$

The simplified function still has $(x-4)$ in the denominator, and so $g(x)$ has a vertical asymptote at $x = 4$. Since the $(x+4)$'s canceled out, that means there is a hole at $x = -4$.

Δ

HORIZONTAL ASYMPTOTES
Suppose for a function $f(x)$, there is a line $y = a$ such that for very large values of x, $f(x)$ approaches $y = a$ very closely but does not touch it. Then $y = a$ is a **horizontal asymptote**.

Note that it is possible for a function to cross a horizontal asymptote for "small" values of x. The horizontal asymptote just describes what is going on for very large values of x, where the function would approach but not cross the asymptote.

EXAMPLE

Find the asymptotes of $f(x) = \frac{2}{x+8}$.

Solution: There is a vertical asymptote when the denominator equals 0, at $x = -8$. As for the horizontal asymptote, note that if x is very large (say one billion), $f(x)$ is a very small number, close to 0. That means that as x gets large, $f(x)$ gets closer to $y = 0$ without touching it, and so there is a horizontal asymptote at $y = 0$.

Δ

There is a way of quickly determining what the horizontal asymptote is, provided $f(x)$ is a fraction where the numerator and denominator are both polynomials. First, recall that the degree of a polynomial is the number of the highest appearing exponent in that polynomial. For instance, if $r(x) = 3x + x^3 - 4x^5$, then $\deg(r(x)) = 5$.

FINDING HORIZONTAL ASYMPTOTES

Suppose $f(x) = N/D$ where N and D are both polynomials with specified degrees. Then the horizontal asymptote, if any, is found as follows.

Criterion 1: If $\deg(N) < \deg(D)$, then the horizontal asymptote is $y = 0$.
Criterion 2: If $\deg(N) = \deg(D)$, then the horizontal asymptote is $y = C_N/C_D$ where C_N is the coefficient in front of the highest exponent in the numerator, and likewise for C_D in the denominator.
Criterion 3: If $\deg(N) > \deg(D)$, then there is no horizontal asymptote.

EXAMPLE

Find the horizontal asymptotes, if any, of the following functions:

$$f(x) = \frac{3x^2 + 2}{x - 1}, \quad g(x) = \frac{x + 1}{7x^3 - x + 8}, \quad \text{and} \quad h(x) = \frac{-4x^3 - x + 5}{3x^3 + 2x - x + 9}$$

Solution: The first function $f(x)$ has numerator degree 2 and denominator degree 1, so the numerator has a higher degree. That means there is no horizontal asymptote.

The second function $g(x)$ has numerator degree 1 and denominator degree 3, so the denominator has a higher degree. That means the horizontal asymptote is $y = 0$.

The third function $h(x)$ has numerator degree 3 and denominator degree 3, so they are equal. Now we look at the coefficients in front of the highest exponents. The numerator coefficient in front of the x^3 is $C_N = -4$, and the denominator coefficient in front of the x^3 is $C_D = 3$, so the horizontal asymptote is

$$y = \frac{C_N}{C_D} = -\frac{4}{3}$$

Δ

In the event your function $f(x) = N/D$ has numerator degree one higher than the denominator degree, then while there is no horizontal asymptote, there is a diagonal one known as an oblique asymptote.

FINDING OBLIQUE (OR SLANT) ASYMPTOTES

Suppose $f(x) = N/D$ where N and D are both polynomials, and $\deg(N) = \deg(D) + 1$. In other words, the numerator's degree is one higher than the denominator's degree (for instance, 3 and 2). Then the **oblique asymptote**, which takes the form $y = mx + b$, is found by doing polynomial long division.

EXAMPLE

Find the oblique asymptote of $f(x) = \frac{3x^2+2}{x-1}$.

Solution: The best way to refresh your memory of how to find an oblique asymptote is to do an example of finding one. The numerator degree is 2, one higher than the denominator degree 1, so let's do polynomial long division (probably not your favorite topic!). We set it up as follows:

$$x - 1 \overline{)3x^2 + 2}$$

It will be easier to insert $0x$ so we can more easily pair up terms:

$$x - 1 \overline{)3x^2 + 0x + 2}$$

Next, ask yourself: x times what is $3x^2$? The answer is $3x$. That number goes above the $3x^2$:

$$\begin{array}{r} 3x \\ x - 1 \overline{)3x^2 + 0x + 2} \end{array}$$

Multiplying $3x$ by $(x - 1)$ results in $3x^2 - 3x$, so we write that on the next line:

$$\begin{array}{r} 3x \\ x - 1 \overline{)3x^2 + 0x + 2} \\ 3x^2 - 3x + 0 \end{array}$$

Again, we inserted 0 just to make it easier to compare terms. Now we subtract the two lines:

$$\begin{array}{r} 3x \\ x - 1 \overline{)3x^2 + 0x + 2} \\ -(3x^2 - 3x + 0) \\ \hline 3x + 2 \end{array}$$

The remainder is $3x + 2$, which now has the same degree as the denominator of $x - 1$. We need to go one step further: x times what is $3x$? The answer is 3, and that number goes above the $0x$:

$$\begin{array}{r} 3x \; + 3 \\ x - 1 \overline{)3x^2 + 0x + 2} \\ -(3x^2 - 3x + 0) \\ \hline 3x + 2 \end{array}$$

Multiplying 3 by $(x - 1)$ results in $3x - 3$, so we write that on the next line:

$$\begin{array}{r} 3x \; + 3 \\ x - 1 \overline{)3x^2 + 0x + 2} \\ -(3x^2 - 3x + 0) \\ \hline 3x + 2 \\ 3x - 3 \end{array}$$

Now we subtract the two lines:

$$
\begin{array}{r}
3x \;\; + 3 \\
x - 1 \overline{)\; 3x^2 + 0x + 2} \\
-(3x^2 - 3x + 0) \\
\hline
3x + 2 \\
-(3x - 3) \\
\hline
5
\end{array}
$$

The remainder is 5, which now has a smaller degree than the denominator of $x - 1$. This means that we have successfully written the function as

$$
f(x) = \frac{3x^2 + 2}{x - 1} = 3x + 3 + \frac{5}{x - 1}
$$

If you want to check your work, combine the pieces back into one fraction, and you'll get the original function. Now, what was the point of all this work? As x gets large in either direction, the remainder piece $5/(x - 1)$ goes to 0, which means that for large values of x, $f(x)$ behaves like $3x + 3$. That means that the oblique asymptote is $y = 3x + 3$ because it "guides" the function for large values of x. The following graph is what this function looks like (the asymptote is indicated with a dashed line, and don't forget about the vertical asymptote at $x = 1$).

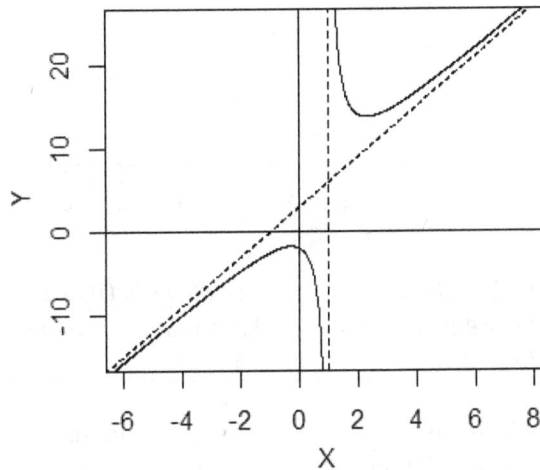

Δ

Let's now turn our attention to exponential rules, which are needed to simplify some expressions.

EXPONENTIAL RULES
For any positive constants a and b, and any real numbers k and l, the following facts are true.

Fact 1: $a^{k+l} = a^k \cdot a^l$

Fact 2: $a^{-k} = \frac{1}{a^k}$

Fact 3: $\left(a^k\right)^l = \left(a^l\right)^k = a^{kl}$

Fact 4: $(ab)^k = a^k \cdot b^k$

EXAMPLE

Rewrite the following expressions: $2x^3x^8$, $5(r^3)^4$, u^7v^7, and $8h^{-1}$.

Solution: We have the following:

$$2x^3x^8 = 2x^{3+8} = 2x^{11}$$
$$5(r^3)^4 = 5r^{3\cdot4} = 5r^{12}$$
$$u^7v^7 = (uv)^7$$
$$8h^{-1} = \frac{8}{h}$$

Δ

_e_ AND _e^x_

A very important number that appears all over mathematics is $e = 2.718281828\ldots$, often approximated as $e \approx 2.718$. This number is a series of never-ending decimals.

The function $f(x) = e^x$ has a graph that looks like this:

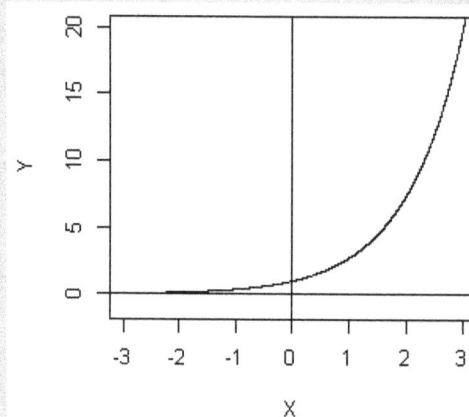

The domain of e^x is all real numbers $(-\infty, \infty)$, while its range is $(0, \infty)$. There is no real value of x for which e^x is negative. The number e is also called Euler's number, studied by the Swiss mathematician Leonhard Euler (pronounced "OIL-er").

This brings us to log rules, which are also needed to simplify certain mathematical expressions. In algebra or pre-calculus, you learned that given the formula $b^x = a$, to solve for x you would have to compute

$$\log_b a = x$$

You have also seen this expressed as

$$\log_{\text{base}}(\text{answer}) = \text{exponent}$$

The simplest way to do this with a calculator would be to type in

$$\frac{\log(a)}{\log(b)} \quad \text{or} \quad \frac{\ln(a)}{\ln(b)}$$

In calculus, we are most often concerned with logs in base e, or in other words logarithms of the form $\log_e a$. These are called natural logs, usually denoted as $\ln(a)$.

DEFINITION
A **natural logarithm** (or **natural log**) is a logarithm with base e. It is denoted as $\ln(a)$, but some textbooks may call it $\log(a)$. Don't let this confuse you; the book will make the distinction!

REVIEW: LOG RULES
The domain of $y = \ln(x)$ is $(0, \infty)$, and the range is all real numbers. To start, $\ln(1) = 0$ and $\ln(e) = 1$. Taking logs is useful because of the following simplifications:

$$\ln(e^x) = x \text{ for all real numbers } x$$
$$e^{\ln(x)} = x \text{ for all } x > 0$$

For any positive constants a and b, and any real number k, the following facts are true.

<u>Fact 1</u>: $\ln(ab) = \ln(a) + \ln(b)$
<u>Fact 2</u>: $\ln(a^k) = k\ln(a)$
<u>Fact 3</u>: $\ln\left(\frac{a}{b}\right) = \ln(a) - \ln(b)$
<u>Fact 4</u>: $\ln\left(\frac{1}{a}\right) = -\ln(a)$

Note that Fact 4 is a special case of Fact 3, taking $a = 1$. The graph of $f(x) = \ln(x)$ looks like this:

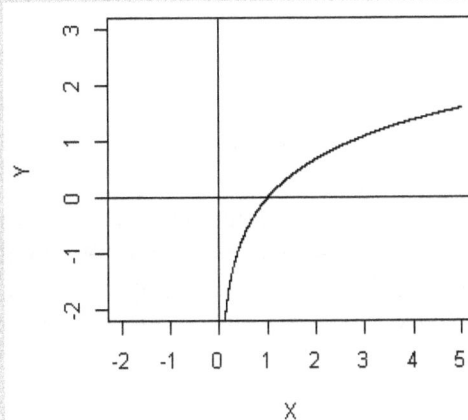

EXAMPLE
Simplify the following expressions, assuming a, b, and c represent positive numbers and that $a > b$:

$$\ln\left(\frac{a^5 b^{-3}}{c^2}\right), \ln\left(\frac{1}{a^4 b}\right), \ln(e^2), \text{ and } \ln(a^2 - b^2)$$

<u>Solution</u>: Using the rules we just saw,

$$\ln\left(\frac{a^5 b^{-3}}{c^2}\right) = \ln(a^5) + \ln(b^{-3}) - \ln(c^2) = 5\ln(a) - 3\ln(b) - 2\ln(c)$$
$$\ln\left(\frac{1}{a^4 b}\right) = -\ln(a^4 b) = -(\ln(a^4) + \ln(b)) = -4\ln(a) - \ln(b)$$
$$\ln(e^2) = 2\ln(e) = 2$$

At first glance there doesn't appear to be an obvious way of simplifying the last expression since $\ln(a^2 - b^2) \neq \ln(a^2) - \ln(b^2)$. However, note that $a^2 - b^2 = (a - b)(a + b)$, a useful factoring formula, so

$$\ln(a^2 - b^2) = \ln\big((a - b)(a + b)\big) = \ln(a - b) + \ln(a + b)$$

This last expression is the reason we needed to state that $a > b$, so that $\ln(a - b)$ could be computed.

Δ

This brings us to some useful factoring formulas.

FACTORING FORMULAS
Given two variables x and y, the following formulas are useful for factoring expressions.

Fact 1: $x^2 - y^2 = (x - y)(x + y)$
Fact 2: $x^3 - y^3 = (x - y)(x^2 + xy + y^2)$
Fact 3: $x^3 + y^3 = (x + y)(x^2 - xy + y^2)$

EXAMPLE
Factor the following expressions: $x^2 - 100$, $t^3 - 125$, $u^6 + 64v^6$, and $16x^4 - 81y^4$.

Solution: The first two expressions factor as follows:

$$x^2 - 100 = x^2 - 10^2 = (x - 10)(x + 10)$$
$$t^3 + 125 = t^3 + 5^3 = (t + 5)(t^2 - t \cdot 5 + 5^2) = (t + 5)(t^2 - 5t + 25)$$

The last two expressions also factor, although it might not be as obvious how. For the third expression, notice that a variable raised to the sixth exponent is the same as a cubed number squared, or indeed a squared number cubed. In other words, $u^6 = (u^3)^2 = (u^2)^3$. Since the expression involves a sum instead of a difference, it would be good to try to use the sum of cubes formula. Also notice that $64 = 2^6$, so

$$\begin{aligned}
u^6 + 64v^6 &= u^6 + (2v)^6 = (u^2)^3 + ((2v)^2)^3 \\
&= (u^2 + (2v)^2)((u^2)^2 - u^2 \cdot (2v)^2 + ((2v)^2)^2) \\
&= (u^2 + 4v^2)(u^4 - u^2 \cdot (4v^2) + (4v^2)^2) \\
&= (u^2 + 4v^2)(u^4 - 4u^2v^2 + 16v^4)
\end{aligned}$$

For the fourth expression, a difference of quartics is also a difference of squares because $x^4 = (x^2)^2$. Also note that $16 = 2^4$ and $81 = 3^4$, so

$$\begin{aligned}
16x^4 - 81y^4 &= (2x)^4 - (3y)^4 = ((2x)^2)^2 - ((3y)^2)^2 \\
&= ((2x)^2 - (3y)^2)((2x)^2 + (3y)^2)
\end{aligned}$$

We can actually go further because notice that the first piece, $(2x)^2 - (3y)^2$, is itself a difference of squares, so the factoring formula can be used a second time.

$$\begin{aligned}
((2x)^2 - (3y)^2)((2x)^2 + (3y)^2) &= (2x - 3y)(2x + 3y)((2x)^2 + (3y)^2) \\
&= (2x - 3y)(2x + 3y)(4x^2 + 9y^2)
\end{aligned}$$

Δ

Speaking of factoring, let's go over another technique that is sometimes needed when other calculations are not obvious at first: completing the square.

COMPLETING THE SQUARE

Suppose you have a parabola $y = x^2 + bx + c$ and want to write it in the form $(x + *)^2 + *$ where the asterisks are placeholders for numbers. This can be accomplished with the following steps:

<u>Step 1</u>: Add and subtract $\left(\frac{b}{2}\right)^2$, as in $x^2 + bx + \left(\frac{b}{2}\right)^2 + c - \left(\frac{b}{2}\right)^2$.

<u>Step 2</u>: The expression can now be written as $\left(x + \frac{b}{2}\right)^2 + c - \left(\frac{b}{2}\right)^2$.

If there is a nonzero constant in front of the squared term, as in $y = ax^2 + bx + c$, one additional step is needed first, and that is to factor out the a from the whole expression. The other two steps follow accordingly.

<u>Step 1</u>: Factor out a, leaving $a\left(x^2 + \frac{b}{a}x + \frac{c}{a}\right)$.

<u>Step 2</u>: Within the parentheses, add and subtract $\left(\frac{b}{2a}\right)^2$, as in $a\left(x^2 + \frac{b}{a}x + \left(\frac{b}{2a}\right)^2 + \frac{c}{a} - \left(\frac{b}{2a}\right)^2\right)$.

<u>Step 3</u>: The expression can now be written as $a\left(\left(x + \frac{b}{2a}\right)^2 + \frac{c}{a} - \left(\frac{b}{2a}\right)^2\right)$.

EXAMPLE

This is one of those techniques that's easier to understand with examples than by memorizing a formula. Complete the square for $y = x^2 - 8x + 10$ and $y = 2x^2 + 10x - 16$.

<u>Solution</u>: For the first one, there is no constant in front of the x^2 (well, there is but it's 1), so note that $b = -8$ and $c = 10$. Half of b is -4, and that number squared is 16, so

$$y = x^2 - 8x + \left(-\frac{8}{2}\right)^2 + 10 - \left(-\frac{8}{2}\right)^2$$
$$= x^2 - 8x + 16 + 10 - 16$$

Factoring the first three terms and combining the last two results in

$$y = (x - 4)^2 - 6$$

The second function is easier than it looks; the only extra step required is to factor out a 2 since there's a 2 in front of the x^2 term. The result is $y = 2(x^2 + 5x - 8)$. Now note that the number left in front of the x term is 5, so we add and subtract the square of $5/2$.

$$y = 2\left(x^2 + 5x + \left(\frac{5}{2}\right)^2 - 8 - \left(\frac{5}{2}\right)^2\right)$$

Factoring the first three terms and combining the last two results in

$$y = 2\left(\left(x + \frac{5}{2}\right)^2 - 8 - \frac{25}{4}\right) = 2\left(\left(x + \frac{5}{2}\right)^2 - \frac{32}{4} - \frac{25}{4}\right) = 2\left(\left(x + \frac{5}{2}\right)^2 - \frac{57}{4}\right)$$

You can also distribute the 2 to get

$$y = 2\left(x + \frac{5}{2}\right)^2 - \frac{57}{2}$$

Δ

Let's also discuss simplifying expressions under radicals, as this comes into play a lot when we are simplifying an answer.

SIMPLIFYING RADICAL EXPRESSIONS

The following facts can be used to simplify radical expressions. Suppose a and b are positive numbers.

<u>Fact 1</u>: If a number can be written as $a^2 b$, then $\sqrt{a^2 b} = a\sqrt{b}$.
<u>Fact 2</u>: It is generally preferred not to have square roots in the denominator of a fraction. To clear any,

$$\frac{1}{\sqrt{a}} = \frac{1}{\sqrt{a}} \cdot \frac{\sqrt{a}}{\sqrt{a}} = \frac{\sqrt{a}}{a}$$

<u>Fact 3</u>: When working with other roots (such a cube roots), factoring out numbers works in similar ways:

$$\sqrt[3]{a^3 b} = a\sqrt[3]{b}, \sqrt[4]{a^4 b} = a\sqrt[4]{b}, \text{etc.}$$

EXAMPLE

Simplify the following expressions: $\sqrt{648}$, $\sqrt{6300}$, and $\sqrt[3]{864}$.

Solution: It would be very helpful to first factor each number into factors with exponents.

$$\sqrt{648} = \sqrt{8 \cdot 81} = \sqrt{2^3 \cdot 9^2} = \sqrt{2^2 \cdot 2 \cdot 9^2} = 2 \cdot 9 \cdot \sqrt{2} = 18\sqrt{2}$$

We continue this procedure with the next number:

$$\sqrt{6300} = \sqrt{4 \cdot 9 \cdot 25 \cdot 7} = \sqrt{2^2 \cdot 3^2 \cdot 5^2 \cdot 7} = 2 \cdot 3 \cdot 5 \cdot \sqrt{7} = 30\sqrt{7}$$

The same technique is used for the cube root, although we now can only factor out cubic numbers.

$$\sqrt[3]{864} = \sqrt[3]{32 \cdot 27} = \sqrt[3]{8 \cdot 27 \cdot 4} = \sqrt[3]{2^3 \cdot 3^3 \cdot 4} = 2 \cdot 3 \cdot \sqrt[3]{4} = 6\sqrt[3]{4}$$

Δ

Section 0.2 – Topics from Pre-calculus

Although pre-calculus covered a lot of topics, the ones we are going to focus on concern trigonometric functions. Calculus is chock-a-block full of trig functions and creative uses of them, so you absolutely must be rock-solid confident with how they work. This of course includes the unit circle, which we will cover very soon.

We start with the geometric interpretation of the sine, cosine, and tangent of the angle of a right triangle.

PYTHAGOREAN THEOREM

Suppose a right triangle (meaning that one of the angles is 90 degrees, or $\pi/2$ radians) has three sides of lengths a, b, and c, where c is the longest side (the hypotenuse) and a and b are the other two sides (the legs), as in the sketch below. Given two sides, the third can be found using the Pythagorean Theorem, named after none other than the Greek philosopher Pythagoras of Samos:

$$c^2 = a^2 + b^2$$

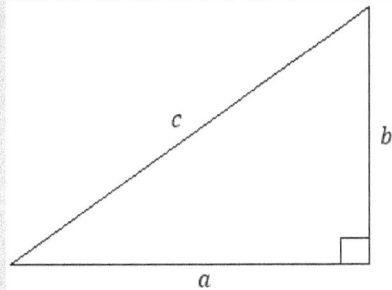

SINE, COSINE, AND TANGENT OF ANGLES OF A TRIANGLE

Given a right triangle as previously described, suppose we want to find the sine, cosine, and tangent of θ (a Greek letter, pronounced "THAY-ta"). By convention, let a be the side adjacent to θ, b the side opposite θ, and c the hypotenuse. Then the following equations hold:

$$\sin(\theta) = \frac{\text{opposite}}{\text{hypotenuse}} = \frac{b}{c} \qquad \cos(\theta) = \frac{\text{adjacent}}{\text{hypotenuse}} = \frac{a}{c} \qquad \tan(\theta) = \frac{\text{opposite}}{\text{adjacent}} = \frac{b}{a}$$

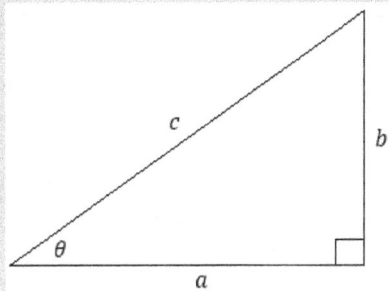

EXAMPLE

Given a right triangle with hypotenuse of length 2 and adjacent side of length 1, find the length of the opposite side and $\sin(\theta)$, $\cos(\theta)$, and $\tan(\theta)$. What is θ, given that $0° \leq \theta \leq 90°$?

Solution: Let's draw what we have:

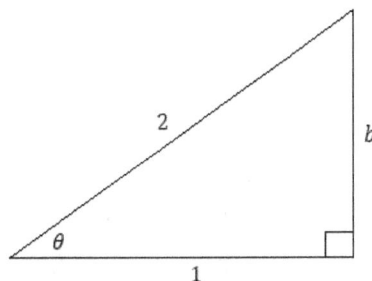

We see that $1^2 + b^2 = 2^2$, and so

$$b^2 = 4 - 1 \Rightarrow b = \sqrt{3}$$

The updated sketch looks like this:

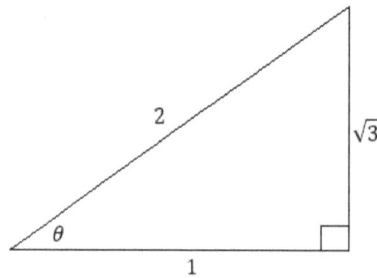

Using the trig formulas,

$$\sin(\theta) = \frac{\text{opposite}}{\text{hypotenuse}} = \frac{\sqrt{3}}{2}$$
$$\cos(\theta) = \frac{\text{adjacent}}{\text{hypotenuse}} = \frac{1}{2}$$
$$\tan(\theta) = \frac{\text{opposite}}{\text{adjacent}} = \frac{\sqrt{3}}{1} = \sqrt{3}$$

Using either your calculator or your knowledge of the unit circle (preferably the latter), $\theta = 60°$ (or $\pi/3$ radians).

$$\Delta$$

Speaking of which, let's have a little talk about radians. You probably know that a circle encompasses 360 degrees, and (for instance) going halfway around the circle in a counterclockwise direction means moving 180 degrees. This is **degree mode**, and in the context of a circle, the possible angles are 0 degrees through 360 degrees.

However, in calculus (unless stated otherwise) you will usually work in **radian mode**, where the possible angles are 0 radians through 2π radians, and going halfway around the circle (counterclockwise) brings you to π radians. You therefore want to keep your graphing calculator in radian mode for the vast majority of calculus problems, if not all of them. (On that note, remember that π is a Greek letter, pronounced "pie," and is equal to 3.141592654 ... with infinitely more decimals, just like e.)

So how do we convert degrees to radians and vice versa? Here's how.

CONVERTING DEGREES TO RADIANS (AND RADIANS TO DEGREES)
Given that the angles of a circle go from 0 degrees to 360 degrees, and from 0 radians to 2π radians, it is clear that 360 degrees corresponds to 2π radians. That means that

$$1 \text{ degree} = \frac{\pi}{180} \text{ radians and therefore } x \text{ degrees} = \frac{\pi}{180} x \text{ radians}$$

In a similar way, if we want to go from radians to degrees,

$$1 \text{ radian} = \frac{180}{\pi} \text{ degrees and therefore } x \text{ radians} = \frac{180}{\pi} x \text{ degrees}$$

EXAMPLE
Convert the angles $\theta = 45$ degrees and $\theta = 5\pi/6$ radians.

Solution: Going from degrees to radians,

$$45 \text{ degrees} = \frac{\pi}{180} \cdot 45 = \frac{\pi}{4} \text{ radians}$$

Going from radians to degrees,

$$\frac{5\pi}{6} \text{radians} = \frac{180}{\pi} \cdot \frac{5\pi}{6} = 30 \cdot 5 = 150 \text{ degrees}$$

Δ

Earlier I mentioned degree mode and radian mode; I was referring to how the TI-84 graphing calculator works with trig functions. See Section 0.3 on how to make sure you are using the correct one, and again, in calculus you will usually want radian mode. On that note, let's turn to the three basic trig functions.

SINE FUNCTION
The sine function $f(x) = \sin(x)$ is shown below, graphed over $-2\pi \leq x \leq 2\pi$. Its domain is all reals, and its range is $[-1, 1]$. This means that the function dips back and forth between -1 and 1 across the entire real domain. Notice that the function passes through $(0, 0)$, $\left(\frac{\pi}{2}, 1\right)$, $(\pi, 0)$, $\left(\frac{3\pi}{2}, -1\right)$, and $(2\pi, 0)$.

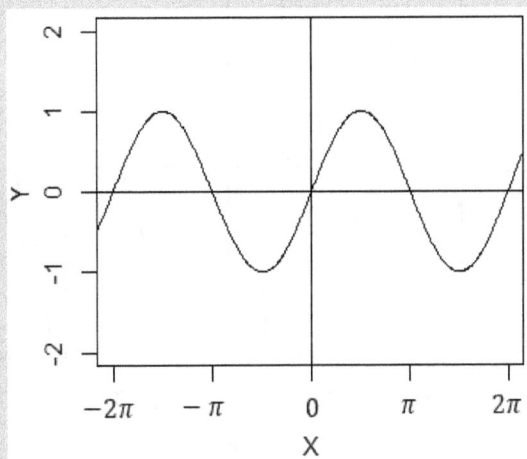

COSINE FUNCTION
The cosine function $f(x) = \cos(x)$ is shown below, graphed over $-2\pi \leq x \leq 2\pi$. Its domain is all reals, and its range is $[-1,1]$ (just like the sine function). This means that the function dips back and forth between -1 and 1 across the entire real domain. However, unlike the sine function, notice that the function passes through different points: $(0, 1)$, $\left(\frac{\pi}{2}, 0\right)$, $(\pi, -1)$, $\left(\frac{3\pi}{2}, 0\right)$, and $(2\pi, 1)$.

COSINE FUNCTION (CONTINUED)

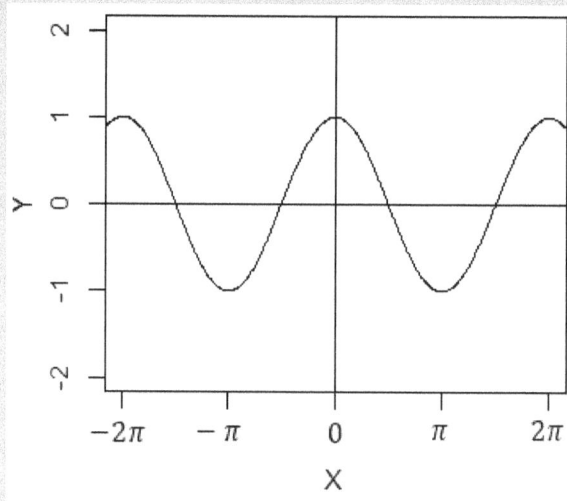

TANGENT FUNCTION

The tangent function $f(x) = \tan(x)$ is shown below, graphed over $-2\pi \leq x \leq 2\pi$.

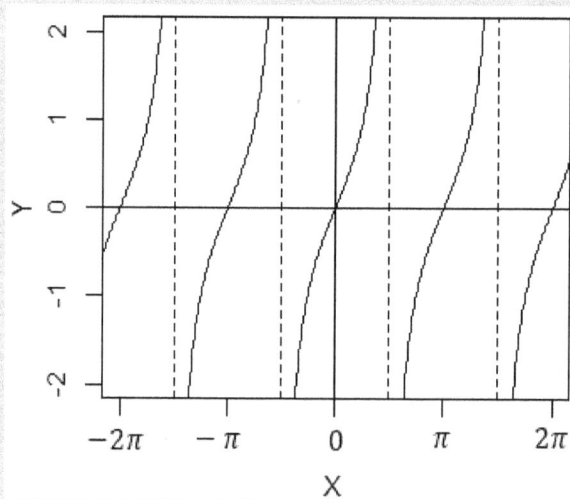

It is also computed as

$$\tan(x) = \frac{\sin(x)}{\cos(x)}$$

As seen on the graph, over $0 \leq x \leq 2\pi$ the tangent function is defined everywhere except at the points $x = \pi/2$ and $x = 3\pi/2$ (marked with vertical asymptotes as dashed lines). As an extension, over $-2\pi \leq x \leq 0$ it is defined everywhere except at the points $x = -3\pi/2$ and $x = -\pi/2$. Judging by the graph, the range is all reals.

The next topic to discuss is one that is crucially important, one that will show up everywhere in calculus – the unit circle! Hopefully you recognize it from pre-calculus, but let's go over it carefully. The following image is of the unit circle; you will also find it in Appendix A. I cannot stress this enough – you must memorize the coordinates and angles on the unit circle; they will come into play so many times in calculus!

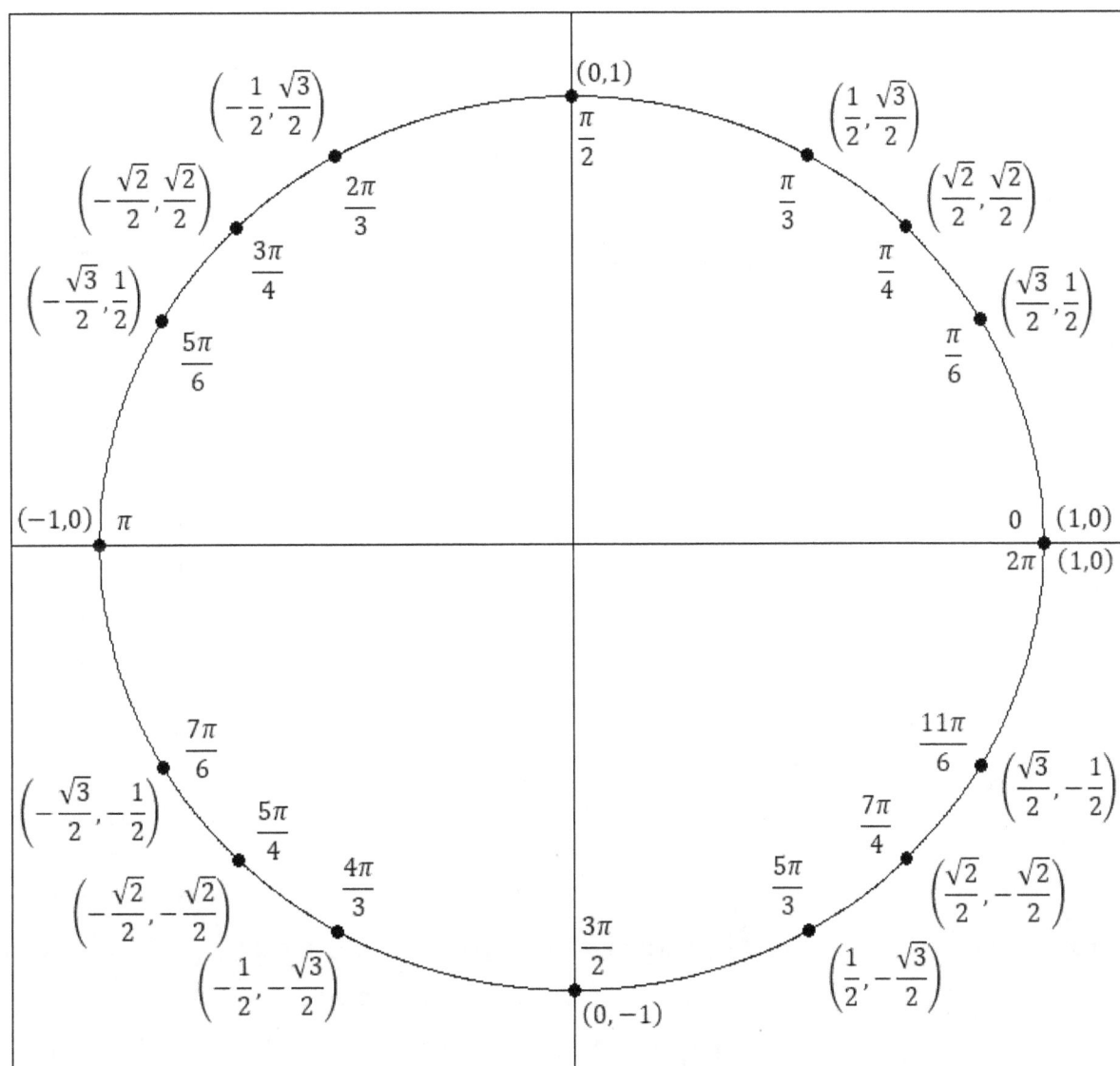

Here's how to use the unit circle. Each pair of numbers in parentheses represents $(\cos(\theta), \sin(\theta))$ for a given θ, or in other words its x- and y-coordinates on the circle $x^2 + y^2 = 1$. For example, for $\theta = \pi/6$, we see that $\cos(\theta) = \sqrt{3}/2$ and $\sin(\theta) = 1/2$. If $\theta = 3\pi/4$, that means that $\cos(\theta) = -\sqrt{2}/2$ and $\sin(\theta) = \sqrt{2}/2$.

EXAMPLE
Find the angles where $\cos(\theta) = -\sqrt{3}/2$, and find the angles where $\sin(\theta) = 1$.

Solution: From the unit circle, the cosine gives the x-coordinate, which is negative in the second and third quadrants. Thus, $\cos(\theta) = -\sqrt{3}/2$ at $\theta = 5\pi/6$ and $\theta = 7\pi/6$.

As for $\sin(\theta) = 1$, there is only one place where sine is equal to 1, and that occurs at the top of the circle, at $\theta = \pi/2$.

Δ

The interesting thing about the unit circle is that every pair of coordinates satisfies the equation $x^2 + y^2 = 1$. For example, let's look at $\theta = \pi/6$, whose coordinates are $\left(\sqrt{3}/2, 1/2\right)$. Squaring both coordinates and adding them results in

$$\left(\frac{\sqrt{3}}{2}\right)^2 + \left(\frac{1}{2}\right)^2 = \frac{3}{4} + \frac{1}{4} = 1$$

There is no reason to limit ourselves to just sine and cosine. How do we find the tangent of an angle? The answer is simple – we use the formula $\tan(\theta) = \sin(\theta) / \cos(\theta)$.

EXAMPLE
Find $\tan(\pi/6)$, and find the angles where $\tan(\theta) = 1$.

Solution: The first question is straightforward enough:

$$\tan(\pi/6) = \frac{\sin(\pi/6)}{\cos(\pi/6)} = \frac{\sqrt{3}/2}{1/2} = \frac{\sqrt{3}}{2} \cdot \frac{2}{1} = \sqrt{3}$$

For the second question, $\tan(\theta) = 1$ whenever $\sin(\theta) / \cos(\theta) = 1$, or in other words when $\sin(\theta) = \cos(\theta)$. The only times this happens are at $\theta = \pi/4$ (where both coordinates are $\sqrt{2}/2$) and at $\theta = 5\pi/4$ (where both coordinates are $-\sqrt{2}/2$).

Δ

There are three more trig functions to know, although they are not as commonly used as sine, cosine, and tangent. Each appears in calculus, however, so we do need to cover them. The good news is that each one is the reciprocal of one of the earlier three trig functions.

COSECANT FUNCTION
The cosecant function $f(x) = \csc(x)$ is shown below, graphed over $-2\pi \leq x \leq 2\pi$.

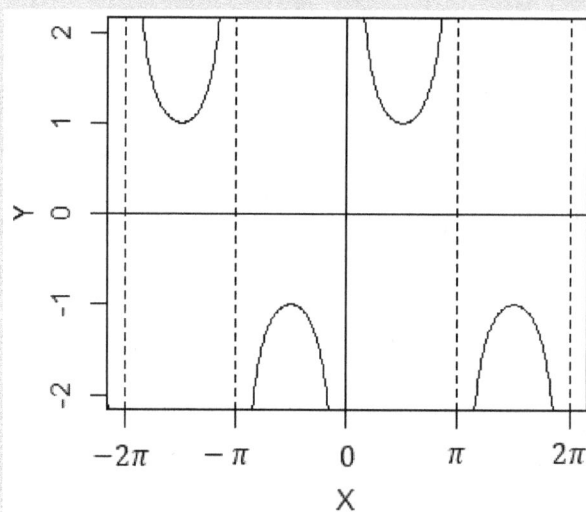

It is also computed as

$$\csc(x) = \frac{1}{\sin(x)}$$

COSECANT FUNCTION (CONTINUED)

As seen on the graph, over $0 \leq x \leq 2\pi$ the cosecant function is defined everywhere except at the points $x = 0$, $x = \pi$, and $x = 2\pi$ (marked with vertical asymptotes as dashed lines). As an extension, over $-2\pi \leq x < 0$ it is defined everywhere except at the points $x = -2\pi$ and $x = \pi$. Judging by the graph, the range is $(-\infty, -1]$ and $[1, \infty)$.

SECANT FUNCTION

The secant function $f(x) = \sec(x)$ is shown below, graphed over $-2\pi \leq x \leq 2\pi$.

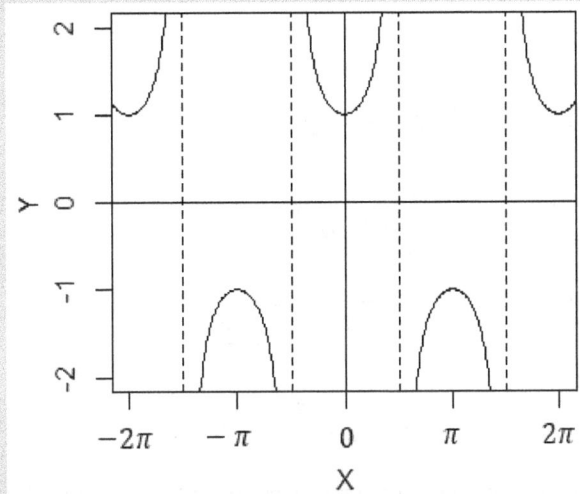

It is also computed as

$$\sec(x) = \frac{1}{\cos(x)}$$

As seen on the graph, over $0 \leq x \leq 2\pi$ the secant function is defined everywhere except at the points $x = \pi/2$ and $x = 3\pi/2$ (marked with vertical asymptotes as dashed lines). As an extension, over $-2\pi \leq x \leq 0$ it is defined everywhere except at the points $x = -3\pi/2$ and $x = -\pi/2$. Judging by the graph, the range is $(-\infty, -1]$ and $[1, \infty)$.

COTANGENT FUNCTION

The cotangent function $f(x) = \cot(x)$ is shown below, graphed over $-2\pi \leq x \leq 2\pi$.

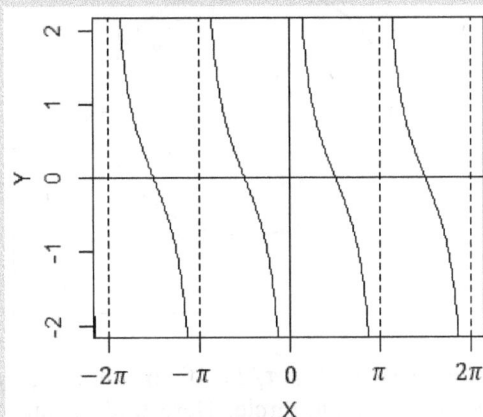

COTANGENT FUNCTION (CONTINUED)

It is also computed as

$$\cot(x) = \frac{\cos(x)}{\sin(x)}$$

As seen on the graph, over $0 \leq x \leq 2\pi$ the cotangent function is defined everywhere except at the points $x = 0$, $x = \pi$, and $x = 2\pi$ (marked with vertical asymptotes as dashed lines). As an extension, over $-2\pi \leq x < 0$ it is defined everywhere except at the points $x = -2\pi$ and $x = \pi$. Judging by the graph, the range is all reals.

EXAMPLE

Compute $\csc(\pi/6)$, $\sec(5\pi/4)$, and $\cot(\pi/2)$.

Solution: Using the unit circle and the formulas we just learned,

$$\csc(\pi/6) = \frac{1}{\sin(\pi/6)} = \frac{1}{\frac{1}{2}} = 2$$

$$\sec(5\pi/4) = \frac{1}{\cos(5\pi/4)} = \frac{1}{-\frac{\sqrt{2}}{2}} = -\frac{2}{\sqrt{2}} = -\sqrt{2}$$

$$\cot(\pi/2) = \frac{1}{\tan(\pi/2)} = \frac{\cos(\pi/2)}{\sin(\pi/2)} = \frac{0}{1} = 0$$

In particular, notice that with the last angle, $\tan(\pi/2) = \sin(\pi/2) / \cos(\pi/2) = 1/0$, which is undefined. However, the reciprocal, $\cot(\pi/2)$, does exist and is 0.

Δ

I'm going to say it again – if you haven't already, please memorize the unit circle; it will make your teacher (and me) proud of you! Use flashcards or other techniques to help learn it. I am including a few pointers below that might help you. Let's start with the four easy points: the right, top, left, and bottom sides of the circle. Using the fact that the unit circle is $x^2 + y^2 = 1$, it should be no surprise that the coordinates are (going counterclockwise) $(1,0)$, $(0,1)$, $(-1,0)$, and $(0,-1)$ before arriving at $(1,0)$ again.

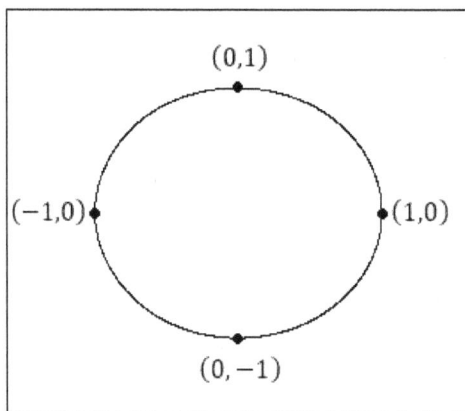

Let's now focus on the first quadrant ($0 \leq \theta \leq \pi/2$). If you thoroughly know this quadrant, you can visualize the answers in the other parts of the circle. Here both cosine and sine are positive (because everything in the first quadrant has positive x- and y-coordinates). Look closely at the coordinates at $\pi/6$, $\pi/4$, and $\pi/3$:

$$\left(\frac{\sqrt{3}}{2},\frac{1}{2}\right) \quad \left(\frac{\sqrt{2}}{2},\frac{\sqrt{2}}{2}\right) \quad \left(\frac{1}{2},\frac{\sqrt{3}}{2}\right)$$

$$\left(\frac{\sqrt{3}}{2},\frac{\sqrt{1}}{2}\right) \quad \left(\frac{\sqrt{2}}{2},\frac{\sqrt{2}}{2}\right) \quad \left(\frac{\sqrt{1}}{2},\frac{\sqrt{3}}{2}\right)$$

Notice how the cosine coordinate numerators go through the square roots as $\sqrt{3}, \sqrt{2}, \sqrt{1}$, while the sine coordinate numerators go in the opposite direction as $\sqrt{1}, \sqrt{2}, \sqrt{3}$. Also notice that the denominator is 2 in all cases. As for the choice of angles $\pi/6$, $\pi/4$, and $\pi/3$, just memorize them since they are easy fractions to remember.

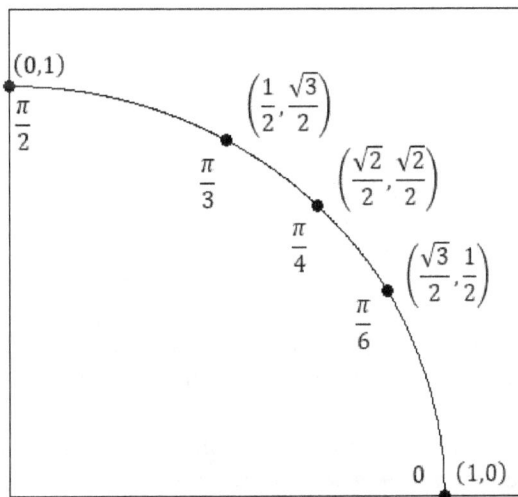

With this in mind, let's hop over to the third quadrant, where the x- and y-coordinates are negative. The coordinates in this quadrant are literally the same of those in the first and in the same order, only with negative signs. As for the angles, you can find them by taking the three angles in the first quadrant and adding π to them. In other words, we have $\pi/6 + \pi = 7\pi/6$, $\pi/4 + \pi = 5\pi/4$, and $\pi/3 + \pi = 4\pi/3$.

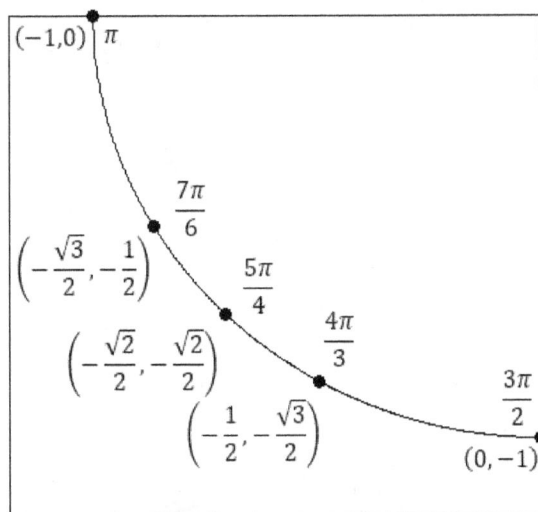

27

Hot-footing it to the second quadrant, the x-coordinates are negative and the y-coordinates are positive. Notice that (ignoring the signs) the coordinates are the same numbers as the mirror-image counterparts from the first quadrant. For instance, the y-coordinate of the first angle, $\theta = 2\pi/3$, is $\sqrt{3}/2$, the same as the y-coordinate of the third angle of the first quadrant, $\theta = \pi/3$. The three angles in the second quadrant are equal to the three angles in the first quadrant but adding $\pi/2$ to them. That means we have $\pi/6 + \pi/2 = 2\pi/3$, $\pi/4 + \pi/2 = 3\pi/4$, and $\pi/3 + \pi/2 = 5\pi/6$.

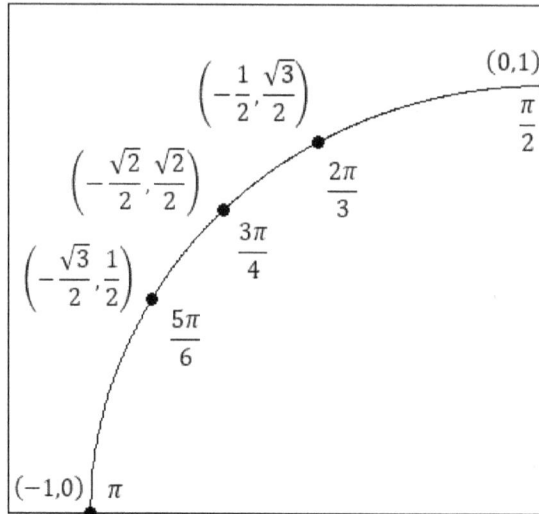

Finally, we arrive at the fourth quadrant, where the coordinates will be the same as those from the second quadrant but with flipped signs. That means the x-coordinates are positive and the y-coordinates are negative, but apart from that the coordinates occur in the same order as those from the second quadrant. You can find the three angles by adding π to the three angles in the second quadrant, obtaining $2\pi/3 + \pi = 5\pi/3$, $3\pi/4 + \pi = 7\pi/4$, and $5\pi/6 + \pi = 11\pi/6$.

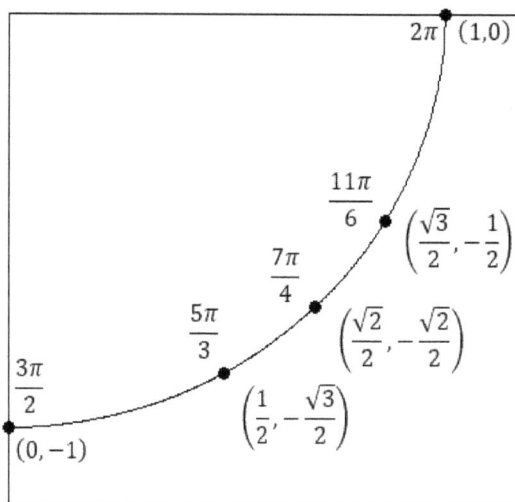

I hope this was a helpful review of the ever-so-important unit circle. As I mentioned, please memorize the angles and coordinates – you will need to know them inside and outside!

The last topic in this section concerns some important trig formulas that will pop up in calculus many times. Appendix B contains many trig formulas that might come up in small corners of calculus such as proofs, but I am including below the ones that are most important to remember.

PYTHAGOREAN IDENTITIES
The following Pythagorean identities are important to remember as they come up a lot in trig simplification.

$$\sin^2(\theta) + \cos^2(\theta) = 1$$
$$1 + \tan^2(\theta) = \sec^2(\theta)$$
$$1 + \cot^2(\theta) = \csc^2(\theta)$$

The most important of these identities to remember is the first one, $\sin^2(\theta) + \cos^2(\theta) = 1$. You will be amazed how frequently it comes up in problems!

DOUBLE-ANGLE FORMULAS
The following double-angle formulas are important to remember as they also appear frequently when it comes to simplifying trig problems.

$$\sin(2\theta) = 2\sin(\theta)\cos(\theta)$$
$$\cos(2\theta) = \cos^2(\theta) - \sin^2(\theta)$$
$$= 2\cos^2(\theta) - 1$$
$$= 1 - 2\sin^2(\theta)$$

Note that $\cos(2\theta)$ has three different forms, depending which one is the most useful for the problem.

EXAMPLE
Simplify the following trig expressions: $3 - 6\cos^2(\theta)$, $2\sin(\theta)\cos(\theta) + \sin^2(\theta) - \cos^2(\theta)$, and $\cos^4(\theta) + 2\cos^2(\theta)\sin^2(\theta) + \cos^2(\theta)$.

Solution: The first expression can be factored as $3(1 - 2\cos^2(\theta))$. Notice we can flip the order by factoring out a negative sign, and the result is $-3(2\cos^2(\theta) - 1)$, which we recognize to be $-3\cos(2\theta)$.

For the second expression, we immediately see that $2\sin(\theta)\cos(\theta) = \sin(2\theta)$, which results in $\sin(2\theta) + \sin^2(\theta) - \cos^2(\theta)$. As for the rest of the expression, notice that $\sin^2(\theta) - \cos^2(\theta)$ can be rewritten as $-(\cos^2(\theta) - \sin^2(\theta))$, which is $-\cos(2\theta)$. That means that

$$2\sin(\theta)\cos(\theta) + \sin^2(\theta) - \cos^2(\theta) = \sin(2\theta) - \cos(2\theta)$$

The last expression looks tricky until you realize that it can be factored. Note that if we instead have the expression $A^4 + 2A^2B^2 + B^4$, it can be factored as $(A^2 + B^2)(A^2 + B^2) = (A^2 + B^2)^2$. Here that means

$$\cos^4(\theta) + 2\cos^2(\theta)\sin^2(\theta) + \cos^2(\theta) = (\cos^2(\theta) + \sin^2(\theta))(\cos^2(\theta) + \sin^2(\theta))$$
$$= (\cos^2(\theta) + \sin^2(\theta))^2$$
$$= 1^2 = 1$$

Δ

> **MNEMONIC**
> I warned you that that Pythagorean identity, $\sin^2(\theta) + \cos^2(\theta) = 1$, would appear many times in this class. A good way to think about it is to imagine a family gathering where lots of photos are taken of each other. This identity can be thought of as an uncle who wants to get in all the photos!

Section 0.3 – Useful TI-84 Commands

This last section of Chapter 0 focuses on certain functions that the TI-84 graphing calculator can do that will be useful in a calculus class. Other graphing calculators likely have very similar commands but possibly in different locations. I should emphasize that a lot of calculus exams forbid the use of calculators on specific sections of the exams, so don't rely on them for all problems. As much as possible, you should see how much of a problem you can do without using a calculator. Nevertheless, I wanted to include a few methods here that you will find useful in some way. See Appendix G for all commands listed in this book.

> **TI-84 COMMAND: CONVERTING DECIMALS TO FRACTIONS**
> Suppose you have a decimal answer on your screen and wish to turn it into a fraction if possible. Calculus problems usually prefer exact answers rather than decimal answers when possible, unless it's an answer that can only be found using a calculator or computer and not by hand.
>
> With a decimal answer already on the screen, press $\boxed{\text{MATH}}$ and under the first menu (MATH), select Option 1: ▷ Frac. Press $\boxed{\text{ENTER}}$, and if possible, the calculator will convert the answer to a fraction.

EXAMPLE
If possible, convert the following numbers into fractions: 6.25, 0.333333333333, and 3.141592654.

Solution: Using the above command, type 6.25 on the main screen. Now choose the ▷ Frac command, press $\boxed{\text{ENTER}}$, and the answer is 25/4.

Now type 0.333333333333 (that's twelve 3s), and the calculator will reveal the fraction to be 1/3. Note that if we put in fewer 3s, the calculator will likely either keep it as a decimal or give us a fraction that wasn't intentional. For instance, if you incorrectly convert 0.33 thinking that that number is the same answer, what you get is 33/100, which is not equal to 1/3.

As for 3.141592654, attempting to convert this decimal to a fraction results in the same decimal number. You (hopefully!) recognize this number to be π, which cannot be expressed as a fraction. (Numbers that cannot be written as fractions are **irrational**; numbers that can are **rational**.)

Δ

Speaking of irrational numbers, in case you didn't know where they were, here's how to type π and e on the calculator.

> **TI-84 COMMAND: π AND e**
> To type π on the home screen, press $\boxed{\text{2nd}}$ and $\boxed{\wedge}$. To type e, press $\boxed{\text{2nd}}$ and $\boxed{\div}$, but if you want to compute e raised to a specific exponent (such as e^x), press $\boxed{\text{2nd}}$ and $\boxed{\text{LN}}$.

EXAMPLE
To find the decimal value of e^π, press $\boxed{\text{2nd}}$ and $\boxed{\text{LN}}$, and the calculator shows $e^\wedge($. Now to call π, press $\boxed{\text{2nd}}$ and $\boxed{\wedge}$, and the calculator now shows $e^\wedge(\pi$. Press $\boxed{\text{ENTER}}$, and the decimal answer is

23.14069263. (It is not necessary to put the closing parenthesis on the screen; the calculator will still do the work.)

Δ

To do calculations using trig functions, usually in calculus you will need to work in radian mode rather than degree mode. As I mentioned in Section 0.2, a circle encompasses 360 degrees, and going halfway around the circle in a counterclockwise direction means moving 180 degrees. This is **degree mode**, and in the context of a circle, the possible angles are 0 degrees through 360 degrees.

However, in calculus (unless stated otherwise) you will usually work in **radian mode**, where the possible angles are 0 radians through 2π radians, and going counterclockwise halfway around the circle brings you to π radians. You therefore want to keep your graphing calculator in radian mode for the vast majority of calculus problems, if not all of them.

TI-84 COMMAND: RADIAN MODE

To make sure your calculator is in **radian mode**, press $\boxed{\text{MODE}}$ and scroll to the third line that says RADIAN and DEGREE. If RADIAN is already highlighted, you are all set. If DEGREE is highlighted, move the cursor over RADIAN and press $\boxed{\text{ENTER}}$. You can then leave the MODE menu by pressing $\boxed{\text{2nd}}$ and $\boxed{\text{MODE}}$, which is the QUIT command. (In the unlikely event you need to do a problem in **degree mode**, do the same instructions but select DEGREE instead.)

EXAMPLE

Find the values $\cos(\pi)$ and $\sin(\pi)$.

Solution: Using the $\boxed{\text{COS}}$ and $\boxed{\text{SIN}}$ buttons, we discover that $\cos(\pi) = -1$ and $\sin(\pi) = 0$, which of course is also what the unit circle tells us. (If you specifically needed to use degree mode, the same answers would result from $\cos(180)$ and $\sin(180)$.)

Δ

It would be very useful to know how to graph functions. Doing so can give us an idea of their shape, maximum and minimum points, possible asymptotes, etc., but we sometimes need to adjust the window of the graph to get a better sense. (Again, you might not be allowed to use a calculator for some problems, but nevertheless it would be good to know how.)

TI-84 COMMAND: GRAPHING FUNCTIONS

To graph a function, press $\boxed{\text{Y} =}$ and type the function next to the first line, $\backslash Y_1 =$. If you have more functions to type, enter them on the subsequent lines. Now press $\boxed{\text{GRAPH}}$, and the function will appear on the graph.

If you need to adjust the viewing window, press $\boxed{\text{WINDOW}}$ and enter the values you think are best. Then press $\boxed{\text{GRAPH}}$, and the function will be drawn using the new window dimensions.

$Xmin =$ lower bound for the x values appearing on the graph
$Xmax =$ upper bound for the x values appearing on the graph
$Xscl =$ axis increment for the x values
$Ymin =$ lower bound for the y values appearing on the graph
$Ymax =$ upper bound for the y values appearing on the graph
$Yscl =$ axis increment for the y values

TI-84 COMMAND: GRAPHING FUNCTIONS (CONTINUED)
To clarify, if $Xscl = 1$, that means that the "tick marks" on the x-axis are spaced apart by 1 unit each (for instance, going from 0 to 1 to 2 and so on through 10). If $Xscl = \pi/4$, then the tick marks would appear at $0, \pi/4, \pi/2, 3\pi/4, \pi$, etc., and similarly for $Yscl$.

If you want to reset the window to the automatic convention without manually typing in those numbers, press ZOOM and choose Option 6: *ZStandard*. Doing so will automatically graph the function over $-10 \le x \le 10$ and $-10 \le y \le 10$, with both axis increments equal to 1.

EXAMPLE
Graph the function $f(x) = 12 - (x - 3)^2$ in such a way so that you can see the highest point.

Solution: Going to Y =, enter the function as $\backslash Y_1 = 12 - (X - 3)^2$, and press GRAPH. If you have the standard window, then your graph will look like this:

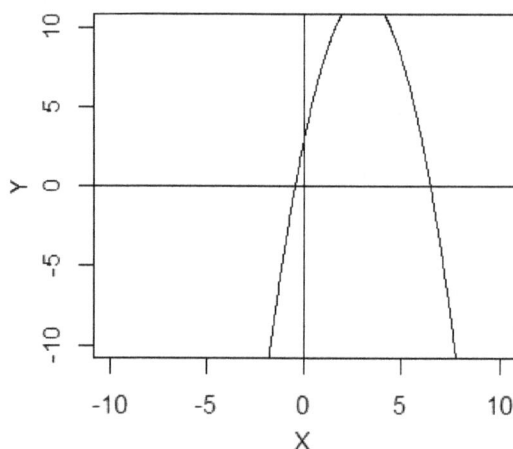

Although it's a start, the vertex (the top of the parabola) clearly goes a little higher than $y = 10$. Let's go to the window and change $Ymax = 10$ to $Ymax = 15$, and see if this is enough to see the vertex (if not, we'll try different values until we are satisfied). Fortunately now the whole top of the parabola is now visible, as seen in the graph below.

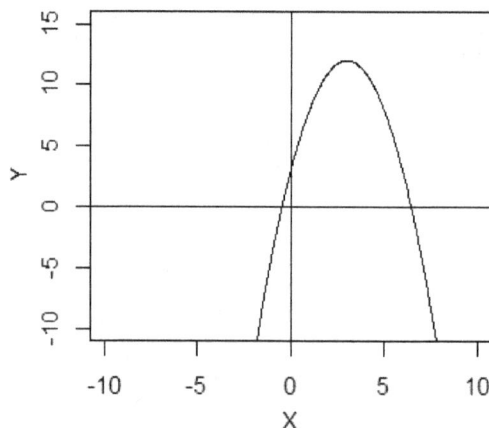

Δ

32

Chapter 1 – Limits

We all know that if we take a function $f(x)$ and evaluate it at a certain point a, then we will get the value $f(a)$, a real number provided that the function is defined at a and we are not dividing by zero. Here we are evaluating the function directly at a.

However, now we want to investigate the behavior of the function as it *approaches* the point a. In some cases this means that even though $f(a) = y$, the value of the function might not be anywhere near y as the function approaches a. This comes up frequently with functions that are not continuous and piecewise functions. Such a concept, likely new for you, is called a limit.

In this chapter we introduce some ideas behind limits and how to use them. Then we explain their connection to differential calculus. As my high school calculus teacher put it, "Calculus is essentially taking a scene in motion – whether it is folding a box or pouring a cup of coffee – and studying just one snapshot of the scene." Limits will show up all over Chapter 2 when we derive important formulas.

Section 1.1 – Introduction to Limits

Before we get started on the main calculus, we first need to get comfortable with the concept of limits. Here is a rough definition:

DEFINITION
The **limit** of a function $f(x)$ is the y-value that function takes on as x approaches the point a.

For example, if we have $f(x) = x^2$, then the limit as x approaches 3 would be 9. Limits describe what the function is doing as it gets closer and closer to a particular point. They do not describe what the function is doing exactly at the point, only what is happening near the point (although in many cases the two concepts give the same answer). Using this example, when I say near $x = 3$, I mean studying what the function is doing at $x = 2.99999$ or $x = 3.00001$, or other numbers that are close by.

ETYMOLOGY
The word **limit** derives from the Latin *limes*, which meant a limit, or more specifically a road or path. In ancient Rome, this word referred to a road or path denoting the boundary between different plots of land.

In addition, the word **calculus** derives from the Latin *calculus*, which meant "a pebble used for counting." This word derived from the Latin *calx*, meaning "limestone." These were the pebbles on an abacus, a centuries-old calculating tool.

While we are on the subject of etymology, the word **algebra** comes from the Arabic الجبر (pronounced *al-jabr*), which translates as "the reunion of broken parts." The Arabic word comes from the title of a book written by the Persian mathematician al-Khwarizmi in the early ninth century. Here the term was referring to the operation of moving a term from one side of an equation to the other side. In fact, when the word first entered the English language, it was also used as a medical term for treating broken bones. This is not as much of a stretch as it might seem because in the subject of algebra, you have "broken equations," as it were, and the goal is to put them back together!

We need to introduce some limit notation.

NOTATION: LIMITS

In general, when working with limits, we write

$$\lim_{x \to a} f(x) = L$$

This is read as "the limit as x approaches a of $f(x)$ equals L."

We also study limits approaching a point from the left or right sides. These are denoted with minus or plus signs in the limit notation. The left limit is written as

$$\lim_{x \to a-} f(x) = L$$

This is read as "the limit as x approaches a from the left of $f(x)$ equals L." The right limit is written as

$$\lim_{x \to a+} f(x) = L$$

This is read as "the limit as x approaches a from the right of $f(x)$ equals L."

For instance, in our first example, we would write $\lim_{x \to 3} x^2 = 9$. We could also note that $\lim_{x \to 3-} x^2 = 9$ and that $\lim_{x \to 3+} x^2 = 9$. Graphically, this looks like the following:

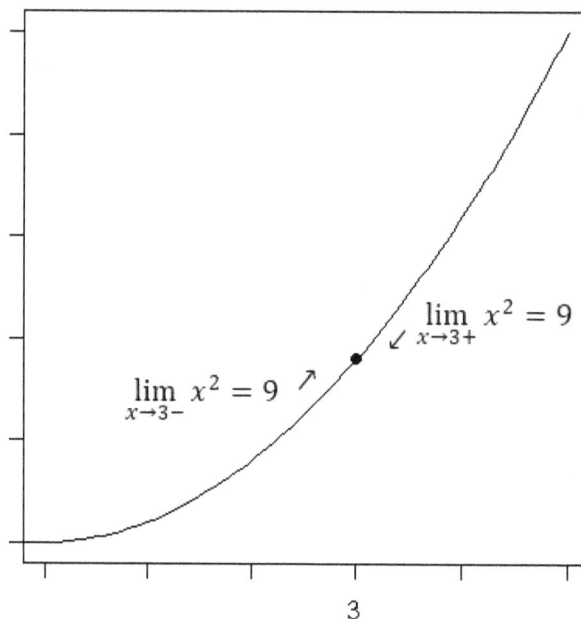

From these definitions we can make our first statement about limits.

CRITERIA FOR A LIMIT TO EXIST

$\lim_{x \to a} f(x) = L$ if and only if $\lim_{x \to a-} f(x) = L$ and $\lim_{x \to a+} f(x) = L$.

34

In other words, for a limit to exist, the value of $f(x)$ must be approaching the same point from both sides of a.

EXAMPLE

Consider the function shown in the following graph.

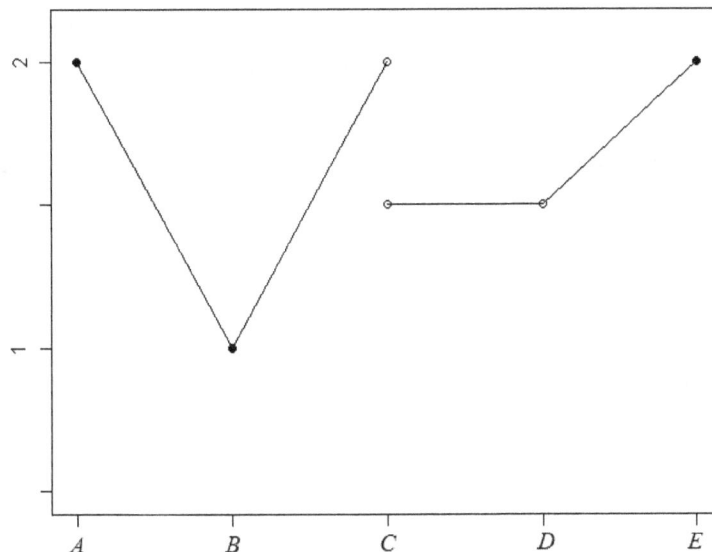

A is an endpoint, so all we have to do here is check the limit as x approaches A from the right. We have $\lim\limits_{x \to A+} f(x) = 2$, and so the limit exists.

The function passes through point B, so we check the limits from the left and the right. We have $\lim\limits_{x \to B-} f(x) = \lim\limits_{x \to B+} f(x) = 1$, and the limit exists.

Now let's consider point C: $\lim\limits_{x \to C-} f(x) = 2$, but $\lim\limits_{x \to C+} f(x) = 1.5$. In this case, $\lim\limits_{x \to C} f(x)$ does not exist.

Even though point D does not actually exist (as indicated by the open circle), we can still check the limit as x approaches D: $\lim\limits_{x \to D-} f(x) = \lim\limits_{x \to D+} f(x) = 1.5$, and so $\lim\limits_{x \to D} f(x) = 1.5$.

Lastly, E is an endpoint, so we just check the limit as x approaches E from the left. We have $\lim\limits_{x \to E-} f(x) = 2$, and so the limit exists.

Δ

Be careful though: a limit is simply the value of a function as x *approaches* a point a, not necessarily when x equals a. For example, if we consider the above example, the point $f(D)$ does not exist, and yet the limit as x approaches D exists. It would have been wrong to declare that $\lim\limits_{x \to D} f(x)$ did not exist simply because the point did not exist.

We now demonstrate four possible simple methods of evaluating limits (even though there are others, as we will soon see).

1) Graphing
2) Evaluating closely
3) Manipulation

4) Substitution

The reader can remember these four methods with the acronym "GEMS" (Graph, Evaluate, Manipulate, Substitute).

EXAMPLE (GRAPHING)

If the student has a graphing calculator, she can simply graph the function and trace out the limit of the function as x approaches a point a. For instance, we can guess that

$$\lim_{x \to 0} \frac{\sin(x)}{x} = 1$$

by examining its graph, as shown. We will actually prove this fact very soon.

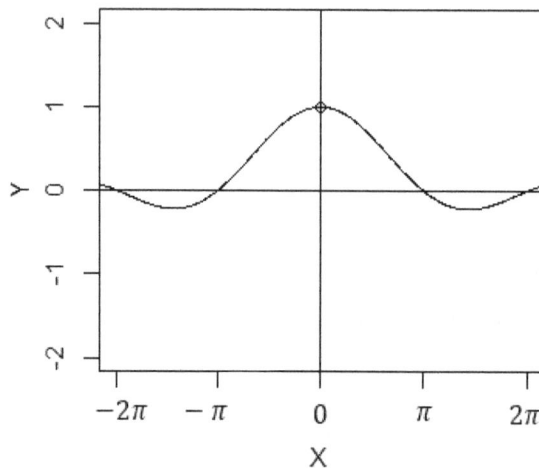

Δ

EXAMPLE (EVALUATING CLOSELY)

If x is approaching a, we can simply evaluate the function at a point very close to a. (For instance, this could be around one-millionth of a point away, if even that far.)

For example, if we want to evaluate $\lim_{x \to 0+} (1/x)$, we could evaluate $f(0.000001)$ and get 1,000,000. The limit, of course, is ∞, so obtaining a number like 1,000,000 makes sense as it is growing very large.

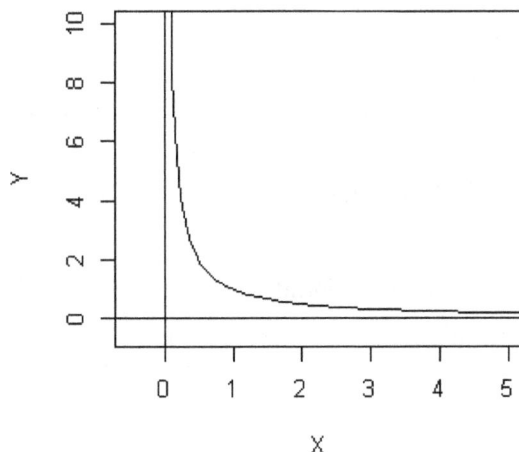

Δ

EXAMPLE (MANIPULATION)

Sometimes if we try to evaluate a limit directly, we get a case when the limit is $0/0$. As we will discuss in detail soon, zero divided by zero is not a number. Usually in such situations, we can manipulate the function to a more manageable one.

Take, for example, $\lim_{x \to 3}(x^2 - 9)/(x - 3)$. If we "plug in" $x = 3$ right away, we get $0/0$. (Caution: We cannot actually write this down as an answer – this is just intuition!) However, we can manipulate the function as follows:

$$\lim_{x \to 3}\frac{x^2 - 9}{x - 3} = \lim_{x \to 3}\frac{(x - 3)(x + 3)}{x - 3} = \lim_{x \to 3}(x + 3) = 6$$

In this case, the function will have a hole at $x = 3$ (as we will see in the next section). Thus, even though there is no point at $x = 3$, the limit still exists.

Δ

EXAMPLE (SUBSTITUTION)

In the simplest of all cases, we can simply substitute the point a which x is approaching into the function and get a proper, real number answer. For example, we have $\lim_{x \to 2} x^3 = 8$. However, we will not always be lucky enough to get such a simple scenario!

Δ

We need to stop and make a couple of comments. First, note that after manipulating a function, we can usually get it down to the point where mere substitution will provide us with the answer. Also note that throughout the problem (such as the manipulation example above), we have to keep writing the limit symbol because, until we get to the end, we have not yet actually evaluated the limit.

Usually what happens is that we will have to manipulate the function in some way in order to evaluate the limit as it approaches a certain point. How do we know when to stop doing this and substitute the point directly? As a general thought process, try this:

1) In your head (or on scrap paper), try substituting the point of interest directly into the function. One of three things will usually happen:
    a) You will get a real number, in which case the limit equals that answer.

b) You will get a nonzero number divided by zero, which is infinity. Or in some cases, you will get an infinite answer directly. In this case, you can automatically conclude that the limit does not exist.

c) You will get 0/0 or ∞/∞, which are not numbers. However, in just about every case, you can manipulate the function somehow and reduce it to an equivalent but simpler function.

2) If Step 1C holds, then repeat Step 1 again. And remember to keep writing "$\lim_{x \to a}$" in front of the function!

Just to be clear again, here is a basic rule: if you intuitively see that $\lim_{x \to a} f(x) = n/0$ where n is any nonzero number, then you can automatically conclude that the limit does not exist (or, equivalently, that $\lim_{x \to a} f(x) = \infty$ or $\lim_{x \to a} f(x) = -\infty$). This is true because a nonzero number divided by zero gives an infinite answer.

We now illustrate a few more properties of limits, accompanying them with examples.

PROPERTIES OF LIMITS

Suppose that $\lim_{x \to a} f(x)$ and $\lim_{x \to a} g(x)$ both exist. Now suppose we know that $\lim_{x \to a} f(x) = A$ and $\lim_{x \to a} g(x) = B$. Then these functions have the following properties:

Fact 1: $\lim_{x \to a} k = k$ where k is a constant

Fact 2: $\lim_{x \to a} kf(x) = k \cdot \lim_{x \to a} f(x) = kA$

Fact 3: $\lim_{x \to a} [f(x) + g(x)] = \lim_{x \to a} f(x) + \lim_{x \to a} g(x) = A + B$

Fact 4: $\lim_{x \to a} [f(x) - g(x)] = \lim_{x \to a} f(x) - \lim_{x \to a} g(x) = A - B$

Fact 5: $\lim_{x \to a} [f(x)g(x)] = \lim_{x \to a} f(x) \cdot \lim_{x \to a} g(x) = A \cdot B$

Fact 6: $\lim_{x \to a} \left(\frac{f(x)}{g(x)} \right) = \frac{\lim_{x \to a} f(x)}{\lim_{x \to a} g(x)} = \frac{A}{B}$ if $B \neq 0$.

EXAMPLE

Evaluate the following limits:

$$\lim_{x \to 3} 8 \,, \lim_{x \to 4} 3x^2 \,, \lim_{x \to 2} (x^2 + 3x^3)$$

Solution: The first limit is easy since it's just a constant:

$$\lim_{x \to 3} 8 = 8$$

The second limit involves pulling out the 3 and evaluating at what remains:

$$\lim_{x \to 4} 3x^2 = 3 \cdot \lim_{x \to 4} x^2 = 3 \cdot 16 = 48$$

The third limit can be split into two limits:

$$\lim_{x \to 2}(x^2 + 3x^3) = \lim_{x \to 2} x^2 + 3 \cdot \lim_{x \to 2} x^3 = 2^2 + 3 \cdot 2^3 = 4 + 24 = 28$$

Δ

EXAMPLE

Here is a case when the limit does not exist:

$$\lim_{x \to 1} \frac{1}{(x-1)^2}$$

Algebraically, if we substitute in $x = 1$ right away, we get $1/0$. Here there is no way of manipulating our way out, for we will always get a zero in the denominator, and the numerator is fixed at 1. In addition, if we evaluate very closely on either side of 1, we will get incredibly huge values. Graphically, we can quickly deduce that the limit does not exist.

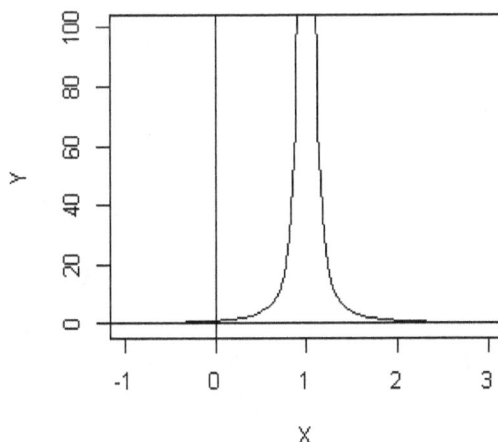

Δ

Section 1.2 – Trigonometric Limits

In this section we turn to perhaps one of the most important limits in calculus. This will enable us to evaluate many limits of functions that are built up from trigonometric functions. First, if you haven't already, please read Section 0.2 for a helpful review of the sine, cosine, and tangent trig functions. And in case you missed my urgent suggestion from that section, please learn the unit circle and its coordinates! See Appendix A for a full graph of the unit circle. The following are some of the important points on the unit circle and ones that are hopefully easy to remember.

$\sin(0) = \sin(\pi) = \sin(2\pi) = 0$ $\cos\left(\frac{\pi}{2}\right) = \cos\left(\frac{3\pi}{2}\right) = 0$ $\tan(0) = \tan(\pi) = 0$

$\sin\left(\frac{\pi}{2}\right) = 1$ $\cos(0) = 1$ $\tan\left(\frac{\pi}{2}\right) = \tan\left(\frac{3\pi}{2}\right) = DNE$

$\sin\left(\frac{3\pi}{2}\right) = -1$ $\cos(\pi) = -1$

For the last result on the right, we write the abbreviation *DNE* to denote "Does Not Exist." Be careful if you choose to write this, for if you are in a hurry and scribble it, "*DNE*" may look remarkably like the word "*ONE!*"

ETYMOLOGY
The word **trigonometry** derives from the Greek τρίγωνον (pronounced *trigonon*), which meant "triangle," and the Greek μέτρον (pronounced *metron*), which meant "measure."

Our goal in this section is to evaluate $\lim\limits_{x\to 0}\dfrac{\sin(x)}{x}$. Recall from earlier that its graph looks like this:

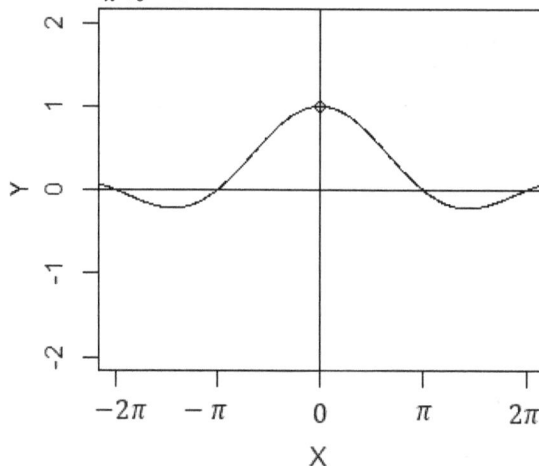

It looks like the function is approaching 1, but how do we prove that it really is 1? If we substitute in $x = 0$, we get $0/0$, and yet there seems to be no obvious way of manipulating this function. We instead need to use another, clever technique which we now talk about.

SANDWICH THEOREM (OR SQUEEZE RULE)
Consider $f(x)$, $g(x)$, and $h(x)$ such that $f(x) \le g(x) \le h(x)$ for all x. Now suppose we are given that $\lim\limits_{x\to a} f(x) = L$ and that $\lim\limits_{x\to a} h(x) = L$. Then it automatically follows that $\lim\limits_{x\to a} g(x) = L$.

The Sandwich Theorem can be a bit hard to digest (pun intended!), so the best way to think about this theorem is to visualize it geometrically.

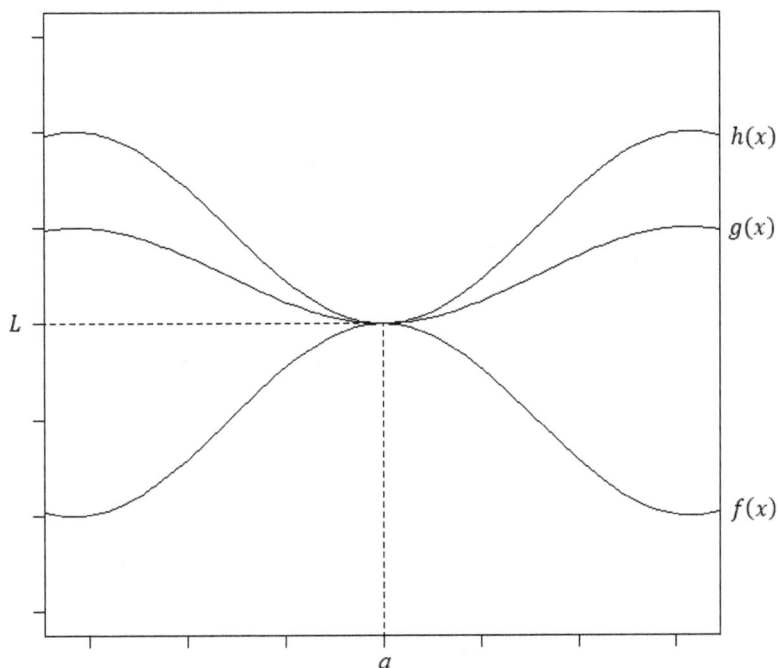

As seen in the above figure, $f(x) \leq g(x) \leq h(x)$ for all x. We see that $\lim\limits_{x \to a} f(x) = L$ and that $\lim\limits_{x \to a} h(x) = L$. It is clear that $\lim\limits_{x \to a} g(x) = L$ also.

Now we can use the Sandwich Theorem to prove the following important theorem.

LIMIT OF $\sin(x)/x$
The following limit is true:

$$\lim_{x \to 0} \frac{\sin(x)}{x} = 1$$

PROOF
We draw the unit circle in the first quadrant with two added triangles, ΔBOA and ΔCOA.

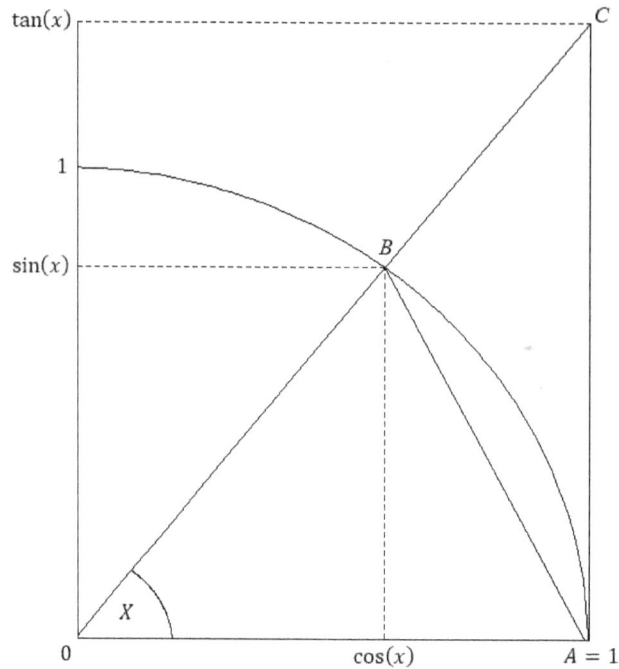

Note that the coordinates of point B are $(\cos(x), \sin(x))$. To see why point C is at $(1, \tan(x))$, observe that if one considers triangle ΔCOA, then

$$\tan(x) = \frac{\overline{AC}}{1} \Rightarrow \overline{AC} = \tan(x)$$

We now compare the areas of triangle ΔCOA, triangle ΔBOA with the circle sector, and triangle ΔCOA.

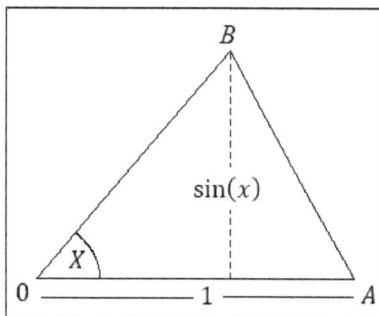

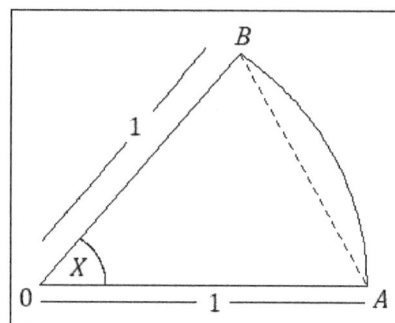

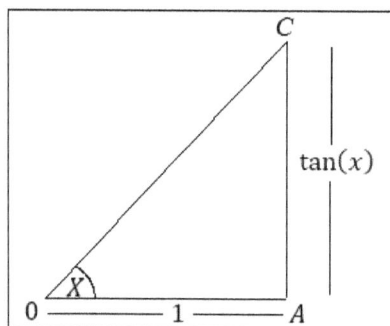

We note the following:

$$
\begin{aligned}
\text{Area } \Delta BOA &= \frac{1}{2} \cdot b \cdot h &&= \frac{1}{2} \cdot 1 \cdot \sin(x) &&= \frac{1}{2}\sin(x) \\
\text{Area } \Delta BOA + \text{Sector} &= \frac{1}{2} \cdot r^2 \cdot \theta &&= \frac{1}{2} \cdot 1 \cdot x &&= \frac{1}{2}x \\
\text{Area } \Delta COA &= \frac{1}{2} \cdot b \cdot h &&= \frac{1}{2} \cdot 1 \cdot \tan(x) &&= \frac{1}{2}\tan(x)
\end{aligned}
$$

We can also see geometrically that Area $\Delta BOA \leq$ Area $\Delta BOA +$ Sector $\leq$ Area ΔCOA, so let's now substitute in these area formulas:

$$
\frac{1}{2}\sin(x) \leq \frac{1}{2}x \leq \frac{1}{2}\tan(x)
$$
$$
\sin(x) \leq x \leq \tan(x)
$$

Next, we rewrite $\tan(x) = \frac{\sin(x)}{\cos(x)}$ and then divide everything by $\sin(x)$.

$$
\sin(x) \leq x \leq \frac{\sin(x)}{\cos(x)}
$$
$$
1 \leq \frac{x}{\sin(x)} \leq \frac{1}{\cos(x)}
$$

Now we flip everything by writing the reciprocal of each term. However, doing this requires us to reverse the direction of the less-than signs.

$$
1 \geq \frac{\sin(x)}{x} \geq \cos(x)
$$
$$
\cos(x) \leq \frac{\sin(x)}{x} \leq 1
$$

Let's look at each of these functions as x approaches zero.

1) $\lim_{x \to 0} \cos(x) = 1$ by direct substitution.
2) $\lim_{x \to 0} 1 = 1$ (obviously).

So we have the following:

$$
\lim_{x \to 0} \cos(x) \leq \lim_{x \to 0} \frac{\sin(x)}{x} \leq \lim_{x \to 0} 1
$$
$$
1 \leq \lim_{x \to 0} \frac{\sin(x)}{x} \leq 1
$$

The middle limit is "sandwiched" in between the 1's, so it has to be 1. Hence, $\lim_{x \to 0} \frac{\sin(x)}{x} = 1$. ∎

Here is a quick observation that follows immediately:

LIMIT OF $x/\sin(x)$
The following limit holds:

$$\lim_{x \to 0} \frac{x}{\sin(x)} = 1$$

PROOF

Since $\lim\limits_{x \to 0} \frac{\sin(x)}{x} = 1$, we simply flip both sides of the equation and get the reciprocals.

$$\lim_{x \to 0} \frac{1}{\left(\frac{\sin(x)}{x}\right)} = \frac{1}{1} \quad \Rightarrow \quad \lim_{x \to 0} \frac{x}{\sin(x)} = 1$$

∎

Here is one more limit that is easy to prove:

LIMIT OF $\tan(x)/x$
The following limit holds:

$$\lim_{x \to 0} \frac{\tan(x)}{x} = 1$$

PROOF

Let's write this in terms of $\sin(x)$ and x.

$$\lim_{x \to 0} \frac{\tan(x)}{x} = \lim_{x \to 0} \frac{\sin(x)}{\cos(x) \cdot x}$$

We rearrange the fraction as follows:

$$\lim_{x \to 0} \frac{\sin(x)}{\cos(x) \cdot x} - \left(\lim_{x \to 0} \frac{\sin(x)}{x} \right) \cdot \left(\lim_{x \to 0} \frac{1}{\cos(x)} \right)$$

We know the left limit, and since $\lim\limits_{x \to 0} \frac{1}{\cos(x)} = \frac{1}{1} = 1$, we end up with

$$\left(\lim_{x \to 0} \frac{\sin(x)}{x} \right) \cdot \left(\lim_{x \to 0} \frac{1}{\cos(x)} \right) = 1 \cdot 1 = 1$$

∎

We spend the rest of this section working out some examples.

EXAMPLE

What is $\lim\limits_{x \to 0} \frac{\cos(x)}{x}$? Notice that if we try to substitute in zero, we get $1/0$, a nonzero number divided by zero. Hence, this limit does not exist.

44

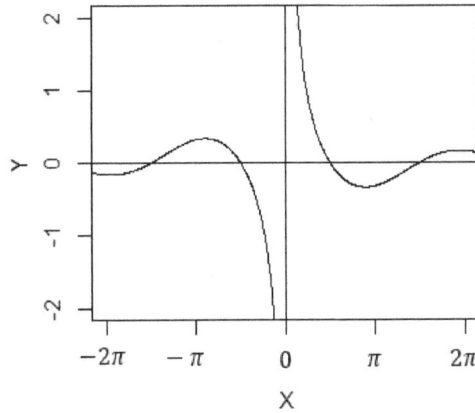

Δ

EXAMPLE

Evaluate the following limit:

$$\lim_{\theta \to 0} \frac{(\sin(3\theta))^2}{\theta^2 \cos(\theta)}$$

Solution: First, θ is a Greek letter (pronounced "THAY-ta") that is sometimes used to denote angles. The first thing to notice is that the sine function is in terms of 3θ, and yet we only have single θs in the denominator. If we want to use the earlier theorem on this limit, we'll have to use 3θ instead of just θ. But this is easy to do: we multiply the whole fraction by 9/9 and then rearrange terms.

$$\lim_{\theta \to 0} \frac{(\sin(3\theta))^2}{\theta^2 \cos(\theta)} = \lim_{\theta \to 0} \frac{(\sin(3\theta))^2}{\theta^2 \cos(\theta)} \cdot \frac{9}{9}$$
$$= \lim_{\theta \to 0} \frac{9 \cdot \sin(3\theta) \cdot \sin(3\theta)}{(3\theta) \cdot (3\theta) \cdot \cos(\theta)}$$

What just happened? By multiplying by 9/9, we have allowed ourselves to rewrite $9\theta^2$ as $3\theta \cdot 3\theta$ on the denominator. We need this to use the theorem: the variable inside the sine function _must_ be the same as the variable by which we divide it! Rearranging terms,

$$\lim_{\theta \to 0} \frac{9 \cdot \sin(3\theta) \cdot \sin(3\theta)}{(3\theta) \cdot (3\theta) \cdot \cos(\theta)} = \left(\lim_{\theta \to 0} \frac{\sin(3\theta)}{(3\theta)} \right) \cdot \left(\lim_{\theta \to 0} \frac{\sin(3\theta)}{(3\theta)} \right) \cdot \left(\lim_{\theta \to 0} \frac{9}{\cos(\theta)} \right)$$

Now we evaluate each of these:

$$\left(\lim_{\theta \to 0} \frac{\sin(3\theta)}{(3\theta)} \right) \cdot \left(\lim_{\theta \to 0} \frac{\sin(3\theta)}{(3\theta)} \right) \cdot \left(\lim_{\theta \to 0} \frac{9}{\cos(\theta)} \right) = 1 \cdot 1 \cdot \frac{9}{1} = 9$$

Here is what the graph of this function looks like:

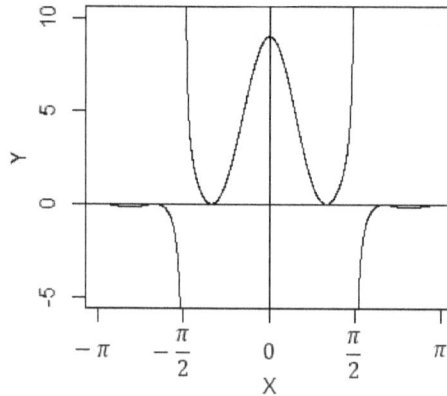

Δ

EXAMPLE

Here is another limit that will appear again later in the notes, when we work with derivatives. Evaluate

$$\lim_{x \to 0} \frac{1 - \cos(x)}{x}$$

Solution: Of course, if we try to substitute in zero, we get $0/0$. But how do we manipulate it? We use a little trick: multiplying by the conjugate of the numerator. In other words, we do the following:

$$\lim_{x \to 0} \frac{1 - \cos(x)}{x} = \lim_{x \to 0} \left(\frac{1 - \cos(x)}{x} \right) \cdot \left(\frac{1 + \cos(x)}{1 + \cos(x)} \right) = \lim_{x \to 0} \frac{1 - \cos^2(x)}{x(1 + \cos(x))}$$

The conjugate of $1 - \cos(x)$ is $1 + \cos(x)$. (In pre-calculus, you learned a similar technique for getting rid of square roots in fractions.)

Now recall the trig formula $\sin^2(x) + \cos^2(x) = 1$. (This is a _very_ important equation to remember!) So we rewrite this as $\sin^2(x) = 1 - \cos^2(x)$. We substitute this in and get

$$\lim_{x \to 0} \frac{1 - \cos^2(x)}{x(1 + \cos(x))} = \lim_{x \to 0} \frac{\sin^2(x)}{x(1 + \cos(x))}$$

We now rearrange the terms to get

$$\lim_{x \to 0} \frac{\sin^2(x)}{x(1 + \cos(x))} = \left(\lim_{x \to 0} \frac{\sin(x)}{x} \right) \cdot \left(\lim_{x \to 0} \frac{\sin(x)}{1 + \cos(x)} \right)$$

We can now evaluate the limits:

$$\left(\lim_{x \to 0} \frac{\sin(x)}{x} \right) \cdot \left(\lim_{x \to 0} \frac{\sin(x)}{1 + \cos(x)} \right) = 1 \cdot \left(\frac{0}{1 + 1} \right) = 0$$

We conclude that $\lim_{x \to 0} \frac{1-\cos(x)}{x} = 0$, which can also be seen in the following graph. (Remember this result for later; we will see it again in Section 2.4.)

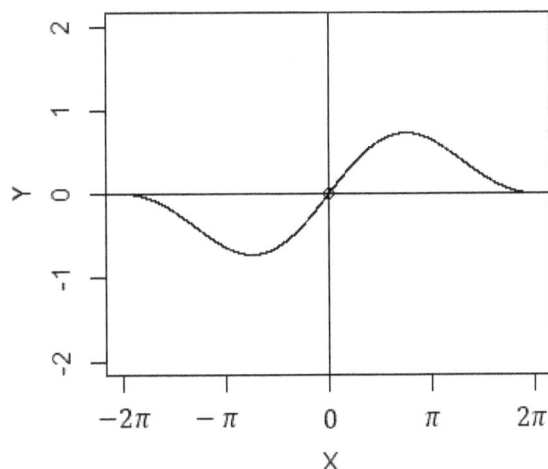

Δ

Section 1.3 – Asymptotes and Behavior at Infinity

In this section we learn how to determine whether a function has any asymptotes and whether they are vertical or horizontal. We then use these facts to enable us to evaluate more limits. See Section 0.1 for more information about asymptotes, but the basic definitions are restated below.

DEFINITION

Let $f(x) = N/D$ where N is the numerator and D is the denominator (both in terms of x). Let x approach a point a. We say that $f(x)$ has a **vertical asymptote** at $x = a$ if and only if $D = 0$ and $N \neq 0$. In other words, there is a vertical asymptote at $x = a$ if the denominator is zero and the numerator is a nonzero real number.

ETYMOLOGY

The word **asymptote** derives from the three Greek words $\grave{\alpha}$ (pronounced a, meaning "not"), $\sigma\acute{\upsilon}\nu$ (pronounced *sun*, meaning "together"), and $\pi\tau\omega\tau\acute{o}\varsigma$ (pronounced *ptotos*, meaning "fallen." Taken together, these three words formed the Greek $\grave{\alpha}\sigma\acute{\upsilon}\mu\tau\omega\tau o\varsigma$ (pronounced *asumptotos*), which meant "not falling together." Although a somewhat strange translation, it makes sense since an asymptote is a vertical or horizontal line that gets closer to but never touches a specific point.

EXAMPLE

The function $f(x) = \frac{1}{(x-1)^2}$ has a vertical asymptote at $x = 1$. We can tell this because

$$f(1) = \frac{1}{(1-1)^2} = \frac{1}{0}$$

The numerator is nonzero, but the denominator is zero.

Δ

EXAMPLE

The function $f(x) = \frac{1}{x-4}$ has a vertical asymptote at $x = 4$, as shown in the following graph (the dashed line represents the asymptote).

47

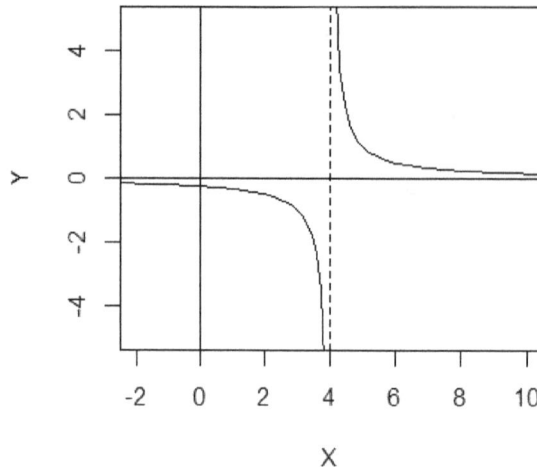

Δ

Here is the next definition we need to know.

DEFINITION
Suppose that $f(x)$ is in the form $f(x) = N/D$ and if we substitute in $x = a$, we get the indeterminate form $0/0$. Now suppose that by using manipulation, we manage to reduce the function to the point where $f(a)$ is now a real number. Then we say that $f(x)$ has a **hole** at $x = a$.

EXAMPLE

Consider the function $f(x) = \frac{x^2+2x}{x+2}$. If we try to substitute in $x = -2$, we will get $0/0$. From pre-calculus, we find that by manipulating the function,

$$f(x) = \frac{x^2 + 2x}{x + 2} = \frac{x(x + 2)}{x + 2} = x$$

Next, if we examine $\lim_{x \to -2} f(x)$, we see that it approaches -2, a real number. However, there is a hole at $x = -2$, as shown below.

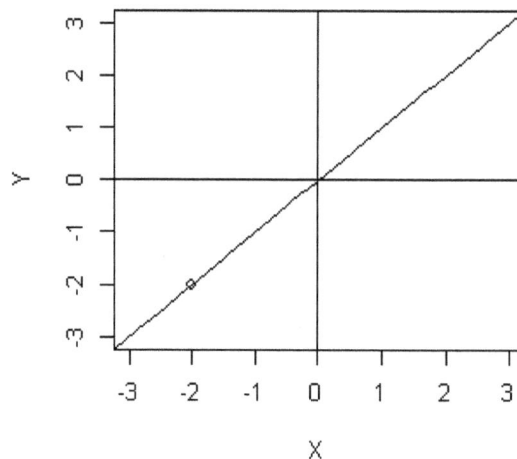

Δ

EXAMPLE

Notice that our definition of a hole does not say that if we get $0/0$ after evaluating the function at a point a, then there absolutely must be a hole at $x = a$ after we reduce the function. Here is an example of a function that behaves this way: take $f(x) = x/x^2$.

We see that evaluating this at zero gives us the indeterminate form $0/0$, and we can easily reduce the function to $f(x) = 1/x$. But now we can quickly see that the function fails to exist at $x = 0$. So instead of a hole, we have a vertical asymptote at $x = 0$.

Δ

Graphically, we can see that vertical asymptotes guide a function to positive and/or negative infinity. Observe the graph of $f(x) = \frac{1}{x-4}$, for instance.

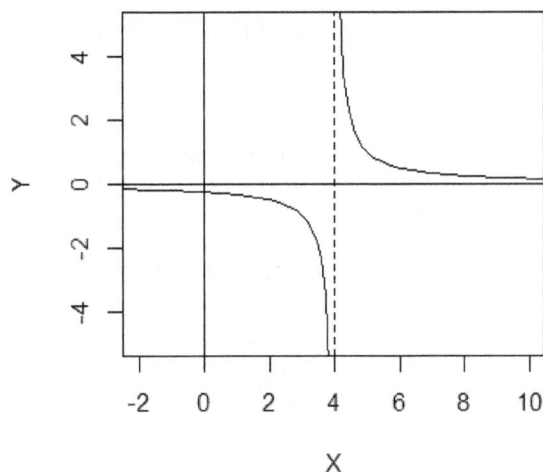

Now let's turn to horizontal asymptotes.

DEFINITION

If $y = a$ is a **horizontal asymptote**, then

$$\lim_{x \to \infty} f(x) = a \quad \text{and/or} \quad \lim_{x \to -\infty} f(x) = a$$

This means that as x grows arbitrarily large, the value of the function will approach a (but of course will never reach it, since infinity is not a number).

In the graph above for $f(x) = 1/(x - 4)$, there appears to be a horizontal asymptote on $y = 0$.

NOTATION: INDETERMINATE FORMS

As we have already hinted, $0/0$ is not a number; it is called an **indeterminate form**. This is somewhat difficult to comprehend at first, for it is not infinity either. Another common indeterminate form is ∞/∞. When you get an answer that is of this form, it usually can somehow be manipulated when taking limits.

We next introduce some techniques of determining where to find horizontal asymptotes. As an extension, this will help us with our study of limits. Before we start, let's make the following definition.

DEFINITION
The **degree** of a polynomial is the number of its highest exponent, usually denoted as $\deg f(x)$.

EXAMPLE
If $f(x) = 3x^4 - x^2 + 2$, then $\deg f(x) = 4$.

Δ

NOTATION
Just as we know that a nonzero number divided by zero is infinity, or does not exist, similarly a nonzero number divided by an infinitely large number goes to zero as the denominator gets larger. In other words, $\lim\limits_{x \to \infty} n/x = 0$ for any nonzero n.

To figure out how to find horizontal asymptotes, let's follow the techniques in the following examples.

EXAMPLE
Let's evaluate the following limit:

$$\lim_{x \to \infty} \frac{3x^5 - 4x^4 + x^2 - 7}{6x^8 + 5x^7 - 1}$$

Solution: What we are going to do is multiply this fraction by another fraction that is equal to 1, but that will help clear up this function.

$$\lim_{x \to \infty} \frac{3x^5 - 4x^4 + x^2 - 7}{6x^8 + 5x^7 - 1} = \lim_{x \to \infty} \frac{3x^5 - 4x^4 + x^2 - 7}{6x^8 + 5x^7 - 1} \cdot \frac{\left(\frac{1}{x^5}\right)}{\left(\frac{1}{x^5}\right)}$$

The reason for our choice will make sense in a moment.

$$\lim_{x \to \infty} \frac{3x^5 - 4x^4 + x^2 - 7}{6x^8 + 5x^7 - 1} \cdot \frac{\left(\frac{1}{x^5}\right)}{\left(\frac{1}{x^5}\right)} = \lim_{x \to \infty} \frac{\left(3 - \frac{4}{x} + \frac{1}{x^3} - \frac{7}{x^5}\right)}{\left(6x^3 + 5x^2 - \frac{1}{x^5}\right)}$$

All we have done so far is distribute the $1/x^5$ in each piece. Now, looking at our new limit, let's first look at the numerator. As x approaches infinity, 3 stays the same, but the other three fractions all go to zero.

However, in the denominator, $6x^3$ and $5x^2$ both go to infinity as x goes to infinity, while the $1/x^5$ goes to 0. Thus, the whole fraction approaches $3/\infty$, which is zero.

To conclude, $\lim\limits_{x \to \infty} \frac{3x^5 - 4x^4 + x^2 - 7}{6x^8 + 5x^7 - 1} = 0$, and there is a horizontal asymptote at $y = 0$ (since the function never actually reaches zero).

Δ

How did we know to multiply by $(1/x^5)/(1/x^5)$? We wanted to reduce this function, so we divided every component by x^5, the degree of the numerator. We would therefore be left with a real number followed by a series of fractions going to zero. Then we could work with the denominator and see what each of its components does at infinity.

EXAMPLE
Let's evaluate

$$\lim_{x \to \infty} \frac{x^4 + 1}{2x^4 - 4x^3 + 3}$$

Solution: Let's start manipulating the limit:

$$\lim_{x \to \infty} \frac{x^4 + 1}{2x^4 - 4x^3 + 3} = \lim_{x \to \infty} \frac{x^4 + 1}{2x^4 - 4x^3 + 3} \cdot \frac{\left(\frac{1}{x^4}\right)}{\left(\frac{1}{x^4}\right)}$$

Again, we pick the degree of the numerator, 4, and divide the numerator and denominator by x^4.

$$\lim_{x \to \infty} \frac{x^4 + 1}{2x^4 - 4x^3 + 3} \cdot \frac{\left(\frac{1}{x^4}\right)}{\left(\frac{1}{x^4}\right)} = \lim_{x \to \infty} \frac{\left(1 + \frac{1}{x^4}\right)}{\left(2 - \frac{4}{x} + \frac{3}{x^4}\right)}$$

As x goes to infinity, the fraction in the numerator and the two fractions in the denominator will all go to zero. Therefore the limit is

$$\lim_{x \to \infty} \frac{\left(1 + \frac{1}{x^4}\right)}{\left(2 - \frac{4}{x} + \frac{3}{x^4}\right)} = \frac{1}{2}$$

This means that there is a horizontal asymptote at $y = 1/2$.

Δ

EXAMPLE
Let's evaluate

$$\lim_{x \to \infty} \frac{5x^6}{4x^4 + 3x - 2}$$

Solution: The degree of the numerator is 6, so let's do our fraction trick.

$$\lim_{x \to \infty} \frac{5x^6}{4x^4 + 3x - 2} \cdot \frac{\left(\frac{1}{x^6}\right)}{\left(\frac{1}{x^6}\right)} = \lim_{x \to \infty} \frac{5}{\left(\frac{4}{x^2} + \frac{3}{x^5} - \frac{2}{x^6}\right)}$$

This time every piece in the denominator goes to zero. Thus, the denominator goes to 0 as x approaches infinity, and so we end up with a non-zero number divided by zero:

$$\lim_{x \to \infty} \frac{5}{\left(\frac{4}{x^2} + \frac{3}{x^5} - \frac{2}{x^6}\right)} = \infty$$

What this tells us is that the limit is infinite (does not exist), and there is no horizontal asymptote.

Δ

Section 1.4 – Continuity and the Intermediate Value Theorem

In this section we introduce the concept of continuity in a simple form. While there is a much more rigorous definition, we will not present it – it will be saved for more advanced classes. We will then tell you cases when a function is discontinuous, and finally we will explain the Intermediate Value Theorem.

DEFINITION

A function $f(x)$ is **continuous** at $x = a$ if all three criteria hold:

Criterion 1: $f(a)$ exists (the point exists).

Criterion 2: $\lim_{x \to a} f(x)$ exists (the limit exists).

Criterion 3: $\lim_{x \to a} f(x) = f(a)$ (the limit equals the point).

ETYMOLOGY

The word **continuous** derives from the Latin *continere*, which meant "to hold together."

EXAMPLE

Let $f(x) = x^2 - 3$. Is $f(x)$ continuous at $x = 1$? Let's check:

1) $f(1) = 1^2 - 3 = -2$, so the point exists.

2) $\lim_{x \to 1}(x^2 - 3) = -2$, so the limit exists.

3) $\lim_{x \to 1}(x^2 - 3) = f(1) = -2$

Thus, $f(x)$ is continuous at $x = 1$.

Δ

EXAMPLE

Let $f(x) = \sin(x)/x$. Is $f(x)$ continuous at $x = 0$? The answer is no, since we have seen that there is a hole at $x = 0$. The point does not exist, and so $f(x)$ is not continuous at $x = 0$. However, it is continuous at all other points.

Δ

DEFINITION

We should stop here and update our terminology. The proper mathematical word for a hole is a **removable discontinuity**.

Let's now state the following facts about continuous functions.

PROPERTIES OF CONTINUOUS FUNCTIONS

Let $f(x)$ and $g(x)$ be continuous functions. The following are all true:

Fact 1: $h(x) = f(x) + g(x)$ is continuous,

PROPERTIES OF CONTINUOUS FUNCTIONS (CONTINUED)

Fact 2: $h(x) = f(x) - g(x)$ is continuous,

Fact 3: $h(x) = f(x) \cdot g(x)$ is continuous, and

Fact 4: $h(x) = f(x)/g(x)$ is continuous except when $g(x) = 0$.

PROOF

We will show that the first statement is true. Let $h(x) = f(x) + g(x)$, and examine point $x = a$.

1) $h(a) = f(a) + g(a)$, so the point exists.

2) $\lim_{x \to a} h(x) = \lim_{x \to a} \big(f(x) + g(x) \big) = f(a) + g(a)$, so the limit exists.

3) $\lim_{x \to a} h(x) = h(a) = f(a) + g(a)$ for all $x = a$.

Thus, $h(x) = f(x) + g(x)$ is continuous everywhere. It is easy to verify this for the other three statements as well.

■

We shall pause for a moment and let the reader know a secret that will save some work. There are some functions that we can simply take for granted are continuous everywhere. For instance, all polynomials are continuous at every point. (Of course, this is assuming we are not dividing by another function.) Intuitively, this should make sense – keep the first example from this section in mind. In a higher-level course, we could rigorously prove this, but here we will just state examples of functions that are continuous everywhere.

CONTINUOUS FUNCTIONS

The following functions are continuous everywhere, on all x:

1) All polynomials
2) $f(x) = \sin(x)$
3) $f(x) = \cos(x)$
4) $f(x) = e^x$

In addition,

5) $f(x) = \sqrt{x}$ is continuous on the interval $[0, \infty)$.
6) $f(x) = \ln(x)$ is continuous on the interval $(0, \infty)$.

The square root function exists when x is 0 or positive, and the natural log function exists when x is strictly positive.

By now the reader should observe that when we write the domain of a function, we sometimes use parentheses, sometimes brackets, and sometimes one of each. Go back to Section 0.1 for more information about how to write domains and what they mean.

We now stop and consider just what criteria might make a function be discontinuous at certain points. There are five major ones, which we present and explain below.

CASES WHEN A FUNCTION IS DISCONTINUOUS
The following are instances when a function $f(x)$ is not continuous at $x = a$.

Case 1: There is a jump at $x = a$.
Case 2: There is a hole / removable discontinuity at $x = a$.
Case 3: There is a vertical asymptote at $x = a$.
Case 4: There is a displaced point at $x = a$.
Case 5: If the y-value of $f(x)$ **oscillates** (jumps back and forth) between two or more points, $f(x)$ is discontinuous everywhere.

EXAMPLE (JUMP)
Consider the following piecewise function whose graph is shown below.

$$f(x) = \begin{cases} a, & x \leq c \\ b, & x > c \end{cases}$$

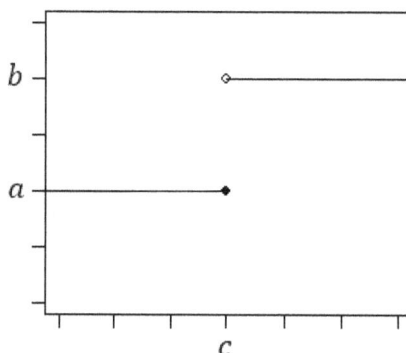

To the left of $x = c$, we have $f(x) = a$. Using domain notation, $f(x) = a$ on $(-\infty, c]$ since it includes the point $f(c) = a$. On the interval (c, ∞), the function has "jumped," and now $f(x) = b$. Clearly the function is discontinuous at $x = a$.

Δ

EXAMPLE (HOLE)
The function $f(x) = (x^2 - 4)/(x - 2)$ can be rewritten as

$$f(x) = \frac{(x - 2)(x + 2)}{x - 2} = x + 2$$

Since the $(x - 2)$ pieces cancel out, that means that there is a hole, or a removable discontinuity, at $x = 2$. Thus, $f(x)$ is discontinuous at $x = 2$ (even though the limit exists).

Δ

EXAMPLE (VERTICAL ASYMPTOTE)
$f(x) = 1/(x - 4)$ has a vertical asymptote at $x = 4$, so it is not continuous at that point. However, it is continuous at all other points.

Δ

EXAMPLE (DISPLACED POINT)

Consider the function

$$f(x) = \begin{cases} x^2 - 1, & x \neq 1 \\ 1, & x = 1 \end{cases}$$

Here $f(-1) = 1$, but looking at points very close to 1 such as 1.00001 or 0.99999, we discover that

$$\lim_{x \to 1} f(x) = \lim_{x \to 1}(x^2 - 1) = 1^2 - 1 = 0$$

Thus, the limit exists and is 0, and the point exists and is $f(1) = 1$, but they don't equal each other. The function is discontinuous at $x = 1$.

Δ

EXAMPLE (OSCILLATION)

This one is somewhat more difficult to explain than the first three. Here is an example:

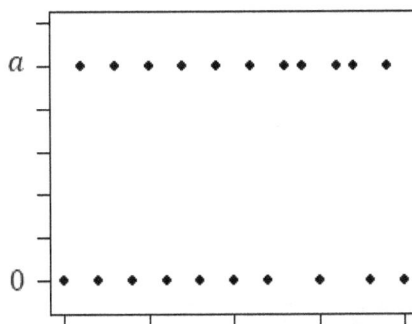

Here the value of $f(x)$ is either 0 or a at all times, so it vacillates between the two. This function has no lines or curves, only oscillating dots, so such a function cannot be continuous *anywhere*. It is somewhat tricky to think of such an example, and we will not be encountering many of them. However, consider the following function, whose sketch is not unlike the one above. (If you want to see more functions like this, you are cordially invited to take a college-level math class called Real Analysis!)

$$f(x) = \begin{cases} 1, & x \text{ is rational} \\ 0, & x \text{ is irrational} \end{cases}$$

Δ

ETYMOLOGY
The word **oscillation** derives from the Latin *oscillare*, which meant "to swing."

As a side note, given a function with a removable discontinuity, we can create a piecewise function that will make the function continuous everywhere by simply adding an extra point.

EXAMPLE

Consider the following function:

$$f(x) = \frac{x^2 - 1}{x + 1} = x - 1$$

Here $f(x)$ has a removable discontinuity at $x = -1$. However, to make it continuous everywhere, we can create a piecewise function that will literally "fill in the hole." The fraction reduces to $x - 1$, and putting in $x = -1$, we get $-1 - 1 = -2$. That means that we can write a new function

$$g(x) = \begin{cases} \dfrac{x^2 - 1}{x + 1}, & x \neq -1 \\ -2, & x = -1 \end{cases}$$

This new function will be continuous everywhere, including at $x = 1$.

Δ

Now we need to introduce the Intermediate Value Theorem (IVT). We will examine first the simple case, and then the general case.

THEOREM (INTERMEDIATE VALUE THEOREM)
Suppose a function $f(x)$ is defined from a to b. Suppose $f(a) < 0$ and $f(b) > 0$, and let $f(x)$ be continuous on $[a, b]$. Then there must be a point c between a and b such that $f(c) = 0$.

Let's sketch a sample function:

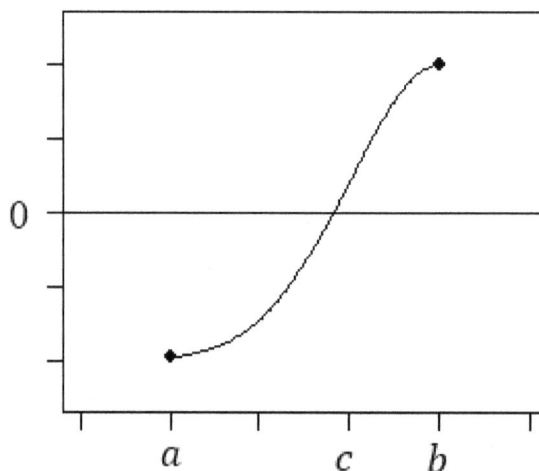

Here $f(a) < 0$, $f(b) > 0$, and the function is clearly continuous. Since the function cannot "jump" over the x-axis, then intuitively it should make sense that there must be some c, lying between a and b, where the function crosses the x-axis (although there is no reason why there cannot theoretically be more such points).

EXAMPLE
Here is a simple example: consider $f(x) = x - 2$ on the interval $[0, 4]$.

1) $f(x)$ is continuous on this interval (and everywhere else).
2) $f(0) = -2$.
3) $f(4) = 2$.

It therefore follows that for some $0 < c < 4$, $f(c) = 0$ (and of course, that occurs at $c = 2$).

Δ

We can state this theorem in a more general setting.

THEOREM (INTERMEDIATE VALUE THEOREM, GENERAL CASE)
Given a y-value d, let a function $f(x)$ be continuous on the interval $[a, b]$. Suppose that $f(a) < d$ and $f(b) > d$. Then it follows that there is some c between a and b such that $f(c) = d$.

A similar sketch will illustrate this idea:

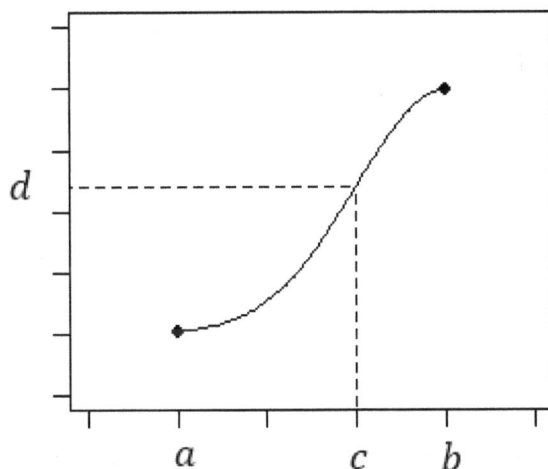

EXAMPLE
Consider $f(x) = \ln(x)$ on $(0, \infty)$. We want to show that there is some c such that $f(c) = 1$.

1. $f(x)$ is continuous on $(0, \infty)$.
2. $f(1) = \ln(1) = 0$
3. $f(3) = \ln(3) > 1$

Then we know that there is some $1 < c < 3$ such that $f(c) = 1$, by the Intermediate Value Theorem. Of course, here $c = e$.

Δ

Section 1.5 – Secant Lines and Tangent Lines

So far we have studied limits and learned techniques of evaluating them and how they might help us in understanding different functions. But what do they have to do with calculus, namely differential calculus? In this section we began to make some connections. We start with a study of slopes and tangent lines, and then we present the definition of the derivative. First, let's briefly review how to find the slope of a line.

REVIEW
Suppose we have two points, (x_1, y_1) and (x_2, y_2), with a line drawn between them, as shown below. We want to find the slope of that line. Then the equation for the slope m is given by

$$m = \frac{y_2 - y_1}{x_2 - x_1}$$

REVIEW (CONTINUED)

The equation of the line passing through those points is

$$y = mx + b$$

We can solve for b by substituting one of the points into the equation.

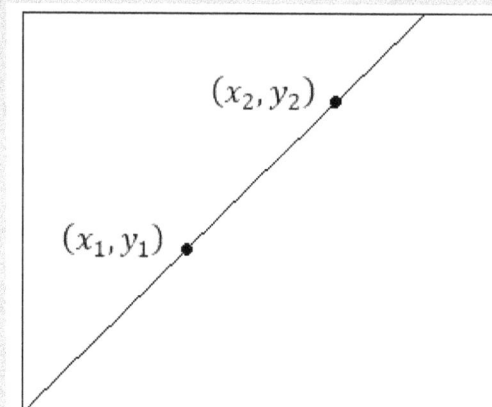

Now consider a curve (instead of just a straight line), and pick two points (x_1, y_1) and (x_2, y_2) on that curve. We want to know the slope of the line that passes through these two points. Of course, this line is not actually part of the curve itself – we are adding it in. Why do we care about this? Take the following visual example:

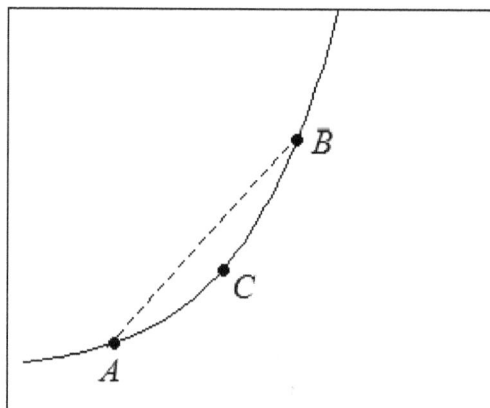

Suppose our function $f(x)$ is represented by the solid curve, and points A, B, and C lie on $f(x)$. We want to know the slope of the function at *any* point on the curve. Unlike the case of the straight line (which you have studied in regular algebra), clearly the slope at point A is not the same as B's slope or C's slope. So how do we calculate the slope at any point on the curve?

Suppose we wish to know the slope at point C. One way to do this is to pick two points (A and B) that are equidistant from C, draw a straight line between these two points, and find the slope of this new line. Since we know the coordinates of A and B, we simply use the slope-intercept formula from above. Of course, this will not necessarily give us the exact slope at point C; it will simply be an approximation.

DEFINITON

Above, we estimated the slope at point C by drawing a line between A and B and using the slope of this line to approximate the slope of $f(x)$ at point C. This line is called a **secant line**, one that intersects the function in more than one spot.

ETYMOLOGY

The word **secant** derives from the Latin *secare*, which meant "to cut."

Now we introduce the formula for calculating the slope of a secant line. It is very similar to the slope-intercept formula.

DEFINITION

Consider the function $f(x)$ and the secant line passing through the two points $(a, f(a))$ and $(b, f(b))$. The equation of the slope of the secant line is

$$\frac{\Delta y}{\Delta x} = \frac{f(b) - f(a)}{b - a}$$

This formula is called the **average rate of change**. You probably recognize the symbol Δ, the Greek letter "delta," which represents a change in something.

Let's also see how to compute a secant line equation.

FINDING THE EQUATION OF A SECANT LINE

Suppose we have a function $f(x)$ and need to find the secant line from $x = a$ to $x = b$.

Step 1: Find m, the slope of the secant line at $x = a$, using the formula

$$m = \frac{\Delta y}{\Delta x} = \frac{f(b) - f(a)}{b - a}$$

Step 2: Find the y-coordinates at $x = a$ and $x = b$ to get the points $(a, f(a))$ and $(b, f(b))$.

Step 3: Use the point-slope method and set up

$$y - f(a) = m(x - a)$$

Step 4: Solve for y to get the secant line equation. (You can use the point $(b, f(b))$ instead; just pick whichever of the two points is easier to use.)

EXAMPLE

Consider $f(x) = x^2 - 3$. We want to calculate the average rate of change from $x = 2$ to $x = 8$ and then write down the equation of the secant line between those points.

Solution: The slope is

$$\frac{\Delta y}{\Delta x} = \frac{f(8) - f(2)}{8 - 2} = \frac{(8^2 - 3) - (2^2 - 3)}{8 - 2} = \frac{61 - 1}{8 - 2} = \frac{60}{6} = 10$$

Thus, the slope of the secant line passing through $(2, 1)$ and $(8, 61)$ is 10. Next, now that we have the slope and both points, pick one of the points and use the point-slope method to find the secant line. Let's pick $(2, 1)$ since it's easier to use:

$$y - 1 = 10(x - 2) \Rightarrow y = 1 + 10x - 20$$
$$\Rightarrow y = 10x - 19$$

The following graph shows the parabola $f(x) = x^2 - 3$, as well as the secant line from through $(2, 1)$ to $(8, 61)$. Notice that it touches the parabola exactly twice, which is why it's a secant line.

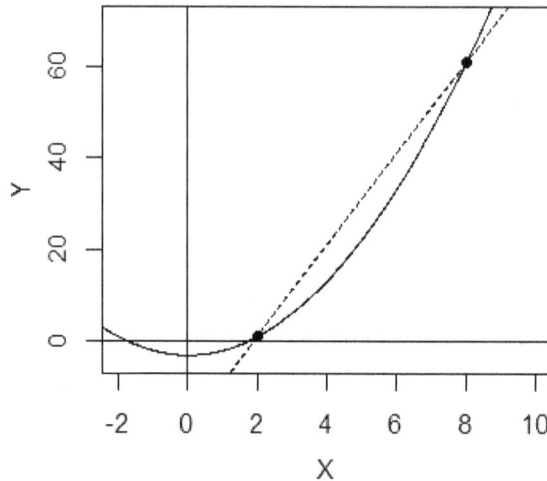

Δ

Now that we know how to find an approximation of the slope of a point on a curve, we seek a way to calculate the exact slope. First, consider the following picture.

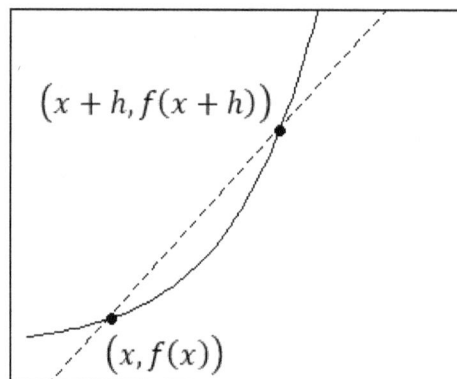

We wish to know the slope of this curve at the point $(x, f(x))$. Here the letter h is just an increment. First, we could find the slope of the secant line passing through the two points $(x, f(x))$ and $(x + h, f(x + h))$. It is just

$$\frac{\Delta y}{\Delta x} = \frac{f(x + h) - f(x)}{x + h - x} = \frac{f(x + h) - f(x)}{h}$$

Now we focus on the point $(x, f(x))$. Intuitively, if we slide the point $(x + h, f(x + h))$ closer to $(x, f(x))$, two things will happen. The value of h will shrink, and the slope of the new secant line will be a closer approximation of the desired slope.

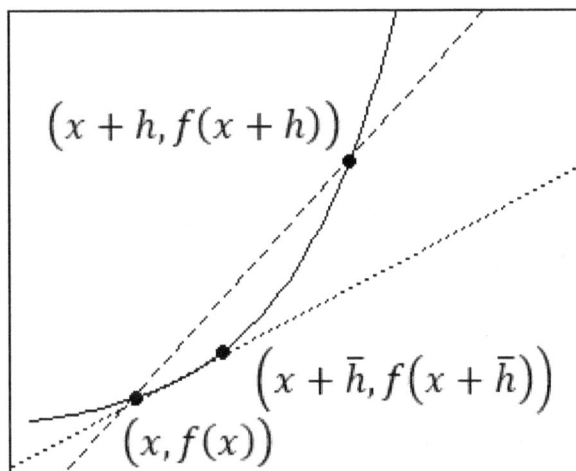

Thus, to calculate the exact slope at the point $(x, f(x))$, we can slide $\left(x + \bar{h}, f\left(x + \bar{h}\right)\right)$ closer and closer to $(x, f(x))$. We do this by letting h approach zero. Does this sound familiar? It should – we are talking about a limit! This means that the slope at $(x, f(x))$ is given by

$$\lim_{h \to 0} \frac{f(x + h) - f(x)}{h}$$

Furthermore, as h approaches 0, the secant line will eventually take on the exact value of the slope at $(x, f(x))$. Here the line will pass through one and only one point: $(x, f(x))$. Hence, this line is no longer a secant line – it is a **tangent line**.

DEFINITION
Consider a point $(x, f(x))$ on a curve. The **tangent line** to $(x, f(x))$ is the unique line passing through that point and no other point nearby on the curve. (If it did pass through a second point nearby, we would instead have a secant line.) The slope of the tangent line gives us the slope of the curve at the point $(x, f(x))$.

ETYMOLOGY
The word **tangent** derives from the Latin *tangere*, which meant "to touch."

DEFINITION
Consider a function $f(x)$. The slope at a point $(a, f(a))$ is

$$\lim_{h \to 0} \frac{f(x + h) - f(x)}{h} \Bigg|_{x=a}$$

The symbolization on the right simply means that after we find the equation of the slope in terms of x, we evaluate it at $x = a$.

DEFINITION
The **instantaneous rate of change** is the slope of the tangent line to a point on a curve. It is given by

$$\lim_{h \to 0} \frac{f(x+h) - f(x)}{h}$$

EXAMPLE
Let's find the slope of $f(x) = 3x$ at the point $(4, 12)$.

Solution: We are after the slope of the tangent line of $f(x) = 3x$ at $x = 4$ using limits. Along the way, we will need $f(x+h)$, but this is easily found by replacing x with $x + h$ in the function. In other words,

$$f(x+h) = 3(x+h)$$

Let's find the limit:

$$\begin{aligned}
\lim_{h \to 0} \frac{f(x+h) - f(x)}{h} &= \lim_{h \to 0} \frac{3(x+h) - 3x}{h} \\
&= \lim_{h \to 0} \frac{3x + 3h - 3x}{h} \\
&= \lim_{h \to 0} \frac{3h}{h} \\
&= \lim_{h \to 0} 3 \\
&= 3
\end{aligned}$$

For the last couple of steps, the h has left the denominator, which means we can finally evaluate the limit by substituting in $h = 0$, leaving 3 as the answer. This means that the slope of the function $f(x) = 3x$ at $x = 4$ is 3, and another way to phrase that is that the instantaneous rate of change at $x = 4$ is 3. (This should be no surprise since $f(x) = 3x$ is a straight line, so it has slope 3 everywhere!)

Δ

We also need to learn how to find a tangent line, so let's go off on a tangent (I'm sorry – I had to say it!) and write down the steps.

FINDING THE EQUATION OF A TANGENT LINE
Suppose we have a function $f(x)$ and need to find the tangent line at $x = a$.

Step 1: Find m, the slope of the tangent line at $x = a$, using the limit analysis.
Step 2: Find the y-coordinate at $x = a$ to get the point $\big(a, f(a)\big)$.
Step 3: Use the point-slope method and set up

$$y - f(a) = m(x - a)$$

Step 4: Solve for y to get the tangent line equation.

EXAMPLE
Find the instantaneous rate of change of $f(x) = x^2 - 3$ at $x = 2$, and find the equation of the tangent line to the function at that point.

Solution: This is a good example of how to find a tangent line. For a start, we want the slope of the tangent line to the point $(2, f(2)) = (2, 1)$. We proceed:

$$\lim_{h \to 0} \frac{f(x + h) - f(x)}{h} = \lim_{h \to 0} \frac{((x + h)^2 - 3) - (x^2 - 3)}{h}$$
$$= \lim_{h \to 0} \frac{x^2 + 2xh + h^2 - 3 - x^2 + 3}{h}$$
$$= \lim_{h \to 0} \frac{2xh + h^2}{h}$$
$$= \lim_{h \to 0} (2x + h)$$
$$= 2x|_{x=2}$$
$$= 2 \cdot 2 = 4$$

This work tells us that the general equation for the slope of a point on $f(x) = x^2 - 3$ is $2x$, and in particular the slope at $x = 2$ is 4. Now let's use this information to calculate the tangent line itself. Once again we use the point-slope method, given that the slope is 4 and the point is $(2, 2^2 - 3) = (2, 1)$:

$$y - 1 = 4(x - 2) \Rightarrow y = 1 + 4x - 8$$
$$\Rightarrow y = 4x - 7$$

The following graph shows the parabola $f(x) = x^2 - 3$, as well as the tangent line at $(2, 1)$. Notice that it touches the parabola exactly once, which is why it's a tangent line instead of a secant line.

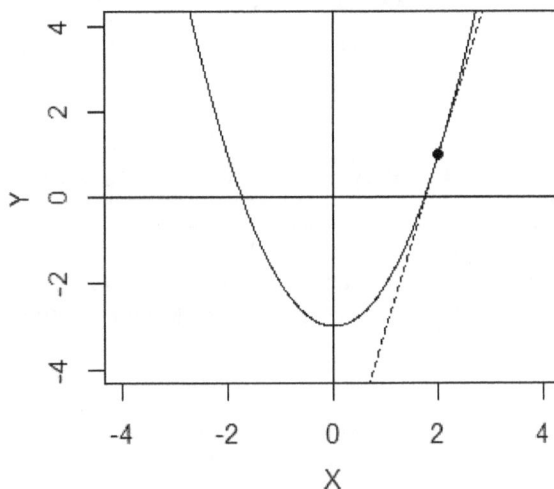

Δ

Section 1.6 – Introduction to Derivatives

As we saw in Section 1.5, the equation for the slope of a line tangent to a given point on a curve $f(x)$ is given by $\lim_{h \to 0} \frac{f(x+h)-f(x)}{h}$. In this section we make the formal definition of a derivative based on this formula.

DEFINITION
Consider the function $f(x)$, which is differentiable at a point a. Then the **derivative** at $x = a$ is the slope of the tangent line at $x = a$. The formula is given by the equation

$$f'(a) = \lim_{h \to 0} \frac{f(x+h) - f(x)}{h}\bigg|_a$$

The notation to the right of the limit means that after we find the general formula for the derivative, we evaluate it at the point $x = a$ to get a numerical answer.

NOTATION
There are several ways of denoting a derivative:

<u>Option 1</u>: Given a function $f(x)$, we may write $f'(x)$. This is read "f-prime x" or "the derivative of $f(x)$ with respect to x."

<u>Option 2</u>: Given a function y, we may write y' or $\frac{dy}{dx}$ (alternatively, dy/dx when written on a line of text). The first symbol is read "y-prime," and the second symbol is read "$dy\,dx$" or "the derivative of y with respect to x."

<u>Option 3</u>: Given a function $f(x)$, we may also write $\frac{d}{dx}\big(f(x)\big)$ or $D_x\big(f(x)\big)$.

In these notes, we will most commonly use $f'(x)$, $\frac{dy}{dx}$, and y'. Which symbol you choose depends on what is convenient for the problem. Of course, if the letters are different, we adjust the letters in the derivative as needed.

ETYMOLOGY
The word **derivative** derives from the Latin *de-* (meaning "down") and *rivus* (meaning "stream"), thereby making the Latin *derivare*, which meant "to derive" or, literally, "to draw off a stream of water from its source."

The previous section dealt with slopes of tangent lines. What we did not say then was that we were actually examining derivatives at the same time! In this section we work out a couple of limit examples to discover the derivatives of a couple of equations.

EXAMPLE
Let's evaluate the derivative of $f(x) = x^3$ at the point $x = 1$.

Solution: We first set up the limit:

$$f'(x) = \lim_{h \to 0} \frac{f(x+h) - f(x)}{h} = \lim_{h \to 0} \frac{(x+h)^3 - x^3}{h}$$

When we have to write $f(x+h)$ above, all we do is take our function and replace all the x's with $(x+h)$'s. In this case, x^3 becomes $(x+h)^3$. Our goal is to get that h out of the denominator and hence avoid having a limit of $0/0$, which is not a number. In this case, we may do it by expanding $(x+h)^3$.

There are two ways to do this. The slower method is to compute the product of each $(x+h)$ individually:

$$(x+h)^3 = (x+h)(x+h)(x+h)$$

$$= (x^2 + 2xh + h^2)(x + h)$$
$$= x^3 + 2x^2h + xh^2 + x^2h + 2xh^2 + h^3$$
$$= x^3 + 3x^2h + 3xh^2 + h^3$$

However, let's choose the quicker method. Recall the binomial expansion formula for $n = 3$:

$$(a + b)^3 = \binom{3}{0}a^3b^0 + \binom{3}{1}a^2b^1 + \binom{3}{2}a^1b^2 + \binom{3}{3}a^0b^3$$
$$= a^3 + 3a^2b + 3ab^2 + b^3$$

Remember that, for instance, $\binom{3}{2} = \frac{3!}{(3-2)!2!} = \frac{3\cdot2\cdot1}{1\cdot2\cdot1} = 3$. (You will find these formulas in Appendix F.) Using this expansion formula, we get

$$(x + h)^3 = x^3 + 3x^2h + 3xh^2 + h^3$$

This time we arrived at the answer in one quick step. Returning to the limit, we have

$$\lim_{h \to 0} \frac{(x + h)^3 - x^3}{h} = \lim_{h \to 0} \frac{(x^3 + 3x^2h + 3xh^2 + h^3) - x^3}{h}$$
$$= \lim_{h \to 0} \frac{3x^2h + 3xh^2 + h^3}{h}$$

Now we may cancel out an h in every term:

$$\lim_{h \to 0} \frac{3x^2h + 3xh^2 + h^3}{h} = \lim_{h \to 0}(3x^2 + 3xh + h^2)$$

We have succeeded in eliminating the h from the denominator, and we no longer have to worry about the limit being $0/0$. Now we can evaluate the limit directly:

$$\lim_{h \to 0}(3x^2 + 3xh + h^2) = 3x^2$$

Hence, the derivative of $f(x) = x^3$ is $f'(x) = 3x^2$. Now we wanted to know the derivative at $x = 1$:

$$f'(x) = 3x^2|_{x=1} = 3 \cdot (1)^2 = 3$$

This tells us that the slope of the tangent line to $f(x) = x^3$ at the point $x = 1$ is 3.

Δ

EXAMPLE

If $f(x) = \sqrt{x}$, then show that $f'(x) = \frac{1}{2\sqrt{x}}$.

Solution: We first set up the limit equation:

$$f'(x) = \lim_{h \to 0} \frac{f(x + h) - f(x)}{h} = \lim_{h \to 0} \frac{\sqrt{x + h} - \sqrt{x}}{h}$$

How do we deal with the radicals in the numerator? We use a little trick from basic algebra, multiplying by the conjugate. Since the limit involves subtracting radicals, the conjugate adds the same radicals.

$$\lim_{h \to 0} \frac{\sqrt{x+h} - \sqrt{x}}{h} = \lim_{h \to 0} \frac{\sqrt{x+h} - \sqrt{x}}{h} \cdot \left(\frac{\sqrt{x+h} + \sqrt{x}}{\sqrt{x+h} + \sqrt{x}} \right)$$

The new fraction we multiply the limit by is just a fancy way of writing 1. After foiling the numerator, we end up with

$$\lim_{h \to 0} \frac{\sqrt{x+h} - \sqrt{x}}{h} \cdot \left(\frac{\sqrt{x+h} + \sqrt{x}}{\sqrt{x+h} + \sqrt{x}} \right) = \lim_{h \to 0} \frac{(x+h) - x}{h\left(\sqrt{x+h} + \sqrt{x}\right)}$$

This is much simpler! The x's cancel out, and afterwards so do the h's. We end up with

$$\lim_{h \to 0} \frac{(x+h) - x}{h\left(\sqrt{x+h} + \sqrt{x}\right)} = \lim_{h \to 0} \frac{h}{h\left(\sqrt{x+h} + \sqrt{x}\right)} = \lim_{h \to 0} \frac{1}{\sqrt{x+h} + \sqrt{x}}$$

Now we can evaluate the limit:

$$\lim_{h \to 0} \frac{1}{\sqrt{x+h} + \sqrt{x}} = \frac{1}{\sqrt{x} + \sqrt{x}} = \frac{1}{2\sqrt{x}}$$

Δ

Next, what does it even mean to say that a function is differentiable? Let's find out.

DEFINITION

We say that a function $f(x)$ is **differentiable** at a point a if the derivative exists at a; that is, if $f'(a)$ exists and is a real number (not infinite).

EXAMPLE

In the most recent example, where $f(x) = \sqrt{x}$, the function is clearly not differentiable when x is negative. The function does not even exist for such values. Also, the function is not differentiable at 0 because, looking at the derivative $f'(x) = \frac{1}{2\sqrt{x}}$, evaluating this at zero will give an undefined answer. (Interestingly, the original function $f(x)$ exists at $x = 0$ since we can compute $\sqrt{0} = 0$, and yet the derivative does not exist there.)

Δ

There is one final statement we must discuss.

DIFFERENTIABILITY IMPLIES CONTINUITY

If a function $f(x)$ is differentiable at a, then $f(x)$ is also continuous at a. In other words, differentiability implies continuity.

A consequence of this statement is that if $f(x)$ is discontinuous at a, then it is not differentiable there.

Thus, if we discover that the derivative at the point a exists, then the function must necessarily be continuous at that point. (Recall the definition of continuity.)

Is the converse true? If a function is continuous at a, does it necessarily follow that the function is differentiable at a? The answer is no, not necessarily. Take, for instance, $f(x) = |x|$.

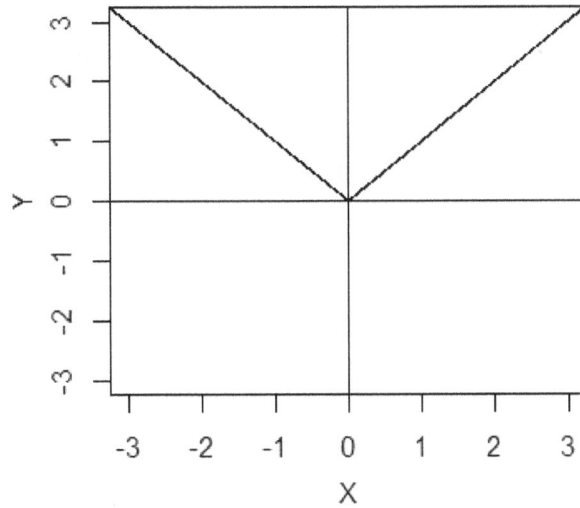

This function is certainly continuous at the origin, for $\lim_{x \to 0} |x| = 0$ and $f(0) = 0$. However, let's now look at the derivative. Recall that this function is really

$$f(x) = \begin{cases} x, & x \geq 0 \\ -x, & x < 0 \end{cases}$$

We need only draw upon basic algebra skills to realize that the slope of the right side of the graph is 1, while the left half's slope is -1. We might sketch this as follows:

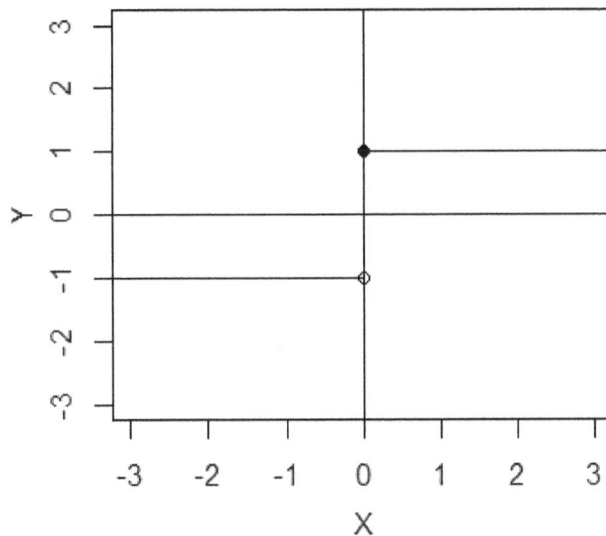

This new function (derivative) is clearly discontinuous at the origin, for there is a jump. Hence, $f(x)$ cannot be differentiable at the origin, even though it is continuous there.

The final topic in this section deals with seven cases when we can know immediately that the derivative does not exist.

CASES WHEN THE DERIVATIVE DOES NOT EXIST
The following are instances when the derivative of a function $f(x)$ at $x = a$ does not exist.
<u>Case 1</u>: There is a corner at $x = a$.
<u>Case 2</u>: There is a cusp at $x = a$.
<u>Case 3</u>: There is a jump at $x = a$.
<u>Case 4</u>: There is a hole / removable discontinuity at $x = a$.
<u>Case 5</u>: There is a displaced point at $x = a$.
<u>Case 6</u>: There is a vertical asymptote at $x = a$.
<u>Case 7</u>: The tangent line at $x = a$ is vertical.

EXAMPLE (CORNER)
The absolute value function $f(x) = |x|$ from the previous example has a corner at $x = 0$, and as we saw, the derivative does not exist there (even though the original function is continuous there).

Δ

EXAMPLE (CUSP)
The function $f(x) = |\sin(x)|$ over $0 \leq x \leq 2\pi$, whose graph looks like the following, has a cusp at $x = \pi$. A cusp is where two curves with different shapes or slopes meet, and that means the derivative cannot exist there.

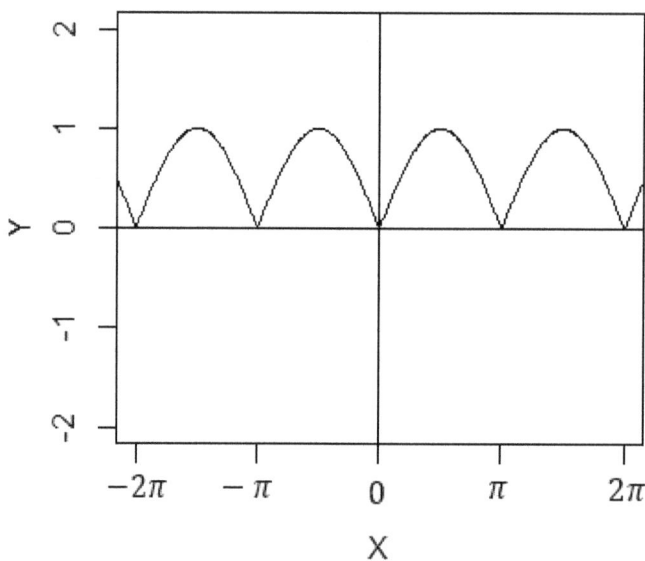

Δ

EXAMPLE (JUMP)
Consider the following piecewise function whose graph is shown below.

$$f(x) = \begin{cases} a, & x \leq c \\ b, & x > c \end{cases}$$

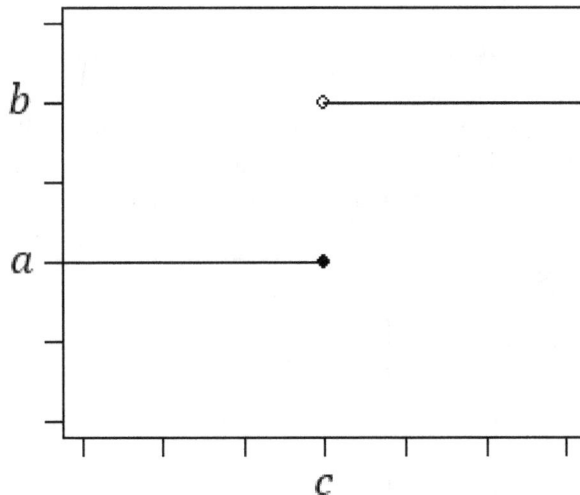

We already know that $f(x)$ is discontinuous at $x = c$, and so it is not differentiable there either.

Δ

EXAMPLE (HOLE)

The function $f(x) = (x^2 - 4)/(x - 2)$ can be rewritten as

$$f(x) = \frac{(x - 2)(x + 2)}{(x - 2)} = x + 2$$

Since the $(x - 2)$ pieces cancel out, that means that there is a hole, or a removable discontinuity, at $x = 2$. We already know that $f(x)$ is not continuous at $x = 2$, and it is also not differentiable there.

Δ

EXAMPLE (DISPLACED POINT)

Consider the function

$$f(x) = \begin{cases} x^2 - 1, & x \neq 1 \\ 1, & x = 1 \end{cases}$$

Here $f(-1) = 1$, but looking at points very close to 1 such as 1.00001 or 0.99999, we discover that

$$\lim_{x \to 1} f(x) = \lim_{x \to 1}(x^2 - 1) = 1^2 - 1 = 0$$

Thus, the limit exists and is 0, and the point exists and is $(1, 1)$, but they don't equal each other. The function is discontinuous at $x = 1$ and is therefore not differentiable there.

Δ

EXAMPLE (VERTICAL ASYMPTOTE)

The function $f(x) = 1/(x - 4)$ has a vertical asymptote at $x = 4$. It is not continuous at that point, and so it is also not differentiable there. However, it is continuous and differentiable at all other points.

Δ

EXAMPLE (VERTICAL TANGENT LINE)

The function $f(x) = \sqrt{x}$ has a derivative of $f'(x) = \frac{1}{2\sqrt{x}}$, as we saw earlier in this section. The original function is continuous at $x = 0$, but the derivative is undefined at $x = 0$ because we would be dividing by 0. Put another way, the derivative there is approaching infinity, and graphically that means that if we drew a tangent line there, it would be vertical. The following graph is of $f'(x)$ and a vertical tangent line at $x = 0$. (Since the vertical tangent line passes through $x = 0$, its equation would be $x = 0$.)

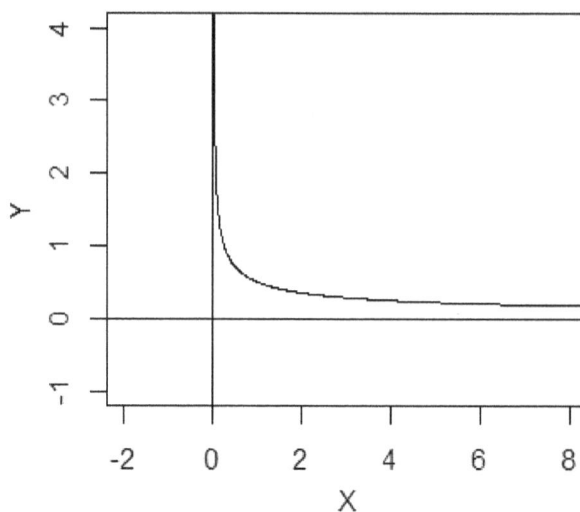

Δ

Chapter 2 – Derivatives

Now that we have seen how to find the derivatives of simple functions like $f(x) = x^2$ and $f(x) = \sqrt{x}$, we wish to find the derivatives of many, more complicated, functions. However, stepping through the whole limit definition each and every time is rough and time consuming, so it would be nice to have some shortcut formulas.

In this chapter we explicitly derive the necessary formulas for derivative operations (such as addition, multiplication, and division). Then we explore how to get the derivatives of algebraic, trigonometric, exponential, and inverse trigonometric formulas. Along the way we will discuss how to compute higher-order derivatives, as well as some applications to physics. We also give an introduction to implicit differentiation, which will enable us to differentiate a formula right away without first isolating y.

Section 2.1 – The Addition, Power, Product, and Quotient Rules

Now that we have officially established the definition of a derivative, it's time to have some shortcut definitions so that we do not have to go through the entire limit definition process each time we compute a derivative. In this section we will begin doing just that, and in future sections, we will derive the formulas for the most common algebraic and trigonometric functions. Let's start with the simplest derivative.

DERIVATIVE OF A CONSTANT
Let $f(x) = c$, where c is some constant real number. Then

$$\frac{d}{dx}(c) = 0$$

PROOF
Here $f(x) = c$ and $f(x + h) = c$ for any h. Then we have

$$\frac{d}{dx}\big(f(x)\big) = \lim_{h \to 0} \frac{f(x + h) - f(x)}{h} = \lim_{h \to 0} \frac{c - c}{h} = 0$$

∎

EXAMPLE
If $f(x) = 314$, then $f'(x) = 0$.

Δ

DERIVATIVE OF A FUNCTION WITH A CONSTANT
Consider the function $cf(x)$, where c is some constant and $f(x)$ is differentiable at x. Then

$$\frac{d}{dx}(cf(x)) = cf'(x)$$

This theorem tells us that if there is a constant in front of a function, then the derivative is equal to the derivative of that function multiplied by that constant. In other words, we compute the derivative of the function, and the constant "comes along for the ride."

PROOF
Using the limit definition of derivative,

$$\frac{d}{dx}(cf(x)) = \lim_{h \to 0} \frac{cf(x+h) - cf(x)}{h} = \lim_{h \to 0} c\left[\frac{f(x+h) - f(x)}{h}\right] = cf'(x)$$

All we do here is factor out c, and we have the normal limit formula.

■

EXAMPLE
Let $f(x) = 5x^2$. As we saw in the previous section, the derivative of x^2 is $2x$, so

$$f'(x) = 5 \cdot 2x = 10x$$

Δ

Now let's consider the function which is the sum of two functions, $h(x) = f(x) + g(x)$. Here is the formula for this derivative.

ADDITION RULE
Let $f(x)$ and $g(x)$ be differentiable at x. Then their sum $h(x) = f(x) + g(x)$ is differentiable at x and

$$\frac{d}{dx}(f(x) + g(x)) = f'(x) + g'(x)$$

Similarly, it follows that

$$\frac{d}{dx}(f(x) - g(x)) = f'(x) - g'(x)$$

PROOF
We begin by writing the derivative formula for the new formula $h(x) = f(x) + g(x)$:

$$\frac{d}{dx}(f(x) + g(x)) = \lim_{h \to 0}\left\{\frac{[f(x+h) + g(x+h)] - [f(x) + g(x)]}{h}\right\}$$

Rearranging terms, we end up with

$$\lim_{h \to 0}\left\{\frac{[f(x+h) + g(x+h)] - [f(x) + g(x)]}{h}\right\} = \lim_{h \to 0}\frac{f(x+h) - f(x)}{h} + \lim_{h \to 0}\frac{g(x+h) - g(x)}{h}$$
$$= f'(x) + g'(x)$$

Of course, the same rule applies when we subtract two functions that are both differentiable at x.

■

EXAMPLE
Let $f(x) = x^2 - 3x + 7$. The functions $g_1(x) = x^2$, $g_2(x) = -3x$, and $g_3(x) = 7$ are all differentiable at any x, and so

72

$$f'(x) = \frac{d}{dx}(x^2) + \frac{d}{dx}(-3x) + \frac{d}{dx}(7)$$
$$= 2x - 3 + 0$$
$$= 2x - 3$$

Δ

The next theorem we present is actually the first of a series of related theorems. Each theorem will build upon itself, and over the next few sections we will introduce a new component until we arrive at the general case. Here is the first (and simplest) case:

POWER RULE (CASE 1: POSITIVE INTEGERS)
Let $f(x) = x^n$ where $n \geq 1$ is a positive integer. Then

$$\frac{d}{dx}(x^n) = nx^{n-1}$$

PROOF
There are several ways to prove this, but we give only one method. Recall the formula for the binomial distribution:

$$(a + b)^n = \binom{n}{0}a^n b^0 + \binom{n}{1}a^{n-1}b^1 + \binom{n}{2}a^{n-2}b^2 + \cdots + \binom{n}{n-1}a^1 b^{n-1} + \binom{n}{n}a^0 b^n$$

Here $\binom{n}{k} = \frac{n!}{(n-k)!k!}$. You have probably seen this notation from pre-calculus. Simplifying the formula slightly, we get

$$(a + b)^n = a^n + na^{n-1}b + \binom{n}{2}a^{n-2}b^2 + \cdots + nab^{n-1} + b^n$$

Returning to the derivative proof, we first set up the formula:

$$f'(x) = \lim_{h \to 0}\frac{f(x + h) - f(x)}{h} = \lim_{h \to 0}\frac{(x + h)^n - x^n}{h}$$

Using the binomial distribution formula, we get

$$\lim_{h \to 0}\frac{(x + h)^n - x^n}{h} = \lim_{h \to 0}\frac{\left[x^n + nx^{n-1}h + \binom{n}{2}x^{n-2}h^2 + \cdots + nxh^{n-1} + h^n\right] - x^n}{h}$$

The x^n's cancel out, and we are left with

$$\lim_{h \to 0}\frac{nx^{n-1}h + \binom{n}{2}x^{n-2}h^2 + \cdots + nxh^{n-1} + h^n}{h}$$

Since each term in the numerator has an h, we may cancel each of these with the denominator:

$$\lim_{h \to 0}\left[nx^{n-1} + \binom{n}{2}x^{n-2}h + \cdots + nxh^{n-2} + h^{n-1}\right] = nx^{n-1}$$

∎

EXAMPLE

Consider $f(x) = x^9 + 4x^5$. Here we use the Power Rule and the Addition Rule:

$$f'(x) = 9 \cdot x^8 + 4 \cdot 5x^4$$
$$= 9x^8 + 20x^4$$

Δ

EXAMPLE

Consider the function $f(x) = 12x^7 - 3x^5 + x^3 - 5x + 18$. Then

$$f'(x) = 12 \cdot 7x^6 - 3 \cdot 5x^4 + 3 \cdot x^2 - 5 \cdot 1$$
$$= 84x^6 - 15x^4 + 3x^2 - 5$$

Δ

Before we go further, we need to introduce a trick called a "clever zero," so called because in the equation, we add in a new term and then subtract it. By doing this, we have not upset the balance of the equation. For instance, if we have $x = 6$ and decide to insert a clever zero, it might look something like this:

$$x + 4 - 4 = 6$$

Since x still equals 6, we have neither changed the value of x nor messed up the equation.

Why would we want to do such a thing to an already simple equation? Sometimes we can perform a sneaky algebraic trick to solve certain problems by using clever zeros. One common example, which you have used before in algebra, is completing the square.

EXAMPLE

If $x^2 + 6x + 2 = 0$, then we complete the square as follows:

$$x^2 + 6x + 2 + 9 - 9 = 0$$
$$x^2 + 6x + 9 - 7 = 0$$
$$(x + 3)^2 = 7$$

The clever zero comes in when we add and subtract the 9's.

Δ

What does this have to do with computing derivatives? We are going to use this trick to derive the Product Rule.

PRODUCT RULE

Let $f(x)$ and $g(x)$ be continuous functions. Then

$$\frac{d}{dx}(f(x) \cdot g(x)) = f(x) \cdot g'(x) + f'(x) \cdot g(x)$$

PROOF

We set up the limit:

$$\frac{d}{dx}[f(x) \cdot g(x)] = \lim_{h \to 0} \frac{f(x+h) \cdot g(x+h) - f(x) \cdot g(x)}{h}$$

Now we are going to insert a clever zero into the numerator. We choose it so that we may rearrange the terms in the numerator. By doing this, we can hopefully find a situation which will make it easier to evaluate the limit.

Although it is not the only choice, consider the clever zero $f(x) \cdot g(x+h) - f(x) \cdot g(x+h)$. How do we spot this? It just takes practice, and hopefully the following will make it clearer.

Inserting this "zero," we get

$$\lim_{h \to 0} \frac{f(x+h) \cdot g(x+h) + [f(x) \cdot g(x+h) - f(x) \cdot g(x+h)] - f(x) \cdot g(x)}{h}$$

Rearrange the terms, and we get

$$\lim_{h \to 0} \frac{f(x) \cdot g(x+h) - f(x) \cdot g(x) + f(x+h) \cdot g(x+h) - f(x) \cdot g(x+h)}{h}$$

Now note that we can factor out $f(x)$ in the first two numerator terms. Similarly, in the third and fourth terms, we can factor out $g(x+h)$. So let's rewrite:

$$\lim_{h \to 0} \frac{f(x)[g(x+h) - g(x)] + g(x+h)[f(x+h) - f(x)]}{h}$$

Now we split this into two limits, obtaining

$$\lim_{h \to 0} \frac{f(x)[g(x+h) - g(x)]}{h} + \lim_{h \to 0} \frac{g(x+h)[f(x+h) - f(x)]}{h}$$

Note that both fractions are now written in terms of derivative definitions. The first fraction is

$$\lim_{h \to 0} \frac{f(x)[g(x+h) - g(x)]}{h} = f(x) \cdot \lim_{h \to 0} \frac{[g(x+h) - g(x)]}{h} = f(x) \cdot g'(x)$$

Since $f(x)$ was not written in terms of h, we could pull it out of the limit. Similarly, for the second fraction,

$$\lim_{h \to 0} \frac{g(x+h)[f(x+h) - f(x)]}{h} = \lim_{h \to 0} g(x+h) \cdot \lim_{h \to 0} \frac{[f(x+h) - f(x)]}{h} = g(x) \cdot f'(x)$$

Combining these, we finally get

$$\frac{d}{dx}(f(x) \cdot g(x)) = f(x) \cdot g'(x) + f'(x) \cdot g(x)$$

■

EXAMPLE

Consider $y = x^4(x+2)^5$. Let's first write the two functions:

$$f(x) = x^4 \qquad\qquad g(x) = (x+2)^5$$

$$f'(x) = 4x^3 \qquad\qquad g'(x) = 5(x+2)^4$$

Applying the Product Rule, we get

$$\begin{aligned} y' &= f(x) \cdot g'(x) + f'(x) \cdot g(x) \\ &= x^4 \cdot 5(x+2)^4 + (x+2)^5 \cdot 4x^3 \\ &= 5x^4(x+2)^4 + 4x^3(x+2)^5 \end{aligned}$$

We may stop here, or we can continue and simplify: by factoring out $x^3(x+2)^4$:

$$\begin{aligned} 5x^4(x+2)^4 + 4x^3(x+2)^5 &= x^3(x+2)^4[5x + 4(x+2)] \\ &= x^3(x+2)^4(9x+8) \end{aligned}$$

Δ

EXAMPLE
Let's find the derivative of $y = 3x^3(4x^5 - 3)$.

Solution: Here are the two functions:

$$\begin{aligned} f(x) &= 3x^3 \\ f'(x) &= 3 \cdot 3x^2 = 9x^2 \\ g(x) &= 4x^5 - 3 \\ g'(x) &= 4 \cdot 5x^4 - 0 = 20x^4 \end{aligned}$$

The derivative is therefore

$$\begin{aligned} y' &= f(x) \cdot g'(x) + f'(x) \cdot g(x) \\ &= 3x^3 \cdot 20x^4 + 9x^2 \cdot (4x^5 - 3) \\ &= 60x^7 + 36x^7 - 27x^2 \\ &= 96x^7 - 27x^2 \end{aligned}$$

We may also pull out some factors:

$$y' = 96x^7 - 27x^2 = 3x^2(32x^5 - 9)$$

Δ

Note that if one of the functions is a constant, then we have the case $y = cf(x)$. Therefore

$$y' = cf'(x) + (0) \cdot f(x) = cf'(x)$$

Here the Product Rule would reduce to the derivative of a function multiplied by a constant.

Sometimes we come across functions that are reciprocals; for instance, $f(x) = 1/x$. It would be nice to have a derivative formula for such a reciprocal function. We can also use this to prove the Quotient Rule as well as establish the next stage of the Power Rule.

RECIPROCAL RULE
Let $y = \dfrac{1}{f(x)}$ where $f(x)$ is differentiable at x and is not equal to zero at x. Then

$$\frac{d}{dx}\left(\frac{1}{f(x)}\right) = -\frac{f'(x)}{f^2(x)} = -\frac{f'(x)}{\big(f(x)\big)^2}$$

PROOF

We start by writing the limit definition.

$$\frac{d}{dx}\left(\frac{1}{f(x)}\right) = \lim_{h \to 0} \frac{\frac{1}{f(x+h)} - \frac{1}{f(x)}}{h} = \lim_{h \to 0} \frac{1}{h} \cdot \left[\frac{1}{f(x+h)} - \frac{1}{f(x)}\right]$$

$$= \lim_{h \to 0} \frac{1}{h} \cdot \left[\frac{f(x) - f(x+h)}{f(x+h) \cdot f(x)}\right]$$

$$= \lim_{h \to 0} \left(\frac{f(x) - f(x+h)}{f(x+h) \cdot f(x) \cdot h}\right)$$

Now we split this into the product of two functions:

$$\lim_{h \to 0} \left(\frac{1}{f(x+h) \cdot f(x)}\right) \cdot \left(\frac{f(x) - f(x+h)}{h}\right) = \lim_{h \to 0} \left(\frac{1}{f(x+h) \cdot f(x)}\right) \cdot \lim_{h \to 0} \left(\frac{f(x) - f(x+h)}{h}\right)$$

Now we can evaluate both of these limits after pulling out a -1 from the second limit:

$$\lim_{h \to 0} \left(\frac{1}{f(x+h) \cdot f(x)}\right) \cdot (-1) \cdot \lim_{h \to 0} \left(\frac{f(x+h) - f(x)}{h}\right) = -\frac{1}{\left(f(x)\right)^2} \cdot f'(x) = -\frac{f'(x)}{\left(f(x)\right)^2}$$

∎

EXAMPLE

Let's compute the derivative for that earlier function, $f(x) = 1/x$. This is equal to $f(x) = 1/g(x)$ where $g(x) = x$ and $x \neq 0$. By using the reciprocal theorem, we have

$$\frac{d}{dx}\left(\frac{1}{x}\right) = -\frac{\frac{d}{dx}(x)}{x^2} = -\frac{1}{x^2}$$

Δ

We can now use this result to prove the next two derivative rules.

QUOTIENT RULE

Let $f(x)$ and $g(x)$ be differentiable at x and $g(x) \neq 0$. Then

$$\frac{d}{dx}\left(\frac{f(x)}{g(x)}\right) = \frac{g(x) \cdot f'(x) - f(x) \cdot g'(x)}{\left(g(x)\right)^2}$$

PROOF

The proof follows from the Reciprocal Rule and the Product Rule. We have

$$y = \frac{f(x)}{g(x)} = f(x) \cdot \frac{1}{g(x)}$$

By the Product Rule, we have

$$\frac{d}{dx}\left(f(x)\cdot\frac{1}{g(x)}\right) = f(x)\cdot\frac{d}{dx}\left(\frac{1}{g(x)}\right) + \frac{d}{dx}(f(x))\cdot\frac{1}{g(x)}$$

$$= f(x)\cdot\frac{d}{dx}\left(\frac{1}{g(x)}\right) + f'(x)\cdot\frac{1}{g(x)}$$

Next, by the Reciprocal Rule,

$$f(x)\cdot\frac{-g'(x)}{(g(x))^2} + \frac{f'(x)}{g(x)} = \frac{f'(x)\cdot g(x)}{(g(x))^2} - \frac{f(x)\cdot g'(x)}{(g(x))^2}$$

$$= \frac{g(x)\cdot f'(x) - f(x)\cdot g'(x)}{(g(x))^2}$$

∎

Of course, we could have proven it by using the "clever zero" trick. However, this proof is much more straightforward.

EXAMPLE

Evaluate $y = \frac{x}{6-x^2}$. Here we have

$$f(x) = x \qquad\qquad g(x) = 6 - x^2$$
$$f'(x) = 1 \qquad\qquad g'(x) = -2x$$

Applying the Quotient Rule, we get

$$y' = \frac{(6-x^2)(1) - x(-2x)}{(6-x^2)^2} = \frac{6+x^2}{(6-x^2)^2}$$

Δ

EXAMPLE

Let's find the derivative of $y = \frac{x^3-6x}{2x+1}$. Here are the two functions:

$$f(x) = x^3 - 6x \qquad\qquad g(x) = 2x + 1$$
$$f'(x) = 3x^2 - 6 \qquad\qquad g'(x) = 2$$

Using the Quotient Rule, the derivative is

$$y' = \frac{g(x)\cdot f'(x) - f(x)\cdot g'(x)}{(g(x))^2}$$

$$= \frac{(2x+1)(3x^2-6) - (x^3-6x)(2)}{(2x+1)^2}$$

Let's simplify this:

$$y' = \frac{(2x+1)(3x^2-6) - (x^3-6x)(2)}{(2x+1)^2}$$

$$= \frac{(6x^3 + 3x^2 - 12x - 6) - (2x^3 - 12x)}{(2x+1)^2}$$

$$= \frac{4x^3 + 3x^2 - 6}{(2x + 1)^2}$$

Δ

And now here is the next part of the Power Rule. We have shown that it works for positive integers above and including 1. We are now going to show that it holds for any integer n.

POWER RULE (CASE 2: INTEGERS)
Let n be any integer, positive or negative. If $f(x) = x^n$, then

$$\frac{d}{dx}(x^n) = nx^{n-1}$$

Additionally, if $n \leq 0$, we have to add the condition that $x \neq 0$.

PROOF
We have three cases to check:

CASE I: $n > 0$
This is the first version of the same theorem that we have already proved.

CASE II: $n = 0$
Here we have $f(x) = x^0 = 1$. By the given formula, $\frac{d}{dx}(x^0) = 0 \cdot x^{-1} = 0$, provided that $x \neq 0$. However, as we already know, $f'(1) = 0$, and so they agree.

CASE III: $n < 0$
Let $n = -a$. Then we have $f(x) = x^n = x^{-a} = \frac{1}{x^a}$, provided $x \neq 0$. We use the Reciprocal Rule:

$$\frac{d}{dx}\left(\frac{1}{x^a}\right) = -\frac{\frac{d}{dx}(x^a)}{(x^a)^2} = -\frac{ax^{a-1}}{x^{2a}}$$

We move the x^{a-1} to the denominator, creating

$$-\frac{ax^{a-1}}{x^{2a}} = -\frac{a}{x^{2a}x^{-(a-1)}} = -\frac{a}{x^{2a-a+1}} = -\frac{a}{x^{a+1}}$$

Next, we move the x^{a+1} back to the numerator.

$$-\frac{a}{x^{a+1}} = -ax^{-(a+1)} = -ax^{-a-1}$$

Substituting $n = -a$ again, we get

$$-ax^{-a-1} = nx^{n-1}$$

Thus, the rule holds when n is a negative integer.

Hence, the derivative $\frac{d}{dx}(x^n) = nx^{n-1}$ also holds for 0 and negative integers if $x \neq 0$.

■

EXAMPLE

Let $f(x) = \frac{x^{-2}-4}{x^2+4}$ and $x \neq 0$. Then by the Power Rule and the Quotient Rule,

$$f'(x) = \frac{(x^2+4) \cdot \frac{d}{dx}(x^{-2}-4) - (x^{-2}-4) \cdot \frac{d}{dx}(x^2+4)}{(x^2+4)^2}$$

$$= \frac{(x^2+4) \cdot (-2x^{-3}) - (x^{-2}-4) \cdot (2x)}{(x^2+4)^2}$$

$$= \frac{-2x^{-3}(x^2+4) - 2x(x^{-2}-4)}{(x^2+4)^2}$$

If we care to distribute and simplify, we end up with

$$f'(x) = \frac{-2x^{-1} - 8x^{-3} - 2x^{-1} + 8x}{(x^2+4)^2}$$

$$= \frac{8x - 4x^{-1} - 8x^{-3}}{(x^2+4)^2}$$

We can also get rid of the negative exponents by multiplying the whole fraction by $\frac{x^3}{x^3}$:

$$f'(x) = \left(\frac{x^3}{x^3}\right) \cdot \left(\frac{8x - 4x^{-1} - 8x^{-3}}{(x^2+4)^2}\right)$$

$$= \frac{8x^4 - 4x^2 - 8}{x^3(x^2+4)^2}$$

Δ

Section 2.2 – The Chain Rule and Derivatives of Inverse Functions

We now turn to one of the most important rules in differential calculus: the Chain Rule. We will not take the time to prove it (see a class on differential calculus with theory for that), but here is how it works.

Suppose we have a function like $y = (x^2 + 3x)^2$ that we wish to differentiate. Given the rules we have seen up to this point, our instinct may be to write $y' = 2(x^2 + 3x)$ by using the Power Rule. However, let's try expanding it out first and differentiating what we get:

$$y = (x^2 + 3x) \cdot (x^2 + 3x)$$
$$= x^4 + 3x^3 + 3x^3 + 9x^2$$
$$= x^4 + 6x^3 + 9x^2$$

And therefore $y' = 4x^3 + 18x^2 + 18x$. We disagree!

What went wrong? The problem is that the derivative rules we have so far learned apply only when the function is of the form $f(x)$. However, here the function takes the form $f(g(x))$, where

$$f(g(x)) = (g(x))^2 \text{ and } g(x) = x^2 + 3x$$

We have a whole new, inner continuous function $g(x)$ to worry about. This function appears underneath the Power Rule. So how do we get around this problem? This is where the Chain Rule comes in.

This special theorem tells us to differentiate the outer term first, and then multiply the result by the derivative of the inner term. In other words, given a composition $y = f(g(x))$, then

$$y' = f(g(x)) \cdot g'(x)$$

In the example above, $f(g(x)) = (x^2 + 3x)^2$ and $g(x) = x^2 + 3x$. Then

$$f'(g(x)) = 2(x^2 + 3x) \qquad g'(x) = 2x + 3$$

So we have

$$y' = f(g(x)) \cdot g'(x)$$
$$= 2(x^2 + 3x)(2x + 3)$$

Does this match what we found earlier? Well, simplifying the second result, the answer is yes:

$$y' = 2(x^2 + 3x)(2x + 3)$$
$$= 2(2x^3 + 3x^2 + 6x^2 + 9x)$$
$$= 2(2x^3 + 9x^2 + 9x)$$
$$= 4x^3 + 18x^2 + 18x$$

Note that with the Chain Rule, we do not have to worry about multiplying the whole problem out before taking the derivative. Not only is that time consuming, it increases the likelihood that we will make a mistake somewhere along the way. The Chain Rule takes care of the derivative much more quickly, provided we use it correctly. Unfortunately it is also one of the easiest rules to overlook in a problem. Here is the Chain Rule stated:

CHAIN RULE

Consider the composition $h(x) = f(g(x))$. (Note that books may also write $h(x) = f \circ g$.) Let $g(x)$ be differentiable at x, and let $f(x)$ be differentiable at $g(x)$. Then

$$h'(x) = f(g(x)) \cdot g'(x)$$

Differentiate first the outside function, and then multiply it by the inner function.

We now turn to a series of examples to illustrate carefully how the chain rule works.

EXAMPLE

Let $y = \sqrt{4x^2 + 3x}$. For every place where y is differentiable, we have

$$f(g(x)) = \sqrt{g(x)} \text{ where } g(x) = 4x^2 + 3x$$

Then

$$f'(g(x)) = \frac{1}{2\sqrt{g(x)}} \qquad g'(x) = 8x + 3$$

And so it follows that

$$y' = f'(g(x)) \cdot g'(x)$$
$$= \frac{1}{2\sqrt{g(x)}} \cdot (8x + 3)$$
$$= \frac{8x + 3}{2\sqrt{4x^2 + 3x}}$$

That's all there is to it! When first starting, it is very helpful to make a list of the functions involved, then differentiating them one at a time.

$$\Delta$$

EXAMPLE
Let's do a more complicated example now. Find the derivative of

$$y = \frac{(1 - x^2)^3}{(4 + 5x + 6x^2)^2}$$

Solution: Here we invoke the Quotient Rule as well as the Chain Rule. There is no need to panic; let's simply start by writing out a way to express this. We will use four functions: f, g, h, and j.

$$y = \frac{f(g(x))}{h(j(x))}$$

Writing this out piece by piece, we see that

$$f(g(x)) = (g(x))^3 \qquad g(x) = 1 - x^2$$
$$h(j(x)) = (j(x))^2 \qquad j(x) = 4 + 5x + 6x^2$$

Now let's compute the derivatives.

$$f'(g(x)) = 3(g(x))^2 \qquad g'(x) = -2x$$
$$h'(j(x)) = 2(j(x)) \qquad j'(x) = 5 + 12x$$

Recall the Quotient Rule with the functions f and h:

$$\text{If } y = \frac{f}{h}, \text{ then } y' = \frac{h \cdot f' - f \cdot h'}{h^2}$$

When we turn these into composition functions, the Quotient Rule becomes

$$y' = \frac{h(j(x)) \cdot f'(g(x)) \cdot g'(x) - f(g(x)) \cdot h'(j(x)) \cdot j'(x)}{[h(j(x))]^2}$$

Using what we listed earlier, we substitute everything in carefully:

$$y' = \frac{(j(x))^2 \cdot 3(g(x))^2 \cdot (-2x) - (g(x))^3 \cdot 2(j(x)) \cdot (5 + 12x)}{\left[(j(x))^2\right]^2}$$

Further substitutions leads to

$$y' = \frac{(4 + 5x + 6x^2)^2 \cdot 3(1 - x^2)^2 \cdot (-2x) - (1 - x^2)^3 \cdot 2(4 + 5x + 6x^2) \cdot (5 + 12x)}{[(4 + 5x + 6x^2)^2]^2}$$

And so the final derivative is

$$y' = \frac{(4 + 5x + 6x^2)^2 \cdot 3(1 - x^2)^2 \cdot (-2x) - (1 - x^2)^3 \cdot 2(4 + 5x + 6x^2) \cdot (5 + 12x)}{(4 + 5x + 6x^2)^4}$$

$$= \frac{(4 + 5x + 6x^2) \cdot 3(1 - x^2)^2 \cdot (-2x) - (1 - x^2)^3 \cdot 2 \cdot (5 + 12x)}{(4 + 5x + 6x^2)^3}$$

$$= \frac{-6x(4 + 5x + 6x^2)(1 - x^2)^2 - 2(5 + 12x)(1 - x^2)^3}{(4 + 5x + 6x^2)^3}$$

It goes without saying that one should take care to simplify carefully!

$$\Delta$$

EXAMPLE

Consider $y = \sqrt{(x^2 + 2)^2 + (2 - 5x)^3}$. This is a new twist, for if we stare at this, we see that it is really a multi-layer composition with two functions inside! This means we will have to use the Chain Rule multiple times. No need to worry – we will look at it piece by piece.

Here there are five different functions going on: the outer square root, the square exponent, its interior function, the cube exponent, and its interior function. Call these five functions f, g, h, j, and k. (In case you are wondering why we skipped the letter i as a function name, this letter is usually reserved for imaginary numbers, something you have probably seen in an algebra class. We will not be using them here!)

Let's name our functions, starting with the middle two.

$$j(x) = x^2 + 2 \qquad\qquad k(x) = 2 - 5x$$

Now we name the two functions wrapping around j and k.

$$g\big(j(x)\big) = \big(j(x)\big)^2 \qquad\qquad h\big(k(x)\big) = \big(k(x)\big)^3$$

And finally, f is the composition

$$f\left(g\big(j(x)\big) + h\big(k(x)\big)\right) = \sqrt{g\big(j(x)\big) + h\big(k(x)\big)}$$

This looks horrible, but it really is not that bad. It can be tackled by taking baby steps. Let's start by computing the derivatives of the five functions.

$$j(x) = x^2 + 2 \qquad\qquad j'(x) = 2x$$
$$k(x) = 2 - 5x \qquad\qquad k'(x) = -5$$

$$g\big(j(x)\big) = \big(j(x)\big)^2 \qquad\qquad g'\big(j(x)\big) = 2j(x)$$

$$h(k(x)) = (k(x))^3 \qquad\qquad h'(k(x)) = 3(k(x))^2$$

$$f\left(g(j(x)) + h(k(x))\right) = \sqrt{g(j(x)) + h(k(x))}$$

$$f'\left(g(j(x)) + h(k(x))\right) = \frac{1}{2\sqrt{g(j(x)) + h(k(x))}}$$

We now write down the formula for y'. In this case, it will be the multi-layer analogue of the Chain Rule, with the added property of the addition of derivatives.

$$y' = f'\left(g(j(x)) + h(k(x))\right) \cdot \left[g'(j(x)) \cdot j'(x) + h'(k(x)) \cdot k'(x)\right]$$

This is simply the Chain Rule added to another Chain Rule, all *within* yet another Chain Rule. Now we substitute in what we know.

$$y' = \frac{1}{2\sqrt{g(j(x)) + h(k(x))}} \cdot \left[2j(x) \cdot 2x + 3(k(x))^2 \cdot -5\right]$$

$$= \frac{4x \cdot j(x) - 15(k(x))^2}{2\sqrt{(j(x))^2 + (k(x))^3}}$$

$$= \frac{4x(x^2 + 2) - 15(2 - 5x)^2}{2\sqrt{(x^2 + 2)^2 + (2 - 5x)^3}}$$

$$\Delta$$

From this point onward, when we use the Chain Rule, we will not actually list all the individual functions. We will simply differentiate the function directly.

EXAMPLE

Differentiate $y = \sqrt{(x^2 + 2)^2 + (2 - 5x)^3}$ again, only this time without writing down all the function pieces.

Solution: Let's write the derivative in pieces with ellipses (...) to indicate that we are not finished. First,

$$y' = \frac{1}{2\sqrt{(x^2 + 2)^2 + (2 - 5x)^3}} \times \dots$$

We now multiply by the derivative of $(x^2 + 2)^2 + (2 - 5x)^3$. Note that both these pieces themselves have Chain Rules:

$$\frac{d}{dx}((x^2 + 2)^2) = 2(x^2 + 2) \times 2x = 4x(x^2 + 2)$$

$$\frac{d}{dx}((2 - 5x)^3) = 3(2 - 5x)^2 \times -5 = -15(2 - 5x)^2$$

Going back to the derivative,

$$y' = \frac{1}{2\sqrt{(x^2+2)^2+(2-5x)^3}} \times \left[\frac{d}{dx}((x^2+2)^2) + \frac{d}{dx}((2-5x)^3)\right]$$

$$= \frac{1}{2\sqrt{(x^2+2)^2+(2-5x)^3}} \times [4x(x^2+2) - 15(2-5x)^2]$$

$$= \frac{4x(x^2+2) - 15(2-5x)^2}{2\sqrt{(x^2+2)^2+(2-5x)^3}}$$

This matches what we found in the previous example.

Δ

We now use the Chain Rule to derive a useful derivative formula that doesn't appear often, but when it does, it can save some messy algebra steps. Given a function $f(x)$, we say it is invertible over a specified domain if its inverse $f^{-1}(x)$ exists over that domain. To remind you how to find inverse functions, suppose $f(x) = 3x - 4$, which is of course a line with slope 3 that passes through the point $(0, -4)$. What you do is write the equation with y instead of $f(x)$ and then interchange the y's with the x's before solving for the new y:

$$y = 3x - 4 \Rightarrow x = 3y - 4 \Rightarrow x + 4 = 3y$$
$$\Rightarrow y = \frac{1}{3}x + \frac{4}{3}$$
$$\Rightarrow f^{-1}(x) = \frac{1}{3}x + \frac{4}{3}$$

This inverse equation is also a line, but this time with slope $1/3$ (the reciprocal of the original line's slope). The other important observation to make concerns the identified point $(0, -4)$ on the original function. If we evaluate the inverse function at $x = -4$, we get

$$f^{-1}(-4) = \frac{1}{3}(-4) + \frac{4}{3} = 0$$

What this means is that $(0, -4)$ lies on the original function, and yet the swapped coordinates $(-4, 0)$ fall on the inverse function. That is exactly how inverses work: if (a, b) is on $f(x)$, then (b, a) falls on $f^{-1}(x)$, provided the inverse exists over the domain of interest.

DEFINITION
Suppose the function $f(x)$ is **invertible** over a specified domain, which means its inverse $f^{-1}(x)$ exists over that domain. Then the following equations are true:

$$f(f^{-1}(x)) = x \quad \text{and} \quad f^{-1}(f(x)) = x$$

Let's check that these equations hold for the line example above, noting that $f(x) = 3x - 4$ and $f^{-1}(x) = \frac{1}{3}x + \frac{4}{3}$:

$$f(f^{-1}(x)) = 3\left(\frac{1}{3}x + \frac{4}{3}\right) - 4 = x + 4 - 4 = x$$
$$f^{-1}(f(x)) = \frac{1}{3}(3x - 4) + \frac{4}{3} = x - \frac{4}{3} + \frac{4}{3} = x$$

Armed with this knowledge, given a function $f(x)$, we now wish to calculate the derivative of the inverse of a function, which we'll denote as $(f^{-1})'(x)$. In the above example, suppose we want to evaluate $(f^{-1})'(-4)$ given that $f(x) = 3x - 4$. Here it is easy since we explicitly found the general inverse function, a line with slope 1/3, which of course means that $(f^{-1})'(-4) = 1/3$. As noted earlier, the slope of the original function was 3 everywhere, and so we start to conjecture that the derivative of an inverse function might be equal to the reciprocal of the derivative of the original function. That statement turns out to be true, although we have to be careful how we define the evaluation point.

Why do we need a shortcut derivative formula for inverses? The answer is that although we can sometimes solve for inverse functions explicitly, in other situations it is too difficult if not impossible. Take, for instance, $g(x) = x^5 + 4x^4 + x^2 + 6$; I wish you luck solving for x explicitly! So now let's find the derivative formula.

Let $f(x)$ be invertible and differentiable over a specified domain, so $f(f^{-1}(x)) = x$. By the Chain Rule,

$$\frac{d}{dx}\left(f(f^{-1}(x))\right) = \frac{d}{dx}(x) \Rightarrow f'(f^{-1}(x)) \cdot (f^{-1})'(x) = 1$$

$$\Rightarrow (f^{-1})'(x) = \frac{1}{f'(f^{-1}(x))}$$

This is in fact the derivative formula for an inverse function, but it's not yet in a format that's user friendly. So now suppose the point (a, b) lies on the original function $f(x)$, which means the point (b, a) lies on $f^{-1}(x)$. To be clear, that means $f(a) = b$, but $f^{-1}(b) = a$. In other words, evaluating the original function at an x-coordinate produces the corresponding y-coordinate, but evaluating the inverse function at a y-coordinate produces the corresponding x-coordinate.

With that said, we wish to calculate the derivative of the inverse function at the y-coordinate b, or in other words $(f^{-1})'(b)$. The above formula tells us to evaluate

$$(f^{-1})'(b) = \frac{1}{f'(f^{-1}(b))} = \frac{1}{f'(a)}$$

To get the answer, find the derivative of the original function, evaluate it at the corresponding x-coordinate a, then take the reciprocal. The result is the derivative of the inverse function evaluated at the y-coordinate b.

DERIVATIVE OF AN INVERSE FUNCTION
Let $f(x)$ be invertible and differentiable over a specified domain, and let (a, b) be a point on $f(x)$. If $f^{-1}(x)$ represents the inverse function, then the derivative of the inverse function is

$$(f^{-1})'(x) = \frac{1}{f'(f^{-1}(x))}$$

Evaluating the derivative of the inverse function at the given point,

$$(f^{-1})'(b) = \frac{1}{f'(a)}$$

If $f'(a) = 0$, then $(f^{-1})'(b)$ does not exist, and the slope of the tangent line to that point is infinite.

EXAMPLE

Let $f(x) = x^2$ over $x \geq 0$. Evaluate $(f^{-1})'(9)$ given that $(3,9)$ lies on the original function.

Solution: The function is obviously a parabola, the right half over nonnegative x-values. We specified the domain $x \geq 0$ so that the inverse could be found without introducing both positive and negative radicals. First, let's find the answer the long way by actually finding the inverse function and differentiating it. Here this is straightforward:

$$y = x^2 \Rightarrow x = y^2 \Rightarrow y = \sqrt{x}$$
$$\Rightarrow f^{-1}(x) = x^{1/2}$$

Note that since $x \geq 0$, we write just the positive radical and not the plus/minus. Differentiating the inverse function and evaluating at 9 (which is actually the y-coordinate on the original function),

$$(f^{-1})'(x) = \frac{1}{2}x^{-1} = \frac{1}{2\sqrt{x}}$$
$$(f^{-1})'(9) = \frac{1}{2\sqrt{9}} = \frac{1}{6}$$

Now let's get the answer again but by using the inverse function derivative formula. To do that, we differentiate the original function, evaluate it at the x-coordinate 3, and then take the reciprocal:

$$f'(x) = 2x$$
$$f'(3) = 6$$
$$(f^{-1})'(9) = \frac{1}{f'(3)} = \frac{1}{6}$$

Δ

EXAMPLE

Returning to the function mentioned earlier, $g(x) = x^5 + 4x^4 + x^2 + 6$, evaluate $(g^{-1})'(12)$.

Solution: This time the inverse function $g^{-1}(x)$ cannot be found explicitly since it's too hard to solve for x in the function. So we have no choice but to use the newly learned derivative formula. First observe that the point of interest has y-coordinate 12, but the x-coordinate is not provided. That's not much of a problem; we just need to solve

$$x^5 + 4x^4 + x^2 + 6 = 12$$

Of course, we cannot explicitly solve for x here either, but what we can do is try evaluating $g(x)$ at various x-values until we find one that produces an evaluation of 12. This doesn't take long to do, because observe that adding the coefficients $1 + 4 + 1 + 6 = 12$, which means $g(1) = 12$. The point of interest on the original curve is therefore $(1,12)$. That means we find the derivative at the original function and evaluate at $x = 1$:

$$g'(x) = 5x^4 + 16x^3 + 2x$$
$$g'(1) = 5(1)^4 + 16(1)^3 + 2(1) = 23$$
$$(g^{-1})'(12) = \frac{1}{g'(1)} = \frac{1}{23}$$

Thus, the slope of the inverse function at the point of interest is $1/23$…without having to suffer a headache trying to explicitly find the inverse and not getting anywhere!

$$\Delta$$

Section 2.3 – The Power Rule Generalized

We have gradually been presenting cases of the Power Rule derivative: if $f(x) = x^n$, then the derivative is $f'(x) = nx^{n-1}$. We have shown this holds when n is any integer, positive or negative, with certain necessary restrictions. In this section, we show that it holds for any rational number. Recall the following definition:

DEFINITION
We say a number is **rational** if it can be written as a fraction, in the form p/q with p, q integers and $q \neq 0$. A number is **irrational** if it is not rational.

EXAMPLE

A) The number 1.5 can be written as $3/2$.
B) The number $0.33333\ \ldots$ (which can also be written as $0.\overline{3}$) can be expressed as $1/3$.
C) The number $\sqrt{2}$ is **irrational** as it cannot be expressed as a fraction of integers. (The reasons why are proved in a higher-level class.)

$$\Delta$$

If you haven't already, go to Section 0.1 and review the algebraic notation with exponents and square roots and other radicals.

To motivate the general formula for the Power Rule, we need to consider how to find derivatives of formulas involving roots. We derived earlier the formula for the derivative of $f(x) = \sqrt{x}$. Now consider this: how can we find the derivative of $f(x) = \sqrt[q]{x}$ with q a positive integer?

EXAMPLE
Let's backtrack for a moment and refresh our memory with how we did the square root case. We multiplied by the conjugate, making the square roots go away:

$$\frac{\left(\sqrt{x+h} - \sqrt{x}\right)}{h} \cdot \frac{\left(\sqrt{x+h} + \sqrt{x}\right)}{\left(\sqrt{x+h} + \sqrt{x}\right)} = \frac{\left(\sqrt{x+h}\right)^2 - \sqrt{x}\sqrt{x+h} + \sqrt{x}\sqrt{x+h} - \left(\sqrt{x}\right)^2}{h\left(\sqrt{x+h} + \sqrt{x}\right)}$$

$$= \frac{(x+h) - x}{h\left(\sqrt{x+h} + \sqrt{x}\right)}$$

Is there an analog for higher roots such as the cube root? Well, let's take a closer look at what we just did. To make notation simpler, let $A = \sqrt{x+h}$ and $B = \sqrt{x}$. Then we may write

$$\sqrt{x+h} - \sqrt{x} = (A - B)$$

We are then presented with this problem:

$$(A - B)(\ast\ast\ast) = A^2 - B^2$$

We want to end up with $A^2 - B^2 = (x + h) - x = h$ so that we may cancel the h with the one in the limit denominator. The question is, what goes in the blank? In this case, the answer is $(A + B)$ because

$$(A - B)(A + B) = A^2 - AB + AB - B^2$$
$$= A^2 - B^2$$

So the missing entity in this case that we need to multiply by is $(A + B)$, or $\sqrt{x + h} + \sqrt{x}$.

Now let's turn to the cube root. Here is the setup:

$$f(x) = \sqrt[3]{x}$$
$$f'(x) = \lim_{h \to 0} \frac{\sqrt[3]{x + h} - \sqrt[3]{x}}{h}$$

We want to multiply this by the conjugate of $\sqrt[3]{x + h} - \sqrt[3]{x}$, so that ultimately we will be left with an h that will cancel out with the h in the denominator. But how exactly do we find the conjugate now? Let's try our simpler notation: let

$$A = \sqrt[3]{x + h}$$
$$B = \sqrt[3]{x}$$

We want $(***)$ such that $(A - B)(***) = A^3 - B^3$. Using a factoring formula from Section 0.1,

$$(A - B)(A^2 + AB + B^2) = A^3 + A^2B + AB^2 - A^2B - AB^2 - B^3$$
$$= A^3 - B^3$$

Here we would multiply by a fraction in which the numerator and denominator are both

$$A^2 + AB + B^2 = \left(\sqrt[3]{x + h}\right)^2 + \sqrt[3]{x + h} \cdot \sqrt[3]{x} + \left(\sqrt[3]{x}\right)^2$$

Returning to the limit, let's multiply by this incredibly ugly fraction.

$$\lim_{h \to 0} \frac{\sqrt[3]{x + h} - \sqrt[3]{x}}{h} = \lim_{h \to 0} \frac{\sqrt[3]{x + h} - \sqrt[3]{x}}{h} \cdot \frac{\left[\left(\sqrt[3]{x + h}\right)^2 + \sqrt[3]{x + h} \cdot \sqrt[3]{x} + \left(\sqrt[3]{x}\right)^2\right]}{\left[\left(\sqrt[3]{x + h}\right)^2 + \sqrt[3]{x + h} \cdot \sqrt[3]{x} + \left(\sqrt[3]{x}\right)^2\right]}$$

And in the end, everything works out.

$$\lim_{h \to 0} \frac{\left(\sqrt[3]{x + h}\right)^3 + \left(\sqrt[3]{x + h}\right)^2\left(\sqrt[3]{x}\right) + \left(\sqrt[3]{x + h}\right)\left(\sqrt[3]{x}\right)^2 - \left(\sqrt[3]{x}\right)\left(\sqrt[3]{x + h}\right)^2 - \left(\sqrt[3]{x + h}\right)\left(\sqrt[3]{x}\right)^2 - \left(\sqrt[3]{x}\right)^3}{h\left[\left(\sqrt[3]{x + h}\right)^2 + \sqrt[3]{x + h} \cdot \sqrt[3]{x} + \left(\sqrt[3]{x}\right)^2\right]}$$

$$= \lim_{h \to 0} \frac{\left(\sqrt[3]{x + h}\right)^3 - \left(\sqrt[3]{x}\right)^3}{h\left[\left(\sqrt[3]{x + h}\right)^2 + \sqrt[3]{x + h} \cdot \sqrt[3]{x} + \left(\sqrt[3]{x}\right)^2\right]}$$

$$= \lim_{h \to 0} \frac{(x + h) - x}{h\left[\left(\sqrt[3]{x + h}\right)^2 + \sqrt[3]{x + h} \cdot \sqrt[3]{x} + \left(\sqrt[3]{x}\right)^2\right]}$$

$$= \lim_{h \to 0} \frac{h}{h\left[\left(\sqrt[3]{x+h}\right)^2 + \sqrt[3]{x+h} \cdot \sqrt[3]{x} + \left(\sqrt[3]{x}\right)^2\right]}$$

$$= \lim_{h \to 0} \frac{1}{\left(\sqrt[3]{x+h}\right)^2 + \sqrt[3]{x+h} \cdot \sqrt[3]{x} + \left(\sqrt[3]{x}\right)^2}$$

All we need to do now is evaluate as h approaches 0:

$$\frac{1}{\left(\sqrt[3]{x}\right)^2 + \sqrt[3]{x} \cdot \sqrt[3]{x} + \left(\sqrt[3]{x}\right)^2} = \frac{1}{\left(\sqrt[3]{x}\right)^2 + \left(\sqrt[3]{x}\right)^2 + \left(\sqrt[3]{x}\right)^2} = \frac{1}{3\left(\sqrt[3]{x}\right)^2}$$

Let's rearrange this just a little to get it in the form we want:

$$\frac{1}{3\left(\sqrt[3]{x}\right)^2} = \frac{1}{3(x^{1/3})^2} = \frac{1}{3x^{2/3}} = \frac{1}{3}x^{-2/3}$$

$$\Delta$$

The derivative we just found is stated below.

DERIVATIVE OF A CUBE ROOT
If $f(x) = \sqrt[3]{x} = x^{1/3}$, then

$$f'(x) = \frac{1}{3}x^{-2/3}$$

Let's establish what we have now observed.

$$f(x) = \sqrt{x} = x^{1/2} \qquad g(x) = \sqrt[3]{x} = x^{1/3}$$
$$f'(x) = \frac{1}{2}x^{-1/2} \qquad g'(x) = \frac{1}{3}x^{-2/3}$$

We seem to be moving the exponent down to be a fraction coefficient and then subtracting 1 from the exponent. This is exactly what we have been doing before with the Power Rule. So let's go ahead and state the next step in the Power Rule saga.

POWER RULE (CASE 3: ROOTS)
Let $f(x) = x^{1/q}$ where q is a nonzero integer, and suppose f is differentiable at x. Then

$$f'(x) = \frac{1}{q}x^{(1/q)-1}$$

Additionally, if q is even (for instance, a square root), then we must add the restriction that $x > 0$. Why? We cannot take even roots of negative numbers.

PROOF
Here is a simplistic way of going through a proof of this. Start by noticing the following:

$$x = \left(x^{1/q}\right)^q$$

This is because $\left(x^{1/q}\right)^q = x^{q/q} = x^1$. Now let f denote $x^{1/q}$. Of course, by doing this, we must assume that f is differentiable at the point we are picking. This means that $x = f^q$.

Now let's differentiate both sides, remembering the Chain Rule:

$$\frac{d}{dx}(x) = \frac{d}{dx}(f^q)$$
$$1 = q \cdot f^{q-1} \cdot f'$$

Now we solve for f'':

$$f' = \frac{1}{q \cdot f^{q-1}} = \frac{1}{q} \cdot f^{-(q-1)}$$
$$= \frac{1}{q} \cdot f^{1-q}$$

Substituting in $f = x^{1/q}$, we arrive at

$$\frac{d}{dx}\left(x^{1/q}\right) = \frac{1}{q} \cdot \left(x^{1/q}\right)^{1-q} = \frac{1}{q} \cdot \left(x^{(1/q)(1-q)}\right) = \frac{1}{q} \cdot x^{\left(\frac{1-q}{q}\right)}$$
$$= \frac{1}{q} \cdot x^{(1/q)-1}$$

∎

EXAMPLE
Find the derivative of $f(x) = 3x^{1/5}$, and find the equation of the tangent line to $x = 32$.

Solution: The derivative is

$$f'(x) = 3 \cdot \frac{1}{5}x^{(1/5)-1} = \frac{3}{5}x^{-4/5} = \frac{3}{5x^{4/5}}$$

It is a matter of personal preference whether you leave the exponent negative or move the term to the denominator to make the exponent positive. Next, in the middle of learning all these derivative rules, let's not forget how to find tangent lines. The slope of the tangent line at $x = 32$ is

$$f'(32) = \frac{3}{5(32)^{4/5}} = \frac{3}{5(32^{1/5})^4}$$

We wrote the denominator this way to make calculation more convenient. While we could just punch the answer into a calculator, let's do it by hand anyway and take advantage of exponential properties. Note that $32 = 2^5$, and so

$$f'(32) = \frac{3}{5(32^{1/5})^4} = \frac{3}{5((2^5)^{1/5})^4} = \frac{3}{5(2)^4} = \frac{3}{5 \cdot 16} = \frac{3}{80}$$

We also need the point at $x = 32$:

$$f(32) = 3(32)^{1/5} = 3(2^5)^{1/5} = 3(2) = 6$$

The point is $(32, 6)$, so we can use the point-slope formula to get the tangent line:

$$y - 6 = \frac{3}{80}(x - 32) \Longrightarrow y = \frac{3}{80}(x - 32) + 6$$
$$\Longrightarrow y = \frac{3}{80}x - \frac{96}{80} + 6$$
$$\Longrightarrow y = \frac{3}{80}x - \frac{6}{5} + 6$$
$$\Longrightarrow y = \frac{3}{80}x + \frac{24}{5}$$

Δ

Before we go further, let's see how the TI-84 can help find derivatives. It will not find the general derivative for us, but what we can do is use the TI-84 to find the derivative at a specified point. I wouldn't recommend using this procedure for each problem, but it is one way of checking your answer, especially in problems involving the slope of a tangent line.

TI-84 COMMAND: FINDING DERIVATIVES AT SPECIFIC POINTS

To find the slope of the tangent line at a specific point $x = a$ on the function $f(x)$, press $MATH$ and choose Option 8: $nDeriv($. Type the following: $nDeriv(f(x), x, a)$.

In other words, you type the function in terms of x followed by a comma, then type x and a comma, and finally type the point a of interest.

EXAMPLE

Use the TI-84 to find the slope of the tangent line to $x = 32$ on $f(x) = 3x^{1/5}$.

Solution: We know from the previous example that the answer is $3/80$, but let's use the TI-84 to check our work. Selecting the $nDeriv($ function, we type the following:

$$nDeriv(3X^{\wedge}(1/5), X, 32)$$

The answer is 0.0375. We can either write that down as the answer, or we can use the $\triangleright Frac$ command to change it to the fraction $3/80$.

Δ

Note that the TI-84 does not always give you a "clean" answer due to its approximation methods. For instance, suppose we want to find the derivative of $f(x) = x^3$ at $x = 2$:

$$nDeriv(X^{\wedge}3, X, 2)$$

The calculator says 12.000001, and so you need to recognize that the answer is really just 12.

Now that we can differentiate $f(x) = x^{1/q}$, let's ask ourselves: how do we differentiate the function $f(x) = x^{p/q}$? This easily follows from the previous theorem. The answer is what you might have already guessed, and we now state it explicitly here.

POWER RULE (CASE 4: RATIONAL NUMBERS)

Let $f(x) = x^{p/q}$ where p and q are integers and $q \neq 0$. Suppose $f(x)$ is differentiable at a point x. Then the derivative is

$$f'(x) = \frac{p}{q} x^{(p/q)-1}$$

PROOF

We are going to use the previous Power Rule result and the Chain Rule. Let's rewrite the function as

$$f(x) = x^{p/q} = \left(x^{1/q}\right)^p$$

Let $g(x) = x^{1/q}$ be the inner function, so let's write $f(x) = x^{p/q} = \left(g(x)\right)^p$. Then by the Chain Rule,

$$f'(x) = p \cdot \left(g(x)\right)^{p-1} \cdot g'(x)$$

We already know that $g'(x) = \frac{1}{q} x^{1/q-1}$, so let's substitute in everything:

$$\begin{aligned}
f'(x) &= p \cdot \left(x^{1/q}\right)^{p-1} \cdot \frac{1}{q} x^{(1/q)-1} \\
&= \frac{p}{q} \cdot x^{\left(\frac{p-1}{q}\right)} \cdot x^{(1/q)-1} \\
&= \frac{p}{q} \cdot x^{\left(\frac{p}{q} - \frac{1}{q} + \frac{1}{q} - 1\right)} \\
&= \frac{p}{q} \cdot x^{(p/q)-1}
\end{aligned}$$

∎

We have now covered all the cases of the Power Rule for the scope of this class, except for one (coming up next). Note that the integer scenario is a special case of the rational number scenario when $q = 1$. If you didn't understand all the steps to these proofs, don't worry – it's more important to know how to use the derivative formulas correctly.

EXAMPLE

Let's find the derivative of $f(x) = \sqrt[4]{x^3 + 2x}$.

Solution: First, let's rewrite this as $f(x) = (x^3 + 2x)^{1/4}$, the form with which we are familiar and with which it is easier to take derivatives. Now let's compute:

$$\begin{aligned}
f(x) &= (x^3 + 2x)^{1/4} \\
f'(x) &= \frac{1}{4}(x^3 + 2x)^{(1/4)-1} \cdot \frac{d}{dx}(x^3 + 2x) \\
&= \frac{1}{4}(x^3 + 2x)^{-3/4} \cdot (3x^2 + 2) = \frac{3x^2 + 2}{4(x^3 + 2x)^{3/4}}
\end{aligned}$$

Δ

EXAMPLE

Let's find the derivative of $f(x) = \sqrt[5]{(x^2 - 4x + 7)^3}$.

Solution: Again, let's rewrite this as $f(x) = (x^2 - 4x + 7)^{3/5}$. Now let's compute:

$$f(x) = (x^2 - 4x + 7)^{3/5}$$
$$f'(x) = \frac{3}{5}(x^2 - 4x + 7)^{(3/5)-1} \cdot \frac{d}{dx}(x^2 - 4x + 7)$$
$$= \frac{3}{5}(x^2 - 4x + 7)^{-2/5} \cdot (2x - 4)$$
$$= \frac{3(2x - 4)}{5(x^2 - 4x + 7)^{2/5}}$$
$$= \frac{6(x - 2)}{5(x^2 - 4x + 7)^{2/5}}$$

Δ

In case you were wondering, the Power Rule can be extended even further to include real numbers such as $\sqrt{2}$, π, or e. We will prove this result in a surprisingly easy way later, but for now, here's the statement.

POWER RULE (CASE 5: REAL NUMBERS)
Let $f(x) = x^r$ where r is any real number (this includes irrational numbers). Suppose $f(x)$ is differentiable at a point x. Then the derivative is

$$f'(x) = rx^{r-1}$$

For instance, if $f(x) = x^\pi$, then the derivative is $f'(x) = \pi x^{\pi-1}$. However, more importantly, ask yourself this: $x^{3/5}$ simply means that we cube the variable x and then take the fifth root of it. But in practical terms, what could it possibly mean to raise x to a power π?

Section 2.4 – Derivatives of Trigonometric Functions

We now derive the derivatives for the six trigonometric functions: $\sin(x)$, $\cos(x)$, $\tan(x)$, $\cot(x)$, $\sec(x)$, and $\csc(x)$. The good news is that we need to use the limit proof to derive just $\sin(x)$ and $\cos(x)$. The other four will follow straight from these first two. Let's begin by listing all the facts we will use. (If you need to review what these six trig functions look like, see Section 0.2.)

REVIEW: TRIGONOMETRIC FORMULAS
Fact 1: $\lim\limits_{x \to 0} \frac{\sin(x)}{x} = 1$

Fact 2: $\lim\limits_{x \to 0} \frac{1-\cos(x)}{x} = 0$ (We saw this in Section 1.2)

Fact 3: $\sin(a + b) = \sin(a)\cos(b) + \cos(a)\sin(b)$

Fact 4: $\cos(a + b) = \cos(a)\cos(b) - \sin(a)\sin(b)$

The last two are both trigonometric formulas that are used sparingly. You do not need to memorize them, but it is helpful to have them written down somewhere. (See Appendix B for more.)

Now we can derive these derivatives.

DERIVATIVE OF SINE FUNCTION
If $f(x) = \sin(x)$, then

$$\frac{d}{dx}\big(\sin(x)\big) = \cos(x)$$

PROOF
Setting up the limit,

$$f'(x) = \lim_{h \to 0} \frac{\sin(x+h) - \sin(x)}{h} = \lim_{h \to 0} \frac{\sin(x)\cos(h) + \cos(x)\sin(h) - \sin(x)}{h}$$

In the second step, we have merely used the above addition trig rule. When we rearrange terms, we can factor out a $\sin(x)$.

$$\lim_{h \to 0} \frac{[\sin(x)\cos(h) - \sin(x)] + \cos(x)\sin(h)}{h} = \lim_{h \to 0} \frac{\sin(x)[\cos(h) - 1] + \cos(x)\sin(h)}{h}$$

Next, we separate the fractions.

$$\lim_{h \to 0} \frac{\sin(x)[\cos(h) - 1]}{h} + \lim_{h \to 0} \frac{\cos(x)\sin(h)}{h}$$

If we pull out -1 from the first limit, we then have it in the form of Fact 2 above.

$$-\sin(x) \cdot \lim_{h \to 0} \frac{1 - \cos(h)}{h} + \cos(x) \cdot \lim_{h \to 0} \frac{\sin(h)}{h}$$

We can now evaluate these:

$$\cos(x) \cdot \lim_{h \to 0} \frac{\sin(h)}{h} - \sin(x) \cdot \lim_{h \to 0} \frac{1 - \cos(h)}{h} = \cos(x) \cdot (1) - \sin(x) \cdot (0)$$
$$= \cos(x)$$

Therefore $\frac{d}{dx}\big(\sin(x)\big) = \cos(x)$.

∎

We next find the derivative for $\cos(x)$. The proof is very similar to the one above.

DERIVATIVE OF COSINE FUNCTION
If $f(x) = \cos(x)$, then

$$\frac{d}{dx}\big(\cos(x)\big) = -\sin(x)$$

PROOF
Here are the first few steps, which we find in the same process as above.

$$f'(x) = \lim_{h \to 0} \frac{\cos(x+h) - \cos(x)}{h} = \lim_{h \to 0} \frac{[\cos(x)\cos(h) - \sin(x)\sin(h)] - \cos(x)}{h}$$

$$= \lim_{h \to 0} \frac{\cos(x)\cos(h) - \cos(x) - \sin(x)\sin(h)}{h}$$

$$= \lim_{h \to 0} \frac{\cos(x)[\cos(h) - 1] - \sin(x)\sin(h)}{h}$$

$$= \lim_{h \to 0} \frac{\cos(x)[\cos(h) - 1]}{h} - \lim_{h \to 0} \frac{\sin(x)\sin(h)}{h}$$

$$= \cos(x) \cdot \lim_{h \to 0} \frac{[\cos(h) - 1]}{h} - \sin(x) \cdot \lim_{h \to 0} \frac{\sin(h)}{h}$$

We have to pull out -1 from the first limit to get it in the form we want. So then we have

$$-\cos(x) \cdot \lim_{h \to 0} \frac{[1 - \cos(h)]}{h} - \sin(x) \cdot \lim_{h \to 0} \frac{\sin(h)}{h}$$

Applying the limit formulas we know, we end up with

$$-\cos(x) \cdot \lim_{h \to 0} \frac{[1 - \cos(h)]}{h} - \sin(x) \cdot \lim_{h \to 0} \frac{\sin(h)}{h} = -\cos(x) \cdot (0) - \sin(x) \cdot (1)$$

$$= -\sin(x)$$

Therefore $\frac{d}{dx}\left(\cos(x)\right) = -\sin(x)$.

∎

EXAMPLE

Consider $y = x^5 \sin(3x)$. We need to use the Power Rule, the Product Rule, and the derivative for $\sin(x)$:

$$y' = x^5 \cdot \frac{d}{dx}\left(\sin(3x)\right) + \frac{d}{dx}(x^5) \cdot \sin(3x)$$

$$= x^5 \cdot \cos(3x) \cdot 3 + \frac{d}{dx}(x^5) \cdot \sin(3x)$$

$$= 3x^5 \cos(3x) + 5x^4 \sin(3x)$$

Note that in the second step we used the Chain Rule for the function $g(x) = 3x$, sitting inside the function $f(g(x)) = \sin\left(g(x)\right)$.

Δ

EXAMPLE

Find the derivative of $y = \frac{\sin(x)}{1 + \cos(x)}$.

Solution: We use the derivatives of $\sin(x)$ and $\cos(x)$, as well as the Quotient Rule. The derivative is

$$y' = \frac{(1 + \cos(x)) \cdot \frac{d}{dx}\left(\sin(x)\right) - \sin(x) \cdot \frac{d}{dx}\left(1 + \cos(x)\right)}{\left(1 + \cos(x)\right)^2}$$

$$= \frac{(1 + \cos(x)) \cdot \cos(x) - \sin(x) \cdot \left(0 - \sin(x)\right)}{\left(1 + \cos(x)\right)^2}$$

$$= \frac{\cos(x) + \cos^2(x) + \sin^2(x)}{\left(1 + \cos(x)\right)^2}$$

We can go further because we spot the most important trigonometric identity formula!

$$y' = \frac{[\cos^2(x) + \sin^2(x)] + \cos(x)}{\left(1 + \cos(x)\right)^2} = \frac{1 + \cos(x)}{\left(1 + \cos(x)\right)^2} = \frac{1}{1 + \cos(x)}$$

Δ

ETYMOLOGY

The word **sine** has perhaps the most interesting history of all the math terms presented in this book. The original term was from the Sanskrit ज्या (*jyā*), which meant "bowstring," as in the string on an archer's bow. It was also the word for the chord of a circle (the dashed line in the graph below). Later, astronomers in India discovered that half the chord was more useful for studying properties of the triangle, and so the similar Sanskrit word जीव (*jīva*) was eventually used to mean half a chord.

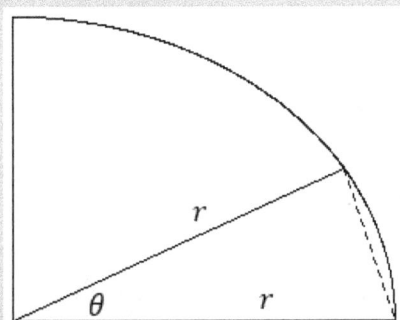

Next, Arab scholars translated the Sanskrit word *jīva* to the Arabic جيب (*jiba*), thereby creating a new word in the Arabic language. However, Arabic vowels are not usually written down, so جيب also represented the already existing word *jaib*. European scholars were unaware that the word *jiba* had been newly added to Arabic, so they instead chose the existing word *jaib*, which translated into Latin as *sinus*, meaning "curved surface" in English. Rather than use this English translation, the Latin word *sinus* was simply added to the English language via the loan word sine.

Put in simpler terms, the word **sine** comes from a mistranslation!

Before we go further, remember the following conversion formulas:

REVIEW: TRIGONOMETRIC FORMULAS

$$\tan(x) = \frac{\sin(x)}{\cos(x)} \qquad \cot(x) = \frac{1}{\tan(x)} = \frac{\cos(x)}{\sin(x)} \qquad \sec(x) = \frac{1}{\cos(x)} \qquad \csc(x) = \frac{1}{\sin(x)}$$

We will use these equations to discover the remaining four derivatives. As we will see, the rest of the trigonometric proofs will follow directly from the two theorems above and the Quotient Rule. This will be much easier than going through the limit definitions.

DERIVATIVE OF TANGENT FUNCTION
If $f(x) = \tan(x)$, then

$$\frac{d}{dx}\big(\tan(x)\big) = \sec^2(x)$$

PROOF

$$\frac{d}{dx}\big(\tan(x)\big) = \frac{d}{dx}\left(\frac{\sin(x)}{\cos(x)}\right) = \frac{\cos(x)\cdot\frac{d}{dx}\big(\sin(x)\big) - \sin(x)\cdot\frac{d}{dx}\big(\cos(x)\big)}{\cos^2(x)}$$

This is just the Quotient Rule. Continuing, we get

$$\frac{\cos(x)\cdot\frac{d}{dx}\big(\sin(x)\big) - \sin(x)\cdot\frac{d}{dx}\big(\cos(x)\big)}{\cos^2(x)} = \frac{\cos(x)\cdot\cos(x) - \sin(x)\cdot\big(-\sin(x)\big)}{\cos^2(x)}$$

$$= \frac{\cos^2(x) + \sin^2(x)}{\cos^2(x)} = \frac{1}{\cos^2(x)} = \sec^2(x)$$

Of course, we used the fact that $\sin^2(x) + \cos^2(x) = 1$.

∎

DERIVATIVE OF COTANGENT FUNCTION
If $f(x) = \cot(x)$, then

$$\frac{d}{dx}\big(\cot(x)\big) = -\csc^2(x)$$

PROOF

$$\frac{d}{dx}\big(\cot(x)\big) = \frac{d}{dx}\left(\frac{\cos(x)}{\sin(x)}\right) = \frac{\sin(x)\cdot\frac{d}{dx}\big(\cos(x)\big) - \cos(x)\cdot\frac{d}{dx}\big(\sin(x)\big)}{\sin^2(x)}$$

$$= \frac{\sin(x)\cdot-\sin(x) - \cos(x)\cdot\cos(x)}{\sin^2(x)} = \frac{-\sin^2(x) - \cos^2(x)}{\sin^2(x)}$$

$$= \frac{-\big(\sin^2(x) + \cos^2(x)\big)}{\sin^2(x)} = -\frac{1}{\sin^2(x)} = -\csc^2(x)$$

∎

DERIVATIVE OF SECANT FUNCTION
If $f(x) = \sec(x)$, then

$$\frac{d}{dx}\big(\sec(x)\big) = \sec(x)\cdot\tan(x)$$

PROOF

$$\frac{d}{dx}\big(\sec(x)\big) = \frac{d}{dx}\left(\frac{1}{\cos(x)}\right) = \frac{\cos(x)\cdot\frac{d}{dx}(1) - 1\cdot\frac{d}{dx}\big(\cos(x)\big)}{\cos^2(x)} = \frac{\cos(x)\cdot 0 + \sin(x)}{\cos^2(x)}$$

$$= \frac{\sin(x)}{\cos^2(x)} = \frac{1}{\cos(x)} \cdot \frac{\sin(x)}{\cos(x)} = \sec(x) \cdot \tan(x)$$

∎

DERIVATIVE OF COSECANT FUNCTION
If $f(x) = \csc(x)$, then

$$\frac{d}{dx}(\csc(x)) = -\csc(x) \cdot \cot(x)$$

PROOF

$$\frac{d}{dx}(\csc(x)) = \frac{d}{dx}\left(\frac{1}{\sin(x)}\right) = \frac{\sin(x) \cdot \frac{d}{dx}(1) - 1 \cdot \frac{d}{dx}(\sin(x))}{\sin^2(x)} = \frac{\sin(x) \cdot 0 - \cos(x)}{\sin^2(x)}$$

$$= -\frac{\cos(x)}{\sin^2(x)} = -\frac{1}{\sin(x)} \cdot \frac{\cos(x)}{\sin(x)} = -\csc(x) \cdot \cot(x)$$

∎

EXAMPLE

Let $f(x) = \frac{\sec(5x)}{\tan(5x)}$. We will first differentiate this function directly.

$$f'(x) = \frac{\tan(5x) \cdot \frac{d}{dx}(\sec(5x)) - \sec(5x) \cdot \frac{d}{dx}(\tan(5x))}{\tan^2(5x)}$$

$$= \frac{\tan(5x) \cdot \sec(5x)\tan(5x) \cdot 5 - \sec(5x) \cdot \sec^2(5x) \cdot 5}{\tan^2(5x)}$$

$$= \frac{5\sec(5x)\tan^2(5x) - 5\sec^3(5x)}{\tan^2(5x)}$$

Remember this answer. Now let's go back and rewrite the original function:

$$f(x) = \frac{\sec(5x)}{\tan(5x)} = \frac{\left(\frac{1}{\cos(5x)}\right)}{\left(\frac{\sin(5x)}{\cos(5x)}\right)} = \frac{1}{\cos(5x)} \cdot \frac{\cos(5x)}{\sin(5x)} = \frac{1}{\sin(5x)} = \csc(5x)$$

Let's now try differentiating $f(x) = \csc(5x)$.

$$f'(x) = -\csc(5x)\cot(5x) \cdot 5$$
$$= -5\csc(5x)\cot(5x)$$

These two answers may look very different, but by using the trigonometric formulas, we can verify that they are in fact equal! Recall the trig identity $1 + \tan^2(u) = \sec^2(u)$. We may rewrite it as $\tan^2(u) - \sec^2(u) = -1$. Now let's turn to our first answer and show that it equals the second:

$$f'(x) = \frac{5\sec(5x)\tan^2(5x) - 5\sec^3(5x)}{\tan^2(5x)} = \frac{5\sec(5x)[\tan^2(5x) - \sec^2(5x)]}{\tan^2(5x)}$$

$$= \frac{5\sec(5x) \cdot (-1)}{\tan^2(5x)} = -\frac{5\sec(5x)}{\tan^2(5x)}$$

We now manipulate this formula:

$$f'(x) = -\frac{5\sec(5x)}{\tan^2(5x)} = -5\sec(5x)\cot^2(5x)$$

$$= -\frac{5}{\cos(5x)} \cdot \frac{\cos^2(5x)}{\sin^2(5x)} = -\frac{5\cos(5x)}{\sin^2(5x)}$$

$$= -5 \cdot \frac{1}{\sin(5x)} \cdot \frac{5\cos(5x)}{\sin(5x)} = -5\csc(5x)\cot(5x)$$

Thus, both derivatives equal each other, as we expect. There are two morals of this example:

1) In some cases, particularly those involving trigonometric formulas, we can discover the derivatives in multiple ways.
2) Sometimes we can turn a seemingly ugly problem into a nice, easy one instead. In the first scenario, we used the Quotient Rule to get a rather nasty-looking answer. However, in the second, we simplified the function to an easier form before differentiating.

Δ

EXAMPLE

Consider $f(x) = \cos^3(\sin(2x))$. Here we actually have a *four*-layered function, so we will have to invoke the Chain Rule three times. Nothing is different; we just have to keep repeating it, starting with the outermost function and working our way inwards. Recall that $\cos^n(u) = (\cos(u))^n$. (Be careful with problems involving trig functions raised to exponents; it is very easy to overlook the exponent when doing the Chain Rule!) Our function therefore looks like

$$f(x) = \Big(\cos\big(\sin(2x)\big)\Big)^3$$

The first function is the cube exponent, followed by the cosine function, and within this the sine function. Inside the sine is the function $2x$. Let's begin calculating the derivative:

$$f'(x) = 3\Big(\cos\big(\sin(2x)\big)\Big)^2 \cdot \ldots$$

Now we have a new function $g_1(x) = \cos(\sin(2x))$. We continue the derivative:

$$f'(x) = 3\Big(\cos\big(\sin(2x)\big)\Big)^2 \cdot \Big(-\sin\big(\sin(2x)\big)\Big) \cdot \ldots$$

Next is the function $g_2(x) = \sin(2x)$:

$$f'(x) = 3\Big(\cos\big(\sin(2x)\big)\Big)^2 \cdot \Big(-\sin\big(\sin(2x)\big)\Big) \cdot \cos(2x) \cdot \ldots$$

Lastly, we have $g_3(x) = 2x$. Thus, the derivative turns out to be

$$f'(x) = 3\Big(\cos\big(\sin(2x)\big)\Big)^2 \cdot \Big(-\sin\big(\sin(2x)\big)\Big) \cdot \cos(2x) \cdot 2$$
$$= -6\cos^2\big(\sin(2x)\big) \cdot \sin\big(\sin(2x)\big) \cdot \cos(2x)$$

Δ

The TI-84 graphing calculator has commands for sine, cosine, and tangent since those are the three most commonly used trig functions. It does not have built-in functions for cotangent, secant, and cosecant. This isn't a problem because you can just compute them by dividing 1 by the appropriate trig function. For example, if you need to compute $\csc(\pi/4)$, you can instead use the calculator to compute $1/\sin(\pi/4)$:

$$\csc\left(\frac{\pi}{4}\right) = \frac{1}{\sin\left(\frac{\pi}{4}\right)} = \frac{1}{\left(\frac{\sqrt{2}}{2}\right)} = \frac{2}{\sqrt{2}} = \sqrt{2}$$

Section 2.5 – Higher Derivatives

Up until now we have been studying derivatives of some common functions. Since we've only been taking the derivative once, we can refer to it as the **first derivative**. However, there is no need to stop there; it is frequently possible to take the derivative of the derivative of a function, and this is called the **second derivative**. Let's study that process next.

DEFINITION

The **second derivative** (if it exists) of a function $f(x)$ is literally the derivative of the first derivative of $f(x)$. There are several ways of writing the second derivative which include all of the following:

$$f''(x) \qquad f^{(2)}(x) \qquad \frac{d^2y}{dx^2} \qquad \frac{d}{dx}\left(\frac{dy}{dx}\right) \qquad D_x\big(f'(x)\big)$$

Which notation you use depends on what happens to be convenient for the problem.

EXAMPLE

Let's find the second derivative of $f(x) = x^3 + 3x^2 + 4x + 6$. The first derivative is

$$f'(x) = 3x^2 + 3 \cdot 2x + 4$$
$$= 3x^2 + 6x + 4$$

And so the second derivative is the derivative of this one:

$$f''(x) = 3 \cdot 2x + 6 = 6x + 6$$

Δ

It should come as no surprise that we can go even further.

DEFINITION

The **third derivative** (if it exists) of a function $f(x)$ is the derivative of the second derivative of $f(x)$. There are several ways of writing the third derivative which include all of the following:

$$f'''(x) \qquad f^{(3)}(x) \qquad \frac{d^3y}{dx^3} \qquad \frac{d}{dx}\left(\frac{d^2y}{dx^2}\right) \qquad D_x\big(f''(x)\big)$$

DEFINITION

In general, the nth derivative (if it exists) of a function $f(x)$ is found by taking the first derivative, then the second derivative, and so on through the $(n-1)$th derivative, and then finally taking one more derivative. The usual notation for the nth derivative when $n > 1$ is

$$f^{(n)}(x) \qquad \frac{d^n y}{dx^n}$$

We usually don't keep writing prime (′) symbols with higher derivatives because the notation quickly becomes horrendous, which is why writing $f^{(n)}(x)$ is more convenient.

EXAMPLE

Let's find the third and fourth derivatives of the same function $f(x) = x^3 + 3x^2 + 4x + 6$.

Solution: We know the second derivative is $f''(x) = 6x + 6$, and so the third derivative is

$$f^{(3)}(x) = 6$$

Since the third derivative is a constant, all higher derivatives will be 0, which means $f^{(4)}(x) = 0$, $f^{(5)}(x) = 0$, etc.

Δ

Notice the previous example was a cubic polynomial, and all derivatives as of the fourth were equal to 0. In general, if $f(x)$ is a polynomial of degree k, then $f^{(n)}(x) = 0$ for all $n \geq k + 1$.

EXAMPLE

Find the first four derivatives of $f(x) = \sin(x)$.

Solution: Using the basic trig derivatives we just learned, let's go for it:

$$\begin{aligned}
f^{(1)}(x) &= \cos(x) \\
f^{(2)}(x) &= -\sin(x) \\
f^{(3)}(x) &= -\cos(x) \\
f^{(4)}(x) &= \sin(x)
\end{aligned}$$

Here we used $f^{(1)}(x)$ for the first derivative to make it easy to compare it to the higher derivatives. Notice that the fourth derivative is equal to the original function, which means if we were to continue differentiating we would go in a four-step cycle. In other words, the eighth derivative would be $f^{(8)}(x) = \sin(x)$, which would be the same as the twelfth derivative $f^{(12)}(x)$, and so on. Similarly, the fifth derivative and ninth derivatives are both equal to $\cos(x)$.

Δ

EXAMPLE

Find the first four derivatives of $f(x) = \sin(ax)$ for any $a > 0$.

Solution: We now have the Chain Rule coming into play:

$$f^{(1)}(x) = \quad a\cos(ax)$$
$$f^{(2)}(x) = -a^2\sin(ax)$$
$$f^{(3)}(x) = -a^3\cos(ax)$$
$$f^{(4)}(x) = \quad a^4\sin(ax)$$

Δ

At this point, you might be wondering if there are cases when the first derivative exists and the second derivative does not. Let's look at an example of such a case.

EXAMPLE
Find the first and second derivatives of the following function, and determine where they exist:

$$f(x) = \begin{cases} -x^2, & x < 0 \\ x^2, & x \geq 0 \end{cases}$$

Solution: When confronted with a piecewise function like this, the derivative will also be piecewise. We simply find the derivative of the first piece and then the derivative of the second piece, keeping the same domains:

$$f'(x) = \begin{cases} -2x, & x < 0 \\ 2x, & x \geq 0 \end{cases}$$

The first derivative obviously exists when $x < 0$ and when $x > 0$. When $x = 0$, we need to take limits from both sides and see whether they equal to each other (using the definition of continuity). Noting that $f'(0) = 0$ from the second piece (due to the $\geq$ sign), we find the left and right limits:

$$\lim_{x \to 0-} f'(x) = \lim_{x \to 0-} -2x = 0$$
$$\lim_{x \to 0+} f'(x) = \lim_{x \to 0+} 2x = 0$$

Thus, the limits match and equal the point, so the first derivative exists everywhere. Now let's find the second derivative, which will also be piecewise:

$$f''(x) = \begin{cases} -2, & x < 0 \\ 2, & x \geq 0 \end{cases}$$

The second derivative exists when $x < 0$ and when $x > 0$. When $x = 0$, we once again take limits from both sides and see whether they equate. Noting that $f''(0) = 2$ from the second piece, we find the limits:

$$\lim_{x \to 0-} f''(x) = \lim_{x \to 0-} -2 = -2$$
$$\lim_{x \to 0+} f''(x) = \lim_{x \to 0+} 2 = 2$$

This time the second derivative is discontinuous at $x = 0$, and so the second derivative exists everywhere except at $x = 0$.

Δ

EXAMPLE
For any integer $n \geq 1$, find a formula for the nth derivative of $f(x) = x^n$.

Solution: This problem isn't as complicated as it looks. For illustrative purposes, take $n = 4$:

$$f^{(1)}(x) = 4x^3$$
$$f^{(2)}(x) = 4 \cdot 3x^2 = 12x^2$$
$$f^{(3)}(x) = 12 \cdot 2x = 24x$$
$$f^{(4)}(x) = 24$$

However, let's look at another way of writing the constants in the derivatives:

$$f^{(1)}(x) = 4x^3$$
$$f^{(2)}(x) = 4 \cdot 3x^2$$
$$f^{(3)}(x) = 4 \cdot 3 \cdot 2x$$
$$f^{(4)}(x) = 4 \cdot 3 \cdot 2 \cdot 1$$

Recognize that the fourth derivative is equal to the product of the numbers 4 down through 1, which is the same thing as 4! (read as "4 factorial" – not as FOUR!!!!). Thus, when $f(x) = x^4$, the 4th derivative is equal to 4!. Generalizing and going through a similar exercise for $n \geq 1$, we see that the nth derivative of $f(x) = x^n$ is

$$f^{(n)}(x) = n!$$

Caution: It should be noted that we answered this question merely by looking at a simple case and then recognizing what the general solution must be. In higher mathematics, we would be expected to prove this in a more rigorous way, and one way to do that is to use a technique called proof by induction. This is beyond the scope of what is normally covered in an introductory calculus class.

Δ

Section 2.6 – Introduction to Derivatives and Physics

In this section we take a perhaps well-needed breather from deriving the derivative formulas and discuss applications of them to physics, a very important field of science. Although there is a lot to learn about how calculus shows up in physics, at this point we can only give an introduction to some basic concepts. More topics will appear later in these notes.

DEFINITION
Physics is the branch of science that deals with topics such as how objects and particles move in time and space, as well as force and energy required to do so. There are plenty of other topics in physics, but we will focus on selective ones that are calculus based.

ETYMOLOGY
The word **physics** derives from the ancient Greek φύσις (pronounced *phusis*), which meant "nature."

The goal in this section is to describe the position of an object as it moves over time, as well as how quickly it is moving and the way it accelerates. On that note, let's make some definitions.

DEFINITION

Suppose an object is moving around and is at specific locations at time t. By convention, unless stated otherwise $t \geq 0$, and $t = 0$ represents the beginning of the analysis of interest.

The **position** of the object is the path it follows with respect to t, and it is usually denoted as $s(t)$ (although you might sometimes see $x(t)$). The units are measurements of length such as feet (ft), meters (m), miles (mi), etc.

The **velocity** of the object is the rate at which the object is moving, or in other words how quickly the object is moving with respect to time. It is usually denoted as $v(t)$. The units are measurements of length per unit of time such as feet per second (ft/s), meters per minute (m/min), miles per hour (mi/h or mph), etc.

The **acceleration** of the object is the rate at which its velocity is changing with respect to time. It is usually denoted as $a(t)$. The units are measurements of length per squared unit of time such as feet per second squared (ft/s^2), meters per minute squared (m/min^2), miles per hour squared (mi/h^2), etc.

ETYMOLOGY

The word **position** derives from the Latin *ponere*, which meant "to place" or "to put," which should make sense as the position function describes the location of an object. The word **velocity** comes from the Latin *velocitas*, which meant "speed." Finally, the word **acceleration** derives from the Latin *accelero*, from *ad* and *celero*, which literally meant "I hasten towards."

When we write $s(0)$, we denote the object's starting position in space (such as its x-coordinate or y-coordinate). Position can be positive, zero, or negative, with the following interpretations:

1) If $s(t) > 0$, the object is to the right (or above) its starting position at time t.
2) If $s(t) = 0$, the object is at its same starting position at time t.
3) If $s(t) < 0$, the object is to the left (or below) its starting position at time t.

Similarly, velocity can be positive, zero, or negative, with the following interpretations:

1) If $v(t) > 0$, the object is moving forward (to the right, or upward) at time t.
2) If $v(t) = 0$, the object is stationary (not moving) at time t.
3) If $v(t) < 0$, the object is moving backward (to the left, or downward) at time t.

Lastly (you guessed it), acceleration can be positive, zero, or negative, with the following interpretations:

1) If $a(t) > 0$, the rate at which the object is moving is increasing at time t.
2) If $a(t) = 0$, the object is moving at a constant rate (or velocity) at time t.
3) If $a(t) < 0$, the rate at which the object is moving is decreasing at time t.

You will note I did not use a word that you may be more comfortable thinking about in practical terms – speed. Here is that definition.

DEFINITION

Suppose $v(t)$ is the rate at which an object is moving at time t (in ft/s, m/min, mi/h, etc. The **speed** of the object at time t is the positive rate at which the object is moving at time t, or in other words $|v(t)|$.

Many people use the terms velocity and speed interchangeably, but technically there is a difference. One easy way to understand the difference is to imagine you are driving a car. If your odometer says 10 mph and you are moving forward (which most of the time you are), then your velocity is 10 mph, and your speed is also 10 mph. If you are parked, then your velocity is 0 mph and your speed is also 0 mph. However, if your odometer says 10 mph and you are reversing, then your velocity is −10 mph but your speed is 10 mph. This is because although speed tells you how quickly you are moving with respect to time, velocity also tells you in which direction (forward or backward).

What do these concepts have to do with derivatives? Let's find out:

DEFINITION
If $s(t)$ describes the position of the object at time t, then $v(t)$ describes the rate at which position is changing at time t. In other words, the derivative of position with respect to time is velocity:

$$v(t) = s'(t) = \frac{d}{dt}\big(s(t)\big)$$

Similarly, $a(t)$ describes the rate at which velocity is changing at time t. In other words, the derivative of velocity with respect to time is acceleration:

$$a(t) = v'(t) = \frac{d}{dt}\big(v(t)\big)$$

This means that the second derivative of position with respect to time squared is acceleration:

$$a(t) = s''(t) = s^{(2)}(t)$$

EXAMPLE
While standing on the ground you throw a pebble in the air, and the pebble's height (in feet) above the ground at time t (in seconds) is given by $s(t) = -16t^2 + 80t$. Neglecting air resistance (a phrase that appears a lot in physics with these types of problems), answer the following questions.

A) At what time does the pebble hit the ground?
B) Find the pebble's velocity and speed after 4 seconds, and describe what the pebble is doing at that instant.
C) At what point in time is the pebble's height above the ground increasing at 16 ft/s?
D) At what point in time is the pebble's velocity 0 ft/s? What is its height at that time?
E) Find the pebble's acceleration at time t.

Solution: This problem is a great example of a calculus exercise that will test your reading skills. You have to carefully work out which function (position, velocity, acceleration) is required in each case; otherwise you will be led astray!

For part A, we want to know when the pebble hits the ground, or in other words when the height is 0. That means we want the position $s(t) = 0$, so we solve that equation:

$$s(t) = -16t^2 + 80t = 0$$
$$80t - 16t^2 = 0$$
$$16t(5 - t) = 0$$
$$t = 0, 5$$

We know that $t = 0$ is the starting time, so $t = 5$ is the ending time, when the pebble hits the ground.

For part B, we find the velocity by taking the derivative of position, then evaluating it at $t = 4$:

$$v(t) = s'(t) = -16 \times 2t + 80 \times 1$$
$$v(t) = -32t + 80$$
$$v(4) = -32(4) + 80 = -48 \text{ ft/s}$$

The pebble's height is decreasing at 48 ft/s after it has been in the air for 4 seconds. The fact that velocity is negative at this instant indicates that the height is decreasing (in this case, falling). Since speed is the absolute value of velocity, the pebble's speed at $t = 4$ is $|v(4)| = |-48| = 48$ ft/s.

For part C, we need to find the time at which the pebble's height is increasing at 16 ft/s. That means we are interested in the rate of change of position (height) and therefore need to use the derivative, which is velocity. Next, we need to know when velocity is equal to 16 (positive since the height is increasing), so we solve $v(t) = 16$:

$$v(t) = -32t + 80 = 16$$
$$-32t = -64$$
$$t = 2$$

This means that 2 seconds after you launch the pebble into the air, its height is increasing at 16 ft/s (which is its velocity at that instant).

For part D, we need to find when the velocity is 0, which indicates that the pebble's height is not changing. (As we shall learn later, this is the maximum height of the pebble). This works in a similar way:

$$v(t) = -32t + 80 = 0$$
$$-32t = -80$$
$$t = \frac{5}{2} = 2.5$$

The height at this moment is found using the position function:

$$x\left(\frac{5}{2}\right) = -16\left(\frac{5}{2}\right)^2 + 80\left(\frac{5}{2}\right) = -16\left(\frac{25}{4}\right) + 80\left(\frac{5}{2}\right)$$
$$= -4 \times 25 + 40 \times 5$$
$$= 100$$

In other words, the pebble's velocity at $t = 2.5$ seconds is 0 ft/s, and it is 100 feet above the ground at that instant.

Finally, part E wants the acceleration at time t. This is the derivative of velocity:

$$v(t) = -32t + 80$$
$$a(t) = v'(t) = -32$$

Thus, the pebble's acceleration is a constant equal to -32 ft/s^2. This means that the pebble's velocity is decreasing at a rate of 32 ft/s^2.

Δ

EXAMPLE
You want to see how deep a well is (in feet), so you drop a pebble into the well and listen for when it hits the ground. After exactly 3 seconds, you hear it hit the ground. Assume the position of the pebble at time t is given by $s(t) = -16t^2$ neglecting air resistance (here a negative position represents feet below ground).

A) How deep is the well?
B) Find the velocity, speed, and acceleration at time t.
C) At what rate is the pebble's velocity changing at $t = 1$?

Solution: Part A is a simple application of the position function. The pebble hits the bottom of the well after 3 seconds (well, well, well!), so

$$s(3) = -16(3^2) = -16 \times 9 = -144$$

The well is 144 feet deep (The negative sign just means that we are below ground).

For part B, we just need the derivatives:

$$v(t) = s'(t) = -16 \times 2t = -32t$$
$$\text{speed}(t) = |v(t)| = |-32t| = 32t$$
$$a(t) = v'(t) = -32$$

Look carefully at the wording of part C – we want to know the rate of change for the velocity. That means we need the derivative of velocity, which is acceleration. Based on our analysis, we know that at any time t, the acceleration is -32 ft/s^2.

Δ

A couple of points should be made here. First, you will note that in both previous examples (both of which involved falling objects) we ended up with an acceleration of -32 ft/s^2. That is not a coincidence; in physics this number is known as the gravitational constant, and it is denoted as $g = -32$ ft/s^2. You might also see it written in the metric system as $g = -9.8$ m/s^2. If you drop an object and you are standing on planet Earth, its acceleration will be equal to this gravitational constant. (The weight of the object does not make a difference.) However, if you stand on the moon and drop a pebble, the gravitational constant will be very different!

Second, the above "free-fall equation" $s(t) = -16t^2$ can be used to find out after how many seconds a dropped object hits the ground. In movies, if someone is pushed off a building, they don't always land on the ground at the exact time they are supposed to. For instance, a person who gets pushed out of a window 80 feet above the ground is supposed to hit the ground after 2.236 seconds, but very few movies accurately show this! (Note that if you are using the metric system, the free-fall equation is instead $s(t) = -4.9t^2$ since finding the second derivative leads to $a(t) = -9.8$ m/s^2.)

EXAMPLE
A dragonfly moves through the air, and its position (in meters) away from its starting point after t seconds is given by

$$s(t) = \frac{t^3 + 3t}{t^2 + 1}, 0 \leq t \leq 5$$

A) Find the dragonfly's velocity at time t. At what times is the dragonfly not moving?

B) Find the dragonfly's acceleration at time t. When is the dragonfly's acceleration 0? What does this mean?

Solution: For part A, let's take the derivative of position using the Quotient Rule:

$$v(t) = s'(t) = \frac{(t^2 + 1)(3t^2 + 3) - (t^3 + 3t)(2t)}{(t^2 + 1)^2}$$

$$= \frac{3t^4 + 3t^2 + 3t^2 + 3 - 2t^4 - 6t^2}{(t^2 + 1)^2}$$

$$v(t) = \frac{t^4 + 3}{(t^2 + 1)^2}$$

If there are any moments when the dragonfly is not moving, that means that velocity is equal to 0, and so we need to solve

$$\frac{t^4 + 3}{(t^2 + 1)^2} = 0 \Rightarrow t^4 + 3 = 0 \Rightarrow t^4 = -3$$

However, this equation cannot be solved without introducing imaginary numbers, and so velocity is never equal to 0 over $0 \leq t \leq 5$. Put another way, the dragonfly is always moving over this time period. (Actually, noting that the numerator and denominator are always positive thanks to the squared terms, we can say that the dragonfly's velocity is always positive, which means it is always moving forward in this time period and never backward. For that reason, here speed is always equal to velocity.)

For part B, we take the derivative of velocity using the Quotient Rule once more:

$$a(t) = v'(t) = \frac{(t^2 + 1)^2(4t^3) - (t^4 + 3) \times 2(t^2 + 1)(2t)}{(t^2 + 1)^4}$$

$$= \frac{4t^3(t^2 + 1) - 4t(t^4 + 3)}{(t^2 + 1)^3} = \frac{4t^5 + 4t^3 - 4t^5 - 12t}{(t^2 + 1)^3}$$

$$a(t) = \frac{4t^3 - 12t}{(t^2 + 1)^3}$$

Next, we need to find when the acceleration is 0:

$$\frac{4t^3 - 12t}{(t^2 + 1)^3} = 0 \Rightarrow 4t^3 - 12t = 0 \Rightarrow 4t(t^2 - 3) = 0$$

$$\Rightarrow t = 0, \sqrt{3}, -\sqrt{3}$$

However, we can discard $t = -\sqrt{3}$ since $0 \leq t \leq 5$, which leaves $t = 0$ and $t = \sqrt{3} \approx 1.73205$. These are the times at which the dragonfly's acceleration is 0. Put another way, these are the moments at which the dragonfly's velocity is not changing.

$$\Delta$$

Although these definitions are covered in more detail in integral calculus, let's introduce two more terms.

DEFINITION

An object's **displacement** between time $t = a$ and $t = b$, $0 \leq a < b$, is the distance between the object's position at $t = b$ and its position at $t = a$, regardless of the path it traveled in between those times.

An object's **total distance traveled** between time $t = a$ and $t = b$, $0 \leq a < b$, is the total distance the object moved between $t = a$ and $t = b$, including distance traveled by reversing at any point along the journey.

There are better, more mathematical definitions of these two terms, but those are best left for an integral calculus class. Right now there isn't much we can do with these definitions other than introduce them and give a basic example.

EXAMPLE

At time $t = 0$ you start driving a car forward in a straight line. At time $t = 10$ seconds you have driven 40 meters, and at this point you reverse the car in a straight line 10 meters before stopping at time $t = 16$ seconds. Find your displacement and total distance traveled from $t = 0$ to $t = 16$.

Solution: There is no complicated mathematics involved here. Observe that you drive forward 40 meters and then reverse 10 meters, and so you've backtracked by 10 meters. That means you end up 30 meters from your starting point, so your displacement is 30 meters.

On the other hand, you move forward 40 meters and then reverse 10 meters. The total distance traveled is 50 meters because we now account for any direction traveled without cancelling out any distance.

Δ

In case you were wondering whether there are real-life applications of derivatives higher than the second, the answer is yes. Let's cover that now (although you will rarely if ever see these in a calculus class).

DEFINITION

The **jerk** of an object is the rate at which its acceleration is changing with respect to time. There isn't a standard notation for jerk, but one common way to write it is $j(t)$. The units are measurements of length per cubed unit of time such as feet per second cubed (ft/s^3), meters per minute cubed (m/min^3), miles per hour cubed (mi/h^3), etc. The derivative of acceleration with respect to time is jerk:

$$j(t) = a'(t) = \frac{d}{dt}\big(a(t)\big)$$

This means that the third derivative of position with respect to time cubed is jerk:

$$j(t) = s^{(3)}(t)$$

It's a little tricky to describe in practical terms what jerk is (it's not your ex-boyfriend!). One way is to imagine two people driving cars. The first driver is experienced, and so she accelerates the car smoothly. Here jerk would be low. The second driver is a beginner, so his acceleration might increase quickly when pressing the pedals (especially if a clutch is involved). The effect here is that the jerk would be higher, and anyone in that car would feel jerky (pun intended!) movements. Severe jerk could in some cases lead to whiplash.

EXAMPLE

Continuing the dragonfly example, find the dragonfly's jerk at time t, $0 \leq t \leq 5$.

Solution: Recall that the acceleration was

$$a(t) = \frac{4t^3 - 12t}{(t^2 + 1)^3}$$

Taking the derivative one more time,

$$\begin{aligned}
j(t) = a'(t) &= \frac{(t^2 + 1)^3(12t^2 - 12) - (4t^3 - 12t) \times 3(t^2 + 1)^2(2t)}{(t^2 + 1)^6} \\
&= \frac{(t^2 + 1)(12t^2 - 12) - 6t(4t^3 - 12t)}{(t^2 + 1)^4} \\
&= \frac{12t^4 + 12t^2 - 12t^2 - 12 - 24t^4 + 72t^2}{(t^2 + 1)^4} \\
j(t) &= \frac{-12t^4 + 72t^2 - 12}{(t^2 + 1)^4}
\end{aligned}$$

Δ

For those of you who simply cannot get enough of higher derivatives, some physics applications go even further. The fourth derivative of position is called **jounce** or **snap**, the fifth derivative of position is **crackle**, while the sixth derivative of position is **pop**. That's all the physics material we can learn for now; we will revisit this topic later when we study vector-valued functions (Section 4.3) and anti-derivatives (Section 5.6).

Section 2.7 – Implicit Differentiation

Until now we have always encountered formulas written strictly in terms of x, such as $y = x^2$ or $y = \sin(\sqrt{5x + 2})$. We have also seen how to compute the slopes at specific points on these functions; for instance, if $y = x^2$ and we want to find the slope of y at $x = 3$, then

$$\frac{dy}{dx} = 2x|_{x=3} = 2 \cdot 3 = 6$$

What we have been practicing up until now is **explicit differentiation** because y has been written in terms of just x. In other words, the left side of the equation has been just y and not, say, y^2 or xy.

Next, suppose we want to compute the derivatives at various points on the unit circle $x^2 + y^2 = 1$. With the techniques we have learned so far, we might be tempted to solve for y and then differentiate the result. Doing this, we would get

$$y = \pm\sqrt{1 - x^2}$$

This is really a group of two functions. Calling these $y_1 = \sqrt{1 - x^2}$ and $y_2 = -\sqrt{1 - x^2}$, the derivatives are

$$\begin{aligned}
\frac{dy_1}{dx} &= \frac{1}{2\sqrt{1 - x^2}} \cdot (-2x) = -\frac{x}{\sqrt{1 - x^2}} \\
\frac{dy_2}{dx} &= -\frac{1}{2\sqrt{1 - x^2}} \cdot (-2x) = \frac{x}{\sqrt{1 - x^2}}
\end{aligned}$$

In this example, we were able to solve for y in terms of x, albeit with the added warning that we get two functions.

Now suppose we were confronted with a function like $x^3 + y^3 = 3xy$. How can we quickly and efficiently isolate y? After a few attempts, you would likely be stymied and give up. Now consider

$$\cos\left(\sqrt{x^2 + y^2}\right) + y = 2x\sin(y^3)$$

It should take only about one second to realize that solving this function for either variable is impossible. And yet mathematicians often need to find derivatives of such functions to study the slopes at certain points. How do they do it?

In this section we practice **implicit differentiation**. This method allows us to differentiate any function without first having to isolate one of its variables. We repeatedly use the Chain Rule to compute dy/dx. The easiest way to see this is to demonstrate with some examples.

1) We have already seen that the derivative of a function y with respect to x is dy/dx, or y'.
2) Now consider y^2. Its derivative is $2y \cdot dy/dx$, or $2y \cdot y'$. Why? We use the Chain Rule:

$$f(g(x)) = (g(x))^2 \text{ where } g(x) = y$$

By the Chain Rule, the derivative is equal to

$$f'(g(x)) \cdot g'(x) = 2g(x) \cdot g'(x)$$
$$= 2y \cdot \frac{dy}{dx}$$

3) The derivative of $x^3\sin(y)$ is $x^3 \cdot \cos(y) \cdot dy/dx + 3x^2 \cdot \sin(y)$. Here we used the Product Rule as well as the Chain Rule with respect to x.

Now let's look at some examples.

EXAMPLE

Let's revisit the unit circle example, $x^2 + y^2 = 1$. We differentiate it with respect to x and then solve for dy/dx, getting

$$2x + 2y \cdot \frac{dy}{dx} = 0 \Rightarrow x + y \cdot \frac{dy}{dx} = 0$$
$$\Rightarrow y \cdot \frac{dy}{dx} = -x \Rightarrow \frac{dy}{dx} = -\frac{x}{y}$$

Does this match what we derived in the two broken formulas above? Recall that we defined $y_1 = \sqrt{1 - x^2}$ and $y_2 = -\sqrt{1 - x^2}$. Then

$$y_1' = -\frac{x}{\sqrt{1 - x^2}} = -\frac{x}{y_1}$$
$$y_2' = \frac{x}{\sqrt{1 - x^2}} = \frac{-x}{-\sqrt{1 - x^2}} = -\frac{x}{y_2}$$

And so we conclude from this old-fashioned method that $y' = -x/y$, which is the same as what we just discovered from implicit differentiation.

Δ

EXAMPLE
We want to know the equation of the tangent line to the point $(\sqrt{2}/2, \sqrt{2}/2)$ on the unit circle from the previous example. We already know that the implicit derivative of $x^2 + y^2 = 1$ is $dy/dx = -x/y$. We can quickly calculate the slope at the given point:

$$\frac{dy}{dx} = -\frac{x}{y}\bigg|_{\left(\frac{\sqrt{2}}{2}, \frac{\sqrt{2}}{2}\right)} = -\frac{\left(\sqrt{2}/2\right)}{\left(\sqrt{2}/2\right)} = -1$$

Thus, the slope of the unit circle at the point $(\sqrt{2}/2, \sqrt{2}/2)$ is -1. Now let's write the equation of the tangent line to this point.

$$-\frac{\sqrt{2}}{2} = -\left(x - \frac{\sqrt{2}}{2}\right) \Rightarrow y = -x + \frac{\sqrt{2}}{2} + \frac{\sqrt{2}}{2}$$

$$\Rightarrow y = -x + \frac{\sqrt{2}}{2} + \frac{\sqrt{2}}{2}$$

The tangent line is therefore $y = -x + \sqrt{2}$.

Δ

EXAMPLE
Let's look at the equation $x^3 + y^3 = 3xy$, which is called the Folium of Descartes. The graph is shown below. (This curve is named after the French mathematician and philosopher René Descartes (pronounced "day-CART"). One of his more well known claims to fame is his famous Latin phrase *cogito, ego sum*, which you know as "I think, therefore I am." The word folium was Latin for "leaf," and the graph certainly resembles a leaf.)

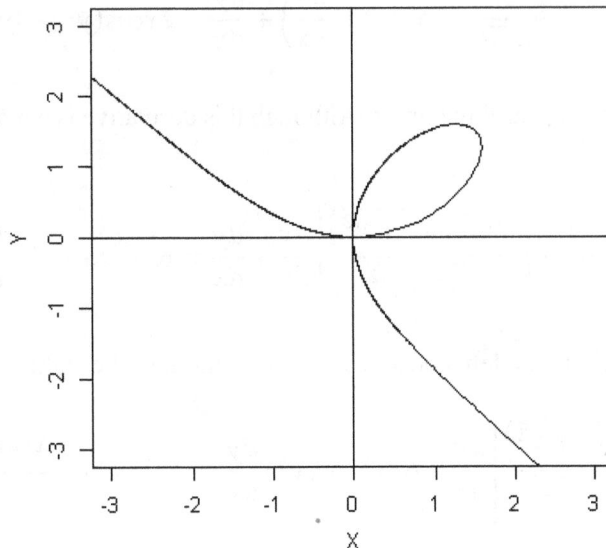

Let's compute its derivative at any point (x, y). We have

$$3x^2 + 3y^2 \cdot \frac{dy}{dx} = 3\left[x \cdot \frac{dy}{dx} + y\right]$$

Note that we used the Product Rule on the right side. Let's get rid of the 3:

$$x^2 + y^2 \cdot \frac{dy}{dx} = x \cdot \frac{dy}{dx} + y$$

Now we group together all terms containing dy/dx and isolate it.

$$y^2 \cdot \frac{dy}{dx} - x \cdot \frac{dy}{dx} = y - x^2$$
$$\frac{dy}{dx}(y^2 - x) = y - x^2$$
$$\frac{dy}{dx} = \frac{y - x^2}{y^2 - x}$$

Δ

MNEMONIC

With problems involving implicit differentiation, note how many times the letter y appears in the original equation. The derivative dy/dx (or y') will usually appear the same number of times in the derivative before you simplify the derivative.

EXAMPLE

Consider the other equation we showed earlier, $\cos\left(\sqrt{x^2 + y^2}\right) + y = 2x\sin(y^3)$. Let's try to differentiate this!

Solution: Using the mnemonic, the letter y appears three times in the function, so we can expect dy/dx to appear three times as well.

$$-\sin\left(\sqrt{x^2 + y^2}\right) \cdot \frac{1}{2\sqrt{x^2 + y^2}} \cdot \left(2x + 2y \cdot \frac{dy}{dx}\right) + \frac{dy}{dx} = 2x\cos(y^3) \cdot 3y^2 \cdot \frac{dy}{dx} + 2\sin(y^3)$$

Note that dy/dx does indeed appear three times. Although this derivative is a real mess, we need to isolate dy/dx (and clean up both sides).

$$-\frac{x\sin\left(\sqrt{x^2 + y^2}\right)}{\sqrt{x^2 + y^2}} - \left[\frac{y\sin\left(\sqrt{x^2 + y^2}\right)}{\sqrt{x^2 + y^2}}\right]\frac{dy}{dx} + \frac{dy}{dx} = 6xy^2\cos(y^3)\frac{dy}{dx} + 2\sin(y^3)$$

Moving all terms with dy/dx to the left side and all terms without to the right side,

$$\frac{dy}{dx} - \left[\frac{y\sin\left(\sqrt{x^2 + y^2}\right)}{\sqrt{x^2 + y^2}}\right]\frac{dy}{dx} - 6xy^2\cos(y^3)\frac{dy}{dx} = 2\sin(y^3) + \frac{x\sin\left(\sqrt{x^2 + y^2}\right)}{\sqrt{x^2 + y^2}}$$

We can factor out dy/dx:

$$\left[1 - \frac{y\sin\left(\sqrt{x^2+y^2}\right)}{\sqrt{x^2+y^2}} - 6xy^2\cos(y^3)\right]\frac{dy}{dx} = 2\sin(y^3) + \frac{x\sin\left(\sqrt{x^2+y^2}\right)}{\sqrt{x^2+y^2}}$$

Isolating dy/dx, we end up with

$$\frac{dy}{dx} = \frac{2\sin(y^3) + \dfrac{x\sin\left(\sqrt{x^2+y^2}\right)}{\sqrt{x^2+y^2}}}{1 - \dfrac{y\sin\left(\sqrt{x^2+y^2}\right)}{\sqrt{x^2+y^2}} - 6xy^2\cos(y^3)}$$

If you don't want fractions in the numerator and denominator, multiply this by the following fraction:

$$\frac{dy}{dx} = \left[\frac{2\sin(y^3) + \dfrac{x\sin\left(\sqrt{x^2+y^2}\right)}{\sqrt{x^2+y^2}}}{1 - \dfrac{y\sin\left(\sqrt{x^2+y^2}\right)}{\sqrt{x^2+y^2}} - 6xy^2\cos(y^3)}\right] \cdot \frac{\sqrt{x^2+y^2}}{\sqrt{x^2+y^2}}$$

Doing so will give the "slightly" cleaner derivative

$$\frac{dy}{dx} = \frac{2\sin(y^3)\sqrt{x^2+y^2} + x\sin\left(\sqrt{x^2+y^2}\right)}{\sqrt{x^2+y^2} - y\sin\left(\sqrt{x^2+y^2}\right) - 6xy^2\cos(y^3)\sqrt{x^2+y^2}}$$

Δ

EXAMPLE
Let's revisit the Folium of Descartes again, $x^3 + y^3 = 3xy$, and this time find the second derivative.

Solution: Recall that the first derivative was

$$\frac{dy}{dx} = \frac{y - x^2}{y^2 - x}$$

Taking the second derivative works the same way; we just treat the right side of the equation as a new function and pretend this is the first time we are differentiating it. Of course, the Quotient Rule will be used, and since the letter y appears twice, so will dy/dx initially before we stop simplifying.

$$\frac{d^2y}{dx^2} = \frac{(y^2-x)\left(\frac{dy}{dx} - 2x\right) - (y-x^2)\left(2y\frac{dy}{dx} - 1\right)}{(y^2-x)^2}$$

$$= \frac{\left(y^2\frac{dy}{dx} - x\frac{dy}{dx} - 2xy^2 + 2x^2\right) - \left(2y^2\frac{dy}{dx} - 2x^2y\frac{dy}{dx} - y + x^2\right)}{(y^2-x)^2}$$

$$= \frac{y^2\frac{dy}{dx} - x\frac{dy}{dx} - 2xy^2 + 2x^2 - 2y^2\frac{dy}{dx} + 2x^2y\frac{dy}{dx} + y - x^2}{(y^2-x)^2}$$

$$= \frac{y^2\frac{dy}{dx} - x\frac{dy}{dx} - 2y^2\frac{dy}{dx} + 2x^2y\frac{dy}{dx} - 2xy^2 + 2x^2 + y - x^2}{(y^2 - x)^2}$$

$$= \frac{2x^2y\frac{dy}{dx} - x\frac{dy}{dx} - y^2\frac{dy}{dx} + x^2 + y - 2xy^2}{(y^2 - x)^2}$$

$$= \frac{(2x^2y - x - y^2)\frac{dy}{dx} + x^2 + y - 2xy^2}{(y^2 - x)^2}$$

Although we could stop here, we typically don't like derivatives to be written in terms of other derivatives when possible. Let's substitute in our previous equation for dy/dx:

$$\frac{d^2y}{dx^2} = \frac{(2x^2y - x - y^2)\left(\frac{y - x^2}{y^2 - x}\right) + x^2 + y - 2xy^2}{(y^2 - x)^2}$$

$$= \frac{(2x^2y - x - y^2)\left(\frac{y - x^2}{y^2 - x}\right) + (x^2 + y - 2xy^2)\left(\frac{y^2 - x}{y^2 - x}\right)}{(y^2 - x)^2}$$

$$= \frac{(2x^2y - x - y^2)(y - x^2) + (x^2 + y - 2xy^2)(y^2 - x)}{(y^2 - x)^3}$$

$$= \frac{(2x^2y^2 - xy - y^3) - (2x^4y - x^3 - x^2y^2) + (x^2y^2 + y^3 - 2xy^4) - (x^3 + xy - 2x^2y^2)}{(y^2 - x)^3}$$

Continuing,

$$\frac{d^2y}{dx^2} = \frac{2x^2y^2 - xy - y^3 - 2x^4y + x^3 + x^2y^2 + x^2y^2 + y^3 - 2xy^4 - x^3 - xy + 2x^2y^2}{(y^2 - x)^3}$$

$$= \frac{6x^2y^2 - 2xy - 2x^4y - 2xy^4}{(y^2 - x)^3}$$

We can actually go even further. Sometimes with second derivatives of implicit differentiation problems, we can use the original equation to simply the second derivative. So here that means we should look for ways to use $x^3 + y^3 = 3xy$:

$$\frac{d^2y}{dx^2} = \frac{6x^2y^2 - 2xy - 2x^4y - 2xy^4}{(y^2 - x)^3}$$

$$= \frac{2xy(3xy - 1 - x^3 - y^3)}{(y^2 - x)^3}$$

Substituting $x^3 + y^3$ into the $3xy$,

$$\frac{d^2y}{dx^2} = \frac{2xy(x^3 + y^3 - 1 - x^3 - y^3)}{(y^2 - x)^3} = \frac{-2xy}{(y^2 - x)^3}$$

Thus, the second derivative started as a complicated expression but ultimately simplifies quite nicely! The moral of this story is that sometimes during implicit differentiation, especially with second derivatives, it doesn't hurt to look for ways to use the original equation for simplification purposes.

Δ

Section 2.8 – Derivatives of Exponential and Logarithmic Functions

In this section we derive the formulas for the derivatives of exponential functions and log functions. First, if you need to review the basic exponential rules and log rules as well as what they look like, please see Section 0.1.

DEFINITION

A **natural logarithm** (or **natural log**) is a logarithm with base e. It is denoted as $\ln(a)$, but some textbooks may call it $\log(a)$. Don't let this confuse you; the book will (hopefully) make the distinction!

ETYMOLOGY

The expression for **natural log** in Latin was *logarithmus naturalis*, which explains why the abbreviation is "ln" and not "nl."

There is one other result we need to state that will be needed when finding the derivative of the natural log function.

FACT: e AS A LIMIT

The following limit is equal to e:

$$\lim_{t \to 0}(1 + t)^{1/t} = e$$

Unfortunately, we are not yet in a position where we can prove this properly. The best way to prove it is to use a certain limit rule that you will learn later in this book, so for now you'll have to take my word that this limit is correct. To see that it is true, use your calculator for values of t that are close to 0, and you'll find that the function gets closer to e. Defining $f(t) = (1 + t)^{1/t}$,

$$f(0.01) = (1 + 0.01)^{1/0.01} = 2.70481$$
$$f(0.001) = (1 + 0.001)^{1/0.001} = 2.71692$$
$$f(0.0001) = (1 + 0.0001)^{1/0.0001} = 2.71815$$
$$f(0.00001) = (1 + 0.00001)^{1/0.00001} = 2.71827$$

We will now derive the derivative for the natural log.

DERIVATIVE OF $\ln(x)$

If $f(x) = \ln(x)$ and $x > 0$, then

$$\frac{d}{dx}\left(\ln(x)\right) = \frac{1}{x}$$

PROOF

Setting up the limit definition of the derivative,

$$\frac{d}{dx}\left(\ln(x)\right) = \lim_{h \to 0}\frac{\ln(x + h) - \ln(x)}{h}$$

Using one of the log rules,

$$\lim_{h \to 0} \frac{\ln(x + h) - \ln(x)}{h} = \lim_{h \to 0} \frac{\ln\left(\frac{x+h}{x}\right)}{h} = \lim_{h \to 0} \frac{1}{h}\ln\left(1 + \frac{h}{x}\right)$$

The next objective is to have x/h on the outside of the natural log so that we can use the limit fact later. Doing so is no problem; we just multiply the $1/h$ by x/x and rearrange terms:

$$\lim_{h \to 0} \frac{1}{h}\ln\left(1 + \frac{h}{x}\right) = \lim_{h \to 0} \frac{x}{x} \cdot \frac{1}{h}\ln\left(1 + \frac{h}{x}\right) = \lim_{h \to 0} \frac{1}{x} \cdot \frac{x}{h}\ln\left(1 + \frac{h}{x}\right)$$

Since the limit is in terms of h and not x, we can pull out the $1/x$:

$$\lim_{h \to 0} \frac{1}{x} \cdot \frac{x}{h}\ln\left(1 + \frac{h}{x}\right) = \frac{1}{x} \cdot \lim_{h \to 0} \frac{x}{h}\ln\left(1 + \frac{h}{x}\right)$$

Using another log rule,

$$\frac{1}{x} \cdot \lim_{h \to 0} \frac{x}{h}\ln\left(1 + \frac{h}{x}\right) = \frac{1}{x} \cdot \lim_{h \to 0} \ln\left(1 + \frac{h}{x}\right)^{x/h}$$

At this point, we are going to make the substitution $t = h/x$, which means we also substitute $1/t = x/h$ and $h = xt$. This may seem like an odd choice, but there is a good reason for it.

$$\frac{1}{x} \cdot \lim_{h \to 0} \ln\left(1 + \frac{h}{x}\right)^{x/h} = \frac{1}{x} \cdot \lim_{xt \to 0} \ln(1 + t)^{1/t}$$

Since x is treated as a constant here and $x > 0$, we can say that $t \to 0$ in the limit instead of $xt \to 0$:

$$\frac{1}{x} \cdot \lim_{xt \to 0} \ln(1 + t)^{1/t} = \frac{1}{x} \cdot \lim_{t \to 0} \ln(1 + t)^{1/t}$$

We are now in the position to use the limit fact, which explains why we were rewriting the limit this way. Recall that the limit fact says that

$$\lim_{t \to 0}(1 + t)^{1/t} = e$$

Remembering the natural log, the limit can now be evaluated as

$$\frac{1}{x} \cdot \lim_{t \to 0} \ln(1 + t)^{1/t} = \frac{1}{x}\ln(e)$$

Finally, using the fact that $\ln(e) = 1$,

$$\frac{1}{x}\ln(e) = \frac{1}{x} \cdot 1 = \frac{1}{x}$$

Thus, we have proven that $\frac{d}{dx}\left(\ln(x)\right) = \frac{1}{x}$.

∎

The previous proof had a lot of steps to it, but the good news is that the next three derivative results can be found using the natural log derivative, thereby cutting down the number of steps required. Let's learn the next one.

DERIVATIVE OF e^x

If $f(x) = e^x$, then

$$\frac{d}{dx}(e^x) = e^x$$

In other words, the derivative of e^x is itself!

PROOF

We will derive this formula using implicit differentiation. Consider

$$y = e^x$$

Taking the natural log of both sides, we have

$$\ln(y) = x$$

Differentiating with respect to x,

$$\frac{1}{y} \cdot \frac{dy}{dx} = 1$$

Solving for dy/dx results in

$$\frac{dy}{dx} = y$$

Since $y = e^x$, we have

$$\frac{dy}{dx} = e^x$$

∎

EXAMPLE

The derivative of $y = e^{x^2}$ is

$$\frac{dy}{dx} = e^{x^2} \cdot \frac{d}{dx}(x^2) = e^{x^2} \cdot 2x = 2xe^{x^2}$$

To be clear, the derivative is the exponential function itself multiplied by the derivative of the exponent, per the Chain Rule.

Δ

EXAMPLE

Find the derivative of $f(x) = \frac{e^{2x}}{\ln(\sqrt{x})}$.

Solution: Before we get started, we can simplify this slightly:

$$f(x) = \frac{e^{2x}}{\ln(\sqrt{x})} = \frac{e^{2x}}{\ln\left(x^{1/2}\right)} = \frac{e^{2x}}{\frac{1}{2}\ln(x)} = \frac{2e^{2x}}{\ln(x)}$$

Now let's differentiate:

$$f'(x) = \frac{\ln(x) \cdot \frac{d}{dx}(2e^{2x}) - 2e^{2x} \cdot \frac{d}{dx}(\ln(x))}{(\ln(x))^2}$$

$$= \frac{\ln(x) \cdot 2e^{2x} \cdot 2 - 2e^{2x} \cdot \frac{1}{x}}{(\ln(x))^2}$$

$$= \frac{2e^{2x}\left(2\ln(x) - \frac{1}{x}\right)}{(\ln(x))^2}$$

If you would rather not have a fraction in the numerator, we can go further by introducing x/x in the numerator:

$$f'(x) = \frac{2e^{2x}\left(\frac{2x\ln(x)}{x} - \frac{1}{x}\right)}{(\ln(x))^2}$$

$$= \frac{\frac{2e^{2x}}{x}(2x\ln(x) - 1)}{(\ln(x))^2}$$

$$= \frac{2e^{2x}(2x\ln(x) - 1)}{x(\ln(x))^2}$$

A word of warning: $(\ln(x))^2 \neq \ln(x^2)$. Be careful not to make this easy mistake!

Δ

EXAMPLE
Find the derivative of $f(x) = \ln\left(e^{\sin(x)+\cos(x^2)}\right)$.

Solution: Before we start, note that we can greatly simplify this!

$$f(x) = \ln\left(e^{\sin(x)+\cos(x^2)}\right)$$
$$= \sin(x) + \cos(x^2)$$

This is much friendlier to differentiate! So then we have

$$f'(x) = \cos(x) - \sin(x^2) \cdot 2x$$
$$= \cos(x) - 2x\sin(x^2)$$

Δ

The moral of these two examples is that sometimes we can simplify the formula before we start differentiating to avoid horribly messy equations later on. If you see a way to simply the original function using exponential rules, log rules, or trig formulas, take advantage of them to make future calculations easier.

Let's prove the next derivative.

DERIVATIVE OF a^x

If $f(x) = a^x$ and $a > 0$ is a constant, then

$$\frac{d}{dx}(a^x) = a^x \ln(a)$$

PROOF

We will derive this formula using implicit differentiation again. Consider

$$y = a^x$$

Taking the natural log of both sides, we have

$$\ln(y) = x\ln(a) = \ln(a) \cdot x$$

Differentiating with respect to x (and remembering that $\ln(a)$ is a constant),

$$\frac{1}{y} \cdot \frac{dy}{dx} = \ln(a) \cdot 1$$

Solving for dy/dx results in

$$\frac{dy}{dx} = y \ln(a)$$

Since $y = a^x$, we have

$$\frac{dy}{dx} = a^x \ln(a)$$

■

EXAMPLE

Let $f(x) = 5^{\tan(x)}$. Then

$$f'(x) = 5^{\tan(x)} \cdot \ln(5) \cdot \sec^2(x)$$

We have to use the Chain Rule on the exponent, but not before we write down $\ln(5)$.

Δ

Some classes might teach the derivative of the log function with other bases. In case you are in such a class, here is that derivative.

DERIVATIVE OF $\log_b(x)$

If $f(x) = \log_b(x)$ where $b > 0$ and $x > 0$, then

$$\frac{d}{dx}(\log_b(x)) = \frac{1}{x\ln(b)}$$

PROOF

Once again, we use implicit differentiation. Consider

$$y = \log_b(x)$$

Using properties of logs, this can be rewritten as

$$b^y = x$$

Taking the natural log of both sides, we have

$$y\ln(b) = \ln(x)$$

Differentiating with respect to x (and remembering that $\ln(b)$ is a constant),

$$\frac{dy}{dx} \cdot \ln(b) = \frac{1}{x}$$

Solving for dy/dx results in

$$\frac{dy}{dx} = \frac{1}{x\ln(b)}$$

■

EXAMPLE

Find the derivative of $f(x) = \log_{10}(x^3 + 1)$.

Solution: If the function were $\log_{10}(x^3)$, we could use log rules to pull down the exponent to simplify it. That is not possible here because of the $+1$ inside the log. No need to worry though; we can still apply the derivative formula we just learned:

$$f'(x) = \frac{1}{(x^3 + 1)\ln(10)} \cdot \frac{d}{dx}(x^3 + 1) = \frac{1}{(x^3 + 1)\ln(10)} \cdot (3x^2)$$
$$= \frac{3x^2}{(x^3 + 1)\ln(10)}$$

We can stop here, or we can use properties of logs to rewrite the denominator:

$$f'(x) = \frac{3x^2}{\ln\left(10^{x^3+1}\right)}$$

The reason we are showing you multiple ways to write the answer is in case you are answering a multiple-choice question, and the correct answer is in an alternative form than what you first derived. Depending what exam you are preparing for, don't be surprised if you see some questions like this!

Δ

There is one other functional form that is worth studying, and that is an exponential function in which both the base and the exponent are functions. Some examples are x^x, x^{x^2}, and $(3x)^x$. Derivatives of these functions are found using implicit differentiation on a case-by-case basis, but let's find the general form of the derivative anyway.

DERIVATIVE OF $(f(x))^{g(x)}$

If $y = (f(x))^{g(x)}$ where $f(x)$ and $g(x)$ are differentiable functions and $f(x) > 0$ at x, then

$$\frac{d}{dx}\left((f(x))^{g(x)}\right) = (f(x))^{g(x)}\left[g'(x) \cdot \ln(f(x)) + \frac{g(x)f'(x)}{f(x)}\right]$$

PROOF

Set up the function as

$$y = (f(x))^{g(x)}$$

Taking the natural log of both sides, we have

$$\ln(y) = g(x)\ln(f(x))$$

Differentiating with respect to x (and remembering to use the Product Rule),

$$\frac{1}{y} \cdot \frac{dy}{dx} = g'(x) \cdot \ln(f(x)) + g(x) \cdot \frac{1}{f(x)} \cdot f'(x)$$

$$\frac{1}{y} \cdot \frac{dy}{dx} = g'(x) \cdot \ln(f(x)) + \frac{g(x)f'(x)}{f(x)}$$

Solving for dy/dx results in

$$\frac{dy}{dx} = y \cdot \left[g'(x) \cdot \ln(f(x)) + \frac{g(x)f'(x)}{f(x)}\right]$$

$$= (f(x))^{g(x)}\left[g'(x) \cdot \ln(f(x)) + \frac{g(x)f'(x)}{f(x)}\right]$$

∎

EXAMPLE

Find the derivative of $y = x^x$.

Solution: Let's first find the derivative using implicit differentiation from scratch. Taking the natural log of both sides,

$$\ln(y) = x\ln(x)$$

Differentiating,

$$\frac{1}{y} \cdot \frac{dy}{dx} = 1 \cdot \ln(x) + x \cdot \frac{1}{x} = \ln(x) + 1$$

Solving for dy/dx results in

$$\frac{dy}{dx} = y[\ln(x) + 1]$$

Using the fact that $y = x^x$, the derivative is

$$\frac{dy}{dx} = x^x[\ln(x) + 1]$$

If you want to use the derivative formula we found earlier, note that $y = (f(x))^{g(x)}$ where $f(x) = x$ and $g(x) = x$. This means that $f'(x) = 1$ and $g'(x) = 1$, and so

$$\frac{d}{dx}\left((f(x))^{g(x)}\right) = (f(x))^{g(x)}\left[g'(x) \cdot \ln(f(x)) + \frac{g(x)f'(x)}{f(x)}\right]$$
$$= x^x\left[1 \cdot \ln(x) + \frac{x \cdot 1}{x}\right]$$
$$= x^x[\ln(x) + 1]$$

Δ

Either method will work to get the answer. If you don't like the idea of memorizing the general derivative formula, you can just use implicit differentiation each time with these functions. The good news is that there is so much more to calculus than just these functions, so you won't run into them too frequently!

There is one more derivative we can prove here. Now that we have learned implicit differentiation and derivatives of natural logs, we can once and for all give a quick, snappy proof of the general Power Rule, even when the exponent is irrational.

POWER RULE (CASE 5: REAL NUMBERS)
Let $f(x) = x^r$ where r is any real number (this includes irrational numbers). Suppose $f(x)$ is differentiable at a point x. Then the derivative is

$$f'(x) = rx^{r-1}$$

PROOF
Define $y = x^r$. Taking the natural log of both sides,

$$\ln(y) = r\ln(x)$$

Differentiating with respect to x,

$$\frac{1}{y} \cdot \frac{dy}{dx} = \frac{r}{x}$$

Solving for dy/dx and using $y = x^r$ results in

$$\frac{dy}{dx} = \frac{r}{x} \cdot y = \frac{r}{x} \cdot x^r = rx^{r-1}$$

$\blacksquare$

This method of proving the Power Rule is so much quicker and easier than all the steps we did earlier. Why didn't we do this sooner? The reason is because at the time, you didn't know how to do implicit differentiation or derivatives of natural logs!

EXAMPLE
Find the derivatives of $y = e$, $y = e^e$, $y = x^e$, and $y = e^x$.

Solution: First things first, don't panic! This problem is a lot easier than it looks. The trick is to recognize where the constants are and how they affect the function. First, $y = e$ is simply a constant, and so

$$\frac{d}{dx}(e) = 0$$

Next, $y = e^e$ may look a little strange, but since e is a constant, e^e is also a constant (equal to approximately 15.15426), so

$$\frac{d}{dx}(e^e) = 0$$

Looking at $y = x^e$, you might instinctively think that the derivative is itself since the function contains an e and an x. The problem is that they are in reverse order! However, remember that e is a constant, which means we can differentiate $y = x^e$ using the Power Rule. Even though e is irrational, the Power Rule still works:

$$\frac{d}{dx}(x^e) = ex^{e-1}$$

Lastly, $y = e^x$ is the familiar exponential function, which means

$$\frac{d}{dx}(e^x) = e^x$$

Δ

Section 2.9 – Derivatives of Inverse Trigonometric Functions
Finally, we discuss how to find the derivatives of inverse trig functions, after reviewing what these are. There are six inverse trig functions that we'll examine, including their graphs and domains, and then we'll see how to differentiate them. Some classes teach all six functions while others concentrate on just the first three, but for completeness you'll find all six below.

REVIEW: INVERSE TRIG FUNCTIONS
Suppose you have the equation $\sin(y) = x$, and you need to solve for y. You learned in pre-calculus how to do this by introducing a new function $\arcsin(x)$, sometimes written as $\sin^{-1}(x)$, that lets you write

$$y = \arcsin(x)$$

This function has the property that $\arcsin(\sin(y)) = y$ for appropriate domain and range of the equation. There are similar functions for the inverses of cosine and tangent, $\arccos(x)$ and $\arctan(x)$.

We now explicitly write down these three functions.

DEFINITION

The function $y = \arcsin(x)$ (pronounced "arc-sine"), or $y = \sin^{-1}(x)$, is equivalent to $\sin(y) = x$. Its domain is $[-1, 1]$, and its range is $[-\pi/2, \pi/2]$, as in the following graph. Notice that its domain is the range of $y = \sin(x)$.

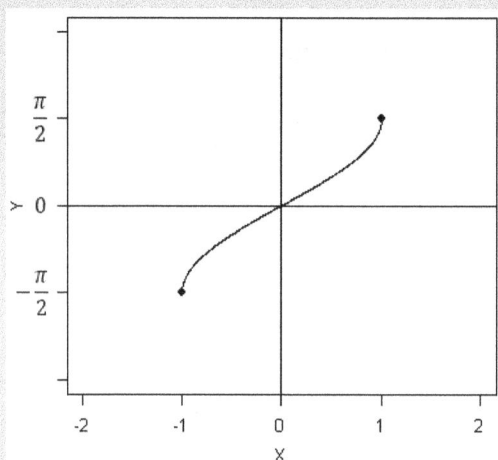

DEFINITION

The function $y = \arccos(x)$ (pronounced "arc-cosine"), or $y = \cos^{-1}(x)$, is equivalent to $\cos(y) = x$. Its domain is $[-1, 1]$, and its range is $[0, \pi]$, as in the following graph. Notice that its domain is the range of $y = \cos(x)$.

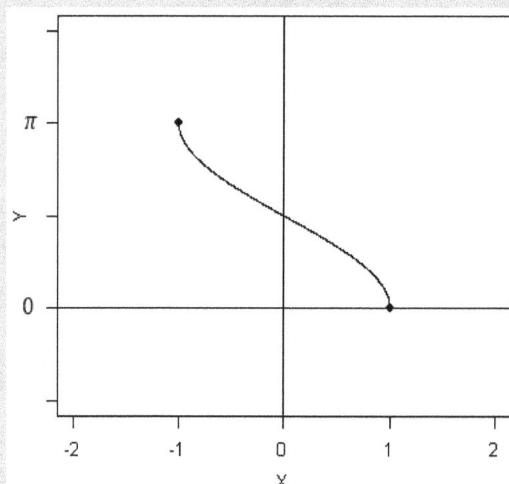

DEFINITION

The function $y = \arctan(x)$ (pronounced "arc-tangent"), or $y = \tan^{-1}(x)$, is equivalent to $\tan(y) = x$. Its domain is all real numbers, and its range is $(-\pi/2, \pi/2)$. Notice that its range does *not* include the endpoints, for there are horizontal asymptotes at $y = \pm\pi/2$.

DEFINITION (CONTINUED)

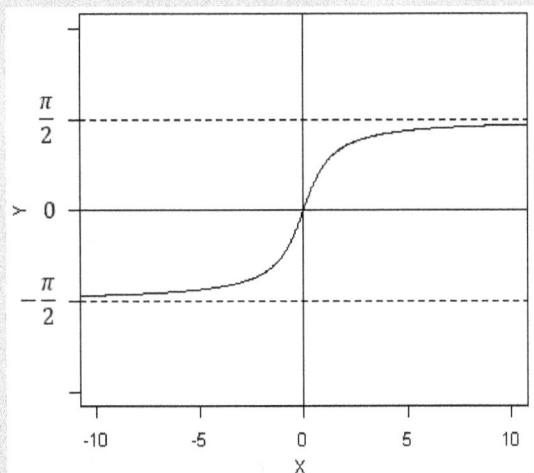

EXAMPLE

We know that $\sin(\pi/4) = \sqrt{2}/2$, so it follows that $\arcsin\left(\sqrt{2}/2\right) = \pi/4$.

In addition, we know from the unit circle that $\cos(\pi/2) = 0$ and $\cos(3\pi/2) = 0$. However, using a calculator, we find that $\arccos(0) = \pi/2$. Why? This is where the range comes in. $3\pi/2$ is out of the range of $y = \arccos(x)$, so we have to choose the angle that is in the range. In this case, the only such angle is $\pi/2$.

$$\Delta$$

While you can write the inverse trig functions using either notation (for instance, $\arcsin(x)$ or $\sin^{-1}(x)$), I recommend sticking with the *arc* notation. The reason is because if you write $\sin^{-1}(x)$, the -1 can easily be confused with a negative exponent, and you could find yourself thinking that the function is $1/\sin(x)$, which of course would be incorrect.

Now let's get the formulas for the derivatives of these three functions. There are a couple of ways of doing this, one of which involves drawing triangle diagrams. However, I'll walk you through what is hopefully an easier approach that uses trig identities.

DERIVATIVE OF ARCSINE

If $f(x) = \arcsin(x)$, then

$$\frac{d}{dx}\left(\arcsin(x)\right) = \frac{1}{\sqrt{1-x^2}} \quad \text{for } |x| < 1$$

PROOF

Let's first write $x = \sin(y)$. Differentiating both sides with respect to x, we get

$$1 = \cos(y) \cdot \frac{dy}{dx} \Rightarrow \frac{dy}{dx} = \frac{1}{\cos(y)}$$

127

Remembering the lovely formula $\cos^2(y) + \sin^2(y) = 1$, we can rearrange it as $\cos(y) = \sqrt{1 - \sin^2(y)}$. Why do we take just the positive square root and not the negative? The reason is because the angles in the range of $\arcsin(x)$ are $[-\pi/2, \pi/2]$, which encompass the 1st and the 4th quadrants, and in these quadrants $\cos(y)$ is positive. Returning to the derivative,

$$\frac{dy}{dx} = \frac{1}{\cos(y)} = \frac{1}{\sqrt{1 - \sin^2(y)}}$$

If $x = \sin(y)$, then

$$\frac{dy}{dx} = \frac{1}{\sqrt{1 - \sin^2(y)}} = \frac{1}{\sqrt{1 - x^2}}$$

Finally, remember that $\arcsin(x)$ is defined over $-1 \le x \le 1$. The derivative exists over that whole interval as well, except for the endpoints (since that would produce a zero denominator). Thus, the derivative exists only for $-1 < x < 1$, or equivalently $|x| < 1$.

∎

This is the strategy for finding the derivatives of these inverse functions. We do a similar process for the other two.

DERIVATIVE OF ARCCOSINE

If $f(x) = \arccos(x)$, then

$$\frac{d}{dx}(\arccos(x)) = -\frac{1}{\sqrt{1 - x^2}} \quad \text{for } |x| < 1$$

Notice that this derivative is the negative of the derivative for $f(x) = \arcsin(x)$.

PROOF

Let's write $x = \cos(y)$. Differentiating both sides with respect to x, we get

$$1 = -\sin(y) \cdot \frac{dy}{dx} \Rightarrow \frac{dy}{dx} = -\frac{1}{\sin(y)}$$

We can rearrange the formula $\cos^2(y) + \sin^2(y) = 1$ as $\sin(y) = \sqrt{1 - \cos^2(y)}$. Why do we take just the positive square root and not the negative? The reason is because the angles in the range of $\arccos(x)$ are $[0, \pi]$, which encompass the 1st and the 2nd quadrants, and in these quadrants $\sin(y)$ is positive. Returning to the derivative and remembering that $x = \cos(y)$,

$$\frac{dy}{dx} = -\frac{1}{\sin(y)} = -\frac{1}{\sqrt{1 - \cos^2(y)}} = -\frac{1}{\sqrt{1 - x^2}}$$

Finally, remember that $\arccos(x)$ is defined over $-1 \le x \le 1$. The derivative exists over that whole interval as well, except for the endpoints. Thus, the derivative exists only for $-1 < x < 1$, or equivalently $|x| < 1$.

∎

DERIVATIVE OF ARCTANGENT
If $f(x) = \arctan(x)$, then

$$\frac{d}{dx}\left(\arctan(x)\right) = \frac{1}{1+x^2}$$

PROOF
Let's write $x = \tan(y)$. Differentiating both sides with respect to x, we get

$$1 = \sec^2(y) \cdot \frac{dy}{dx} \Rightarrow \frac{dy}{dx} = \frac{1}{\sec^2(y)}$$

Using the trig identity $\tan^2(y) = \sec^2(y) - 1$, we have $\sec^2(y) = 1 + \tan^2(y)$ and

$$\frac{dy}{dx} = \frac{1}{1 + \tan^2(y)} = \frac{1}{1+x^2}$$

Note that $\arctan(x)$ is defined over all real numbers, and so is the derivative since the denominator is never zero.

■

EXAMPLE
Let's find the derivative of $f(x) = x^2 \arctan(x)$.

Solution: Using the Product Rule,

$$f'(x) = x^2 \cdot \frac{1}{1+x^2} + 2x \cdot \arctan(x) = \frac{x^2}{1+x^2} + 2x\arctan(x)$$

Δ

EXAMPLE
Find the derivative of $f(x) = \arcsin(x) / \arccos(x)$.

Solution: Using the Quotient Rule,

$$f'(x) = \frac{\arccos(x) \cdot \dfrac{1}{\sqrt{1-x^2}} - \arcsin(x) \cdot \left(-\dfrac{1}{\sqrt{1-x^2}}\right)}{\left(\arccos(x)\right)^2}$$

$$= \frac{\arccos(x) \cdot \dfrac{1}{\sqrt{1-x^2}} + \arcsin(x) \cdot \dfrac{1}{\sqrt{1-x^2}}}{\left(\arccos(x)\right)^2}$$

$$= \frac{\dfrac{1}{\sqrt{1-x^2}}\left(\arccos(x) + \arcsin(x)\right)}{\left(\arccos(x)\right)^2}$$

$$= \frac{\arccos(x) + \arcsin(x)}{\sqrt{1-x^2}\left(\arccos(x)\right)^2}$$

Δ

Let's pause for a moment to point out a subtle but important fact. You might have been tempted to rewrite $f(x) = \arcsin(x) / \arccos(x)$ as $\arctan(x)$; after all, $\sin(x) / \cos(x) = \tan(x)$, so would the same statement carry over for these inverse trig functions? The answer is no, $\arcsin(x) / \arccos(x) \neq \arctan(x)$. This can easily be seen by noting that the derivative of $\arctan(x)$ is $1/(1 + x^2)$, which certainly does not equal the derivative we found in the previous example.

EXAMPLE
Find the derivative of $f(x) = \arctan(x^2 - 4x)$.

Solution: Using the Chain Rule,

$$f'(x) = \frac{1}{1 + (x^2 - 4x)^2} \cdot (2x - 4)$$
$$= \frac{2(x - 2)}{1 + (x^2 - 4x)^2}$$

$$\Delta$$

There are in fact three more inverse trig functions that you may or may not see in your calculus class, and they take the names you are perhaps expecting (based on the other three standard trig functions). If your class does not cover these three derivatives, then you may skip the rest of this section. We now explicitly write down these other three functions.

DEFINITION
The function $y = \text{arccot}(x)$ (pronounced "arc-cotangent"), or $y = \cot^{-1}(x)$, is equivalent to $\cot(y) = x$. Its domain is all real numbers, and its range is $(0, \pi)$, as in the following graph. Notice that its domain is the range of $y = \cot(x)$.

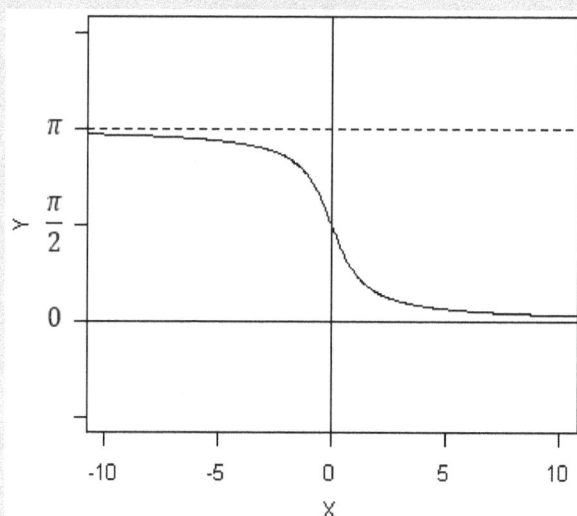

DEFINITION
The function $y = \text{arcsec}(x)$ (pronounced "arc-secant"), or $y = \sec^{-1}(x)$, is equivalent to $\sec(y) = x$. Its domain is $(-\infty, -1)$ and $(1, \infty)$, so the numbers $[-1, 1]$ are *not* in the domain. Its range is $[0, \pi/2)$ and $(\pi/2, \pi]$, so $y = \pi/2$ is *not* in the range (there is a horizontal asymptote at $y = \pi/2$), as in the following graph. Notice that its domain is the range of $y = \sec(x)$.

DEFINITION (CONTINUED)

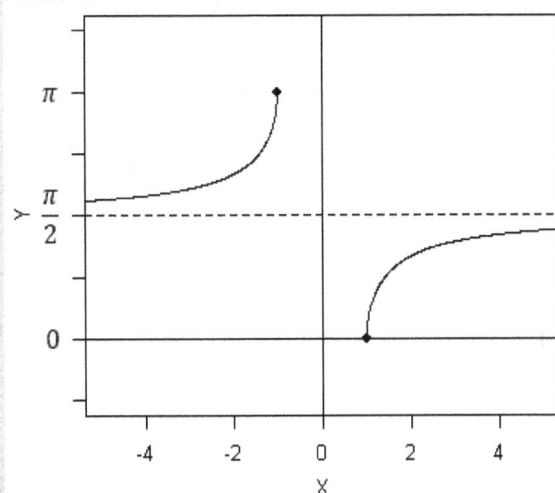

DEFINITION

The function $y = \text{arccsc}(x)$ (pronounced "arc-cosecant"), or $y = \csc^{-1}(x)$, is equivalent to $\csc(y) = x$. Its domain is $(-\infty, -1)$ and $(1, \infty)$, so the numbers $[-1,1]$ are *not* in the domain. Its range is $[-\pi/2, 0)$ and $(0, \pi/2]$, so $y = 0$ is *not* in the range (there is a horizontal asymptote at $y = 0$), as in the following graph. Notice that its domain is the range of $y = \csc(x)$.

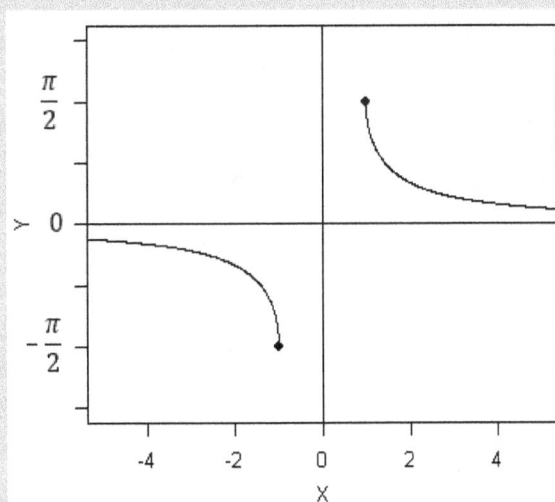

The last three derivatives in this section can be proven using similar methods as before.

DERIVATIVE OF ARCCOTANGENT

If $f(x) = \text{arccot}(x)$, then

$$\frac{d}{dx}(\text{arccot}(x)) = -\frac{1}{1 + x^2}$$

Notice that this derivative is the negative of the derivative for $f(x) = \arctan(x)$.

PROOF

Let's first write $\cot(y) = x$. Differentiating both sides with respect to x, we get

$$-\csc^2(y) \cdot \frac{dy}{dx} = 1 \Rightarrow \frac{dy}{dx} = -\frac{1}{\csc^2(y)}$$

We need to eliminate the y term from the derivative. Using the trig identity $\csc^2(y) = 1 + \cot^2(y)$,

$$\frac{dy}{dx} = -\frac{1}{1 + \cot^2(y)} = -\frac{1}{1 + x^2}$$

Note that $\mathrm{arccot}(x)$ is defined over all real numbers, and so is the derivative since the denominator is never zero.

■

DERIVATIVE OF ARCSECANT

If $f(x) = \mathrm{arcsec}(x)$, then

$$\frac{d}{dx}\left(\mathrm{arcsec}(x)\right) = \frac{1}{|x|\sqrt{x^2 - 1}} \quad \text{for } |x| > 1$$

PROOF

Let's first write $\sec(y) = x$. Differentiating both sides with respect to x, we get

$$\sec(y)\tan(y) \cdot \frac{dy}{dx} = 1 \Rightarrow \frac{dy}{dx} = \frac{1}{\sec(y)\tan(y)}$$

We need to eliminate the y terms from the derivative. To do this, let's first square both sides (the reason will become clear very soon):

$$\left(\frac{dy}{dx}\right)^2 = \frac{1}{\sec^2(y)\tan^2(y)}$$

Using the trig identity $\tan^2(y) = \sec^2(y) - 1$,

$$\left(\frac{dy}{dx}\right)^2 = \frac{1}{\sec^2(y)\left(\sec^2(y) - 1\right)}$$

We did this so that we can then substitute $\sec(y) = x$:

$$\left(\frac{dy}{dx}\right)^2 = \frac{1}{x^2(x^2 - 1)}$$

To get back to dy/dx, we square root both sides and use absolute values in doing so. Notice that since $x > 1$ or $x < -1$, $x^2 - 1$ is always positive and therefore does not require absolute values.

$$\left|\frac{dy}{dx}\right| = \frac{1}{|x|\sqrt{x^2 - 1}}$$

Next, notice that the derivative is always positive. We can see this by looking at the graph of $y = \text{arcsec}(x)$ and observing that as x increases within the allowed domain, y always increases, as seen in the following graph. That means we need to keep the absolute values around x to force the derivative to be positive.

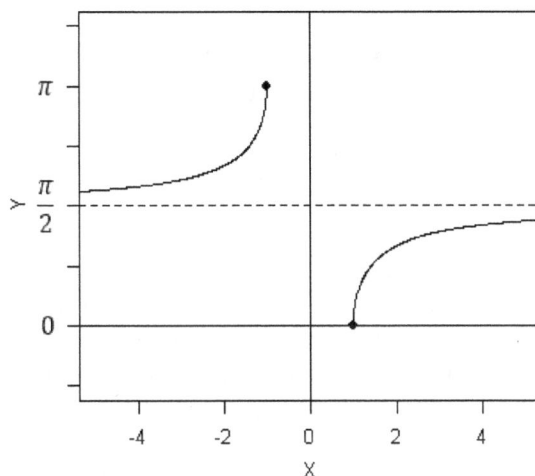

Finally, remember that $\text{arcsec}(x)$ is defined if $x \leq -1$ or $x \geq 1$. The derivative exists over that whole interval as well, except for the endpoints (because they cause the denominator to be zero). Thus, the derivative $\frac{dy}{dx} = \frac{1}{|x|\sqrt{x^2-1}}$ exists only for $x < -1$ or $x > 1$, or equivalently $|x| > 1$.

■

One more to go!

DERIVATIVE OF ARCCOSECANT
If $f(x) = \text{arccsc}(x)$, then

$$\frac{d}{dx}\big(\text{arccsc}(x)\big) = -\frac{1}{|x|\sqrt{x^2-1}}$$

Notice that this derivative is the negative of the derivative for $f(x) = \text{arcsec}(x)$.

PROOF
Let's first write $\csc(y) = x$. Differentiating both sides with respect to x, we get

$$-\csc(y)\cot(y)\cdot\frac{dy}{dx} = 1 \Rightarrow \frac{dy}{dx} = -\frac{1}{\csc(y)\cot(y)}$$

We need to eliminate the y terms from the derivative. Once again, let's first square both sides:

$$\left(\frac{dy}{dx}\right)^2 = \frac{1}{\csc^2(y)\cot^2(y)}$$

Using the trig identity $\cot^2(y) = \csc^2(y) - 1$,

$$\left(\frac{dy}{dx}\right)^2 = \frac{1}{\csc^2(y)\,(\csc^2(y) - 1)}$$

133

We did this so that we can then substitute $\csc(y) = x$:

$$\left(\frac{dy}{dx}\right)^2 = \frac{1}{x^2(x^2 - 1)}$$

To get back to dy/dx, we square root both sides and use absolute values in doing so. Notice that since $x > 1$ or $x < -1$, $x^2 - 1$ is always positive and therefore does not require absolute values.

$$\left|\frac{dy}{dx}\right| = \frac{1}{|x|\sqrt{x^2 - 1}}$$

Next, notice that the derivative is always negative. We can see this by looking at the graph of $y = \text{arccsc}(x)$ and observing that as x increases within the allowed domain, y always decreases, as seen in the following graph. (We also know this because of the original negative sign before we squared both sides.) That means we need to keep the absolute values around x to force the denominator to be positive, and then remember to put the -1 back in the derivative to force it to be negative.

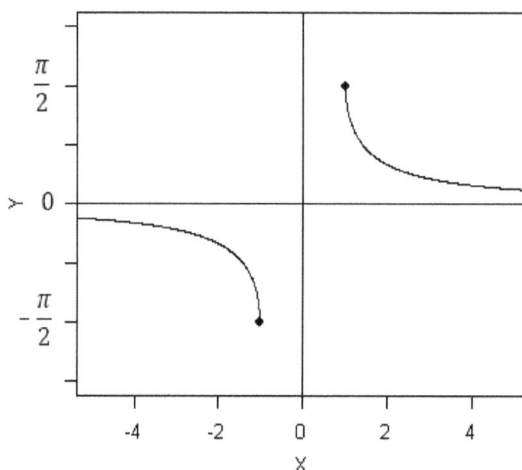

Finally, remember that $\text{arccsc}(x)$ is defined if $x \le -1$ or $x \ge 1$. The derivative exists over that whole interval as well, except for the endpoints. Thus, the derivative $\frac{dy}{dx} = -\frac{1}{|x|\sqrt{x^2-1}}$ exists only for $|x| > 1$.

∎

EXAMPLE

Find the derivatives of $f(x) = \text{arccot}(4x)$, $g(x) = x\,\text{arcsec}(x^2)$, and $h(x) = \frac{\text{arccsc}(2x)}{e^{2x}}$.

Solution: Let's tackle these one at a time:

$$f'(x) = -\frac{1}{1 + (4x)^2} \cdot 4 = -\frac{4}{1 + 16x^2}$$

Next,

$$g'(x) = 1 \cdot \text{arcsec}(x^2) + x \cdot \frac{1}{|x^2|\sqrt{(x^2)^2 - 1}} \cdot 2x$$

$$= \text{arcsec}(x^2) + \frac{2x^2}{|x^2|\sqrt{x^4 - 1}}$$

Notice that $|x^2| = x^2$ because x^2 is never negative, and so

$$g'(x) = \text{arcsec}(x^2) + \frac{2}{\sqrt{x^4 - 1}}$$

Finally,

$$h'(x) = \frac{e^{2x} \cdot \left(\dfrac{-1}{|2x|\sqrt{(2x)^2 - 1}}\right) - \text{arccsc}(2x) \cdot e^{2x} \cdot 2}{(e^{2x})^2}$$

$$= \frac{\dfrac{-1}{2|x|\sqrt{4x^2 - 1}} - 2\,\text{arccsc}(2x)}{e^{2x}}$$

$$= \frac{\dfrac{-1}{2|x|\sqrt{4x^2 - 1}} - \dfrac{2\,\text{arccsc}(2x) \cdot 2|x|\sqrt{4x^2 - 1}}{2|x|\sqrt{4x^2 - 1}}}{e^{2x}}$$

$$= \frac{-1 - 4|x|\,\text{arccsc}(2x)\,\sqrt{4x^2 - 1}}{2|x|e^{2x}\sqrt{4x^2 - 1}}$$

The reason $|2x| = 2|x|$ is because the 2 is already positive.

Δ

Section 2.10 – Derivatives of Hyperbolic Functions and their Inverses*

This final section discusses a series of functions with which you may or may not be familiar, the hyperbolic functions. They are written in terms of the exponential functions e^x and e^{-x} and often arise in physics applications such as electromagnetic theory. There are six main functions that take the names of the six trigonometric functions, but with the letter h added to the end (for instance, $y = \sinh(x)$, which is pronounced "hyperbolic sine"). If your class does not cover these functions, let alone their derivatives, then you may skip this section.

You may remember that the sine and cosine functions are determined from the unit circle angles, and that they satisfy the formula $\cos^2(x) + \sin^2(x) = 1$. This trig formula is equivalent to the unit circle formula $x^2 + y^2 = 1$. Now it's time to meet their hyperbolic cousins, $\sinh(x)$ and $\cosh(x)$.

DEFINITION
A **hyperbolic function** is defined in terms of the exponential functions e^x and e^{-x}. Specifically, the **hyperbolic sine** and **hyperbolic cosine** are defined in the following way:

$$\sinh(x) = \frac{e^x - e^{-x}}{2} \qquad \cosh(x) = \frac{e^x + e^{-x}}{2}$$

Their graphs are shown below. The domain and range for $\sinh(x)$ are both all real numbers ($\mathbb{R}$). For $\cosh(x)$, the domain is all real numbers, while the range is $[1, \infty)$.

DEFINITION (CONTINUED)

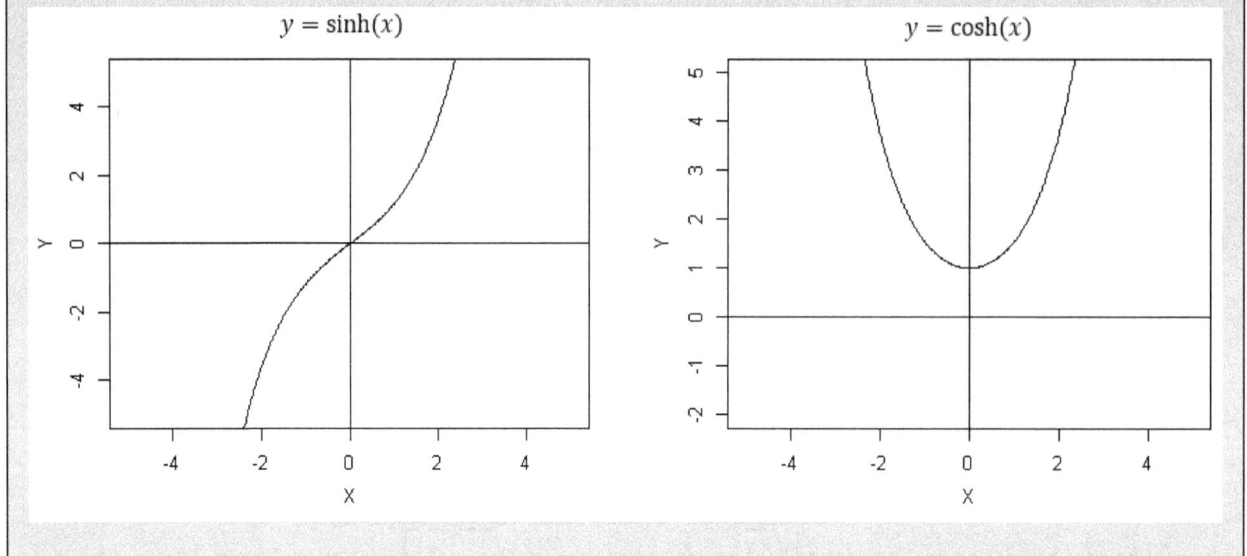

$y = \sinh(x)$ $y = \cosh(x)$

Instead of the unit circle formula, the hyperbolic sine and hyperbolic cosine satisfy the equation $\cosh^2(x) - \sin^2(x) = 1$. This is the formula for the hyperbola that opens to the left and right, which is $x^2 - y^2 = 1$, as seen in the following graph.

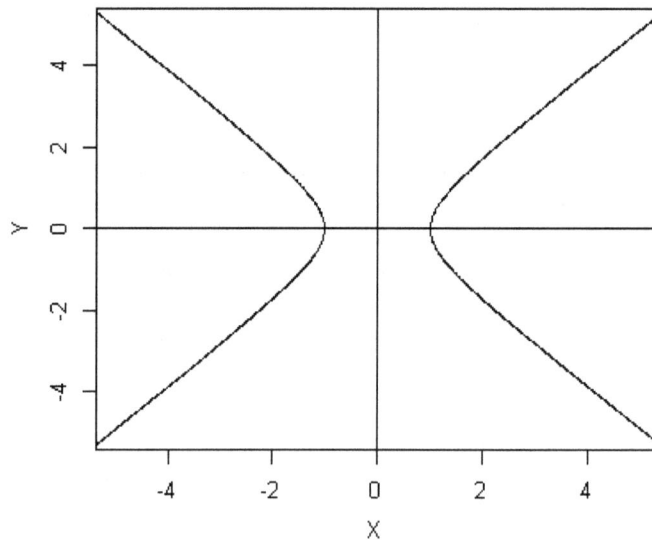

EXAMPLE

To find $\cosh(0)$ and $\sinh(1)$, we simply compute as

$$\cosh(0) = \frac{e^0 + e^{-0}}{2} = \frac{1+1}{2} = 1$$

$$\sinh(1) = \frac{e^1 - e^{-1}}{2} = \frac{e - \dfrac{1}{e}}{2} = \frac{e^2 - 1}{2e} \approx 1.17520$$

Δ

There are four more hyperbolic functions, and you can probably guess what they are called. The good news is that they are defined in the same ways the six trig functions are defined. We just have to get used to how their graphs look!

DEFINITION

The **hyperbolic tangent** and **hyperbolic cotangent** are defined in the following way:

$$\tanh(x) = \frac{\sinh(x)}{\cosh(x)} = \frac{e^x - e^{-x}}{e^x + e^{-x}} \qquad \coth(x) = \frac{\cosh(x)}{\sinh(x)} = \frac{e^x + e^{-x}}{e^x - e^{-x}}$$

Their graphs are shown below. For $\tanh(x)$, the domain is all real numbers, and the range is $(-1, 1)$. For $\coth(x)$, the domain is $(-\infty, 0) \cup (0, \infty)$, while the range is $(-\infty, -1) \cup (1, \infty)$.

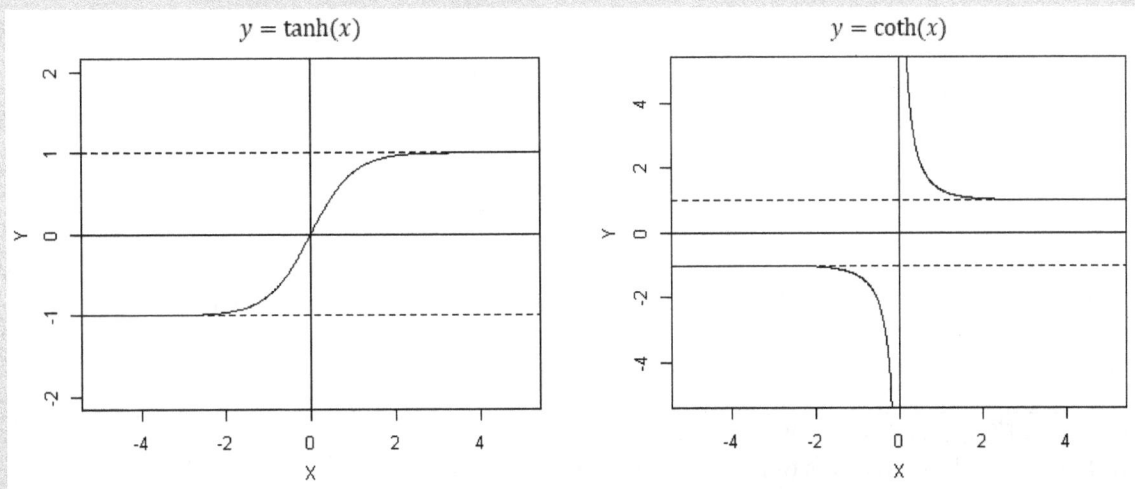

And now for the last two.

DEFINITION

The **hyperbolic secant** and **hyperbolic cosecant** are defined in the following way:

$$\text{sech}(x) = \frac{1}{\cosh(x)} = \frac{2}{e^x + e^{-x}} \qquad \text{csch}(x) = \frac{1}{\sinh(x)} = \frac{2}{e^x - e^{-x}}$$

Their graphs are shown below. For $\text{sech}(x)$, the domain is all real numbers, and the range is $(0, 1]$. For $\text{csch}(x)$, the domain is $(-\infty, 0) \cup (0, \infty)$, while the range is $(-\infty, 0) \cup (0, \infty)$.

DEFINITION (CONTINUED)

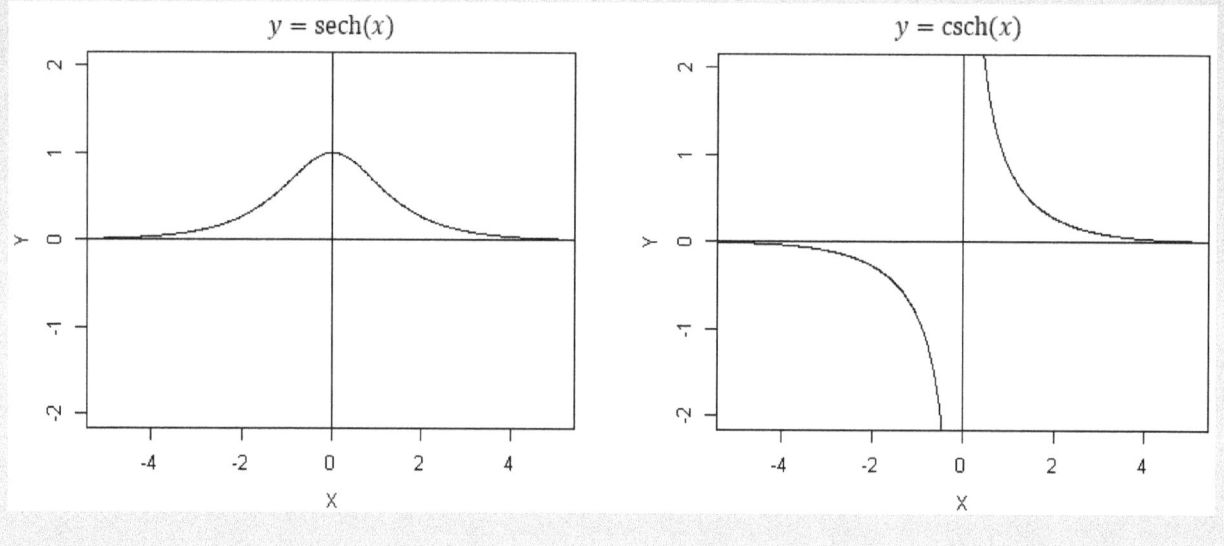

You know what's coming next…we need to have a little chitchat about their derivatives! (In earlier sections we focused on one derivative at a time, boxing each result individually. Since the hyperbolic functions are not as common in a calculus class, we will just treat all six together. You will not see them in this book anywhere else, apart from Appendices B and C.)

DERIVATIVES OF HYPERBOLIC FUNCTIONS

The following are the derivatives of the six hyperbolic functions:

$$\frac{d}{dx}(\sinh(x)) = \cosh(x) \qquad \frac{d}{dx}(\coth(x)) = -\operatorname{csch}^2(x)$$

$$\frac{d}{dx}(\cosh(x)) = \sinh(x) \qquad \frac{d}{dx}(\operatorname{sech}(x)) = -\operatorname{sech}(x)\tanh(x)$$

$$\frac{d}{dx}(\tanh(x)) = \operatorname{sech}^2(x) \qquad \frac{d}{dx}(\operatorname{csch}(x)) = -\operatorname{csch}(x)\coth(x)$$

PROOF

The good news is that we don't need to use that limit definition! The derivatives of the first two functions are easy to find:

$$\frac{d}{dx}(\sinh(x)) = \frac{d}{dx}\left(\frac{e^x - e^{-x}}{2}\right) = \frac{e^x - e^{-x} \cdot -1}{2} = \frac{e^x + e^{-x}}{2} = \cosh(x)$$

$$\frac{d}{dx}(\cosh(x)) = \frac{d}{dx}\left(\frac{e^x + e^{-x}}{2}\right) = \frac{e^x + e^{-x} \cdot -1}{2} = \frac{e^x - e^{-x}}{2} = \sinh(x)$$

To find the derivative of $\tanh(x)$, we rewrite it and then differentiate:

$$\frac{d}{dx}(\tanh(x)) = \frac{d}{dx}\left(\frac{\sinh(x)}{\cosh(x)}\right) = \frac{\cosh(x) \cdot \cosh(x) - \sinh(x) \cdot \sinh(x)}{\cosh^2(x)} = \frac{\cosh^2(x) - \sinh^2(x)}{\cosh^2(x)}$$

138

Using the fact that $\cosh^2(x) - \sinh^2(x) = 1$,

$$\frac{\cosh^2(x) - \sinh^2(x)}{\cosh^2(x)} = \frac{1}{\cosh^2(x)} = \text{sech}^2(x)$$

Next,

$$\frac{d}{dx}(\coth(x)) = \frac{d}{dx}\left(\frac{\cosh(x)}{\sinh(x)}\right) = \frac{\sinh(x) \cdot \sinh(x) - \cosh(x) \cdot \cosh(x)}{\sinh^2(x)} = \frac{\sinh^2(x) - \cosh^2(x)}{\sinh^2(x)}$$

Since $\cosh^2(x) - \sinh^2(x) = 1$, we have $\sinh^2(x) - \cosh^2(x) = -1$ and therefore

$$\frac{\sinh^2(x) - \cosh^2(x)}{\sinh^2(x)} = -\frac{1}{\sinh^2(x)} = -\text{csch}^2(x)$$

For the hyperbolic secant derivative,

$$\frac{d}{dx}(\text{sech}(x)) = \frac{d}{dx}\left(\frac{1}{\cosh(x)}\right) = -\frac{\sinh(x)}{\cosh^2(x)} = -\frac{1}{\cosh(x)} \cdot \frac{\sinh(x)}{\cosh(x)} = -\text{sech}(x)\tanh(x)$$

Finally, the hyperbolic cosecant derivative is

$$\frac{d}{dx}(\text{csch}(x)) = \frac{d}{dx}\left(\frac{1}{\sinh(x)}\right) = -\frac{\cosh(x)}{\sinh^2(x)} = -\frac{1}{\sinh(x)} \cdot \frac{\cosh(x)}{\sinh(x)} = -\text{csch}(x)\coth(x)$$

∎

There are two important points to make here. First, notice how we repeatedly used the $\cosh^2(x) - \sinh^2(x) = 1$ identity to get some of these results. This is analogous to the use of the $\cos^2(x) + \sin^2(x) = 1$ for the regular trig functions. You have heard me say that the $\cos^2(x) + \sin^2(x) = 1$ formula is the uncle who wants to be in all your family photos. Well, in the hyperbolic world, the $\cosh^2(x) - \sinh^2(x) = 1$ identity can be thought of as the nephew who wants to be in every photo!

Second, notice how the six derivatives are very similar to the analogous derivatives for the trig functions. For instance, the derivative of $\tan(x)$ is $\sec^2(x)$, while the derivative of $\tanh(x)$ is $\text{sech}^2(x)$. However, be especially careful about the positive and negative signs. For instance, the derivative of $\cos(x)$ is $-\sin(x)$, but the derivative of $\cosh(x)$ is $\sinh(x)$!

EXAMPLE
Find the derivatives of $f(x) = \ln(\text{sech}(x))$ and $g(x) = \sinh^3(x)\cosh^2(x)$.

Solution: The derivative of the first function uses the Chain Rule (and don't forget the negative sign!):

$$f'(x) = \frac{1}{\text{sech}(x)} \cdot -\text{sech}(x)\tanh(x) = -\tanh(x)$$

The second function requires the Product Rule as well as the Chain Rule:

$$\begin{aligned}g'(x) &= 3\sinh^2(x)\cosh(x) \cdot \cosh^2(x) + \sinh^3(x) \cdot 2\cosh(x)\sinh(x) \\ &= 3\sinh^2(x)\cosh^3(x) + 2\sinh^4(x)\cosh(x) \\ &= \sinh^2(x)\cosh(x)\,[3\cosh^2(x) + 2\sinh^2(x)]\end{aligned}$$

139

Δ

The six trig functions also brought along their friends, the six inverse trig functions that we studied in Section 2.9. I'm terribly sorry to inform you, but there are also six inverse hyperbolic functions! Let's cover what these six functions look like, and then we'll go to their derivatives.

DEFINITION

The function $y = \text{arcsinh}(x)$ (the **inverse hyperbolic sine**), or $y = \sinh^{-1}(x)$, is equivalent to $\sinh(y) = x$. Its domain and range are both all real numbers. The function $y = \text{arccosh}(x)$ (the **inverse hyperbolic cosine**), or $y = \cosh^{-1}(x)$, is equivalent to $\cosh(y) = x$. Its domain is $[1, \infty)$, and its range is $[0, \infty)$.

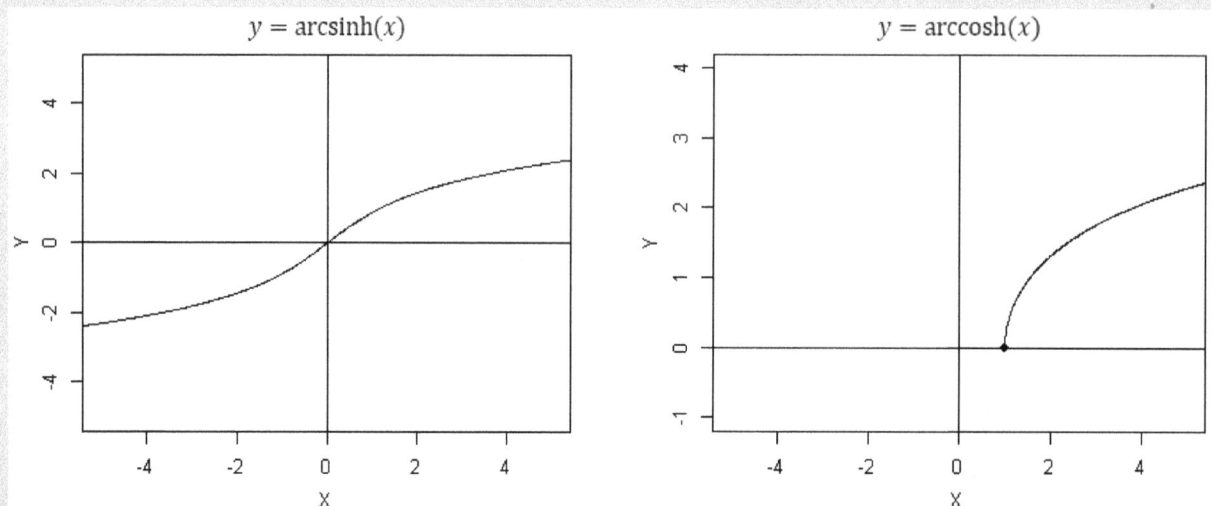

DEFINITION

The function $y = \text{arctanh}(x)$ (the **inverse hyperbolic tangent**), or $y = \tanh^{-1}(x)$, is equivalent to $\tanh(y) = x$. Its domain is $(-1, 1)$, and its range is all real numbers. The function $y = \text{arccoth}(x)$ (the **inverse hyperbolic cotangent**), or $y = \coth^{-1}(x)$, is equivalent to $\coth(y) = x$. Its domain is $(-\infty, -1) \cup (1, \infty)$, and its range is $(-\infty, 0) \cup (0, \infty)$.

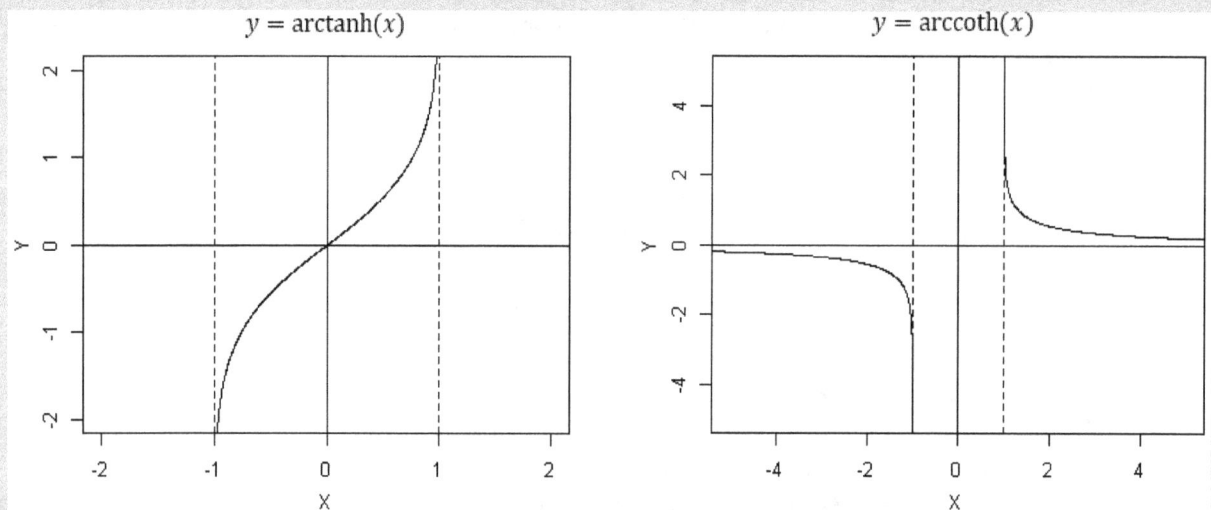

DEFINITION

The function $y = \text{arcsech}(x)$ (the **inverse hyperbolic secant**), or $y = \text{sech}^{-1}(x)$, is equivalent to $\text{sech}(y) = x$. Its domain is $(0, 1]$, and its range is $[0, \infty)$. The function $y = \text{arccsch}(x)$ (the **inverse hyperbolic cosecant**), or $y = \text{csch}^{-1}(x)$, is equivalent to $\text{csch}(y) = x$. Its domain is $(-\infty, 0) \cup (0, \infty)$, and its range is $(-\infty, 0) \cup (0, \infty)$.

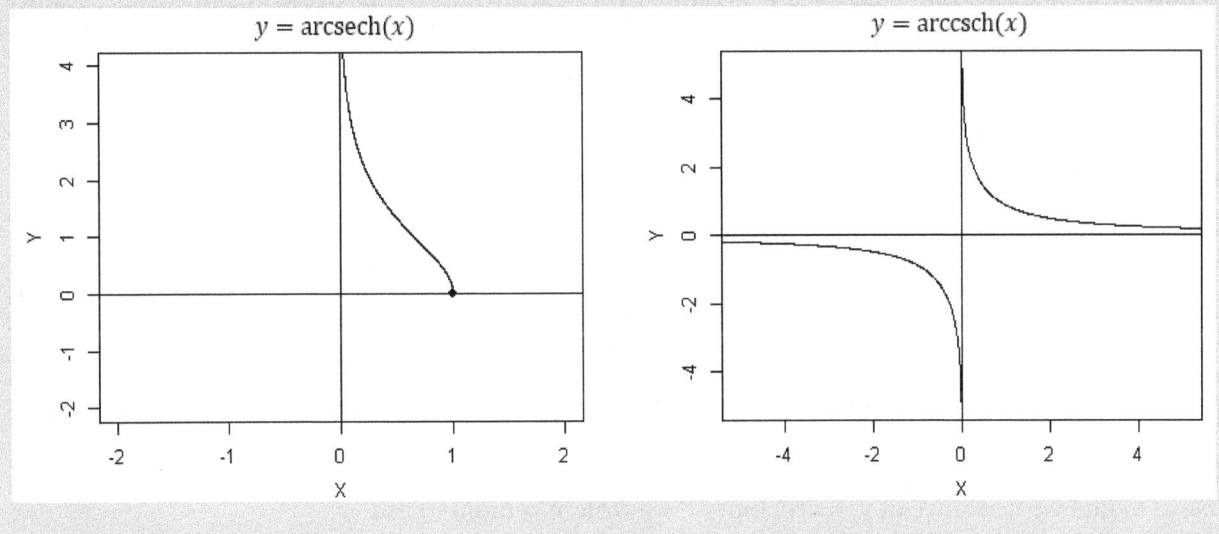

$y = \text{arcsech}(x)$

$y = \text{arccsch}(x)$

As before, while you can write the inverse hyperbolic functions using either notation (for instance, $\text{arcsinh}(x)$ or $\sinh^{-1}(x)$), I recommend sticking with the *arc* notation. For instance, if you write $\sinh^{-1}(x)$, the -1 can easily be confused with a negative exponent, and you could find yourself thinking that the function is $1/\sinh(x)$, which of course would be incorrect.

Let's now see the derivatives of these inverse functions.

DERIVATIVES OF INVERSE HYPERBOLIC FUNCTIONS

The following are the derivatives of the six inverse hyperbolic functions:

$$\frac{d}{dx}(\text{arcsinh}(x)) = \frac{1}{\sqrt{1 + x^2}}$$

$$\frac{d}{dx}(\text{arccosh}(x)) = \frac{1}{\sqrt{x^2 - 1}}, x > 1$$

$$\frac{d}{dx}(\text{arctanh}(x)) = \frac{1}{1 - x^2}, |x| < 1$$

$$\frac{d}{dx}(\text{arccoth}(x)) = \frac{1}{1 - x^2}, |x| > 1$$

$$\frac{d}{dx}(\text{arcsech}(x)) = -\frac{1}{x\sqrt{1 - x^2}}, 0 < x < 1$$

$$\frac{d}{dx}(\text{arccsch}(x)) = -\frac{1}{|x|\sqrt{1 + x^2}}, x \neq 0$$

PROOF

The strategy with these proofs is to use implicit differentiation carefully. Let's start with the derivative of $y = \text{arcsinh}(x)$. Recognize that this formula is the same as $x = \sinh(y)$, and so

$$1 = \cosh(y) \cdot \frac{dy}{dx} \Rightarrow \frac{dy}{dx} = \frac{1}{\cosh(y)}$$

Since $\cosh^2(y) - \sinh^2(y) = 1$ and therefore $\cosh(y) = \sqrt{1 + \sinh^2(y)}$, along with the fact that $x = \sinh(y)$,

$$\frac{dy}{dx} = \frac{1}{\sqrt{1 + \sinh^2(y)}} = \frac{1}{\sqrt{1 + x^2}}$$

There are no domain restrictions for $y = \text{arcsinh}(x)$. The derivative of $y = \text{arccosh}(x)$ works in a similar way: starting with $x = \cosh(y)$,

$$1 = \sinh(y) \cdot \frac{dy}{dx} \Rightarrow \frac{dy}{dx} = \frac{1}{\sinh(y)}$$

Since $\cosh^2(y) - \sinh^2(y) = 1$ and therefore $\sinh(y) = \sqrt{\cosh^2(y) - 1}$, along with the fact that $x = \cosh(y)$,

$$\frac{dy}{dx} = \frac{1}{\sqrt{\cosh^2(y) - 1}} = \frac{1}{\sqrt{x^2 - 1}}$$

Remembering that the domain of $y = \text{arccosh}(x)$ is $[1, \infty)$, the derivative is defined on this domain except at $x = 1$, so it exists when $x > 1$.

Next, to find the derivative of $y = \text{arctanh}(x)$, we write $x = \tanh(y)$ and

$$1 = \text{sech}^2(y) \cdot \frac{dy}{dx} \Rightarrow \frac{dy}{dx} = \frac{1}{\text{sech}^2(y)} = \cosh^2(y)$$

Dividing the identity $\cosh^2(y) - \sinh^2(y) = 1$ by $\cosh^2(y)$ results in

$$1 - \tanh^2(y) = \frac{1}{\cosh^2(y)} \Rightarrow \cosh^2(y) = \frac{1}{1 - \tanh^2(y)}$$

We can substitute this rearranged expression:

$$\frac{dy}{dx} = \frac{1}{1 - \tanh^2(y)} = \frac{1}{1 - x^2}$$

Noting that the domain of $y = \text{arctanh}(x)$ is $(-1, 1)$, the derivative also exists on this domain, or equivalently when $|x| < 1$. Similarly, to find the derivative of $y = \text{arccoth}(x)$, write $x = \coth(y)$ and

$$1 = -\text{csch}^2(y) \cdot \frac{dy}{dx} \Rightarrow \frac{dy}{dx} = -\frac{1}{\text{csch}^2(y)} = -\sinh^2(y)$$

Dividing the identity $\cosh^2(y) - \sinh^2(y) = 1$ by $\sinh^2(y)$ results in

$$\coth^2(y) - 1 = \frac{1}{\sinh^2(y)} \Rightarrow \sinh^2(y) = \frac{1}{\coth^2(y) - 1}$$

Substituting,

$$\frac{dy}{dx} = -\frac{1}{\coth^2(y) - 1} = -\frac{1}{x^2 - 1} = \frac{1}{1 - x^2}$$

Noting that the domain of $y = \operatorname{arccoth}(x)$ is $(-\infty, -1) \cup (1, \infty)$, the derivative also exists on this domain, or equivalently when $|x| > 1$. Curiously, the derivative formulas of $\operatorname{arctanh}(x)$ and $\operatorname{arccoth}(x)$ are the same; they only difference is where they are defined!

Continuing our adventure, the next derivative is for $y = \operatorname{arcsech}(x)$. Working with $x = \operatorname{sech}(y)$,

$$1 = -\operatorname{sech}(y)\tanh(y) \cdot \frac{dy}{dx} \Rightarrow \frac{dy}{dx} = -\frac{1}{\operatorname{sech}(y)\tanh(y)}$$

Dividing the identity $\cosh^2(y) - \sinh^2(y) = 1$ by $\cosh^2(y)$ results in

$$1 - \tanh^2(y) = \frac{1}{\cosh^2(y)} \Rightarrow \tanh^2(y) = 1 - \operatorname{sech}^2(y) \Rightarrow \tanh(y) = \sqrt{1 - \operatorname{sech}^2(y)}$$

We can substitute this rearranged expression:

$$\frac{dy}{dx} = -\frac{1}{\operatorname{sech}(y)\sqrt{1 - \operatorname{sech}^2(y)}} = -\frac{1}{x\sqrt{1 - x^2}}$$

The domain of $y = \operatorname{arcsech}(x)$ is $(0, 1]$, which applies for the derivative as well except for $x = 1$. That means the derivative exists over $0 < x < 1$. Observe that the derivative is always negative, as can be seen in the graph of $y = \operatorname{arcsech}(x)$. Since $0 < x < 1$, there is no need to write $|x|$ in the derivative formula.

Nearly there! The final derivative is for $y = \operatorname{arccsch}(x)$. Working with $x = \operatorname{csch}(y)$,

$$1 = -\operatorname{csch}(y)\coth(y) \cdot \frac{dy}{dx} \Rightarrow \frac{dy}{dx} = -\frac{1}{\operatorname{csch}(y)\coth(y)}$$

Dividing the identity $\cosh^2(y) - \sinh^2(y) = 1$ by $\sinh^2(y)$ results in

$$\coth^2(y) - 1 = \operatorname{csch}^2(y) \Rightarrow \coth^2(y) = 1 + \operatorname{csch}^2(y) \Rightarrow \coth(y) = \sqrt{1 + \operatorname{csch}^2(y)}$$

Substituting,

$$\frac{dy}{dx} = -\frac{1}{\operatorname{csch}(y)\sqrt{1 + \operatorname{csch}^2(y)}} = -\frac{1}{x\sqrt{1 + x^2}}$$

The domain of $y = \operatorname{arccsch}(x)$ is all real numbers except for $x = 0$, and the derivative likewise exists everywhere except at $x = 0$. Noting that the derivative is always negative as seen in the graph of $y = \operatorname{arccsch}(x)$, we need to ensure that the x in the denominator stays positive so that the whole derivative can be negative. That's why we need to write $|x|$, arriving at

$$\frac{dy}{dx} = -\frac{1}{|x|\sqrt{1 + x^2}}$$

■

EXAMPLE

Find the derivatives of $f(x) = \text{arcsinh}(x)\,\text{arcsin}(x)$ and $g(x) = \text{arccosh}(x)\,/\,\text{arctanh}(x)$. You may ignore the step about stating the domains of the derivatives.

Solution: For the first function, be careful with notation since one piece is an inverse hyperbolic function and the other an inverse trig function!

$$f'(x) = \frac{1}{\sqrt{1+x^2}} \cdot \text{arcsin}(x) + \text{arcsinh}(x) \cdot \frac{1}{\sqrt{1-x^2}} = \frac{\text{arcsin}(x)}{\sqrt{1+x^2}} + \frac{\text{arcsinh}(x)}{\sqrt{1-x^2}}$$

If you want to combine fractions, you would have

$$f'(x) = \frac{\text{arcsin}(x)\sqrt{1-x^2} + \text{arcsinh}(x)\sqrt{1+x^2}}{\sqrt{(1+x^2)(1-x^2)}} = \frac{\text{arcsin}(x)\sqrt{1-x^2} + \text{arcsinh}(x)\sqrt{1+x^2}}{\sqrt{1-x^4}}$$

Use the Quotient Rule on the next function:

$$g'(x) = \frac{\text{arctanh}(x) \cdot \dfrac{1}{\sqrt{x^2-1}} - \text{arccosh}(x) \cdot \dfrac{1}{1-x^2}}{(\text{arctanh}(x))^2} = \frac{\dfrac{\text{arctanh}(x)}{\sqrt{x^2-1}} - \dfrac{\text{arccosh}(x)}{1-x^2}}{(\text{arctanh}(x))^2}$$

Simplifying the numerator,

$$g'(x) = \frac{\left(\dfrac{\text{arctanh}(x)\,(1-x^2) - \text{arccosh}(x)\sqrt{x^2-1}}{(1-x^2)\sqrt{x^2-1}}\right)}{(\text{arctanh}(x))^2}$$

$$= \frac{\text{arctanh}(x)\,(1-x^2) - \text{arccosh}(x)\sqrt{x^2-1}}{(1-x^2)\sqrt{x^2-1}(\text{arctanh}(x))^2}$$

$$\Delta$$

Chapter 3 – Applications of the Derivative

Now that we are familiar with finding derivatives of the most common functions, how do we use these findings? In pre-calculus, for instance, you learned how to sketch graphs of functions, but with few exceptions you were never taught how to find the points where the function "peaked," or in other words obtained a maximum. Now we can use our calculus knowledge to find these points.

In this chapter we first introduce some definitions concerning maximum and minimum points and values of a function. We then learn how to use the derivative to find these points, as well as the exact places where the function is increasing and decreasing (where the slope of the tangent line is positive and where it is negative). We can also examine just how the function curves. In addition, we learn how to solve problems involving optimization, related rates, as well as other applications of the derivative. Also, we discuss how to sketch a careful graph of functions using calculus.

Section 3.1 – The Basic Definitions of Max-Min Problems

In this section we give some basic definitions concerning extremum values, and then we begin to learn how to find them in functions. First, recall the following definitions from Section 0.1:

1) A **closed interval** $[a, b]$ contains the points $a \leq x \leq b$, and most importantly, it includes both endpoints a and b.
2) An **open interval** (a, b) contains the points $a < x < b$, but it does *not* include either endpoint a or b.

DEFINITION

Consider the function $f(x)$ on the closed interval $[a, b]$. Suppose there is some $x = c$ in the interval $[a, b]$. Now suppose that c is such that for enough points to the left and to the right of c, $f(c) \leq f(x)$. (The function dips down, stops decreasing at c, and starts rising again after c.) Then we say that $f(c)$ is the **minimum value** of $f(x)$ on the interval $[a, b]$.

Similarly, suppose there is a $x = d$ such that $f(d) \geq f(x)$ for enough points x to the left and right of d. Then we say that $f(d)$ is the **maximum value** of $f(x)$ on the interval $[a, b]$. (The function rises, stops rising at d, and starts falling again after d.) A graph should help clarify these meanings.

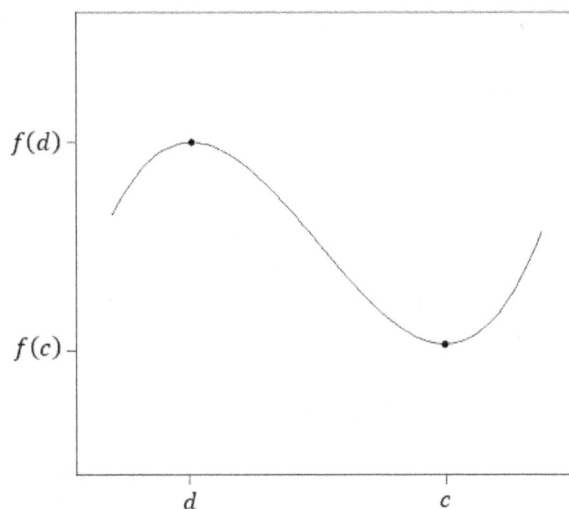

Be careful, though – the maximum value is $f(d)$, *not* d itself! So the maximum (or minimum) value is the y-coordinate of the highest (or lowest) point of $f(x)$.

DEFINITION

Consider the function $f(x)$ on the closed interval $[a, b]$. Given a c in $[a, b]$, suppose that $f(c) \leq f(x)$ for *all* other x in $[a, b]$. Then $f(c)$ is the **absolute minimum value**, or the **global minimum value**, of $f(x)$ on the interval $[a, b]$.

Similarly, given a d in $[a, b]$, suppose that $f(d) \geq f(x)$ for *all* other x in $[a, b]$. Then $f(d)$ is the **absolute (global) maximum value** of $f(x)$ on the interval $[a, b]$.

On the other hand, there is no reason why there cannot be any other maximum or minimum values on the function. Absolute values are merely the highest maximum or lowest minimum values. However, there could certainly be other x's such that $f(x)$ is a "peak" or a "trough" in the graph. These values might not come as high (or low) as the absolute values, but they still count as maximum (or minimum) values. We give these a definition.

DEFINITION

Consider the function $f(x)$ on the closed interval $[a, b]$. Given a c in $[a, b]$, suppose that $f(c) \leq f(x)$ for enough x's close to c. Then $f(c)$ is a **local minimum value** of $f(x)$.

Similarly, given a d in $[a, b]$, suppose that $f(d) \geq f(x)$ for enough x's close to d. Then $f(d)$ is a **local maximum value** of $f(x)$.

We use the term **local extremum** to describe a value of $f(x)$ that is either a local minimum or a local maximum.

ETYMOLOGY

The words **extremum**, **minimum**, and **maximum** all come from the Latin *extremus*, *minimus*, and *magnus*, which meant "extreme," "smallest," and "large," respectively. Due to the Latin declensions of these words, the English plurals are **extrema**, **minima**, and **maxima**.

Keep in mind that endpoints can be maxima or minima also! Here is a graph to illustrate the differences among all these terms.

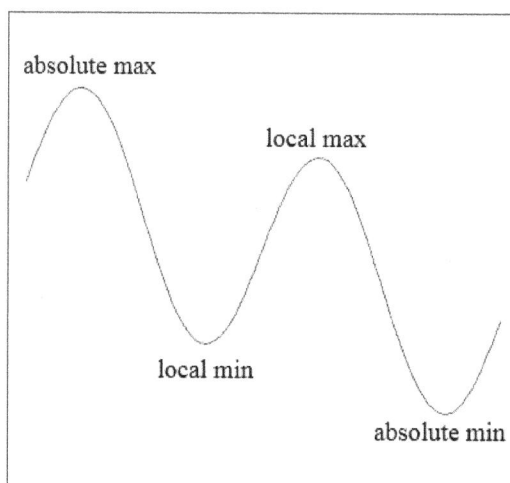

Now that we are familiar with all these terms, we need to introduce some theorems before we can start working with problems.

THEOREM (EXTREME VALUE THEOREM)

Consider the function $f(x)$, which satisfies these two properties:

     1) We are examining $f(x)$ on a *closed* interval $[a, b]$.
     2) On this interval $[a, b]$, $f(x)$ is continuous.

Then we are guaranteed the existence of two numbers c and d, both in $[a, b]$, such that

     1) $f(c)$ is the minimum value of f on $[a, b]$.
     2) $f(d)$ is the maximum value of f on $[a, b]$.

In other words, the function is guaranteed to have at least one maximum value and at least one minimum value on $[a, b]$. Note that either or both of these may be the endpoints.

Why must the function be continuous, and why must the interval be closed? Here are two examples that illustrate why.

EXAMPLE
Consider the following function, whose graph is shown.

$$f(x) = \begin{cases} \dfrac{1}{x}, & 0 < x \leq 2 \\ \dfrac{1}{2}, & x = 0 \end{cases}$$

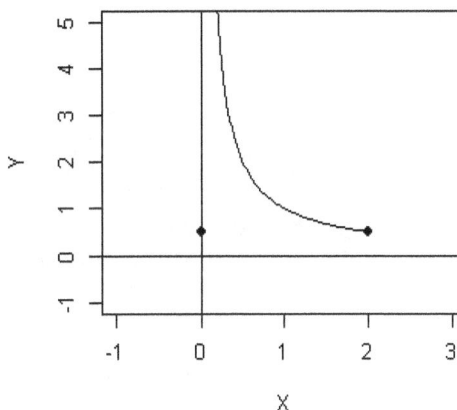

While $f(x)$ exists on the closed interval $[0, 2]$, it is not continuous at $x = 0$. Let's check for minimum and maximum values:

1) $f(x)$ does have a minimum value at $x = 2$ (and actually, at $x = 0$ also).
2) $f(x)$ does not have a maximum value on $[0, 2]$. By choosing very small x greater than zero, we can make $1/x$ arbitrarily large.

Δ

EXAMPLE
Consider $f(x) = x$ on the interval $0 < x \leq 1$. Here the function is continuous, but the interval is not closed.

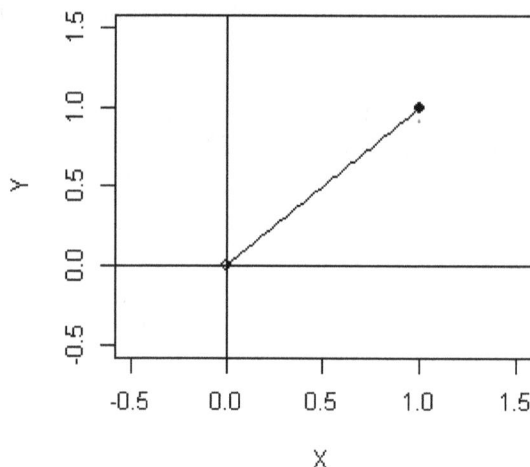

Does $f(x)$ attain maximum and minimum values?

1) There is a maximum value at the point $x = 1$.
2) There is no minimum value of $f(x)$ on this interval. There normally would be one at $x = 0$, but $f(0)$ does not exist because we have excluded this endpoint.

Δ

We can now see that to have both a maximum and a minimum value, $f(x)$ has to be continuous on a closed interval. Now we turn to the next important theorem.

THEOREM
Suppose a function $f(x)$ is differentiable at a point c within an *open* interval (a, b) (so now we exclude the endpoints). Suppose $f(c)$ is either a local maximum or a local minimum value of $f(x)$. Then $f'(c) = 0$.

Thus, if $f(c)$ is a local extremum, then the slope of the tangent line to the point c is zero (and therefore horizontal). To get an idea of why this theorem is true, consider the following graphs of a local minimum value $f(c)$.

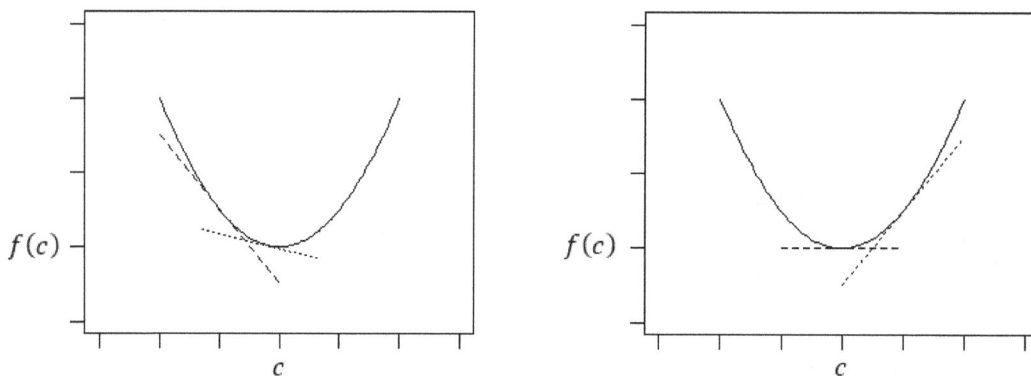

As we approach c from the left, the slope of the tangent line starts out steeply but gradually levels. When we get to c, the tangent is a horizontal line. When we pass c, the tangent starts to grow again (only this time it is positive), and as we move away from c, it becomes steeper. The same idea applies for a local maximum.

Why do we exclude the endpoints in the above theorem? If an endpoint ends up being a local extremum, then the tangent line to that point may or may not have a slope of zero. But if the extremum occurs elsewhere in the interval, then its tangent has to be horizontal.

Is the converse true? If $f'(c) = 0$ for some $a < c < b$, is $f(c)$ a local extremum? The answer is no; this does not necessarily follow. Take the function $f(x) = x^3$.

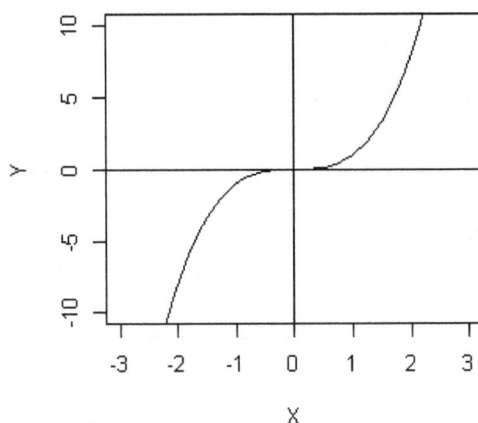

Even though the derivative at $x = 0$ is clearly zero, we can quickly see that $f(0)$ is neither a local minimum nor a local maximum value.

Before we go on, we need to stop and give a new definition.

DEFINITION
Consider the continuous function $f(x)$ on the closed interval $[a, b]$. If the point c is within $[a, b]$, then we say that c is a **critical point** if one of the following holds:

    1) $f'(c) = 0$
    2) $f'(c)$ does not exist

One way that $f'(c)$ could not exist is if the slope of the tangent line at $x = c$ is vertical. However, remember that the derivative also does not exist at corners, cusps, and holes.

Now we state our final theorem of this section.

THEOREM
Consider the continuous function $f(x)$ on the closed interval $[a, b]$. Suppose that $f(c)$ is an absolute minimum (or maximum) value. Then one of the following holds:

    1) c is a critical point.
    2) c is one of the endpoints (a or b).

This is essentially an extension of the previous theorem, only this time taking into account the endpoints.

Section 3.2 – Finding Absolute Maximum and Minimum Values

In this section we learn how to actually pinpoint the absolute maximum and absolute minimum values of a function on a closed interval. Then we work through several examples.

METHOD FOR FINDING ABSOLUTE EXTREMA

Given a continuous function $f(x)$ on a closed interval $[a, b]$, we do the following steps:

Step 1: Find the derivative $f'(x)$.
Step 2: Set $f'(x) = 0$.
Step 3: Find all values of x that make $f'(x)$ equal to 0.
Step 4: Find all values of x that make $f'(x)$ undefined. This most often occurs if $f'(x)$ is a fraction, in which case we set the denominator equal to zero. But don't forget, there are also functions such as $\tan(x)$ and $\ln(x)$ that have some undefined values.
Step 5: List the critical points you have found, as well as the two endpoints $x = a$ and $x = b$.
Step 6: Evaluate the *original* function at each of the critical and endpoints. In other words, given the critical point c, evaluate $f(c)$ and not $f'(c)$!
Step 7: Identify which of these points is the highest and lowest in value.
Step 8: Write a concluding statement.

EXAMPLE

Find the absolute maximum and minimum values of $f(x) = 2x^3 - 9x^2 + 12x$ on the interval $[0, 5]$.

Solution: We first find the derivative:

$$f'(x) = 6x^2 - 18x + 12$$

Then we set it equal to zero and find the critical points.

$$6x^2 - 18x + 12 = 0$$
$$x^2 - 3x + 2 = 0$$
$$(x - 2)(x - 1) = 0$$

Thus, two of the critical points are $x = 1$ and $x = 2$. Since the function is not undefined anywhere, these are the only critical points. Now we need to check the function at the points $x = 0, 1, 2, 5$ (including the endpoints).

$$f(0) = 2(0)^3 - 9(0)^2 + 12(0) = 0$$
$$f(1) = 2(1)^3 - 9(1)^2 + 12(1) = 5$$
$$f(2) = 2(2)^3 - 9(2)^2 + 12(2) = 4$$
$$f(5) = 2(5)^3 - 9(5)^2 + 12(5) = 85$$

The lowest and highest values occur at $x = 0$ and $x = 5$, respectfully. Thus, on the interval $[0, 5]$, the absolute maximum value of $f(x)$ is 85, and the absolute minimum value of $f(x)$ is 0.

Δ

EXAMPLE

Find the absolute maximum and minimum values of the function $f(x) = |\sin(x)|$ on the interval $[0, 2\pi]$.

Solution: This is a new twist because until now we have not seen many examples of taking derivatives of functions involving absolute values. Let's first start by graphing the normal function $f(x) = \sin(x)$.

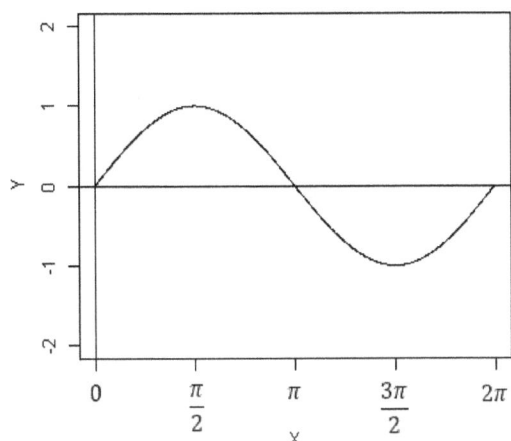

Now we sketch $f(x) = |\sin(x)|$, which will make all the negative y-values of the above graph positive.

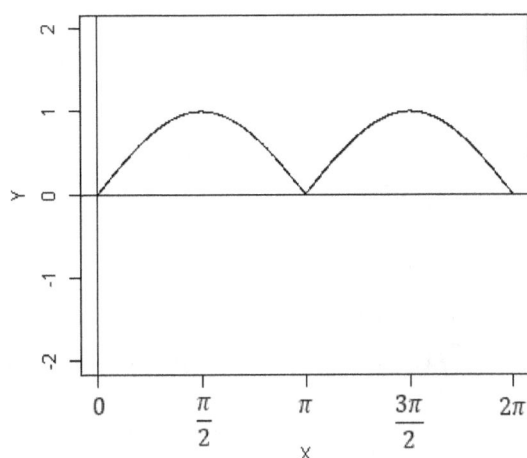

Observe that on the interval $[0, \pi]$, the function is identical to $f(x) = \sin(x)$. The second half of the graph, on $[\pi, 2\pi]$, is the absolute value of $f(x) = \sin(x)$. So we might think of this piece as a new function $f_2(x) = -\sin(x)$.

Now we write this as a piecewise function (we arbitrarily put $x = \pi$ for the first piece):

$$f(x) = \begin{cases} \sin(x), & 0 \le x \le \pi \\ -\sin(x), & \pi < x \le 2\pi \end{cases}$$

Let's now take the derivative of each piece.

$$f'(x) = \begin{cases} \cos(x), & 0 \le x \le \pi \\ -\cos(x), & \pi < x \le 2\pi \end{cases}$$

This derivative resembles the following graph. Note that the filled circle goes with the first piece since $\cos(x)$ is used at the point $x = \pi$.

151

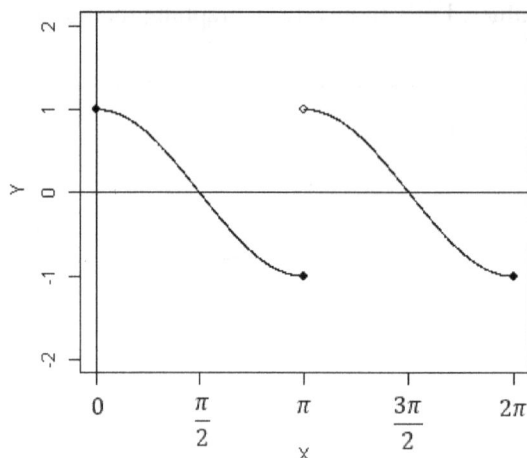

We set $f'(x) = 0$ but do it in two parts. First, $\cos(x) = 0$ at the point $x = \pi/2$ (here we only check between 0 and π). Second, $-\cos(x) = 0$ at the point $x = 3\pi/2$ (here we only check between π and 2π).

Next, is the derivative undefined anywhere? It clearly does not exist at $x = \pi$, for it is not continuous there.

Thus, we have three critical points: $x = \pi/2, \pi, 3\pi/2$. We also have to check the endpoints $x = 0, 2\pi$. Now we evaluate the original function at each of these five points.

$$f(0) = |\sin(0)| = |0| = 0$$
$$f\left(\frac{\pi}{2}\right) = \left|\sin\left(\frac{\pi}{2}\right)\right| = |1| = 1$$
$$f(\pi) = |\sin(\pi)| = |0| = 0$$
$$f\left(\frac{3\pi}{2}\right) = \left|\sin\left(\frac{3\pi}{2}\right)\right| = |-1| = 1$$
$$f(2\pi) = |\sin(2\pi)| = |0| = 0$$

To conclude, the function $f(x) = |\sin(x)|$ on the interval $[0, 2\pi]$ has the following:

1) The absolute maximum value 1 occurs at $x = \pi/2, 3\pi/2$.
2) The absolute minimum value 0 occurs at $x = 0, \pi, 2\pi$.

Δ

EXAMPLE

Let's find the absolute maximum and minimum values on $f(x) = x + \frac{2}{x}$ on the interval $[1, 4]$.

Solution: It might help to rewrite $f(x) = x + 2x^{-1}$.

$$f'(x) = 1 + 2 \cdot (-x^{-2}) = 1 - \frac{2}{x^2}$$

Now we get the critical points:

$$f'(x) = 1 - \frac{2}{x^2} = 0 \Rightarrow 1 = \frac{2}{x^2}$$
$$\Rightarrow x^2 = 2$$

$$\Rightarrow x = \pm\sqrt{2}$$

However, $x = -\sqrt{2}$ is out of the domain, so we reject it. While the derivative does not exist at $x = 0$, this too is out of the domain. So the only points we need to check are $x = 1, \sqrt{2}, 4$.

$$f(1) = 1 + \frac{2}{1} = 3$$
$$f(\sqrt{2}) = \sqrt{2} + \frac{2}{\sqrt{2}} = \sqrt{2} + \frac{2\sqrt{2}}{2} = \sqrt{2} + \sqrt{2} = 2\sqrt{2} \approx 2.82843$$
$$f(4) = 4 + \frac{2}{4} = \frac{9}{2} = 4.5$$

This tells us that the absolute maximum value of $f(x)$ on the interval $[1, 4]$ is $9/2$, while the absolute minimum value is $2\sqrt{2}$.

Δ

Section 3.3 – Optimization Problems
Now that we know how to find the absolute maximum and minimum values on a closed interval, how do we apply this? One such topic is called optimization. The idea behind this topic is this: given a situation involving some sort of geometric shape, what variable(s) will maximize or minimize a certain quantity. For instance, if we are going to construct a box out of a certain sized piece of cardboard, what dimensions will yield the maximum possible volume for the box? If we have a set amount of fencing, what is the maximum possible area of the rectangle we could form with the fence? Here is a general process of solving such problems (and note what I call Step 0, which means do this before anything else!):

> **METHOD FOR SOLVING OPTIMIZATION PROBLEMS**
> The following process should be used when solving optimization problems.
>
> Step 0: When possible, draw a picture of what is happening. For instance, if the problem involves a rectangle, sketch a rectangle and write down the formulas for its length and width as you proceed. If there is a cylinder involved, sketch a cylinder with its radius and height.
> Step 1: Write down any constraint equations given (for instance, whether the numbers are positive).
> Step 2: Write down any formulas, geometric or otherwise, that may help with the problem.
> Step 3: Write down the formula that you are trying to optimize.
> Step 4: If there is more than one variable in the optimization formula, use the other known formulas to reduce it to one variable.
> Step 5: Determine the domain of this formula. This is often the hardest step, but it involves finding how low and how high the independent variable x can get. Then write out the domain, and *include the endpoints*.
> Step 6: Find the derivative of the optimization formula and get the critical points. Reject any that are not in the domain.
> Step 7: Find the value of the optimization at each of the critical points *and* the endpoints.
> Step 8: Write down what the absolute maximum/minimum value is and what conditions give it.
> Step 9: Lastly, answer the original question in a sentence or two.

Of course, knowing what formulas to begin with often requires knowledge of basic geometry.
Why does this process work? To answer that, we turn to the domain. Note that we include the endpoints in the domain, even though the endpoints might not give us a suitable answer. We do this because we turn it

into a closed interval, so by the theorem from Section 3.1, the function is guaranteed to have a maximum and a minimum value on the closed interval.

EXAMPLE

Find two positive real numbers x and y so that their sum is 100 and their product is as high as possible.

Solution: Let's start by writing down the formulas we have:

$$x + y = 100$$
$$P = xy$$

Here we chose P for "product." Although P is a function of two variables x and y, we need to reduce this to one variable so that we can perform calculus. Note that by the first formula, $y = 100 - x$. So now the product formula is

$$P = x(100 - x)$$
$$P = 100x - x^2$$

Now let's think about the domain of this formula.

1) We are given that x and y are positive, so obviously $0 < x$.
2) Now note that the highest x can get is 100 because this forces y to be zero.

So the domain for the product formula is $[0, 100]$. We include the endpoints to insure that a maximum value exists. Now let's compute the derivative:

$$P = 100x - x^2$$
$$\frac{dP}{dx} = 100 - 2x$$

The sole critical point is

$$100 - 2x = 0$$
$$x = 50$$

We now need to check the points $x = 0, 50, 100$ (including the endpoints).

$$P(0) = (0)(100 - 0) = 0$$
$$P(50) = (50)(100 - 50) = 50 \cdot 50 = 2500$$
$$P(100) = (100)(100 - 100) = 0$$

The maximum value of 2500 occurs at $x = 50$. Therefore, by the first formula, $y = 100 - 50 = 50$.

Now we answer the question. The two positive numbers satisfying the conditions that their sum is 100 and their product is as high as possible are $x = 50$ and $y = 50$. Their product is 2,500.

$$\Delta$$

EXAMPLE

We have an 8-foot by 5-foot piece of cardboard. We are going to make it into an open-topped box by first slicing off congruent squares from the four corners, then folding up the newly formed sides. Where should we cut the squares so we can maximize the volume of the box?

Solution: First, here's a sketch of what we are about to do.

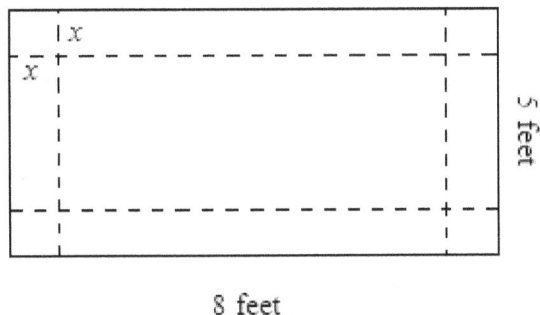

8 feet

We are going to cut off identical squares, each of length x, off each corner. The end result will be a sheet of cardboard with the corners cut out. Then we will fold up the four sides and get an open-topped box.

What sort of formula should we aim to use? Since we are finding the volume of a box with a length, width, and height, we would think of using the formula

$$V = L \cdot W \cdot H$$

However, we need to get the length, width, and height in terms of one variable. So let's turn back to our sketch, where we have already defined the length of the cut square x.

1) Let's start with the length. The cardboard was originally 8 feet long. If we remove a measurement x on both sides of the sheet, we are taking away a total of $2x$. Thus, our length is $L = 8 - 2x$.
2) The width of the cardboard was originally 5 feet. If we take away a measurement x on both sides, we are removing $2x$ again, so the width of the adjusted cardboard is $W = 5 - 2x$.
3) Finally, when we fold the cardboard into a box, its height will be the length of whatever x we will end up using. Thus, we have $H = x$.

Once cut, the cardboard will look something like this:

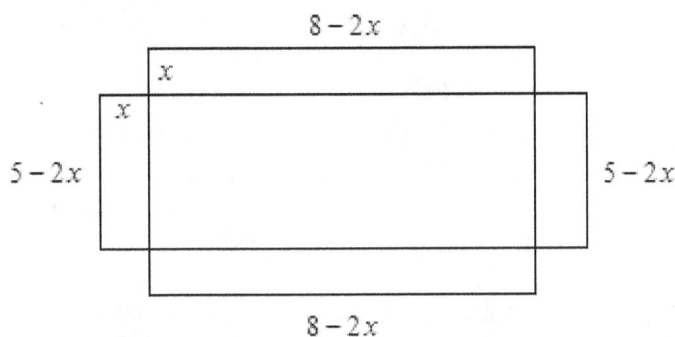

Now our formula for volume is the following:

$$\begin{aligned}
V &= L \cdot W \cdot H \\
&= (8 - 2x)(5 - 2x)x \\
&= (40 - 10x - 16x + 4x^2)x \\
&= (40 - 26x + 4x^2)x \\
&= 4x^3 - 26x^2 + 40x
\end{aligned}$$

Next comes the tricky part: determining the domain of this function. To answer this, we need to think about the smallest and largest values x can be.

1) How small can x get? Well, if we do nothing to the cardboard, then x will be zero and thus there is no height (and no box!) If x is just above zero, we will have a height. So the lower endpoint is 0, and therefore $0 < x$.

2) How large can x be? Note that the smaller of the side lengths is $W = 5 - 2x$. If $x = 2.5$, then the width becomes zero (again, no box!) since $W = 5 - 2(2.5) = 0$. So 2.5 is the upper limit, and therefore $x < 2.5$.

However, in an optimization problem, we actually do include the endpoints. The reason we do this is to guarantee that the function does in fact have a maximum and a minimum value on the domain. So the domain for this problem is $[0, 2.5]$. (To be clear, in practical terms x must be higher than 0 and smaller than 2.5 so that a box can be formed, but to guarantee a maximum or minimum, we need to include the endpoints. But we could theoretically make a box with, say, $x = 0.001$ – a pathetic box, but a box nonetheless!)

Now comes the calculus. We find the derivative and the critical points.

$$V = 4x^3 - 26x^2 + 40x$$
$$\frac{dV}{dx} = 12x^2 - 52x + 40$$
$$= 4(3x^2 - 13x + 10)$$
$$= 4(3x - 10)(x - 1)$$

The last step requires you to recognize how to factor that polynomial (but even if you had not spotted it, there is always the quadratic formula as a last resort.) Now here are the critical points:

$$\frac{dV}{dx} = 4(3x - 10)(x - 1) = 0$$
$$\Rightarrow x = \frac{10}{3} \text{ and } x = 1$$

However, $x = 10/3 = 3.\overline{3}$ is outside the domain, so we reject it. Thus, the points we have to check are $x = 0, 1, 2.5$ once we include the endpoints. Now substitute each of these values into the original formula:

$$V(0) = \big(8 - 2(0)\big)\big(5 - 2(0)\big)(0) = 0$$
$$V(1) = \big(8 - 2(1)\big)\big(5 - 2(1)\big)(1) = 6 \cdot 3 \cdot 1 = 18$$
$$V(2.5) = \big(8 - 2(2.5)\big)\big(5 - 2(2.5)\big)(2.5) = 0$$

The highest value, 18, occurs at $x = 1$.

Now we answer the question. To maximize the volume of the box, we need to cut squares of length 1 foot off each of the corners. This will give us a box with dimensions 6 feet by 3 feet by 1 foot, with a maximum volume of 18 cubic feet.

As a side note, if you didn't know how to factor $3x^2 - 13x + 10$, the quadratic formula is always there to save you. (You cannot go through a calculus class and not use the quadratic formula somewhere!) To review, recall that given $ax^2 + bx + c = 0$, the two solutions are

$$x = \frac{-b \pm \sqrt{b^2 - 4ac}}{2a}$$

Putting in $a = 3$, $b = -13$, and $c = 10$,

$$x = \frac{-(-13) \pm \sqrt{(-13)^2 - 4(3)(10)}}{2(3)} = \frac{13 \pm \sqrt{169 - 120}}{6} = \frac{13 \pm \sqrt{49}}{6} = \frac{13 \pm 7}{6}$$

$$x = \frac{13 - 7}{6} = 1 \quad \text{and} \quad x = \frac{13 + 7}{6} = \frac{20}{6} = \frac{10}{3}$$

Δ

EXAMPLE

Here is a tougher example. Suppose a right circular cylinder has surface area 150π, including both circular ends. Find the maximum possible volume of the cylinder. Here is a sample sketch:

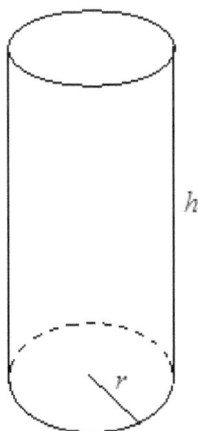

Solution: To solve this problem, we need to remember the necessary formulas for the volume and the surface area of a right cylinder:

$$V = \pi r^2 h$$
$$A = 2\pi r^2 + 2\pi rh$$

As it stands, our volume formula is in terms of two variables. We need to figure out how to express one variable in terms of the other. So let's use the given surface area to help:

$$150\pi = 2\pi r^2 + 2\pi rh$$
$$150 = 2r^2 + 2rh$$
$$150 = 2r(r + h)$$
$$h = \frac{150}{2r} - r$$
$$h = \frac{75}{r} - r$$

Now that we can express h in terms of r, we substitute this into the volume formula:

$$V = \pi r^2 h = \pi r^2 \left(\frac{75}{r} - r \right)$$
$$= 75\pi r - \pi r^3$$

Next comes the domain of r.

1) If r is zero, then the cylinder will have no radius, so we know $0 < r$.
2) The upper limit is trickier. But if you think carefully, you will realize that the largest possible radius corresponds to the smallest possible height. The smallest height we could have is zero, so we work with that:

$$h = \frac{75}{r} - r$$
$$0 = \frac{75}{r} - r$$
$$r = \frac{75}{r}$$
$$r^2 = 75 \Rightarrow r = \pm\sqrt{75}$$

We disregard $r = -\sqrt{75}$ because we cannot have a negative radius. Thus, the highest radius we could have is $r = \sqrt{75}$. This means that our domain, including the endpoints, is $\left[0, \sqrt{75}\right]$ for r.

Here is the derivative of the volume:

$$V = 75\pi r - \pi r^3$$
$$\frac{dV}{dr} = 75\pi - 3\pi^2$$

The critical points are

$$75\pi - 3\pi r^2 = 0$$
$$25 - r^2 = 0$$
$$r = \pm 5$$

We disregard the negative critical point, so the only points we need to work with are $r = 0, 5, \sqrt{75}$.

$$V(0) = 75\pi(0) - \pi(0)^3 = 0$$
$$V(5) = 75\pi(5) - \pi(5)^3 = 375\pi - 125\pi = 250\pi$$
$$V\left(\sqrt{75}\right) = 75\pi\left(\sqrt{75}\right) - \pi\left(\sqrt{75}\right)^3 = 0$$

And so we find that $r = 5$ gives the maximum volume of 250π. This means that the height is

$$h = \frac{75}{5} - 5 = 15 - 5 = 10$$

To conclude, the maximum possible volume of a cylinder with surface area 150π squared units is 250π squared units, with a radius of 5 units and a height of 10 units. (We are saying "units" since none were specified.)

Δ

EXAMPLE
Let's do one more example that appears sometimes in calculus problems. A Norman window is one where the lower part is a rectangle and the upper part is a semicircle. You need to construct a Norman window with total perimeter equal to 24 feet. Find the dimensions of the window that maximize the window's area.

Solution: Before making a sketch, we need to get a sense of what the perimeters look like. A rectangle with sides x and y normally has perimeter $2x + 2y$. If we define the rectangle to have short (horizontal) length x and long (vertical) length y, we can see that there are two y lengths and only one x length. The reason is because the top of the rectangle is connected to the semicircle, so we don't count that side in the perimeter.

Next, the perimeter (or circumference) of a full circle with radius r is $2\pi r$, and so the circumference of the top half of a circle is half that, πr. Let's stop and make our sketch to see what is going on.

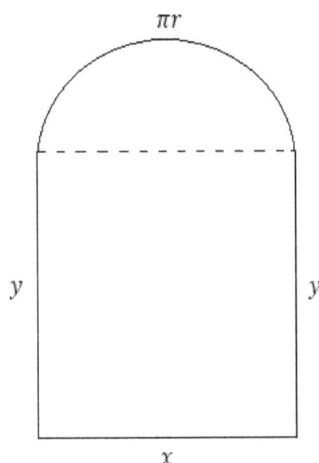

We can see that the outer perimeter of the Norman window consists of the two long sides and one short side of the rectangle, plus the top half of the circle's circumference. Given that perimeter is 24 feet, we have

$$24 = x + 2y + \pi r$$

The goal is to find the optimal area of the window. Here the area is equal to the area of the rectangle (xy) plus the area of the semicircle (half of πr^2), and so using the current letters,

$$A = xy + \frac{1}{2}\pi r^2$$

The problem here is that the area is currently a function of three variables, and we want it to be a function of one variable. If you go on to take multivariable calculus, you will learn techniques that will enable you to solve the problem directly, but for now we have to use creativity to get it down to one variable. Looking at the sketch we made, notice that the radius of the semicircle (r) is also equal to half the length of the rectangle's short side (x). In other words, $r = x/2$. (If you don't understand why, observe that the diameter of the semicircle is equal to x, and therefore the radius is half of x.) Now let's update the perimeter and area formulas.

$$24 = x + 2y + \frac{\pi}{2}x \Rightarrow 24 = \left(1 + \frac{\pi}{2}\right)x + 2y$$
$$A = xy + \frac{1}{2}\pi\left(\frac{1}{2}x\right)^2 \Rightarrow A = xy + \frac{\pi}{8}x^2$$

This is better, but the area is still a function of two variables. Now we use the perimeter as a constraint equation to solve for one of x or y. Looking at the formula, I would say that it's easier to solve for y:

$$24 = \left(1 + \frac{\pi}{2}\right)x + 2y \Rightarrow 2y = 24 - \left(\frac{2+\pi}{2}\right)x$$
$$\Rightarrow y = 12 - \left(\frac{2+\pi}{4}\right)x$$

Substitute this into the area formula and simplify:

$$A = x\left(12 - \left(\frac{2+\pi}{4}\right)x\right) + \frac{\pi}{8}x^2$$
$$A = 12x - \left(\frac{2+\pi}{4}\right)x^2 + \frac{\pi}{8}x^2$$
$$A = 12x + \left(\frac{\pi}{8} - \frac{2}{2}\cdot\left(\frac{2+\pi}{4}\right)\right)x^2 = 12x + \left(\frac{\pi - 2(2+\pi)}{8}\right)x^2 = 12x + \left(\frac{-4-\pi}{8}\right)x^2$$
$$A = 12x - \left(\frac{4+\pi}{8}\right)x^2$$

A lot of work so far, and not one bit of it has been calculus! We do need the domain of x, however. Since x is a side length, we know that $0 < x$. The upper limit of x corresponds to the lower limit of y. Since $0 < y$ as well, we can find what x value corresponds to $y = 0$ by using the perimeter equation:

$$24 = \left(1 + \frac{\pi}{2}\right)x + 2(0) \Rightarrow \left(\frac{2+\pi}{2}\right)x = 24 \Rightarrow x = \frac{48}{2+\pi} \approx 9.33563$$

This means that the domain of x is $\left[0, \frac{48}{2+\pi}\right]$ (again, including the endpoints). At last, we use calculus:

$$\frac{dA}{dx} = 12 - 2\left(\frac{4+\pi}{8}\right)x = 12 - \left(\frac{4+\pi}{4}\right)x = 0$$
$$\Rightarrow \left(\frac{4+\pi}{4}\right)x = 12 \Rightarrow x = 12\left(\frac{4}{4+\pi}\right)$$
$$\Rightarrow x = \frac{48}{4+\pi} \approx 6.72119$$

There are no places where the derivative is undefined, so the points to check are 0, $\frac{48}{4+\pi}$, and $\frac{48}{2+\pi}$. Let's carefully put these into the original area equation.

$$A(0) = 12(0) - \left(\frac{4+\pi}{8}\right)(0)^2 = 0$$
$$A\left(\frac{48}{4+\pi}\right) = 12\left(\frac{48}{4+\pi}\right) - \left(\frac{4+\pi}{8}\right)\left(\frac{48}{4+\pi}\right)^2 = \frac{576}{4+\pi} - \frac{48^2}{8(4+\pi)}$$
$$= \frac{576}{4+\pi} - \frac{288}{4+\pi} = \frac{288}{4+\pi} \approx 40.32714$$
$$A\left(\frac{48}{2+\pi}\right) = 12\left(\frac{48}{2+\pi}\right) - \left(\frac{4+\pi}{8}\right)\left(\frac{48}{2+\pi}\right)^2 = \frac{576}{2+\pi} - \frac{(4+\pi)}{(2+\pi)^2}\left(\frac{48^2}{8}\right)$$
$$= \frac{576}{2+\pi} - \frac{288(4+\pi)}{(2+\pi)^2} \approx 34.22528$$

The maximum area is $\frac{288}{4+\pi}$, or about 40.32714 ft^2. Going back to the original question, we need to state the dimensions of the window with maximum area. Let's state what x, y, and r are:

$$x = \frac{48}{4 + \pi} \approx 6.72119$$

$$y = 12 - \left(\frac{2 + \pi}{4}\right)\left(\frac{48}{4 + \pi}\right) = 12 - 12\left(\frac{2 + \pi}{4 + \pi}\right) = \frac{12(4 + \pi) - 12(2 + \pi)}{4 + \pi}$$

$$= \frac{48 + 12\pi - 24 - 12\pi}{4 + \pi} = \frac{24}{4 + \pi} \approx 3.36059$$

$$r = \frac{1}{2}\left(\frac{48}{4 + \pi}\right) = \frac{24}{4 + \pi} \approx 3.36059$$

Thus, the Norman window has maximum area when the rectangular section is $\frac{48}{4+\pi}$ feet by $\frac{24}{4+\pi}$ feet and when the semicircular section has radius $\frac{24}{4+\pi}$ feet.

$$\Delta$$

One final word: in all these examples, we could have solved for either variable in the optimization formula. How do we decide which one to work with? The answer is that it does not matter which variable you pick; if you do the steps correctly, you will get the same answer. However, your domain will be different because you are working with a different variable.

As a rule of thumb, if solving for one variable is easy while isolating the other variable is tough, then choose the easier of the two. In the cylinder example, we could have solved for r in terms of h, and then written our volume formula with h as the independent variable. However, this would have required more steps involving completing the square, as well as some square roots. Take the easier path instead – it is not the lazy way, it is the smart way!

Section 3.4 – The Mean Value Theorem

Now we present one of the most important theorems in differential calculus. It will enable us to find maximum and minimum values, as well as intervals in which a function is increasing and decreasing.

Consider a function $f(x)$ on a closed interval $[a, b]$. Suppose the function is continuous on that interval, and everywhere in the open interval (a, b) the function is differentiable. Let's draw such a function.

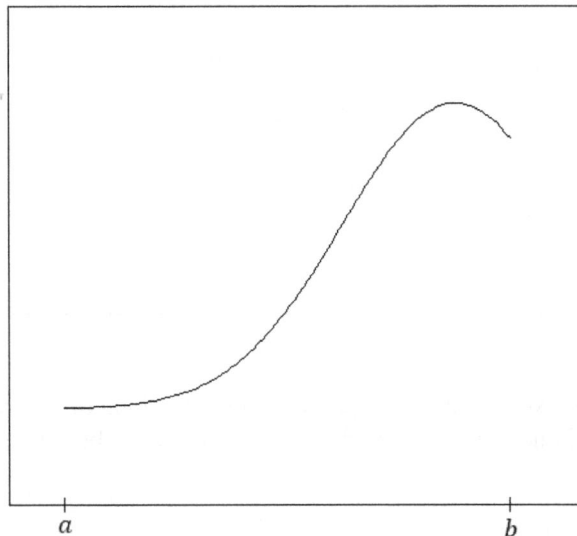

Suppose we now decide to calculate the slope between $(a, f(a))$ and $(b, f(b))$. This will give us a secant line through the graph.

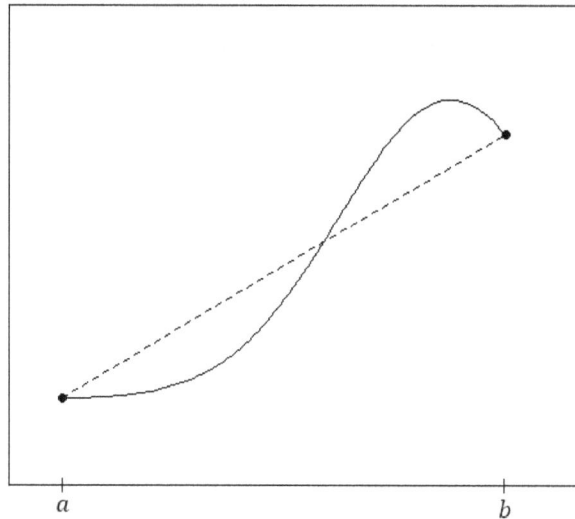

The dashed line is the secant line from $(a, f(a))$ to $(b, f(b))$. The slope of this straight line is simply $\frac{f(b)-f(a)}{b-a}$, straight from regular algebra.

Now we might ask ourselves: is there some point c, between a and b, such that the slope of the tangent line at $(c, f(c))$ is equal to the slope $\frac{f(b)-f(a)}{b-a}$? The Mean Value Theorem tells us that there is such a point. There could be more than one, but this theorem guarantees us the existence of at least one. If we return to our sketch, by eyeballing the function we might spot two possible points, drawn with solid tangent lines.

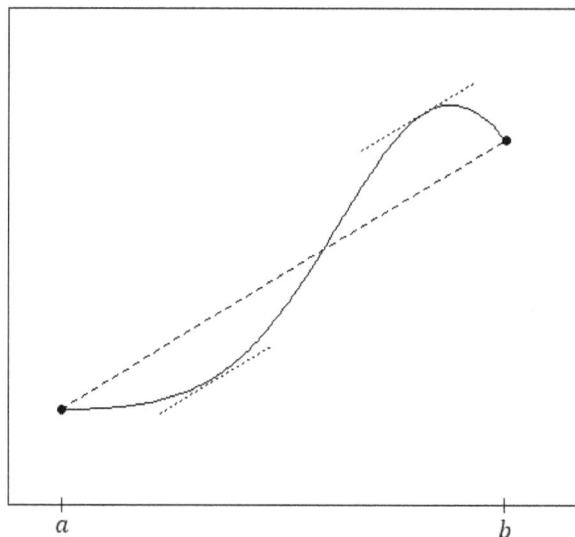

Just to reiterate, here it looks like we have two points where the slope of the tangent line equals the slope of the secant line. There might not always be two points in each case, but there will always be *at least one* point provided that

    1) $f(x)$ is continuous on $[a, b]$, and

2) $f(x)$ is differentiable on (a, b).

Let's state the theorem explicitly (without proof).

THEOREM (MEAN VALUE THEOREM)

Let a function $f(x)$ be continuous on the closed interval $[a, b]$ and differentiable on the open interval (a, b). Then there exists a point c, $a < c < b$, such that

$$\frac{f(b) - f(a)}{b - a} = f'(c)$$

That is, there is a point c such that the slope of the tangent line at $(c, f(c))$ is equal to the slope $\frac{f(b) - f(a)}{b - a}$, the secant line running from $(a, f(a))$ to $(b, f(b))$.

Note that the Mean Value Theorem does not tell us what the c value is or how to find it, or even how many such points there are. It simply tells us that at least one point c exists.

EXAMPLE

Let $f(x) = \sqrt{x} + x$ on the interval $[1, 4]$. Prove that there is a point c, $1 < c < 4$, such that $f'(c) = 4/3$, and find c.

Solution: First, $f(x)$ is continuous on the closed interval $[1, 4]$. While it is not continuous for negative values of x, we don't have to worry about that for this problem. It is also differentiable on the open interval $(1, 4)$. We first calculate the slope of the secant line running from $x = 1$ to $x = 4$.

$$\frac{f(4) - f(1)}{4 - 1} = \frac{\left(\sqrt{4} + 4\right) - \left(\sqrt{1} + 1\right)}{4 - 1} = \frac{6 - 2}{3} = \frac{4}{3}$$

Thus, by the Mean Value Theorem, there is definitely at least one point c, between 1 and 4, with a tangent line whose slope is equal to $4/3$. Now let's find that c. We compute the derivative:

$$f'(x) = \frac{1}{2\sqrt{x}} + 1$$

Then we evaluate it at the point c, at which we know the derivative is equal to $4/3$.

$$f'(x) = \frac{1}{2\sqrt{x}} + 1 \bigg|_{x=c} = \frac{1}{2\sqrt{c}} + 1 = \frac{4}{3}$$

Now we solve for c:

$$\frac{1}{2\sqrt{c}} + 1 = \frac{4}{3} \Rightarrow \frac{1}{2\sqrt{c}} = \frac{1}{3}$$
$$\Rightarrow 2\sqrt{c} = 3$$
$$\Rightarrow \sqrt{c} = \frac{3}{2} \Rightarrow c = \left(\frac{3}{2}\right)^2 = 9/4$$

Thus, we have shown that $\frac{f(4) - f(1)}{4 - 1} = f'\left(\frac{9}{4}\right)$, and note that $1 < 9/4 < 4$.

Δ

EXAMPLE
A police helicopter watches a car enter a mile-long tunnel. Sixty seconds later (one minute), the helicopter clocks the car emerging from the other end of the tunnel. If the speed limit inside the tunnel is 50 miles per hour, show that the policeman can prove that the car was speeding at some point inside the interval.

Solution: Think about this intuitively: if the car took one minute to drive through a mile long tunnel, then it must have been driving at 60 miles per hour (if it was driving at a constant speed). Alternatively, by using the Mean Value Theorem, we could argue that it averaged 60 miles per hour, meaning that at some point in the tunnel, it was traveling at exactly 60 miles per hour. Thus, it was breaking the speed limit!

How might we actually use the Mean Value Theorem formula here? We could use the car's time in minutes (independent) and miles traveled (dependent), starting at the beginning of the tunnel. Then $f(0) = 0$, the number of miles traveled in 0 minutes. At the end of the tunnel, the car has traveled one mile in one minute, so $f(1) = 1$. Then in one minute,

$$\frac{f(1) - f(0)}{1 - 0} = \frac{1 - 0}{1 - 0} = 1 \text{ mile/minute}$$

We get the units from the fact that the numerator is in miles and the denominator in minutes. Multiplying this by 60, we have 60 miles per hour. Therefore the car must have been speeding at least once in this one-minute interval, even though the policeman couldn't actually see it! (Some road systems really can catch speeding cars with a method similar to this one.)

Δ

There is in fact a special case of the Mean Value Theorem where the slope of the tangent line, $f'(c)$, is 0. It is called Rolle's Theorem, named after the French mathematician Michel Rolle (although a primitive form of this result was studied over five hundred years earlier by the Indian mathematician Bhāskara II).

THEOREM (ROLLE'S THEOREM)
Let a function $f(x)$ be continuous on the closed interval $[a, b]$ and differentiable on the open interval (a, b), and suppose $f(a) = f(b)$. Then there exists a point c, $a < c < b$, such that

$$f'(c) = 0$$

In other words, given the above conditions, there must be a point c where the function stops increasing (or decreasing), reaches a critical point, and turns around, reversing direction.

Section 3.5 – Increasing and Decreasing Intervals
In the previous section we introduced the Mean Value Theorem and hinted that it would help us discover the intervals in which a function is increasing and decreasing. Here we officially learn how to pinpoint these intervals.

The bottom line behind all this is that if the derivative of a function is positive at x, then the function is increasing at x. Similarly, if the derivative of $f(x)$ is negative at x, then $f(x)$ is decreasing at x. And if the derivative at x is 0, then the function is constant, or flat (and there is a critical point at x).

Suppose we know that $f'(x) > 0$ in the interval $[a, b]$. How do we actually prove that the function $f(x)$ is increasing on $[a, b]$? One way we might tackle this problem is the following method.

Let $[k, l]$ be a "subinterval" in $[a, b]$. That is, $a < k < l < b$. If the function really is increasing in $[a, b]$, then $f(k) < f(l)$ because the values get higher. So let's use the Mean Value Theorem to derive the fact that $f(k) < f(l)$.

First, since $f(x)$ is differentiable on $[a, b]$, it is continuous on $[a, b]$ and thus is continuous on the subinterval $[k, l]$. It is also differentiable on $[k, l]$. Now let's set up what we know:

$$\frac{f(l) - f(k)}{l - k} = f'(c)$$
$$f(l) - f(k) = f'(c) \cdot (l - k)$$

That is, given the slope $\frac{f(l) - f(k)}{l - k}$, we are guaranteed that for some point c in the interval $[k, l]$, $f'(c) = \frac{f(l) - f(k)}{l - k}$.

Now, since $k < l$, then the difference $(l - k)$ is positive. We already know that $f'(c)$ is positive, so the product $f'(c) \cdot (l - k)$ is also positive.

Since $f'(c) \cdot (l - k) = f(l) - f(k)$, it follows that $f(l) - f(k) > 0$. From this, we conclude that $f(l) > f(k)$, which is what we wanted.

Thus, if $f'(x) > 0$ in $[k, l]$, then $f(k) < f(l)$ and therefore the function is increasing.

We can run through an analogous proof to show that if $f'(x) < 0$ on an interval, then $f(x)$ is decreasing. Let's formally state this result, along with some diagram aids.

INTERPRETATION OF SIGN OF FIRST DERIVATIVE
If $f'(x) > 0$ (positive) throughout the interval $[a, b]$, then $f(x)$ is increasing on $[a, b]$.
If $f'(x) < 0$ (negative) throughout the interval $[a, b]$, then $f(x)$ is decreasing on $[a, b]$.

The following graph should make things clear:

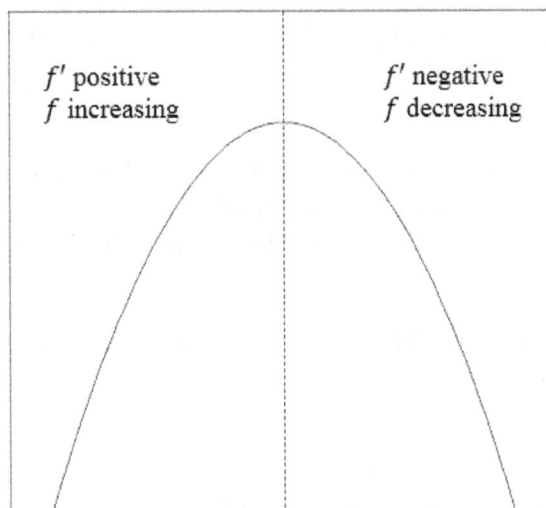

And finally, here's a table:

$f'(x)$	$f(x)$
Positive	Increasing
Negative	Decreasing

Now this new tool allows us to find the intervals of increasing and decreasing, which in turn will let us find the maximum and minimum values of the entire function, and not just on a restricted interval.

How do we actually find such intervals? Let's walk through an example to see how it works.

EXAMPLE

Find the intervals on which the function $f(x) = 6x - 2x^2$ is increasing and decreasing.

Solution: We are going to use a very similar process from Section 3.2. First we find the derivative, set it equal to zero, and find the critical points.

$$f'(x) = 6 - 4x = 0 \Rightarrow 4x = 6$$
$$\Rightarrow x = \frac{3}{2}$$

Since there are no points where the derivative does not exist, $x = 3/2$ is the only critical point.

However, here is where the process differs. Previously we were given a closed interval to work with, complete with two endpoints. Here we are working across all real numbers, represented by the interval $(-\infty, \infty)$ (or the notation $\mathbb{R}$, which means "all reals"). Here is what we do:

We sketch a number line and plot the critical points. Here we only have one to work with: $x = 3/2$.

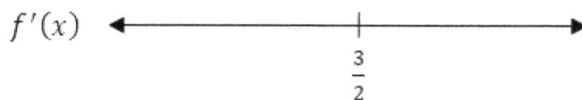

$$f'(x) \quad \longleftarrow \!\!\!\!\!\!\!\!\!\! \underset{\frac{3}{2}}{\rule{0pt}{0pt}\quad\quad\quad\quad\quad\quad +\quad\quad\quad\quad\quad\quad} \!\!\!\!\!\!\!\!\!\! \longrightarrow$$

Our goal is to find out whether the value of $f'(x)$ is positive or negative to the left and right of the critical point. Obviously, at $x = 3/2$ the derivative is zero. Since it is the only critical point, we have two intervals to check: $(-\infty, 3/2)$ and $(3/2, \infty)$.

The question is: are these increasing or decreasing intervals, and how can we tell? The answer is simple. We pick one point in each interval and evaluate the derivative at that point. In other words, given $-\infty < a < 3/2$, we calculate $f'(a)$. The numerical answer itself is irrelevant; all we care about is whether $f'(a)$ is positive or negative.

So let's pick a point in the interval $(-\infty, 3/2)$. A good tactic is to pick a point that is easy to work with, so here we might pick 0. Then

$$f'(0) = 6 - 4(0) = 6$$

Since $f'(0)$ is positive, then all numbers in the interval $(-\infty, 3/2)$ are positive. We indicate this on the number line as follows:

$$f'(x) \qquad \xleftarrow{\qquad\qquad \overset{+}{\rule{0pt}{0pt}} \qquad\qquad \underset{\frac{3}{2}}{|} \qquad\qquad} \rightarrow$$

Now let's examine the interval $(3/2, \infty)$. Choose one point in this interval that will be easy to work with, say $x = 2$. Then

$$f'(2) = 6 - 4(2) = -2$$

Thus, the derivative is negative in the interval $(3/2, \infty)$. Let's indicate this on the number plot.

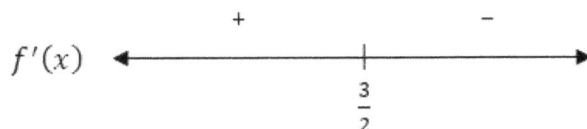

$$f'(x) \qquad \xleftarrow{\qquad\qquad \overset{+}{\rule{0pt}{0pt}} \qquad\qquad \underset{\frac{3}{2}}{|} \qquad \overset{-}{\rule{0pt}{0pt}} \qquad} \rightarrow$$

Now let's use what we have just learned in this section.

1) The derivative in $(-\infty, 3/2)$ is positive, so $f(x)$ is increasing in this interval.
2) The derivative in $(3/2, \infty)$ is negative, so $f(x)$ is decreasing in this interval.

To summarize, $f(x)$ is increasing in $(-\infty, 3/2)$ and decreasing in $(3/2, \infty)$.

Δ

It was probably easier to follow an example before seeing the explicit process written down. Let's state the steps officially now.

METHOD FOR FINDING INCREASING AND DECREASING INTERVALS
The following procedure is used for finding increasing and decreasing intervals for a function $f(x)$.

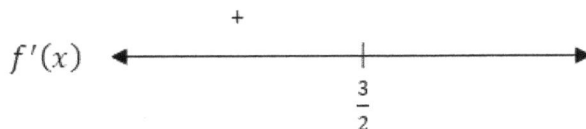

Step 1: Find $f'(x)$, set it equal to zero, and find all critical points.
Step 2: Find all points at which $f'(x)$ does not exist.
Step 3: Draw a number plot, label it $f'(x)$, and plot all these points from Steps 1 and 2.
Step 4: Pick a number a within each interval and evaluate $f'(a)$. Whenever possible, pick a such that evaluating $f'(a)$ is easy.
Step 5: Record the sign ($+$ or $-$) above that interval on the number line.
Step 6: Interpret each sign appropriately ($+$ for increasing and $-$ for decreasing)
Step 7: Write down which intervals are increasing and which are decreasing.

EXAMPLE
Find the increasing and decreasing intervals for $f(x) = x^3 - 12x + 10$.

Solution: Let's find the critical points:

$$f'(x) = 3x^2 - 12 = 0 \Rightarrow x^2 - 4 = 0$$
$$\Rightarrow (x - 2)(x + 2) = 0$$
$$\Rightarrow x = \pm 2$$

The derivative exists everywhere, so these are the only two critical points. Here is our number plot:

$$f'(x) \xleftarrow{\hspace{1cm}} \overset{\displaystyle \quad +\quad\quad +}{\underset{\underset{\textstyle -2 \qquad\quad 2}{\big|\qquad\quad\big|}}{\rule{5cm}{0.4pt}}} \xrightarrow{\hspace{1cm}}$$

Let's examine each of the three intervals.

1) $(-\infty, 2)$, pick $x = -3$
$$f'(-3) = 3((-3)^2 - 4) = 15, \text{ positive}$$

2) $(-2, 2)$, pick $x = 0$
$$f'(0) = 3((0)^2 - 4) = -12, \text{ negative}$$

3) $(2, \infty)$, pick $x = 3$
$$f'(3) = 3((3)^2 - 4) = 15, \text{ positive}$$

$$f'(x) \xleftarrow{\hspace{1cm}} \overset{\displaystyle \quad +\qquad\quad -\qquad\quad +}{\underset{\underset{\textstyle -2 \qquad\quad 2}{\big|\qquad\quad\big|}}{\rule{5cm}{0.4pt}}} \xrightarrow{\hspace{1cm}}$$

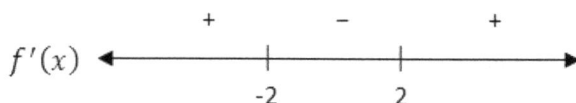

Thus, $f(x)$ is increasing on $(-\infty, 2)$ and $(2, \infty)$, and $f(x)$ is decreasing on $(-2, 2)$.

Δ

EXAMPLE

Let's find the increasing and decreasing intervals for $f(x) = x\sqrt{x^2 - 1}$.

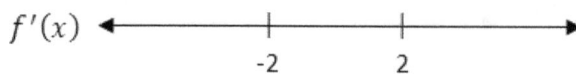

Solution: We first get all the critical points:

$$f'(x) = x \cdot \left(\frac{2x}{2\sqrt{x^2 - 1}}\right) + 1 \cdot \sqrt{x^2 - 1}$$
$$= \frac{x^2}{\sqrt{x^2 - 1}} + \sqrt{x^2 - 1}$$

It would be in our best interest to simplify this before setting it equal to zero.

$$f'(x) = \frac{x^2}{\sqrt{x^2 - 1}} + \sqrt{x^2 - 1} \cdot \left(\frac{\sqrt{x^2 - 1}}{\sqrt{x^2 - 1}}\right)$$
$$= \frac{x^2}{\sqrt{x^2 - 1}} + \frac{x^2 - 1}{\sqrt{x^2 - 1}}$$
$$= \frac{2x^2 - 1}{\sqrt{x^2 - 1}}$$

We now find the critical points.

$$\frac{2x^2 - 1}{\sqrt{x^2 - 1}} = 0 \Rightarrow 2x^2 - 1 = 0$$
$$\Rightarrow x^2 = \frac{1}{2}$$

$$\Rightarrow x = \pm\frac{1}{\sqrt{2}} = \pm\frac{\sqrt{2}}{2} \approx \pm0.70711$$

Does the derivative not exist anywhere? Let's set the denominator equal to zero.

$$\sqrt{x^2 - 1} = 0 \Rightarrow x^2 - 1 = 0$$
$$\Rightarrow x = \pm1$$

There is one other oddity lurking here. Note that if $-1 < x < 1$, then $x^2 - 1$ is negative, and therefore we would have to take the square root of a negative number. Thus, not only does the derivative not exist at $x = \pm1$, it also does not exist on the whole interval $-1 \leq x \leq 1$!

Since the first critical points ±0.70711 are within the interval $-1 \leq x \leq 1$, we can ignore them since the derivative does not exist at those points. This means that we have only two points left to check: ±1. Here is our number plot:

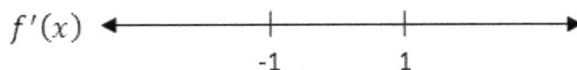

$$f'(x) \xleftarrow{\hspace{1cm}} \underset{-1}{+} \hspace{1cm} \underset{1}{+} \xrightarrow{\hspace{1cm}}$$

We need to examine just two intervals. Let's go from left to right.

1) $(-\infty, -1)$, pick $x = -2$
$$f'(-2) = \frac{2(-2)^2 - 1}{\sqrt{(-2)^2 - 1}} = \frac{7}{\sqrt{3}}, \text{ positive}$$

2) $(-1, 1)$, the derivative does not exist

3) $(1, \infty)$, pick $x = 2$
$$f'(2) = \frac{2(2)^2 - 1}{\sqrt{(2)^2 - 1}} = \frac{7}{\sqrt{3}}, \text{ positive}$$

The number plot looks like this, and remember that DNE stands for Does Not Exist.

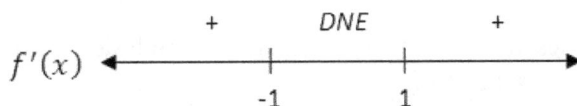

$$f'(x) \xleftarrow{\hspace{1cm}} \overset{+}{\underset{-1}{|}} \quad \overset{DNE}{} \quad \overset{+}{\underset{1}{|}} \xrightarrow{\hspace{1cm}}$$

Thus, the two intervals $(-\infty, -1)$ and $(1, \infty)$ are both increasing. There are no decreasing intervals.

What if we had missed the fact that the derivative did not exist on $(-1, 1)$? We would have had four numbers to check: ±1 and ±0.70711. We would plot these all on the number line and checked a total of five intervals. At that point we would have discovered, by picking points in the intervals, that the derivative did not exist on $(-1, -0.70711)$, $(-0.70711, 0.70711)$, and $(0.70711, 1)$. So even if we had missed it at first, we would have picked it up here.

Δ

Section 3.6 – The First Derivative Test

In the previous section we showed how to find the intervals where a function $f(x)$ is increasing and decreasing. We used a number plot to illustrate, with $(+)$ or $(-)$ signs, which intervals of the derivative were positive or negative. Now we are going to use this information to quickly identify all the maximum and minimum values of $f(x)$.

At the beginning of the chapter, we could simply evaluate the function at each critical point. From that information, we could identify the absolute maximum value because it was the highest value, and similarly for the absolute minimum value. However, what about the other critical points? Are they local maxima or local minima? In this section we will discover how to tell.

Let's start backwards. We already know that if $f(a)$ is a maximum value of the function, then f is increasing to the left of $x = a$ and decreasing to the right. Thus, with the help of the charts from Section 3.5, we can conclude that the derivative is positive to the left of $x = a$ and negative to the right.

Similarly, if $f(a)$ is a minimum value of the function, then $f(x)$ is decreasing to the left of $x = a$ and increasing to the right. Thus, the derivative is negative to the left of $x = a$ and positive to the right.

$f'(x)$	$f(x)$
Positive	Increasing
Negative	Decreasing

Here is a theorem stating how to spot the maximum and minimum values of $f(x)$.

THEOREM: CLASSIFYING CRITICAL POINTS

If $f'(x)$ is positive to the left of a and $f'(x)$ is negative to the right of a, then $f(a)$ is a **local maximum value** of $f(x)$.

If $f'(x)$ is negative to the left of a and $f'(x)$ is positive to the right of a, then $f(a)$ is a **local minimum value** of $f(x)$.

If $f'(x)$ is positive on both sides of a, or if $f'(x)$ is negative on both sides of a, then $f(a)$ is neither a local maximum nor a local minimum value of $f(x)$.

Let's look at a sample number plot and how to interpret it.

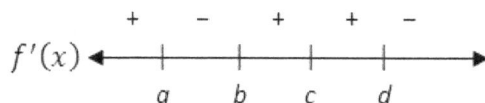

1) The point a is a local maximum value because $f'(x)$ is positive to the left and negative to the immediate right.
2) The point b is a local minimum value since $f'(x)$ is negative to the left and positive to the right.
3) The point c, while a critical point, is neither a local minimum nor a local maximum. It simply means that the function increases, comes to a horizontal tangent at c, and then begins increasing again rather than reversing direction.
4) The point d is a local maximum value.

EXAMPLE

We mentioned this function earlier, but here is an example of a function with a critical point that is neither a minimum nor a maximum. Take $f(x) = x^3$.

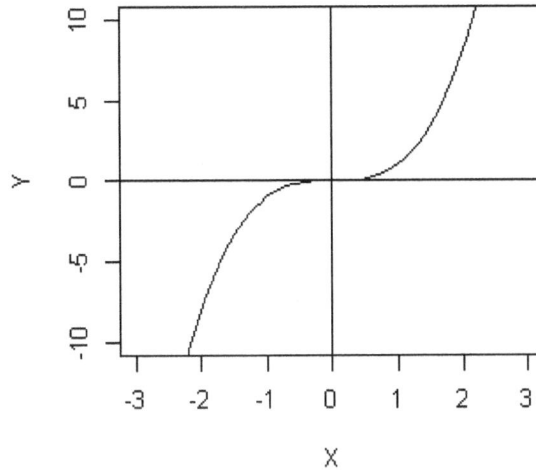

As you can see, $f(x)$ increases, stops at $x = 0$, and then continues increasing afterwards. Here is a graph of the derivative $f'(x) = 3x^2$.

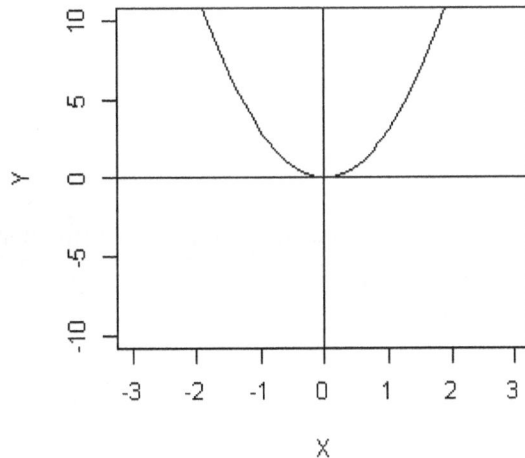

Δ

EXAMPLE

Let's classify the critical points of $f(x) = 2x^3 - 9x^2 - 60x + 2$.

Solution: We find the critical points first:

$$\begin{aligned}
f'(x) &= 6x^2 - 18x - 60 \\
&= 6(x^2 - 3x - 10) \\
&= 6(x - 5)(x + 2) = 0 \\
&\Rightarrow x = 5, x = -2
\end{aligned}$$

The critical points are $x = -2, 5$. Let's plot them:

$$f'(x) \longleftarrow \underset{\substack{| \\ -2}}{} \underset{\substack{| \\ 5}}{} \longrightarrow$$

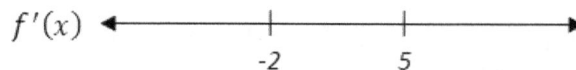

We now examine the three intervals.

1) $(-\infty, -2)$, pick $x = -3$
$$f'(-3) = 6(-3 - 5)(-3 + 2) = 6(-8)(-1) = 48, \text{ positive}$$

2) $(-2, 5)$, pick $x = 0$
$$f'(0) = 6(0 - 5)(0 + 2) = 6(-5)(2) = -60, \text{ negative}$$

3) $(5, \infty)$, pick $x = 6$

$$f'(6) = 6(6 - 5)(6 + 2) = 6(1)(8) = 48, \text{ positive}$$

Let's draw our results:

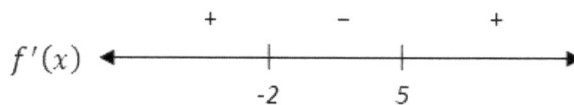

$$f'(x) \longleftarrow \underset{\substack{| \\ -2}}{\overset{+}{}} \underset{\substack{| \\ 5}}{\overset{-}{}} \overset{+}{\longrightarrow}$$

What does this plot tell us? By the theorem at the beginning, $f(-2)$ is a local maximum value, and $f(5)$ is a local minimum value. To sum up:

1) The local maximum of f is $f(-2) = 70$.
2) The local minimum of f is $f(50) = -273$.

Δ

EXAMPLE

Let's classify the critical points of $f(x) = \frac{\ln(x)}{x^2}$, with the added condition that $x > 0$.

Solution: We first get the critical points:

$$f'(x) = \frac{x^2 \cdot \frac{1}{x} - \ln(x) \cdot 2x}{x^4} = \frac{x - 2x \ln(x)}{x^4}$$
$$= \frac{1 - 2\ln(x)}{x^3}$$

Setting this equal to zero, we have

$$\frac{1 - 2\ln(x)}{x^3} = 0 \Rightarrow 1 - 2\ln(x) = 0$$
$$\Rightarrow \ln(x) = \frac{1}{2}$$
$$\Rightarrow x = e^{1/2} = \sqrt{e} \approx 1.64872$$

We are additionally writing the critical point in decimal form merely to make it easier to pick points in the intervals for sign testing. Picking correct points might not be as obvious when the critical points are in exact form.

While the derivative is undefined at $x = 0$, this point is not within the domain, and so we can ignore it. Hence, our only critical point is $x = \sqrt{e}$.

$$f'(x) \quad \overleftarrow{\underset{0}{} \underset{1.649}{+} } \rightarrow$$

Note that we have drawn the left endpoint differently. Since our interval is $(0, \infty)$, we start at $x = 0$ instead of at negative infinity. And since the interval is open, we indicate this with a bowed curve. (If it had been closed, we would have drawn a straight bracket instead.)

1) $\left(0, \sqrt{e}\right)$, pick $x = 1$

$$f'(1) = \frac{1 - 2\ln(1)}{1^3} = 1, \text{ positive}$$

2) $\left(\sqrt{e}, \infty\right)$, pick $x = 2$

$$f'(2) = \frac{1 - 2\ln(2)}{2^3} \approx -0.04829, \text{ negative}$$

The number plot looks like this:

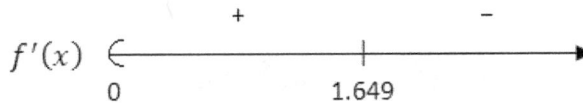

$$f'(x) \quad \overleftarrow{\underset{0}{} \overset{+}{} \underset{1.649}{|} \overset{-}{}} \rightarrow$$

The sole critical point $x = \sqrt{e}$ is therefore a local maximum. The maximum value is thus

$$f\left(\sqrt{e}\right) = \frac{\ln\left(e^{1/2}\right)}{\left(e^{1/2}\right)^2} = \frac{\frac{1}{2}\ln(e)}{e} = \frac{1}{2e}$$

Δ

EXAMPLE
Classify the critical points of $f(x) = \sin^3(x)$ on the open interval $(-3, 3)$.

Solution: At last, some trig! Let's get the critical points.

$$f'(x) = 3\sin^2(x)\cos(x)$$

We need to set both trig formulas equal to 0 to find the critical points. First,

$$3\sin^2(x) = 0 \Rightarrow \sin(x) = 0$$
$$\Rightarrow \sin(x) = 0, \pm\pi, \pm2\pi$$

However, $\pm\pi$ and $\pm2\pi$ are outside the domain $(-3, 3)$, so we reject them and keep $x = 0$. Next,

$$\cos(x) = 0 \Rightarrow = \pm\frac{\pi}{2}, \pm\frac{3\pi}{2}$$

Note that $\pm3\pi/2$ is outside the domain, so we reject those points. The derivative is not undefined anywhere, so our critical points are $x = -\pi/2, 0, \pi/2$. (Note that because we are on an open interval, we do not have to check the endpoints!)

Section 3.6 – The First Derivative Test

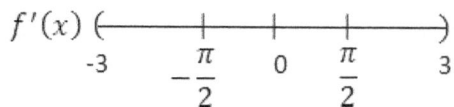

$$f'(x) \longleftarrow | \quad | \quad | \quad \longrightarrow$$
$$-3 \quad -\frac{\pi}{2} \quad 0 \quad \frac{\pi}{2} \quad 3$$

We have four intervals to check. Before doing so, let me show you a great shortcut. Remember that when picking test points, all we really care about is whether the answer in each interval is positive or negative. Notice that the first part of the derivative, $3\sin^2(x)$, is positive (except for at least some of the critical points, in which case it could be 0). That means that the sign of the derivative evaluation depends entirely on the sign on $\cos(x)$. So to make things easier, let's for this part of the problem write $f'(x) = K\cos(x)$ where $K = 3\sin^2(x)$. Remember, we don't care what the number itself is, just the sign!

1) $\left(-3, -\frac{\pi}{2}\right)$, pick $x = -\frac{2\pi}{3}$ (since $\cos\left(-\frac{2\pi}{3}\right) = \cos\left(\frac{4\pi}{3}\right) = -\frac{1}{2}$ is easy to work with)

$$f'\left(-\frac{2\pi}{3}\right) = K\cos\left(-\frac{2\pi}{3}\right) = K\cos\left(\frac{4\pi}{3}\right) = K\left(-\frac{1}{2}\right), \text{negative}$$

2) $\left(-\frac{\pi}{2}, 0\right)$, pick $x = -\frac{\pi}{3}$ so that $\cos\left(-\frac{\pi}{3}\right) = \cos\left(\frac{5\pi}{3}\right) = \frac{1}{2}$

$$f'\left(-\frac{\pi}{3}\right) = K\cos\left(-\frac{\pi}{3}\right) = K\cos\left(\frac{5\pi}{3}\right) = K\left(\frac{1}{2}\right), \text{positive}$$

3) $\left(0, \frac{\pi}{2}\right)$, pick $x = \frac{\pi}{3}$

$$f'\left(\frac{\pi}{3}\right) = K\cos\left(\frac{\pi}{3}\right) = K\left(\frac{1}{2}\right), \text{positive}$$

4) $\left(\frac{\pi}{2}, 3\right)$, pick $x = \frac{2\pi}{3}$

$$f'\left(\frac{2\pi}{3}\right) = K\cos\left(\frac{2\pi}{3}\right) = K\left(-\frac{1}{2}\right), \text{negative}$$

Our number plot will summarize all this:

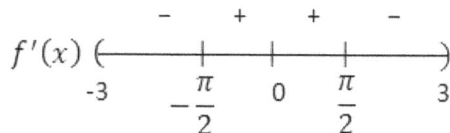

$$\quad - \quad + \quad + \quad -$$
$$f'(x) \longleftarrow | \quad | \quad | \quad \longrightarrow$$
$$-3 \quad -\frac{\pi}{2} \quad 0 \quad \frac{\pi}{2} \quad 3$$

What can we draw from this?

1) $f(-\pi/2) = -1$ is a local minimum value of $f(x)$.
2) $f(\pi/2) = 1$ is a local maximum of $f(x)$.
3) $f(0) = 0$ is neither a maximum nor a minimum value of $f(x)$.

Here is what the graph looks like:

174

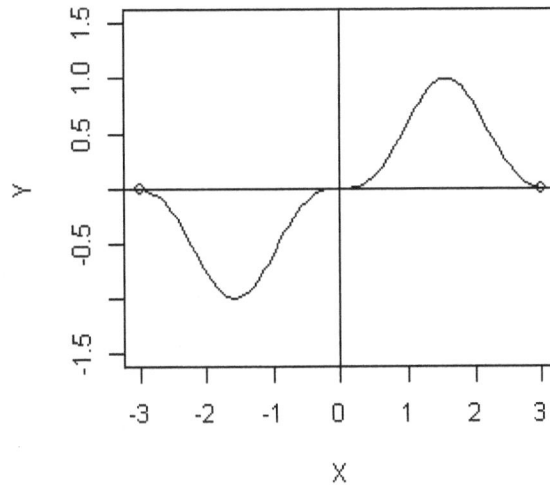

Δ

Section 3.7– Concavity and the Second Derivative Test

So far we have seen that the first derivative can tell us where a function is increasing and where it is decreasing. As a consequence, we can use this information to discover where the maximum and minimum values are.

Earlier in Chapter 2 we introduced the concept of higher derivatives, including applications to physics. But do higher derivatives tell us anything important about functions? The answer is yes, and in this section we see how. Let's examine a new concept called **concavity**. We will make a formal definition of it shortly, but for now concavity is essentially the study of how a curve curves. Does it curve upwards (**concave up**) or downwards (**concave down**)? Here are some sketches to illustrate these curves.

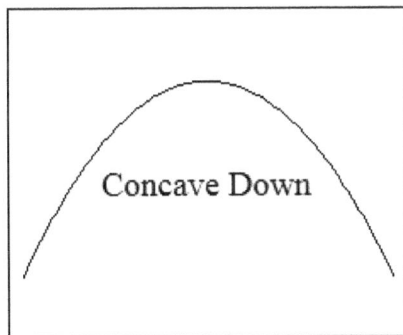

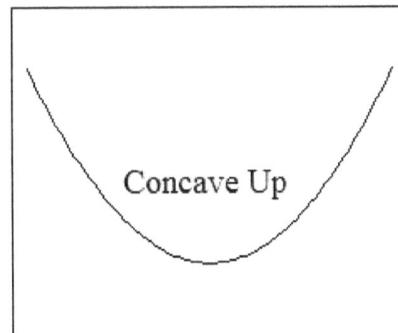

The curve on the left is bowed downwards the whole time, while the curve on the right is bowed upwards. It is very helpful to remember these images; they will prove to be very useful in the concavity problems coming up.

MNEMONIC

Here is a little rhyme to help you remember the shape of concavity:

"If you put it in a crown, it's concave down. If you put it in a cup, it's concave up."

(Think of someone's head going into a crown and how a cup is open upwards!)

175

EXAMPLE

The function $y = -x^2$ is concave down everywhere, while $y = x^2$ is concave up everywhere.

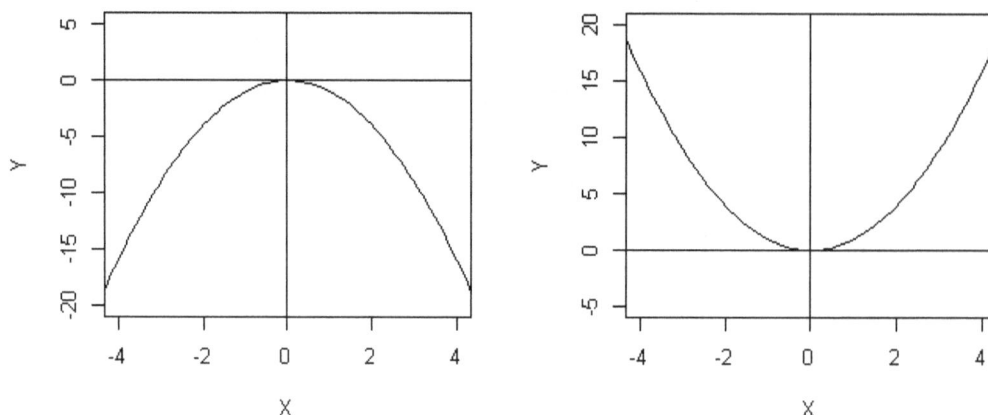

Δ

EXAMPLE

Let's revisit $y = x^3$. Although it may be difficult to tell from its graph at this point, this function is concave down to the left of the origin and concave up to the right.

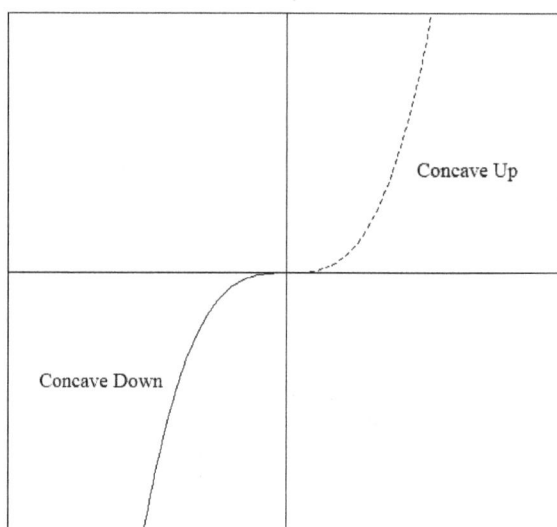

The left, solid segment is concave down, while the right, dotted portion is concave up. We will prove this very shortly, but for now we are just examining the graph itself. (If you are having trouble seeing this, compare both halves of the graph to the images above.)

Δ

Now that we have some idea of concavity, we ask ourselves: how do we actually find the intervals where a function is concave up and where it is concave down? We cannot always rely on a graph to tell us, although we can use one to get an idea. This is where the second derivative comes in.

When we examined first derivatives, we discovered that a negative derivative indicates that the function is decreasing, while a positive derivative tells us that the function's increasing. Now let's look at the second derivative. Here is what it tells us:

1) If the second derivative is positive on the interval (a, b), then the function is concave up on (a, b).
2) If the second derivative is negative on the interval (a, b), then the function is concave down on (a, b).
3) If the second derivative is equal to zero at the point c, and the second derivative is positive on one side of c and negative on the other side, then the function has an **inflection point** at c.

DEFINITION

An **inflection point** at $x = c$ is a point where $f''(x) < 0$ on one side of c and $f''(x) > 0$ on the other side of c. Be careful though – just because the second derivative is zero at c does not automatically make it an inflection point! It has to obey the above criteria.

More precisely, if the function is concave up on (a, c) and concave down on (c, b) (or the other way around), then at the point $x = c$ the function switches concavity, making $x = c$ an inflection point.

A word of warning here: we also need to check where the second derivative does not exist. If the second derivative switches signs at a point c, but the original function does not exist at c (for instance, a vertical asymptote), then concavity indeed changes at c but c is not an inflection point. (The first example of Section 3.8 illustrates these circumstances.)

ETYMOLOGY

The word **concave** comes from the Latin *concavus*, meaning "hollow" or "arched," while the word **inflection** comes from the Latin *inflexion*, meaning "a bending." These original definitions should make sense since a curve that is concave down or up is arched, in a sense, and when the curve "bends" (i.e. changes concavity), this occurs at an inflection point.

In the sketch of $y = x^3$, for example, the origin is an inflection point because here concavity changes.

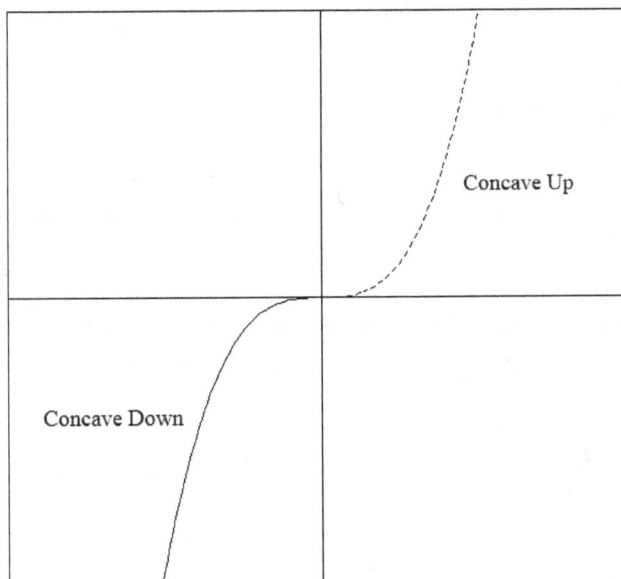

Here is a little chart to remember, not unlike the one we saw for first derivatives.

$f''(x)$	$f(x)$
Positive	Concave Up
Negative	Concave Down

And here are some official definitions.

DEFINITION

A function $f(x)$ is **concave up** on (a, b) if $f''(x) > 0$ for all x in (a, b).

A function $f(x)$ is **concave down** on (a, b) if $f''(x) < 0$ for all x in (a, b).

EXAMPLE

Here is the official proof that the origin is an inflection point of $f(x) = x^3$. The first derivative is $f'(x) = 3x^2$, while the second is $f''(x) = 6x$. The only possible inflection point here is $x = 0$. Now we sketch a number plot for the second derivative to see if $x = 0$ really is an inflection point.

$f''(x)$ ←———————————|———————————→
                     0

Just like we did earlier with the first derivative test, we now pick points within the intervals $(-\infty, 0)$ and $(0, \infty)$. Substitute them into the *second* derivative equation and record the sign. Again, try to pick easy points whenever possible.

1) $(-\infty, 0)$, pick $x = -1$
    $f''(-1) = 6(-1) = -6$, negative

2) $(0, \infty)$, pick $x = 1$
    $f''(1) = 6(1) = 6$, positive

$f''(x)$ ←————————$-$————|————$+$————→
                        0

Since the sign of the second derivative does indeed change at 0, we conclude that $x = 0$ is an inflection point of f. Furthermore, the function is concave down on $(-\infty, 0)$ and concave up on $(0, \infty)$.

Δ

Caution: When sketching your number plot, take care to label it correctly as the first or second derivative! Otherwise it tells the reader nothing.

EXAMPLE

Let's find the intervals where the function $f(x) = x^3 - 3x^2 - 45x$ is concave up and concave down. Along the way, also find the maximum and minimum values.

Solution: Let's start by finding the first derivative and its critical points.

$$f'(x) = 3x^2 - 6x - 45$$

$$= 3(x^2 - 2x - 15)$$
$$= 3(x - 5)(x + 3) = 0$$

The critical points are $x = -3, 5$. We therefore have three intervals to examine.

1) $(-\infty, -3)$, pick $x = -4$
$$f'(-4) = 3(-4 - 5)(-4 + 3) = 3(-9)(-1) = 27, \text{ positive}$$

2) $(-3, 5)$, pick $x = 0$
$$f'(0) = 3(0 - 5)(0 + 3) = 3(-5)(3) = -45, \text{ negative}$$

3) $(5, \infty)$, pick $x = 6$
$$f'(6) = 3(6 - 5)(6 + 3) = 3(1)(9) = 27, \text{ positive}$$

The number plot looks like this:

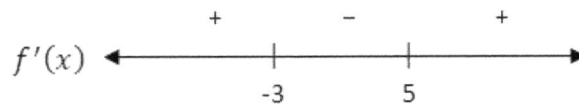

To sum up, $f(-3) = 81$ is a maximum value, while $f(5) = -175$ is a minimum value. The intervals $(-\infty, -3)$ and $(5, \infty)$ are increasing, and the function is decreasing on $(-3, 5)$. Now for the new stuff!

$$f'(x) = 3x^2 - 6x - 45$$
$$f''(x) = 6x - 6$$
$$= 6(x - 1) = 0$$

The only possible inflection point is $x = 1$. Let's check the two intervals:

1) $(-\infty, 1)$, pick $x = 0$
$$f''(0) = 6(0) - 6 = -6, \text{ negative}$$

2) $(1, \infty)$, pick $x = 2$
$$f''(2) = 6(2) - 6 = 6, \text{ positive}$$

Here is the next number plot:

So $x = 1$ is indeed an inflection point since concavity changes here. Since $f(1) = 47$, the point is $(1, -47)$. To answer the original question, $f(x)$ is concave down on $(-\infty, 1)$ and concave up on $(1, \infty)$.

Δ

EXAMPLE

Let's find where the function $f(x) = \dfrac{\ln(x)}{x}$ is concave up and concave down, with $x > 0$. This time, we will skip the maximum and minimum values.

Solution: The first derivative is

$$f'(x) = \frac{x\left(\frac{1}{x}\right) - \ln(x)}{x^2} = \frac{1 - \ln(x)}{x^2}$$

Then the second derivative is

$$f''(x) = \frac{x^2 \cdot \frac{d}{dx}(1 - \ln(x)) - (1 - \ln(x)) \cdot \frac{d}{dx}(x^2)}{(x^2)^2}$$

$$= \frac{x^2 \cdot \left(-\frac{1}{x}\right) - (1 - \ln(x)) \cdot 2x}{x^4}$$

$$= \frac{-x - 2x(1 - \ln(x))}{x^4}$$

$$= \frac{-x - 2x + 2x\ln(x)}{x^4}$$

$$= \frac{2x\ln(x) - 3x}{x^4}$$

$$= \frac{2\ln(x) - 3}{x^3}$$

We find the potential inflection points:

$$f''(x) = \frac{2\ln(x) - 3}{x^3} = 0$$
$$2\ln(x) = 3$$
$$\ln(x) = \frac{3}{2}$$
$$x = e^{3/2} \approx 4.48169$$

While the second derivative is undefined at 0, this is outside the interval, so we have just one point to check.

1) $\left(0, e^{3/2}\right)$, pick $x = 1$
$$f''(1) = \frac{2\ln(1) - 3}{1^3} = -3, \text{ negative}$$

2) $\left(e^{3/2}, \infty\right)$, pick $x = e^2$
$$f''(e^2) = \frac{2\ln(e^2) - 3}{e^6} = \frac{4\ln(e) - 3}{e^6} = \frac{1}{e^6} \approx 0.00248, \text{ positive}$$

Our choice for the latter interval might seem a bit odd. But remember, we know that $\ln(e) = 1$. If we do not have a calculator handy, we at least know this relationship, so we can get $f''(e^2)$ down to $1/e^6$. We don't care what the value is; we just want to know whether it is positive or negative. Since e^6 is positive, so is $1/e^6$. The number plot therefore looks like this:

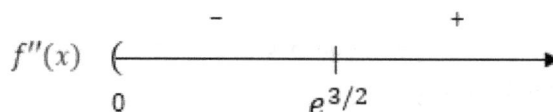

$$f''(x) \quad \overset{\displaystyle -}{\underset{0}{\longleftarrow}} \quad \overset{\displaystyle +}{\underset{e^{3/2}}{\mid}} \quad \longrightarrow$$

Thus, $f(x)$ is concave down on $\left(0, e^{3/2}\right)$ and concave up on $\left(e^{3/2}, \infty\right)$.

Δ

EXAMPLE
Here's an example that ties everything together in an interesting way. Consider the following graph of the first derivative y' of a function. Classify the critical points, find the intervals where the original function y is increasing and decreasing, and find the intervals where the original function is concave up and concave down. (You'll need to estimate where the critical points and potential inflection points occur by looking at the graph.)

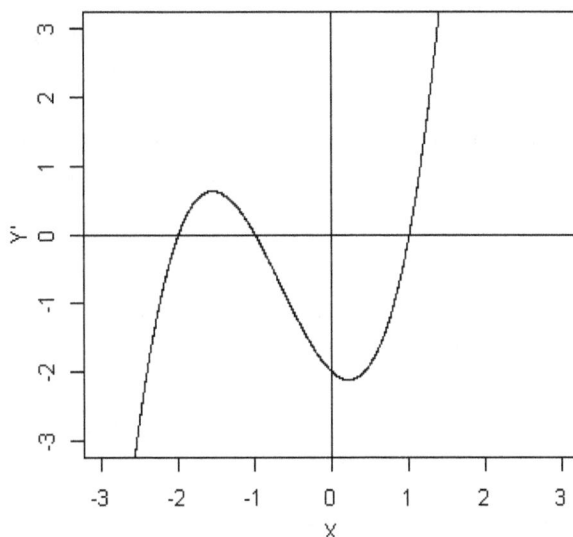

Solution: This is a good example because calculus exams at some point tend to include problems that don't actually give the function but ask you to analyze a graph of it anyway. In this case, note that we are looking at the graph of the first derivative y' and not the original function y (as indicated by the y-axis label). Since no numbers are given, we'll have to do our best to estimate the necessary ones.

For a start, critical points occur when the first derivative is equal to 0. Looking at the graph, the derivative function is 0 around $x = -2, -1$, and 1, so there are three critical points. (To be clear, we are *not* examining the "peak" on the left side and the "trough" on the right like we normally would because we are not looking at the original function.)

Having found the three critical points, there are four regions to check. All we have to do is look at the graph and note whether the function is positive (above the x-axis) or negative (below the x-axis).

1) On $(-\infty, -2)$ the function is below the x-axis, so y' is negative.
2) On $(-2, -1)$ the function is above the x-axis, so y' is positive.
3) On $(-1, 1)$ the function is below the x-axis, so y' is negative.
4) On $(1, \infty)$ the function is above the x-axis, so y' is positive.

The corresponding number line for the first derivative is as follows (and note we found it without having to plug in numbers since there's no function to plug numbers into!).

$$\begin{array}{ccccc} - & + & - & + \\ \end{array}$$

y' number line with marks at -2, -1, 1 and signs $-$, $+$, $-$, $+$.

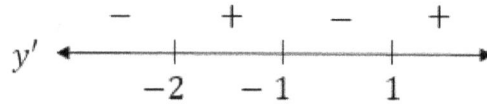

Based on our analysis, we can say that $x = -2$ and $x = 1$ are minima while $x = -1$ is a maximum. We also conclude the following:

1) y is increasing on $(-2, -1)$ and $(1, \infty)$.
2) y is decreasing on $(-\infty, -2)$ and $(-1, 1)$.

Now let's go for the second derivative. Earlier you might have been tempted to go for the peak and the trough on the graph, but because it's the first derivative, those two spots actually indicate where the potential inflection points occur. We'll have to use our own judgment for the x-coordinates, and they seem to occur at $x = -1.5$ and 0.2. Observe that the first derivative is increasing until $x = -1.5$, then decreasing until $x = 0.2$, then increasing afterwards. The corresponding number line for the second derivative is as follows (and again, we didn't need to plug in numbers).

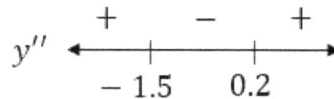

$$\begin{array}{ccc} + & - & + \\ \end{array}$$

y'' number line with marks at -1.5, 0.2 and signs $+$, $-$, $+$.

Based on our analysis, we can say that $x = -1.5$ and $x = 0.2$ are indeed points of inflection, and we also conclude the following:

1) y is concave up on $(-\infty, -1.5)$ and $(0.2, \infty)$.
2) y is concave down on $(-1.5, -0.2)$.

Δ

We have seen how to use the first derivative to find the critical points and then classify them as maxima and minima with a number line test. There is in fact an alternative way of classifying the critical points that instead utilizes the second derivative. Although you might not see it too often in introductory calculus, it is a useful extra skill to have in your back pocket, so let's conclude the section with this method.

The idea is that if a point on a function is a local maximum, then judging by the shape of the curve at that point, the curve must be concave down. Similarly, a local minimum would necessarily indicate that the curve is shaped in a concave up fashion, as seen in the same diagram that was shown earlier.

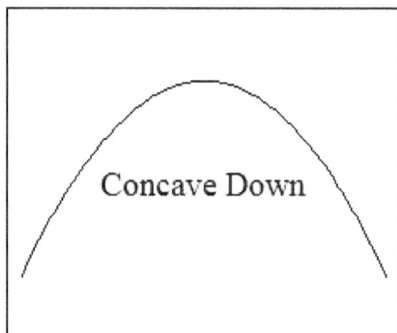

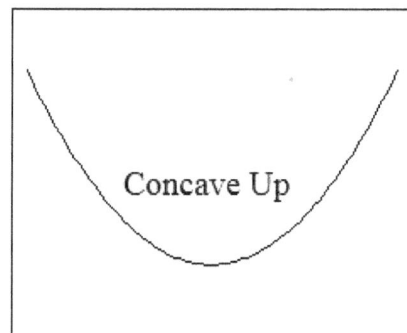

Concave Down

Concave Up

What we can do is find the second derivative and then evaluate it at the critical points and note whether the outcome is positive or negative. A negative second derivative indicates that the function is concave down at the critical point, making it a local maximum (left graph), while a positive second derivative shows that the function is concave up at the critical point, making it a local minimum (right graph). And if the second derivative is zero at the critical point, then it's neither a maximum nor a minimum. (Although it's rare, if the second derivative doesn't exist at the critical point, then you'd have to go back to the first derivative analysis to make a decision.)

CLASSIFYING CRITICAL POINTS WITH THE SECOND DERIVATIVE
Suppose $f(x)$'s first and second derivatives exist and that $x = a$ is a critical point identified from the first derivative. Then $x = a$ can be classified as follows:

If $f''(a) > 0$, then $f(x)$ is concave up at $x = a$, which means $x = a$ is a local minimum.
If $f''(a) < 0$, then $f(x)$ is concave down at $x = a$, which means $x = a$ is a local maximum.
If $f''(a) = 0$, then $x = a$ is a potential inflection point of $f(x)$, which means $x = a$ is neither a maximum nor a minimum.
If $f''(a)$ does not exist or is infinite, then no conclusion can be made, in which case go back to the first derivative number line test.

EXAMPLE
Use the second derivative to classify the critical points of $f(x) = \sin^3(x)$ on the open interval $(-3, 3)$.

Solution: We already solved this problem in Section 3.6, but let's repeat the last part about classifying the critical points. As a reminder, the first derivative is $f'(x) = 3\sin^2(x)\cos(x)$ and the critical points in the open interval are $x = -\pi/2, 0, \pi/2$. The goal is to identify whether each is a maximum, minimum, or neither, but this time using the second derivative evaluated at each point. Let's first find the second derivative:

$$\begin{aligned}
f''(x) &= 3 \times 2\sin(x)\cos(x) \times \cos(x) + 3\sin^2(x) \times -\sin(x) \\
&= 6\cos^2(x)\sin(x) - 3\sin^3(x) = 3\sin(x)\left(2\cos^2(x) - \sin^2(x)\right) \\
&= 3\sin(x)\left(\cos^2(x) + \cos^2(x) - \sin^2(x)\right) \\
&= 3\sin(x)\left(\cos^2(x) + \cos(2x)\right)
\end{aligned}$$

The next step is to evaluate the second derivative at the three critical points identified from the first derivative, and the sign of the answer is what we are after. As with the first derivative test, we don't really care what the numerical answer itself is, just whether it's positive or negative.

$$\begin{aligned}
f''\left(-\frac{\pi}{2}\right) &= 3\sin\left(-\frac{\pi}{2}\right)\left(\cos^2\left(-\frac{\pi}{2}\right) + \cos\left(2\left(-\frac{\pi}{2}\right)\right)\right) = 3(-1)(0^2 + (-1)) = 3(-1)(-1) \\
&= 3, \text{positive}
\end{aligned}$$

The critical point $x = -\pi/2$ is associated with a positive second derivative, so the function is concave up there and therefore a local minimum. Repeating this procedure,

$$\begin{aligned}
f''(0) &= 3\sin(0)\left(\cos^2(0) + \cos(0)\right) = 3(0)(1^2 + 1) = 3(0)(2) \\
&= 0, \text{zero}
\end{aligned}$$

The critical point $x = 0$ corresponds to a zero second derivative, which means it's also a potential inflection point (which still needs to be checked). However, here a zero second derivative means that $x = 0$ is neither a maximum nor a minimum. Lastly,

$$f''\left(\frac{\pi}{2}\right) = 3\sin\left(\frac{\pi}{2}\right)\left(\cos^2\left(\frac{\pi}{2}\right) + \cos\left(2\left(\frac{\pi}{2}\right)\right)\right) = 3(1)\left(0^2 + (-1)\right) = 3(1)(-1)$$
$$= -3, \text{negative}$$

The critical point $x = \pi/2$ is associated with a negative second derivative, so the function is concave down there and therefore a local maximum. All these answers agree with what we discovered earlier from using the first derivative number line test.

Δ

Section 3.8 – Sketching Curves

We now give some guidelines on sketching rough graphs of functions. We do it here because by now we have seen how to find intercepts, asymptotes, maximum and minimum values, and inflection points. You must be comfortable with this process – you won't always have that graphing calculator to save you!

This entire section focuses on two examples for illustrative purposes. If you want further examples, pick any example function shown in these notes and try to work out all possible elements of the graph that will be helpful in sketching the function. Here is a general plan of action to use when sketching a function.

METHOD FOR SKETCHING CURVES
The following procedure should be used when sketching curves.

Step 1: Solve for the y-intercept and plot it. (Set $x = 0$ and solve for y.)
Step 2: Solve for the x-intercept(s) and plot them. (Set $y = 0$ and solve for x.)
Step 3: Find the vertical asymptote(s), if any, and sketch them with dotted lines.
Step 4: Find the horizontal asymptote(s), if any, and sketch them with dotted lines.
Step 5: Find the maximum and minimum points of the function. (Use the first derivative test.)
Step 6: Find the inflection points of the function. (Use the second derivative test.)
Step 7: The previous two steps will tell you where the function is increasing and decreasing, as well as where it is concave up and concave down.

EXAMPLE

Let's sketch a graph for $y = \frac{1}{x^2-4}$.

Solution: We first get the y-intercept:

$$y = \frac{1}{0^2 - 4} = -\frac{1}{4}$$

This means that the y-intercept is $(0, -1/4)$.

When we solve for the x-intercept, we get $0 = \frac{1}{x^2-4}$. However, multiplying both sides by $(x^2 - 4)$ results in $0 = 1$, which is obviously a false statement. Hence, there is no x-intercept.

Now it is time for the asymptotes. Setting the denominator equal to zero, we find that

$$x^2 - 4 = 0$$
$$x = \pm 2$$

Thus, there are vertical asymptotes at $x = \pm 2$. Now we examine the function at infinity: as x grows large, the denominator approaches infinity while the numerator remains fixed at 1, so

$$\lim_{x \to \infty} \frac{1}{x^2 - 4} = 0$$

This means that there is a horizontal asymptote at $y = 0$. Let's write down and draw what we know so far:

y-intercept: $(0, -1/4)$ Vertical asymptotes: $x = \pm 2$
x-intercept: none   Horizontal asymptote: $y = 0$

Now we go for the maximum and minimum points.

$$\frac{dy}{dx} = \frac{(x^2 - 4) \cdot 0 - 1 \cdot (2x)}{(x^2 - 4)^2} = -\frac{2x}{(x^2 - 4)^2}$$

The critical point is

$$-\frac{2x}{(x^2 - 4)^2} = 0$$
$$-2x = 0$$
$$x = 0$$

The derivative is undefined at $x = \pm 2$, so we have three critical points: $x = -2, 0, 2$.

1) $(-\infty, -2)$, pick $x = -3$
$$f'(-3) = \frac{-2(-3)}{((-3)^2 - 4)^2} = \frac{6}{25}, \text{ positive}$$

2) $(-2, 0)$, pick $x = -1$
$$f'(-1) = \frac{-2(-1)}{((-1)^2 - 4)^2} = \frac{2}{9}, \text{ positive}$$

3) $(0, 2)$, pick $x = 1$
$$f'(1) = \frac{-2(1)}{((1)^2 - 4)^2} = -\frac{2}{9}, \text{ negative}$$

4) $(2, \infty)$, pick $x = 3$

$$f'(3) = \frac{-2(3)}{((3)^2-4)^2} = -\frac{6}{25}, \text{ negative}$$

Here is the first derivative number plot:

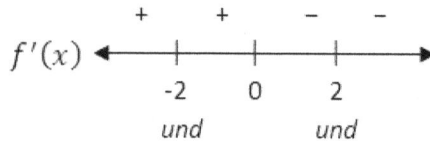

$$f'(x) \quad \begin{array}{ccccc} + & + & - & - \\ \hline & -2 & 0 & 2 \\ & und & & und \end{array}$$

We are writing "*und*" for "undefined" for -2 and 2 simply to point out that they are asymptotes. We can quickly see that 0 is the only place where the slope changes sign, and it is a maximum. Then $f(0) = -1/4$ is the maximum value, and this happens to be the y-intercept.

The function is increasing on $(-\infty, -2)$ and $(-2, 0)$, and it is decreasing on $(0, 2)$ and $(2, \infty)$.

And now we go for the inflection points.

$$\frac{d^2y}{dx^2} = \frac{(x^2-4)^2 \cdot (-2) + 2x \cdot 2(x^2-4) \cdot 2x}{(x^2-4)^4}$$
$$= \frac{(x^2-4) \cdot (-2) + 2x \cdot 2 \cdot 2x}{(x^2-4)^3}$$
$$= \frac{-2(x^2-4) + 8x^2}{(x^2-4)^3}$$
$$= \frac{-2x^2 + 8 + 8x^2}{(x^2-4)^3}$$
$$= \frac{6x^2 + 8}{(x^2-4)^3}$$

Again, the derivative does not exist at $x = \pm 2$, and this time we have

$$8 + 6x^2 = 0 \Rightarrow x^2 = -\frac{8}{6}$$

This result tells us that the second derivative never equals zero (since otherwise we would be introducing complex numbers). However, since the second derivative doesn't exist at $x = \pm 2$, the vertical asymptotes, we do need to see if concavity changes there. Let's now find how the function curves.

1) $(-\infty, -2)$, pick $x = -3$
$$f''(x) = \frac{8+6(-3)^2}{((-3)^2-4)^3} = \frac{62}{125}, \text{ positive}$$

2) $(-2, 2)$, pick $x = 0$
$$f''(x) = \frac{8+6(0)^2}{((0)^2-4)^3} = -\frac{8}{64}, \text{ negative}$$

3) $(2, \infty)$, pick $x = 3$
$$f''(x) = \frac{8+6(3)^2}{((3)^2-4)^3} = \frac{62}{125}, \text{ positive}$$

Here is the second derivative plot:

$$f''(x)$$

(sign chart)

$+$ ———— $-$ ———— $+$

-2 2

und   *und*

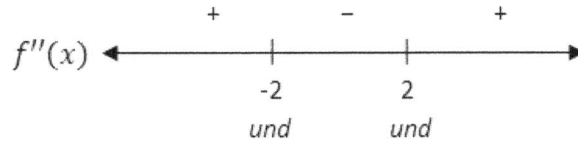

There are no inflection points because the only two candidates are both asymptotes. However, the function is concave up on $(-\infty, -2)$ and $(2, \infty)$, and concave down on $(-2, 2)$. This is a good example of a function where concavity switches in two locations, and yet the two locations are not inflection points!
Let's write a summary of the intervals:

Increasing: $(-\infty, -2)$ and $(-2, 0)$ <u>Concave up</u>: $(-\infty, -2)$ and $(2, \infty)$
Decreasing: $(0, 2)$ and $(2, \infty)$ <u>Concave down</u>: $(-2, 2)$

Let's start with the middle part of the graph in between the asymptotes. We know that $(0, -1/4)$ is a maximum, and that in this area the function is concave down. So we will sketch this region:

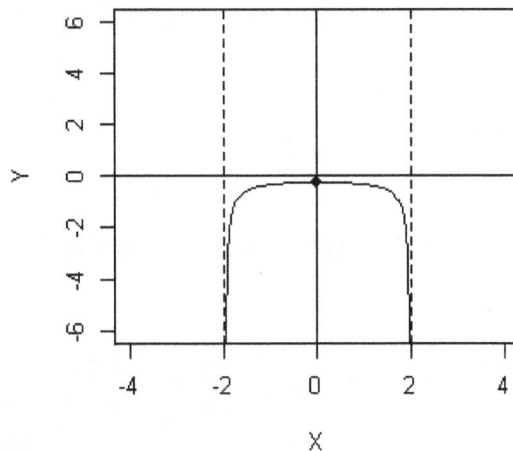

We can tell by substituting in appropriate points that f is positive to the left of $x = -2$, is increasing, and is concave up. Similarly, to the right of $x = 2$, f is positive, decreasing, and concave up. Thus, our final sketch looks something like this:

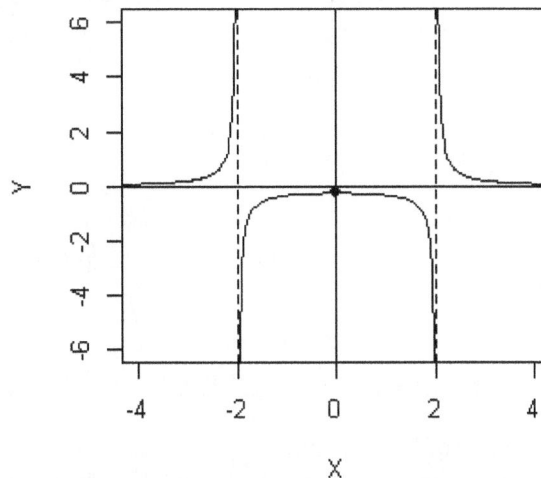

Δ

EXAMPLE

Sketch the graph for $f(x) = \frac{x^3+3x}{x^2+1}$. You might recognize this function as the same one we used for the position of a dragonfly back in Section 2.6, only now we are writing it in terms of x and over all reals rather than having a restricted domain.

Solution: First, the y-intercept is at $f(0) = \frac{0^3+3(0)}{0^2+1} = 0$, or at $(0,0)$. Next, any x-intercepts occur when $f(x) = 0$:

$$0 = \frac{x^3 + 3x}{x^2 + 1} \Rightarrow 0 = x^3 + 3x \Rightarrow 0 = x(x^2 + 3)$$

The only real solution is at $x = 0$, and so the origin is the x-intercept as well as the y-intercept. Next, let's have a go at the asymptotes. Setting the denominator equal to zero,

$$x^2 + 1 = 0 \Rightarrow x^2 = -1$$

Again, there is no solution without introducing complex numbers, so there are no vertical asymptotes. Next, examining the function at infinity, we see that the numerator grows larger than the denominator:

$$\lim_{x\to\infty} \frac{x^3 + 3x}{x^2 + 1} = \lim_{x\to\infty} \frac{(x^3 + 3x)\cdot\left(\frac{1}{x^2}\right)}{(x^2 + 1)\cdot\left(\frac{1}{x^2}\right)} = \lim_{x\to\infty} \frac{x + \frac{3}{x}}{1 + \frac{1}{x^2}} = \infty$$

The same is true as x approaches negative infinity, only in the negative direction.

$$\lim_{x\to-\infty} \frac{x^3 + 3x}{x^2 + 1} = \lim_{x\to-\infty} \frac{(x^3 + 3x)\cdot\left(\frac{1}{x^2}\right)}{(x^2 + 1)\cdot\left(\frac{1}{x^2}\right)} = \lim_{x\to-\infty} \frac{x + \frac{3}{x}}{1 + \frac{1}{x^2}} = -\infty$$

This tells us that there are no horizontal asymptotes either. However, don't celebrate just yet – you might recall at some point learning in an algebra class that when a function's numerator has degree one higher than the denominator's degree, there is an **oblique asymptote**, or a **slant asymptote**. Since the numerator is a cubic (degree 3) and the denominator is a quadratic (degree 2), this function will have an oblique asymptote. Forgive me making this definition in the middle of an example, but we need to mention it. (There's also an example of this in Section 0.1.)

DEFINITION

Let a function be defined as a polynomial divided by a polynomial where the degree of the numerator is one higher than the degree of the denominator. That is,

$$f(x) = \frac{g(x)}{h(x)} \quad \text{where} \quad \deg(g(x)) = \deg(h(x)) + 1$$

Then $f(x)$ has an **oblique asymptote** (or **slant asymptote**) written in the form $y = mx + b$. This "diagonal asymptote" guides the function's path as $f(x)$ approaches positive and negative infinity.

The best way to refresh your memory of how to find an oblique asymptote is to do an example of finding one. Since the numerator is $x^3 + 3x$ and the denominator is $x^2 + 1$, the best way to find it is to do polynomial long division, not the most popular procedure among math students. We set it up as follows:

$$x^2 + 1 \overline{)x^3 + 3x}$$

It will be easier to insert $0x^2$ and 0 so we can more easily pair up terms:

$$x^2 + 1 \overline{)x^3 + 0x^2 + 3x + 0}$$

Next, ask yourself: x^2 times what is x^3? The answer is x. That number goes above the x^3:

$$\begin{array}{r} x \\ x^2 + 1 \overline{)x^3 + 0x^2 + 3x + 0} \end{array}$$

Multiplying x by $(x^2 + 1)$ results in $x^3 + x$, so we write that on the next line:

$$\begin{array}{r} x \\ x^2 + 1 \overline{)x^3 + 0x^2 + 3x + 0} \\ x^3 + 0x^2 + x \end{array}$$

Again, we inserted $0x^2$ just to make it easier to compare terms. Now we subtract the two lines:

$$\begin{array}{r} x \\ x^2 + 1 \overline{)x^3 + 0x^2 + 3x + 0} \\ -(x^3 + 0x^2 + x) \\ \hline 2x \end{array}$$

The remainder is $2x$, which now has a smaller degree than the denominator of $x^2 + 1$. This means that we have successfully written the function as

$$f(x) = \frac{x^3 + 3x}{x^2 + 1} = x + \frac{2x}{x^2 + 1}$$

If you want to check your work, combine the two pieces back into one fraction, and you'll get the original function. Now, what was the point of all this work? As x gets large in either direction, the $2x/(x^2 + 1)$ piece goes to 0, which means that for large values of x, $f(x)$ behaves like x. That means that the oblique asymptote here is $y = x$ because it "guides" the function for large values of x.

Let's take a breather and record what we've found so far:

<u>y-intercept</u>: $(0,0)$	<u>Vertical asymptotes</u>: None
<u>x-intercept</u>: $(0,0)$	<u>Horizontal asymptotes</u>: None
	<u>Oblique asymptote</u>: $y = x$

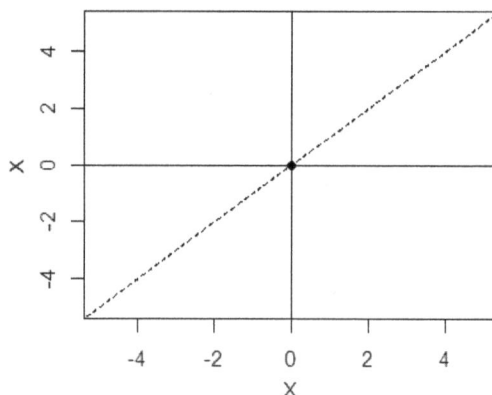

A natural question to ask is does the function ever cross the oblique asymptote; that is, are there any points where $f(x) = x$. The answer is yes, and finding the point is straightforward – just set the function equal to the asymptote.

$$x + \frac{2x}{x^2 + 1} = x \Rightarrow \frac{2x}{x^2 + 1} = 0 \Rightarrow x = 0$$

The origin is the x- and y-intercept, and it also happens to be where $f(x)$ crosses the oblique asymptote. Next, let's find the increasing and decreasing intervals. We found the first derivative in Section 2.6 (the velocity function), so I'll just state it here without deriving it again:

$$f'(x) = \frac{x^4 + 3}{(x^2 + 1)^2}$$

The critical points are when $f'(x) = 0$, and so we need to see where $x^4 + 3 = 0$. This is impossible without introducing complex numbers, so the derivative is never 0. To see if it's ever undefined, we need to see if $(x^2 + 1)^2 = 0$. The denominator is never 0; in fact, like the numerator, it's always positive, so the derivative is never undefined. That means that this function has no critical points, which means that the derivative is either always positive or always negative and never switches. To find out which one it is, pick one point and put it into the derivative. Let's use $x = 0$; we might as well make it easy!

$$f'(0) = \frac{(0)^4 + 3}{((0)^2 + 1)^2} = \frac{3}{1} = 3, \text{positive}$$

Thus, the function is increasing over the entire domain of all real numbers, over $(-\infty, \infty)$. Let's now study concavity by finding the second derivative. We found it in Section 2.6 (the acceleration function), so again I'll just state it below:

$$f''(x) = \frac{4x^3 - 12x}{(x^2 + 1)^3}$$

To find the potential inflection points, set it equal to 0.

$$\frac{4x^3 - 12x}{(x^2 + 1)^3} = 0 \Rightarrow 4x^3 - 12x = 0 \Rightarrow 4x(x^2 - 3) = 0$$
$$\Rightarrow x = 0, \sqrt{3}, -\sqrt{3}$$

To see where the second derivative is undefined,

190

$$(x^2 + 1)^3 = 0 \Rightarrow x^2 + 1 = 0$$

This cannot be solved without complex numbers (not again!), so the second derivative is never undefined. Let's now study the three potential inflection points we found.

1) $\left(-\infty, -\sqrt{3}\right)$, pick $x = -2$
$$f''(x) = \frac{4(-2)^3 - 12(-2)}{((-2)^2 + 1)^3} = -\frac{8}{125}, \text{ negative}$$

2) $\left(-\sqrt{3}, 0\right)$, pick $x = -1$
$$f''(x) = \frac{4(-1)^3 - 12(-1)}{((-1)^2 + 1)^3} = \frac{8}{8} = 1, \text{ positive}$$

3) $\left(0, \sqrt{3}\right)$, pick $x = 1$
$$f''(x) = \frac{4(1)^3 - 12(1)}{((1)^2 + 1)^3} = -\frac{8}{8} = -1, \text{ negative}$$

4) $\left(\sqrt{3}, \infty\right)$, pick $x = 2$
$$f''(x) = \frac{4(2)^3 - 12(2)}{((2)^2 + 1)^3} = \frac{8}{125}, \text{ positive}$$

Here is the second derivative plot:

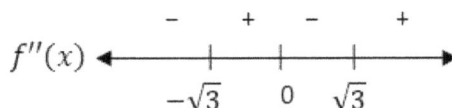

This means that the function is concave down on $\left(-\infty, -\sqrt{3}\right)$ and $\left(0, \sqrt{3}\right)$, and concave up on $\left(-\sqrt{3}, 0\right)$ and $\left(\sqrt{3}, \infty\right)$. Let's write a summary of the intervals:

<u>Increasing:</u>	$(-\infty, \infty)$
<u>Concave down:</u>	$\left(-\infty, -\sqrt{3}\right)$ and $\left(0, \sqrt{3}\right)$
<u>Concave up:</u>	$\left(-\sqrt{3}, 0\right)$ and $\left(\sqrt{3}, \infty\right)$.

Since there are no maxima or minima, we might as well find the y-coordinates of the three inflection points and plot them instead. Let's do that by putting the three values into the original function, and because of the square roots it might be helpful to factor an x out of the numerator so that we have x^2 terms left over. In other words, let's work with $f(x) = \frac{x(x^2+3)}{x^2+1}$.

$$f(-\sqrt{3}) = \frac{(-\sqrt{3})\left((-\sqrt{3})^2 + 3\right)}{(-\sqrt{3})^2 + 1} = \frac{(-\sqrt{3})(3 + 3)}{3 + 1} = -\frac{6\sqrt{3}}{4} = -\frac{3\sqrt{3}}{2} \approx -2.59808$$

$$f(0) = \frac{(0)((0)^2 + 3)}{(0)^2 + 1} = 0$$

$$f(\sqrt{3}) = \frac{(\sqrt{3})\left((\sqrt{3})^2 + 3\right)}{(\sqrt{3})^2 + 1} = \frac{(\sqrt{3})(3 + 3)}{3 + 1} = \frac{6\sqrt{3}}{4} = \frac{3\sqrt{3}}{2} \approx 2.59808$$

Noting that $\sqrt{3} \approx 1.73205$, the inflection points are located at $(-1.73205, -2.59808)$, $(0,0)$, and $(1.73205, 2.59808)$. Next, for graphing purposes it might be helpful to plot a few more points located within the four identified intervals. Let's use the same ones we used for testing concavity $(-2, -1, 1, 2)$ but this time put them into the original function.

$$f(-2) = \frac{(-2)((-2)^2 + 3)}{(-2)^2 + 1} = \frac{(-2)(4 + 3)}{4 + 1} = -\frac{14}{5} = -2.8$$

$$f(-1) = \frac{(-1)((-1)^2 + 3)}{(-1)^2 + 1} = \frac{(-1)(1 + 3)}{1 + 1} = -\frac{4}{2} = -2$$

$$f(1) = \frac{(1)((1)^2 + 3)}{(1)^2 + 1} = \frac{(1)(1 + 3)}{1 + 1} = \frac{4}{2} = 2$$

$$f(2) = \frac{(2)((2)^2 + 3)}{(2)^2 + 1} = \frac{(2)(4 + 3)}{4 + 1} = \frac{14}{5} = 2.8$$

Our extra "test points" are $(-2, -2.8)$, $(-1, -2)$, $(1, 2)$, and $(2, 2.8)$. Let's start with the left side of the graph, noting that it's concave down and then concave up.

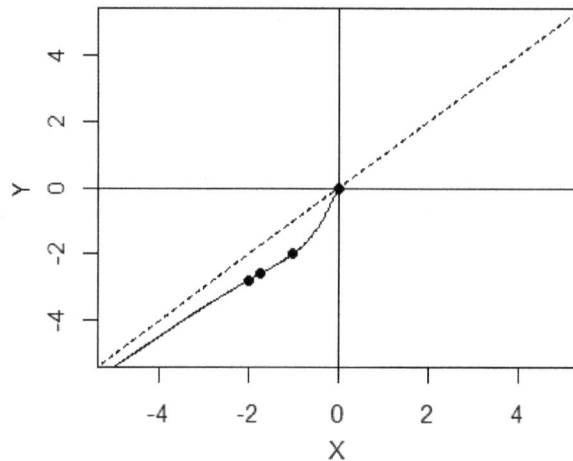

The right side of the graph is concave down and then concave up.

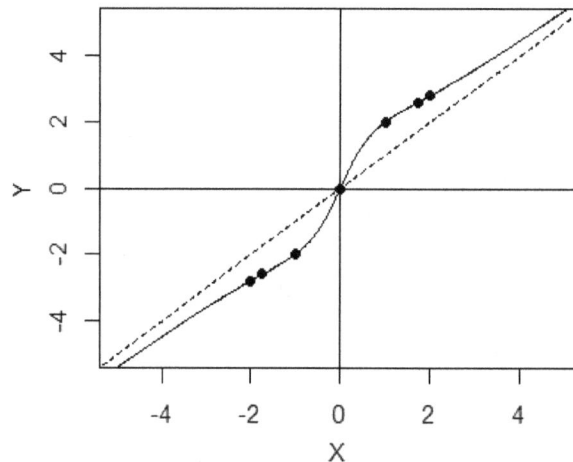

Δ

Section 3.9 – Related Rates

This section contains a fun application of derivatives. It is sometimes taught after you learn implicit differentiation, but we instead include it in this chapter because it is an application. If your class teaches this topic along with implicit differentiation, you can jump from Section 2.7 to this section without worrying about the previous content in Chapter 3.

A related rate problem involves a situation that takes place over time. It is about studying just one snapshot of the problem at a given moment in time. For instance, if a coffee maker is pouring coffee into the glass container, how quickly is the coffee rising when the container is 5 cm full of coffee? We will work through a simple example before outlining the rules.

The first thing you have to learn is that whatever we are studying, we are examining its behavior over time. As a result, we will be taking derivatives with respect to time, so our derivatives will be of the form df/dt.

EXAMPLE

A spaceship is rising vertically from the ground at a rate of 8000 miles per hour. A radar is situated 6 miles away from the launch pad, and it is tracking the distance the spaceship is moving away from the radar. When the ship is 8 miles above the ground, how quickly is it moving away from the radar?

Solution: We first draw a picture of what is happening.

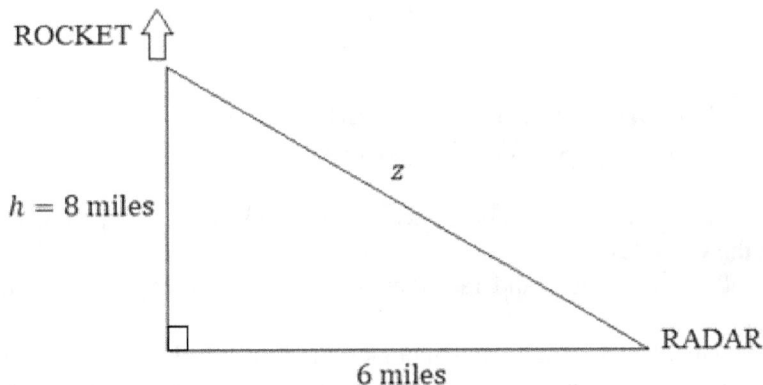

Let z denote the distance from the spaceship to the radar, and let h be the height of the spaceship off the ground. In this particular snapshot, $h = 8$. Meanwhile, the distance from the radar to the launch pad is fixed at 6 miles. Also, the statement about the spaceship rising at 8000 miles per hour tells us that this number is a rate. Specifically, the height is increasing at 8000 mph, so we write $dh/dt = 8000$.

Now let's think about a mathematical relationship between z and h. Since we have a triangle image, let's use the Pythagorean Theorem.

$$h^2 + 6^2 = z^2$$

This is the relationship! We also need to know what z is at this moment. This is not difficult:

$$8^2 + 6^2 = z^2$$
$$100 = z^2$$
$$z = 10$$

(Although $z = -10$ is another solution, it does not apply here since distance cannot be negative.) Now we differentiate $h^2 + 6^2 = z^2$ with respect to time t, and we use implicit differentiation. That means we will use the derivative of h with respect to time (dh/dt) and the derivative of z with respect to time (dz/dt).

$$2h \cdot \frac{dh}{dt} + 0 = 2z \cdot \frac{dz}{dt}$$
$$h \cdot \frac{dh}{dt} + 0 = z \cdot \frac{dz}{dt}$$

Now let's substitute in what we already know: $h = 8$, $z = 10$, and $dh/dt = 8000$.

$$(8)(8000) = (10) \cdot \frac{dz}{dt}$$
$$\frac{dz}{dt} = 6400$$

To answer the question, the spaceship is moving away from the radar at 6400 miles per hour when it is 8 miles above the ground.

Δ

And that is how related rates work! Here is a little process to follow (and again, Step 0 is so called because I want you to make a sketch before doing anything else; that way you'll more easily see what needs to be done).

METHOD FOR SOLVING RELATED RATE PROBLEMS
The following procedure should be used for solving related rate problems.

Step 0: Draw a sketch so you can see for yourself what is going on. This will also be useful in spotting any relationships among the variables.
Step 1: Make a list of every variable and rate that is given. Variables will be letters, while rates are derivatives with respect to time t.
Step 2: Spot a mathematical relationship that includes the non-rate letters. This could be an equation involving the Pythagorean Theorem, a volume or area formula, or sometimes it may involve similar triangles.
Step 3: Find the values of any missing variables before you take the derivative of anything.
Step 4: You should have the formulas in terms of two variables, dependent and independent. If there are any more, you will have to write them in terms of one variable.
Step 5: Find the derivative of the related rate formula with respect to time.
Step 6: Substitute in the known values *after* you find the derivative. Don't do it before!
Step 7: Find the missing value/rate you are after. Make sure you name the units correctly (miles per hour, centimeters per second, liters per minute, etc.).
Step 8: If you get a negative answer, it means that the rate is decreasing rather than increasing.
Step 9: Answer the original question in a sentence or two.

EXAMPLE
All the edges of a cube are increasing at a rate of 4 cm per second. When the edge measures 6 cm, how fast is the volume of the cube changing?

Solution: Here is a sketch:

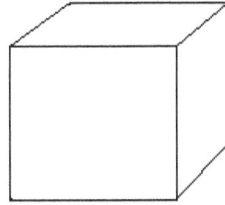

$$w = 5\text{cm}$$

Let's use w (for "width") to represent the length of an edge. (We are not using e for "edge" to avoid confusion with $e = 2.718$!) We are given the following:

1) $dw/dt = 4$ cm/s
2) $w = 5$ cm
3) $dV/dt = ?$ cm^3/s

We are interested in the volume of the cube since we are trying to find dV/dt. Since the edges all have the same length, the volume of the cube is $V = w^3$. Then the derivative is

$$\frac{dV}{dt} = 3w^2 \cdot \frac{dw}{dt}$$

Substituting in our known variables, we get

$$\frac{dV}{dt} = 3(5)^2 \cdot 4 = 300$$

The volume of the box is therefore increasing at a rate of 300 cm^3/s (cubic centimeters per second) when the edges are 5 cm.

Δ

EXAMPLE
A coffeemaker is pouring coffee into a cylindrical glass pot at the rate of 1400 cubic centimeters per minute. When the pot is 6 centimeters full of coffee, how quickly is the coffee rising if 1200 cubic centimeters of coffee are in the pot at that moment?

Solution: Here is a sketch. Notice we have a cylinder where the coffee has height h, and we want to know how the height is changing.

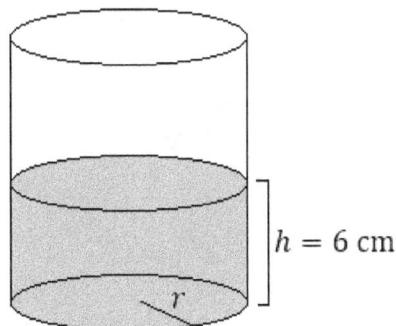

$$h = 6 \text{ cm}$$

Let's list the variables we have been given.

1) $dV/dt = 1400$ cm^3/min
2) $h = 6$ cm
3) $V = 1200$ cm^3
4) $dh/dt =?$ cm/min

Using our knowledge of geometry, the volume of a cylinder is $V = \pi r^2 h$ where r is the radius of the coffee pot. If you think about it, as the coffee rises, the radius of the pot will stay the same, so we can use the volume formula to solve for r:

$$V = \pi r^2 h \Rightarrow 1200 = \pi r^2 \cdot 6 \Rightarrow r^2 = \frac{200}{\pi}$$
$$\Rightarrow r \approx 7.97885$$

Next, we differentiate volume with respect to time. Be careful – here radius is constant, so we don't differentiate it!

$$\frac{dV}{dt} = \pi r^2 \cdot \frac{dh}{dt}$$
$$1400 = \pi \left(\frac{200}{\pi}\right) \cdot \frac{dh}{dt}$$

Actually, since radius appears as r^2, we didn't need to find the square root of it; we just needed r^2. This makes calculations considerably easier!

$$1400 = \pi \left(\frac{200}{\pi}\right) \cdot \frac{dh}{dt} \Rightarrow 1400 = 200 \cdot \frac{dh}{dt}$$
$$\Rightarrow \frac{dh}{dt} = 7$$

The height of the coffee is rising at 7 centimeters per minute when the coffee pot has 6 centimeters of coffee inside. (Since I am English, may I suggest tea instead!)

Δ

EXAMPLE
Sand is falling onto a cone-shaped pile at the rate of 10 cubic feet per minute. Suppose the diameter of the base of this cone is always 3 times the height of the cone. At what rate is the height of the sand pile changing when the pile is 5 feet high? (This is actually a classic calculus problem!)

Solution: Here is a sketch of the cone-shaped pile of sand.

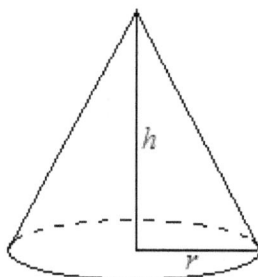

We have a bit more work to do here. Let's start by listing what we know:

1) Since sand is falling onto the cone, and we are given the value in cubic feet per minute, we are discussing how the volume is changing. So the volume of the cone is increasing at 10 cubic feet per minute, which means $dV/dt = 10$.
2) The diameter (twice the radius) is 3 times the cone's height, so $2r = 3h$.
3) At this snapshot in time, $h = 5$.
4) We want to find dh/dt.

Said more succinctly,

1) $dV/dt = 10 \text{ft}^3/\text{min}$
2) $2r = 3h$
3) $h = 5 \text{ ft}$
4) $dh/dt = ? \text{ ft/min}$

Next, we need to know the formula for the volume of a right cone. That formula is

$$V = \frac{1}{3}\pi r^2 h$$

Before we do anything to this, we need to get rid of one of the variables, r or h. Choosing to solve for r in terms of h, we use the radius-height relationship to get $r = \frac{3}{2}h$. We substitute this into the volume:

$$V = \frac{1}{3}\pi r^2 h = \frac{1}{3}\pi \left(\frac{3}{2}h\right)^2 h = \frac{1}{3}\pi \cdot \frac{9}{4}h^2 \cdot h$$
$$V = \frac{3}{4}\pi h^3$$

Differentiating this, we get

$$\frac{dV}{dt} = \frac{3}{4}\pi \cdot 3h^2 \cdot \frac{dh}{dt}$$
$$\frac{dV}{dt} = \frac{9}{4}\pi h^2 \cdot \frac{dh}{dt}$$

Substituting in the known variables, we have

$$10 = \frac{9}{4}\pi \cdot (5)^2 \cdot \frac{dh}{dt}$$
$$10 = \frac{225}{4}\pi \cdot \frac{dh}{dt}$$
$$10 \cdot \frac{4}{225\pi} = \frac{dh}{dt}$$
$$\frac{dh}{dt} = \frac{40}{225\pi} = \frac{8}{45\pi} \approx 0.05659$$

The height of the sand pile is increasing at $8/45\pi$ ft/min (feet per minute) when the pile is 5 feet high.

Δ

EXAMPLE
It would be good to see an example where the rates are negative. A spherical medicinal tablet is submersed in a glass of water and is dissolving at a rate of 0.02 cubic centimeters per second. When the tablet's radius is 0.5 centimeters, how quickly is the radius shrinking?

Solution: We are told the following.

1) $dV/dt = -0.02$ cm^3/s
2) $r = 0.5$ cm
3) $dr/dt =?$ cm/s

Note the negative sign for dV/dt because the tablet is dissolving and therefore losing volume. Since the tablet is spherical, we can use the volume for a sphere:

$$V = \frac{4}{3}\pi r^3$$

Differentiating with respect to time,

$$\frac{dV}{dt} = \frac{4}{3}\pi \cdot 3r^2 \cdot \frac{dr}{dt} = 4\pi r^2 \cdot \frac{dr}{dt}$$

Substituting in what we know,

$$-0.02 = 4\pi(0.5)^2 \cdot \frac{dr}{dt} \Rightarrow -0.02 = 1 \cdot \pi \cdot \frac{dr}{dt}$$
$$\Rightarrow \frac{dr}{dt} = -\frac{0.02}{\pi} = -\frac{1}{50\pi} \approx -0.00637$$

The tablet's radius is decreasing at the rate of $1/50\pi$ centimeters per second when the tablet's radius is 0.5 centimeters. Notice that instead of writing the negative sign, we remove it and use the word "decreasing" in the sentence. That's the practical interpretation of a negative rate in this case.

Δ

Section 3.10 – Applications of Derivatives to Other Subjects
In this fun section we go through several examples of real-life problems that involve differential calculus using tools we have learned up until now.

EXAMPLE (APPLICATION TO ART)
Find the critical points for $g(x) = \frac{1}{3}x^3 - \frac{1}{2}x^2 - x$.

Solution: This is straightforward: we just find the derivative and set it equal to 0.

$$g'(x) = \frac{1}{3}\cdot 3x^2 - \frac{1}{2}\cdot 2x - 1 = x^2 - x - 1 = 0$$

Using the quadratic formula, the two critical points are

$$x = \frac{-(-1) \pm \sqrt{(-1)^2 - 4(1)(-1)}}{2} = \frac{1 \pm \sqrt{5}}{2} \approx -0.61803, 1.61803$$

What, you ask, does this problem have to do with art? One of the critical points (to three decimals) is 1.618, and this number is called the Golden Ratio, often denoted by the Greek letter ϕ (pronounced "fai"). This number (sometimes called the divine proportion) shows up a lot in nature, sometimes in unexpected ways, and consequently in art and architecture. It typically arises when considering the ratio of the length of something to the length of a similar object, and in the context of art, such proportions often look appealing and aesthetically pleasing. The following are just a few of many examples of when the Golden Ratio appears.

1) If you look at the height of a typical Christian cross or crucifix and divide it by the length of the crossbeam, chances are good the ratio will be close to 1.618.
2) Given a colony of bees, the number of females divided by the number of males is usually close to 1.618.
3) Rectangles, triangles, and even star shapes exhibiting the Golden Ratio can be drawn over many famous paintings to illustrate how people or parts of their bodies were sketched. Artists of such paintings include Leonardo da Vinci, Raphael, Michelangelo, and Salvador Dali, among many others.
4) Spirals drawn in certain ways according to the Golden Ratio appear a lot in nature, for instance in sunflowers, pine cones, nautilus shells, hurricanes, and even galaxies.

Δ

EXAMPLE (APPLICATION TO LINGUISTICS)
In linguistics (the study of languages, especially their structure), there is a well-known formula called Zipf's Law (named after the American linguist George Zipf) that gives a relationship between the frequency of a word in a language (f) and its rank (r). In the English language, it has been shown that this relationship can be approximated by $f = 0.1/r$. For instance, the most common word in English is *the* ($r = 1$) with an estimated frequency of $f = 0.1$ (or 10%), and the second most common word is *of* ($r = 2$) with an estimated frequency of $f = 0.05$ (or 5%).

A) Find the derivative of frequency with respect to rank.
B) Find the equation of the tangent line for the tenth most common English word.

Solution: Part A is a straightforward derivative after rewriting $f = 0.1r^{-1}$:

$$\frac{df}{dr} = -0.1r^{-2} = -\frac{0.1}{r^2}$$

For part B, the slope of the tangent line at $r = 10$ is

$$\frac{df}{dr}\bigg|_{r=10} = -\frac{0.1}{10^2} = -0.001 = -\frac{1}{1000}$$

The point at $r = 10$ is

$$f(10) = \frac{0.1}{10} = 0.01 = \frac{1}{100}$$

Thus, the tangent line at $r = 10$ (using f instead of y and r instead of x) is

$$f - 0.01 = -0.001(r - 10) \Rightarrow f = -0.001r + 0.01 + 0.01$$
$$\Rightarrow f = -0.001r + 0.02$$
$$\Rightarrow f = -\frac{1}{1000}r + \frac{1}{50}$$

Δ

EXAMPLE (APPLICATION TO ECONOMICS)

Economics is the study of using limited resources and applying them to supply and demand. One application concerns finding the optimal number of units to sell that will maximize a company's profit on an item. Suppose a company sells x lawnmowers and makes a revenue of $R(x) = 300x - 2x^2$, but the cost of producing x mowers is $C(x) = 5000 + 40x$. Find the number of mowers this company should sell to maximize profit, and find the maximum profit.

Solution: The key to solving these profit problems is to recognize that profit is equal to revenue minus cost. (For instance, if you sell something for \$20 that cost you \$12 to make, your profit would be \$8.) Let's state our revenue and cost functions:

$$R(x) = 300x - 2x^2$$
$$C(x) = 5000 + 40x$$

The profit function $P(x)$ is then revenue minus cost:

$$P(x) = (300x - 2x^2) - (5000 + 40x)$$
$$P(x) = -2x^2 + 260x - 5000$$

Recognize that the lowest number of mowers we can sell is 0, while there technically is no upper bound. That means the domain is $[0, \infty)$. Since we want to maximize the profit, we take the derivative and find the critical points.

$$P'(x) = -4x + 260 = 0$$
$$x = 65$$

Thus, $P(65) = -2(65)^2 + 260(65) - 5000 = 3450$. This means that to get the maximum profit, we should sell 65 mowers, making the maximum profit \$3,450.

Of course, to be really official, we need to check the endpoints of the profit function to verify that $x = 65$ really is a maximum. We can easily see that $P(0) = -2(0)^2 + 260(0) - 5000 = -5000$, which is lower than 3450. As for the upper endpoint, rather than evaluating at infinity, let's just pick an x larger than 65, say $x = 100$. That means the profit is $P(100) = -2(100)^2 + 260(100) - 5000 = 1000$, so selling $x = 65$ mowers still results in a higher profit. We are in business – literally!

Δ

EXAMPLE (APPLICATION TO CRYPTOGRAPHY)

Cryptography is the mathematical study of building and deciphering codes. One application in this field is called an elliptic curve, whose general equation is given by $y^2 = x^3 + ax + b$ where a and b are given constants. (One use of elliptic curves is to ensure that a message can be transmitted online with hopefully little chance that the wrong person intercepts the message and decodes it.) Find the first and second derivatives of y with respect to x. The graph for $a = 2$ and $b = 0$ is shown below.

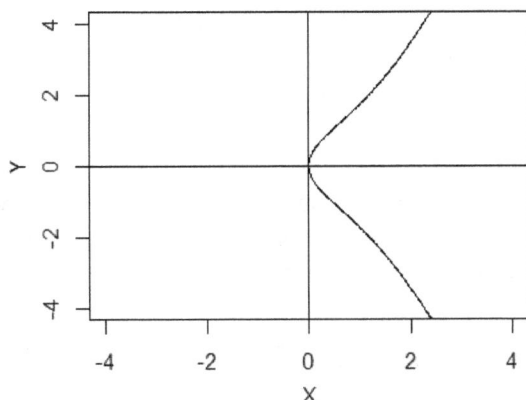

Solution: Using implicit differentiation (and treating a and b as constants), the first derivative is

$$2yy' = 3x^2 + a$$
$$y' = \frac{3x^2 + a}{2y}$$

The second derivative is

$$y'' = \frac{(2y)(6x) - (3x^2 + a)2y'}{(2y)^2} = \frac{12xy - 2(3x^2 + a)y'}{4y^2}$$
$$= \frac{6xy - (3x^2 + a)y'}{2y^2}$$

Since we don't usually want first derivatives as part of the answer, let's push on:

$$y'' = \frac{6xy - (3x^2 + a)\left(\frac{3x^2 + a}{2y}\right)}{2y^2} = \frac{6xy\left(\frac{2y}{2y}\right) - (3x^2 + a)\left(\frac{3x^2 + a}{2y}\right)}{2y^2}$$
$$= \frac{12xy^2 - (3x^2 + a)^2}{(2y)(2y^2)} = \frac{12xy^2 - (3x^2 + a)^2}{4y^3}$$

We can stop here, or we can use the fact that $y^2 = x^3 + ax + b$ to further simplify our answer. Let's substitute that into the numerator and leave the denominator alone because there the y is cubed:

$$y'' = \frac{12x(x^3 + ax + b) - (3x^2 + a)^2}{4y^3}$$
$$= \frac{(12x^4 + 12ax^2 + 12bx) - (9x^4 + 6ax^2 + a^2)}{4y^3}$$
$$= \frac{12x^4 + 12ax^2 + 12bx - 9x^4 - 6ax^2 - a^2}{4y^3}$$
$$= \frac{3x^4 + 6ax^2 + 12bx - a^2}{4y^3}$$

This is probably the cleanest we can get for the second derivative. If you wanted to substitute in $y^2 = x^3 + ax + b$ on the denominator as well, the result would be

$$y'' = \frac{3x^4 + 6ax^2 + 12bx - a^2}{4(x^3 + ax + b)y}$$

Δ

EXAMPLE (APPLICATION TO STATISTICS)

This last example is from my field of expertise! Statistics is the science of studying numerical characteristics of a population by examining random samples and making conclusions about the population. Many problems in statistics involve the normal distribution, also known as a bell curve, whose function is defined by

$$f(x) = \frac{1}{\sqrt{2\pi}} e^{-x^2/2}, \quad -\infty < x < \infty$$

This function is called the standard normal distribution with mean 0 and standard deviation 1.

A) Find the y-intercept and x-intercepts, if any, as well as any vertical and horizontal asymptotes.
B) Find where the standard normal distribution achieves its maximum, and state the maximum value.
C) Describe the concavity of the standard normal distribution.

Solution: For part A, the y-intercept is at

$$f(0) = \frac{1}{\sqrt{2\pi}} e^{-(0)^2/2} = \frac{1}{\sqrt{2\pi}} \cdot 1 = \frac{1}{\sqrt{2\pi}}$$

Thus, the y-intercept is $\left(0, 1/\sqrt{2\pi}\right)$, or approximately $(0, 0.39894)$. Noting that $e^{-x^2/2} > 0$ for all real values of x, that means $f(x) > 0$ for all x, and therefore there are no x-intercepts.

As for the asymptotes, the function exists everywhere, so there are no vertical asymptotes. However, as x goes to positive infinity, the function approaches 0, and the same is true as x goes to negative infinity. (You can see this by substituting large positive or negative values for x and seeing that the answer is very close to 0.) For that reason, there is a horizontal asymptote at $y = 0$. (If it helps, recognize that $1/\sqrt{2\pi}$ is just a constant, which makes finding the derivatives easier.)

For part B, the first derivative is

$$f'(x) = \frac{1}{\sqrt{2\pi}} e^{-x^2/2} \cdot -\frac{2x}{2}$$
$$= -\frac{1}{\sqrt{2\pi}} x e^{-x^2/2}$$

Setting this equal to 0 results in

$$xe^{-x^2/2} = 0$$

Since $e^{-x^2/2}$ is always positive, the first derivative is 0 only at $x = 0$. Picking points on either side establishes the nature of this critical point.

1) $(-\infty, 0)$, pick $x = -1$
$$f'(-1) = -\frac{1}{\sqrt{2\pi}} \cdot (-1) \cdot e^{-(-1)^2/2} = \frac{1}{\sqrt{2\pi}} \cdot e^{-1/2} > 0, \text{ positive}$$

2) $(0, \infty)$, pick $x = 1$

$$f'(1) = -\frac{1}{\sqrt{2\pi}} \cdot (1) \cdot e^{-\frac{(1)^2}{2}} = -\frac{1}{\sqrt{2\pi}} \cdot e^{-1/2} < 0, \text{ negative}$$

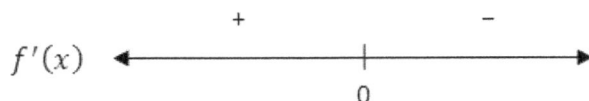

$$f'(x) \qquad \xleftarrow{\qquad + \qquad | \qquad - \qquad} $$
$$\qquad\qquad\qquad\qquad 0$$

Thus, $f(x)$ is increasing on $(-\infty, 0)$ and decreasing on $(0, \infty)$, which makes $x = 0$ a maximum. This happens to be the same as the y-intercept, $(0, 1/\sqrt{2\pi})$. For part C, the second derivative is

$$f''(x) = -\frac{1}{\sqrt{2\pi}}\left[1 \cdot e^{-x^2/2} + x \cdot e^{-x^2/2} \cdot -\frac{2x}{2}\right]$$
$$= -\frac{1}{\sqrt{2\pi}} e^{-x^2/2}(1 - x^2)$$

Setting this equal to 0 results in

$$e^{-x^2/2}(1 - x^2) = 0$$

Since $e^{-x^2/2} > 0$, that means the only two points where the second derivative is 0 are $x = -1$ and $x = 1$. Let's do our second derivative test.

1) $(-\infty, -1)$, pick $x = -2$
$$f''(-2) = -\frac{1}{\sqrt{2\pi}} e^{-(-2)^2/2}(1 - (-2)^2) = \frac{3}{\sqrt{2\pi}} \cdot e^{-2} > 0, \text{ positive}$$

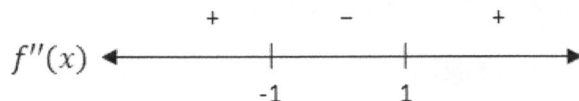

2) $(-1, 1)$, pick $x = 0$
$$f''(0) = -\frac{1}{\sqrt{2\pi}} e^{-(0)^2/2}(1 - (0)^2) = -\frac{1}{\sqrt{2\pi}} \cdot 1 < 0, \text{ negative}$$

3) $(1, \infty)$, pick $x = 2$
$$f''(2) = -\frac{1}{\sqrt{2\pi}} e^{-(2)^2/2}(1 - (2)^2) = \frac{3}{\sqrt{2\pi}} \cdot e^{-2} > 0, \text{ positive}$$

$$f''(x) \qquad \xleftarrow{\qquad + \qquad | \qquad - \qquad | \qquad + \qquad}$$
$$\qquad\qquad\qquad\qquad -1 \qquad\quad 1$$

Thus, $f(x)$ is concave up on $(-\infty, 1)$ and $(1, \infty)$ and concave down on $(-1, 1)$, which makes $x = -1$ and $x = 1$ inflection points. The y-coordinates are

$$f(-1) = \frac{1}{\sqrt{2\pi}} e^{-(-1)^2/2} = \frac{1}{\sqrt{2\pi}} e^{-1/2} = \frac{1}{\sqrt{2\pi e}} \approx 0.24197$$
$$f(1) = \frac{1}{\sqrt{2\pi}} e^{-(1)^2/2} = \frac{1}{\sqrt{2\pi}} e^{-1/2} = \frac{1}{\sqrt{2\pi e}} \approx 0.24197$$

The last step came from noting that $e^{-1/2}$ is the same as $1/\sqrt{e}$, and so we can multiply that by $1/\sqrt{2\pi}$. Thus, the two inflection points are $(-1, 1/\sqrt{2\pi e})$ and $(1, 1/\sqrt{2\pi e})$, or $(-1, 0.24197)$ and $(1, 0.24197)$. The graph of the standard normal distribution looks like the following.

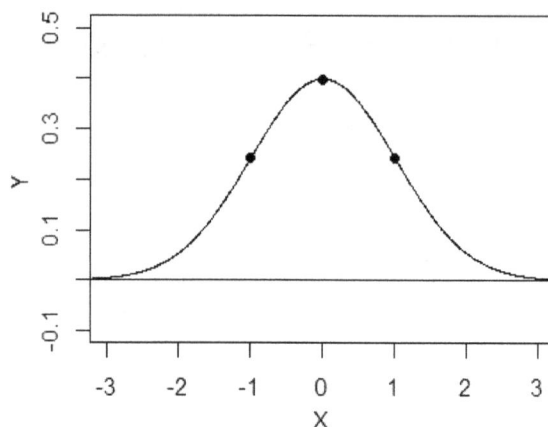

If you want to learn more about statistics (from a non-calculus point of view), then I recommend a really good book called *Chris Notes! A Set of Notes for Introductory Statistics*, written by someone you might have heard of!

Δ

Section 3.11 – Newton's Method

Here we discuss an algorithm to find the roots of functions using the calculator, so let's first remind ourselves of what a root is.

DEFINITION

The **roots** of a function $f(x)$, if any exist, are the x-coordinates at which $f(x) = 0$.

There are some functions for which we can easily find the roots with formulas, and good examples of these are lines, quadratics, and certain simple trig functions. However, there are plenty of functions where it is difficult or impossible to find the roots on paper, in which case a computer or graphing calculator can come to the rescue. There are many different computational algorithms that can be used, but the one we focus on in this section is called Newton's Method (sometimes called the Newton-Raphson Method), named after the English mathematicians Sir Isaac Newton and Joseph Raphson.

We won't go into a rigorous proof of this algorithm, but here's an idea of how it works. First, suppose we want to estimate the root of $f(x) = 0$. Looking at a graph, suppose we have made an initial guess x_0 for where the root is (it does not have to be an accurate guess, but for technical reasons it should be relatively near). Then the point of the function at x_0 is given by $(x_0, f(x_0))$, and the slope of the tangent line at that point is $f'(x_0)$. Using the point-slope formula with the tangent line's slope, the tangent line equation is

$$y - f(x_0) = f'(x_0)(x - x_0)$$
$$y = f(x_0) + f'(x_0)(x - x_0)$$

The following graph shows where this tangent line might fall.

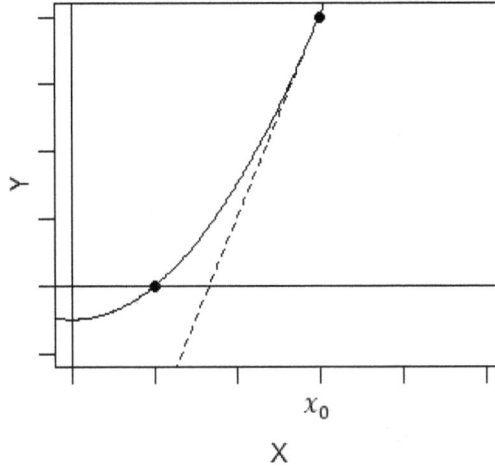

Remember that x_0 is the initial guess for the root. We are now going to define the coordinate $(x_1, 0)$ (note the 0 y-coordinate since this point is assumed to be the root). Putting this into the above formula and rearranging the formula results in

$$0 = f(x_0) + f'(x_0)(x_1 - x_0)$$
$$0 = f(x_0) + x_1 f'(x_0) - x_0 f'(x_0)$$
$$x_1 f'(x_0) = x_0 f'(x_0) - f(x_0)$$
$$x_1 = \frac{x_0 f'(x_0)}{f'(x_0)} - \frac{f(x_0)}{f'(x_0)}$$
$$x_1 = x_0 - \frac{f(x_0)}{f'(x_0)}$$

Thus, we have written the new point x_1 in terms of the initial guess x_0. That means that (hopefully) x_1 will be a better guess than x_0 was, as can be seen in the following graph.

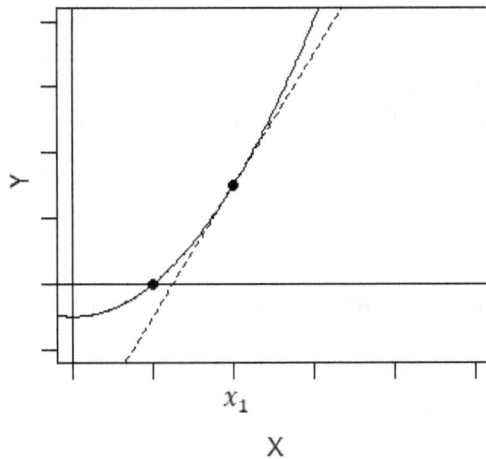

Next, we can improve our guess by putting x_1 into the same formula to arrive at a better guess x_2:

$$x_2 = x_1 - \frac{f(x_1)}{f'(x_1)}$$

We can do this again to get an even better guess x_3, and by repeatedly using this "recursive" formula, the algorithm (usually) settles down at a specific answer after a certain number of iterations. This is how Newton's Method finds a root to a function!

NEWTON'S METHOD

Let $f(x)$ be a differentiable function, and it is of interest to find the roots; that is, the x-values where $f(x) = 0$. Let x_0 be reasonably close to one of the roots. Then that root can be numerically approximated in a recursive manner using the formula

$$x_{n+1} = x_n - \frac{f(x_n)}{f'(x_n)}$$

The more iterations performed (as n increases), usually the better the approximation to the root.

To start the algorithm, given an initial value x_0, the first iteration is computed as

$$x_1 = x_0 - \frac{f(x_0)}{f'(x_0)}$$

If x_0 was "reasonable enough," then x_1 will be a better approximation to the root. The next step is

$$x_2 = x_1 - \frac{f(x_1)}{f'(x_1)}$$

Hence, x_2 should be an even better approximation to the root. By repeating these steps, the approximation will generally get more accurate. It is up to us to decide how close is close. As you probably have guessed, we will need to use our calculator to perform this algorithm.

EXAMPLE

Find the positive root of the function $f(x) = x^2 - 16$ using Newton's Method.

Solution: Of course, we can quickly see that the two roots are $x = 4$ and $x = -4$, but this is a good starting example because it will be easy to illustrate how to use Newton's Method on something for which we already know the answer. We want to end up with the positive root $x = 4$. First, let's determine the recursive formula to use. We know that $f(x) = x^2 - 16$ and therefore $f'(x) = 2x$, so

$$x_{n+1} = x_n - \frac{(x_n^2 - 16)}{2x_n}$$

Let's choose an initial guess of $x_0 = 10$. Then x_1 is computed as

$$x_1 = x_0 - \frac{(x_0^2 - 16)}{2x_0} = 10 - \frac{((10)^2 - 16)}{2(10)} = 10 - 4.2 = 5.8$$

We have $x_1 = 5.8$, which is a closer approximation to the positive root than $x_0 = 10$ was. Let's get the next iteration now:

$$x_2 = x_1 - \frac{(x_1^2 - 16)}{2x_1} = 5.8 - \frac{((5.8)^2 - 16)}{2(5.8)} \approx 4.279310345$$

Thus, $x_2 \approx 4.279310345$ is a better approximation than $x_1 = 5.8$. Continuing,

$$x_3 = x_2 - \frac{(x_2^2 - 16)}{2x_2} \approx 4.279310345 - \frac{((4.279310345)^2 - 16)}{2(4.279310345)} \approx 4.009115285$$

$$x_4 = x_3 - \frac{(x_3^2 - 16)}{2x_3} \approx 4.009115285 - \frac{((4.009115285)^2 - 16)}{2(4.009115285)} \approx 4.000010362$$

$$x_5 = x_4 - \frac{(x_4^2 - 16)}{2x_4} \approx 4.000010362 - \frac{((4.000010362)^2 - 16)}{2(4.000010362)} \approx 4.000000000$$

After only five iterations, it is clear that Newton's Method is going toward 4 as the positive root. What if we had started with a different initial guess? Usually the algorithm will still give you the root you need. For instance, suppose we instead used $x_0 = 20$. Then the following happens:

$$x_1 = x_0 - \frac{(x_0^2 - 16)}{2x_0} = 20 - \frac{((20)^2 - 16)}{2(20)} = 10.4$$

$$x_2 = x_1 - \frac{(x_1^2 - 16)}{2x_1} = 10.4 - \frac{((10.4)^2 - 16)}{2(10.4)} \approx 5.969230769$$

$$x_3 = x_2 - \frac{(x_2^2 - 16)}{2x_2} \approx 5.969230769 - \frac{((5.969230769)^2 - 16)}{2(5.969230769)} \approx 4.3248215$$

$$x_4 = x_3 - \frac{(x_3^2 - 16)}{2x_3} \approx 4.32482157 - \frac{((4.32482157)^2 - 16)}{2(4.32482157)} \approx 4.012198082$$

$$x_5 = x_4 - \frac{(x_4^2 - 16)}{2x_4} \approx 4.012198082 - \frac{((4.012198082)^2 - 16)}{2(4.012198082)} \approx 4.000018543$$

$$x_6 = x_5 - \frac{(x_5^2 - 16)}{2x_5} \approx 4.000018543 - \frac{((4.000018543)^2 - 16)}{2(4.000018543)} \approx 4.000000000$$

This time it took six iterations, but we still got the answer. As a side note, I also tried using $x_0 = 1,000,000$, and Newton's Method still resulted in 4.000000000 as the approximation, although doing so required 22 iterations!

Δ

At this point, it would be good to describe an efficient way to use the TI-84 to perform Newton's Method. There are a few ways to do this, but the following method is very straightforward.

TI-84 COMMAND: NEWTON'S METHOD

First know what your $f(x)$ and $f'(x)$ functions are. Type your initial guess as a number and press $\boxed{\text{ENTER}}$. Your number will appear on the screen as is. Next, we are going to repeatedly use the *Ans* (answer) feature that uses the previously found answer (in this case, the initial guess you just entered). Pressing $\boxed{\text{2nd}}$ and $\boxed{\text{(-)}}$ puts Ans on the screen. Using this feature, type

$$\text{Ans} - f(\text{Ans})/f'(\text{Ans})$$

Of course, you will replace the $f(\text{Ans})$ with the given function with Ans as the variable, and likewise for the derivative. Press $\boxed{\text{ENTER}}$, and the calculator gives you the first iteration x_1. Now press $\boxed{\text{ENTER}}$ repeatedly until the answer shown no longer changes.

EXAMPLE

Using your calculator, find the only real root of $f(x) = 2x^3 - x^2 + 3x + 1$.

Solution: We want to see where $f(x) = 0$. Just to see what we are up against, let's graph this cubic function to get an idea of where the root might be. Using your calculator, the graph looks like this:

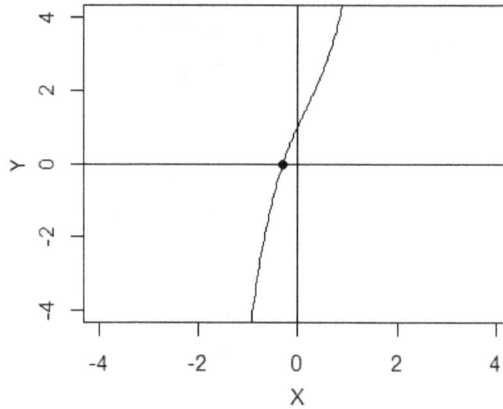

The root is clearly between -1 and 0, so let's use $x_0 = -1$ as an initial guess. The derivative is $f'(x) = 6x^2 - 2x + 3$, and so the formula to work with is

$$x_{n+1} = x_n - \frac{2x_n^3 - x_n^2 + 3x_n + 1}{6x_n^2 - 2x_n + 3}$$

Type -1 and press $\boxed{\text{ENTER}}$. Now using the $\boxed{\text{2nd}}$ and $\boxed{(-)}$ buttons a total of six times, type the following onto your calculator screen:

$$\text{Ans} - (2\text{Ans}^\wedge 3 - \text{Ans}^2 + 3\text{Ans} + 1)/(6\text{Ans}^2 - 2\text{Ans} + 3)$$

Press $\boxed{\text{ENTER}}$, and the answer is -0.5454545455. Press $\boxed{\text{ENTER}}$ again, and this time you get -0.3312875591 for the next iteration. Keep pressing $\boxed{\text{ENTER}}$, and you will end up with -0.2904800418, -0.2892960106, and -0.2892950691. If you keep going, the answer will be the same, which means to ten decimal places we have arrived at the root to the cubic function. That means with an initial guess of $x_0 = -1$, after five iterations we ended up with $x_5 \approx -0.2892950691$, which intuitively makes sense based on the earlier graph.

If we had tried a different initial guess, then most likely we would end up with the same answer, albeit possibly after a different number of iterations. (As a side note, this cubic function in fact has three roots, only one of which is real, the one we found. The other two roots are complex, which we don't worry about in this class.)

Δ

You might be wondering why we looked at a graph to get an initial guess. That is not cheating; it ensures that our guess is relatively close to the true root. Why do more calculator iterations than we need? In the previous example, choosing $x_0 = -1$ or $x_0 = 0$ would be good choices based on the graph, but it would be foolish to choose, say, $x_0 = 1000$. We might as well start our "journey" close to the root to cut down on the number of steps needed. You need a calculator to do Newton's Method, so why not use it effectively?

EXAMPLE

Let's try a problem that is set up differently. Find the x-value at which the functions $f(x) = x^5 + 2x^3 - 3x^2 + 2x - 1$ and $g(x) = 4$ intersect.

Solution: A root, by definition, is an x-value at which a function is equal to 0. To use that idea here, we need to find the x-value where $f(x) = g(x)$. The graph from the TI-84 looks like the following.

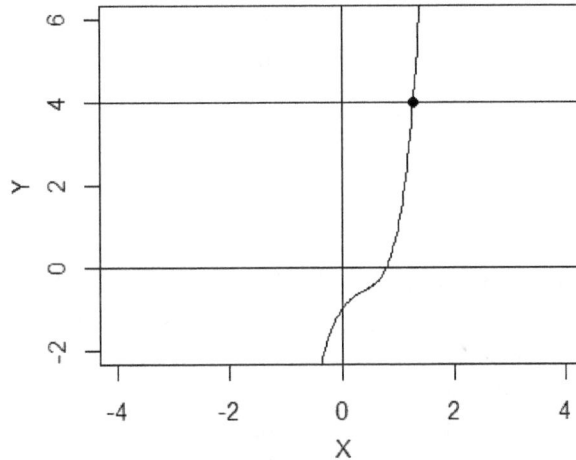

The intersection point appears to be between 1 and 2. The way to solve this problem is to define a new function $h(x) = f(x) - g(x) = x^5 + 2x^3 - 3x^2 + 2x - 5$, and the goal is to find where $h(x) = 0$. Now that we have the function of interest, Newton's Method can be used. We have

$$h(x) = x^5 + 2x^3 - 3x^2 + 2x - 5$$
$$h'(x) = 5x^4 + 6x^2 - 6x + 2$$

The recursive formula is

$$x_{n+1} = x_n - \frac{x_n^5 + 2x_n^3 - 3x_n^2 + 2x_n - 5}{5x_n^4 + 6x_n^2 - 6x_n + 2}$$

Going for the root, let's choose $x_0 = 2$. Using the TI-84 method described earlier, the resulting calculations are 1.627659574, 1.388071378, 1.283093428, 1.264500309, 1.263975654, and 1.263975247, and any subsequent iterations give the same number. Thus, after six iterations, we have determined that $f(x)$ and $g(x)$ intersect at $x \approx 1.263975247$.

Δ

You will note I have been saying that Newton's Method generally or usually works. Are there instances when it fails to give the correct root? The answer is yes – there are certain situations when the method will not stop at the root, although we won't go into the exact circumstances when this happens. One example is $f(x) = x^4 + 2x - \sin(x) - 1$, which has two roots. The positive root is between 0 and 1, so for illustration let's choose $x_0 = 1$.

Using the TI-84 method described earlier, the first ten calculations (to three decimals) are 0.421, -0.635, -3.483, -2.634, -2.003, -1.532, -1.174, -0.871, -0.405, and -1.155. You can see that here Newton's Method is bouncing around and not "settling" to a specific number. The same thing happens when we try a different starting value. Thus, it's important to realize that this numerical method of finding roots is very useful but not entirely foolproof.

While we are on the subject of numerical methods, let's go over a couple of useful TI-84 commands to find roots of a function, as well as where two curves intersect.

TI-84 COMMAND: FINDING ROOTS OF A FUNCTION

To find an x-value at which a function $f(x) = 0$, first press $\boxed{Y =}$ and type the function next to Y_1. Adjust the window as necessary, and press $\boxed{\text{GRAPH}}$. If the window is appropriate, you will see the function and the general area at which it crosses the x-axix.

Next, press $\boxed{\text{2nd}}$ and $\boxed{\text{TRACE}}$ to go to the CALC menu. Select Option 2: *zero*, and you'll return to the graph. The calculator says "Left Bound?", so type a guess and press $\boxed{\text{ENTER}}$. The calculator then says "Right Bound?", so type a guess and press $\boxed{\text{ENTER}}$ again. Finally, the calculator says "Guess?", so type an x-value that looks to be close to the root and press $\boxed{\text{ENTER}}$. The calculator then shows you the approximate x-coordinate of the root.

TI-84 COMMAND: FINDING INTERSECTION POINTS OF TWO FUNCTIONS

To find the x-values at which two functions $f(x)$ and $g(x)$ intersect, first press $\boxed{Y =}$ and type the two functions next to Y_1 and Y_2. Adjust the window as necessary, and press $\boxed{\text{GRAPH}}$. If the window is appropriate, you will see the two functions and the general area at which they intersect.
Next, press $\boxed{\text{2nd}}$ and $\boxed{\text{TRACE}}$ to go to the CALC menu. Select Option 5: *intersect*, and you'll return to the graph. The calculator says "First curve?", and press $\boxed{\text{ENTER}}$. The calculator then says "Second curve?", and press $\boxed{\text{ENTER}}$ again. Finally, the calculator says "Guess?", so type an x-value that looks to be close to the intersection point and press $\boxed{\text{ENTER}}$. The calculator then shows you the approximate (x, y) coordinates.

EXAMPLE

Using the second example in this section, type in the function $Y_1 = 2X^\wedge 3 - X^2 + 3X + 1$. Looking at the graph, it appears the root is between -1 and 0. Selecting the *zero* feature, enter a reasonable left bound (say -1) and press $\boxed{\text{ENTER}}$. Next, enter a reasonable right bound (say 0) and press $\boxed{\text{ENTER}}$. Finally, enter a reasonable guess for the root (say -0.5) and press $\boxed{\text{ENTER}}$ one more time. The answer is $x \approx -0.2892951$ and $y = 0$.

Using the third example in this section, type in the functions $Y_1 = X^\wedge 5 + 2X^\wedge 3 - 3X^2 + 2X - 1$ and $Y_2 = 4$. Looking at the graph, it appears they intersect between $x = 1$ and $x = 2$. Selecting the *intersect* feature, press $\boxed{\text{ENTER}}$ and $\boxed{\text{ENTER}}$, then enter a reasonable guess for the intersection (say 1) and press $\boxed{\text{ENTER}}$ one more time. The answer is $x \approx 1.2639752$ and $y = 4$.

Δ

We close this section with an interesting afterthought. I mentioned earlier that given a line ($f(x) = ax + b$) or a quadratic function ($f(x) = ax^2 + bx + c$), we can find the roots using established formulas. There is a cubic formula to solve cubic functions ($f(x) = ax^3 + bx^2 + cx + d$), but it should be no surprise to hear that the cubic formula is very complicated. In case you were wondering, there is also a quartic formula to solve quartic functions (fourth-degree polynomials), but it is absolutely horrendous to write down.

Are there general formulas for solving quintic functions (fifth-degree polynomials) or polynomials with higher degrees? The answer is no; the Norwegian mathematician Niels Henrik Abel and the French mathematician Évariste Galois proved that such formulas cannot exist. However, the point is that even if there are formulas, they often get complicated to work on paper, which is why technology can be so useful for solving some equations. If you will excuse me, I won't be writing down the cubic and quartic formulas here!

Section 3.12 – L'Hôpital's Rule

It is now time for a dose of limits. Back in Chapter 1, many of the limits presented needed to be solved by somehow manipulating the function being evaluated. This involved factoring and canceling terms, multiplying by conjugates, and even using geometry of triangles (remember the Sandwich Theorem?). Admittedly, it was a lot of work at the time, but we needed to do it to arrive at the answers. What if there was a shortcut that made evaluating limits easier? We now present it, and the good news is that it is fairly straightforward to use! First, let's define a term we briefly used in Chapter 1, an indeterminate form.

DEFINITION

Suppose we need to evaluate $\lim_{x \to a} f(x)$. The result of substituting a directly into $f(x)$ is called an **indeterminate form** if it takes any of the following seven forms:

$$\frac{0}{0}, \ \frac{\infty}{\infty}, \ 0^0, \ \infty^0, \ \infty - \infty, \ 0 \times \infty, \ 1^\infty$$

An answer appearing in one of these indeterminate forms, by definition, is not a number. Consider the following examples:

$$\lim_{x \to 0} \frac{\sin(x)}{x}, \ \lim_{x \to \infty} \frac{x^2}{x}, \ \lim_{x \to 0} x^x, \ \lim_{x \to 0} (1 + x)^{1/x}$$

If we were to substitute the approaching point of interest for these limits, we would get $0/0$, ∞/∞, 0^0, and 1^∞, respectively. Of course, we cannot write these down and declare them to be our answers to the limits. Fortunately, there is a really useful limit result we can use when substituting right away results in an indeterminate form.

L'HÔPITAL'S RULE

Consider the limit $\lim_{x \to a} f(x)/g(x)$ where $f(x)$ and $g(x)$ are both differentiable at $x = a$ and a can be any number, including positive or negative infinity. Suppose if we evaluated the limit at a, one of the following is true:

$$\lim_{x \to a} \frac{f(x)}{g(x)} = \frac{0}{0} \quad \text{or} \quad \lim_{x \to a} \frac{f(x)}{g(x)} = \frac{\infty}{\infty}$$

Then the limit can be simplified to

$$\lim_{x \to a} \frac{f(x)}{g(x)} = \lim_{x \to a} \frac{f'(x)}{g'(x)}$$

The limit is equal to the limit as x approaches a of the derivative of the numerator divided by the derivative of the denominator.

ETYMOLOGY
I think we need an etymology lesson for the name of this rule! This important calculus result was named after the French mathematician Guillaume Francoid Antoine, Marquis de l'Hôpital, who is credited with using this theorem in his work. (Interestingly, he did not discover this rule; the Swiss mathematician Johann Bernoulli introduced him to it.)

L'Hôpital is pronounced "LOW-pee-tal," and if it's not the first word of a sentence, only the H is capitalized, as in l'Hôpital. An alternative spelling of the name is l'Hospital and therefore l'Hospital's Rule. For consistency, in this book I will refer to it as l'Hôpital's Rule, with the circumflex written over the letter o.

Let's launch straight into some examples!

EXAMPLE
Let's evaluate the following limit:

$$\lim_{x \to 0} \frac{\sin(x)}{x}$$

Solution: You might recall from Section 1.2 that we evaluated this limit, but it required some creative applications of geometry of the triangle, as well as the delicious Sandwich Theorem. The reason is because if we try to evaluate the limit, the answer would be 0/0. However, let's find the limit using l'Hôpital's Rule. The derivative of the numerator is $\cos(x)$, and the derivative of the denominator is 1:

$$\lim_{x \to 0} \frac{\sin(x)}{x} = \lim_{x \to 0} \frac{\cos(x)}{1}$$

Let's try to evaluate the limit again. If we substitute $x = 0$, we now get $\cos(0) = 1$, making the answer 1:

$$\lim_{x \to 0} \frac{\cos(x)}{1} = \frac{1}{1} = 1$$

Thus, the original limit is equal to 1, as we already know. This method of evaluating the limit is so much easier than using the Sandwich Theorem! Why, you ask, did we not use l'Hôpital's Rule back in Chapter 1 when we first studied limits? The answer is simple: at that time, you didn't know how to find derivatives!

Δ

Two important points should be noted in the above example. First, we used l'Hôpital's Rule once, and then the "transformed" limit could then be evaluated in a straightforward manner. It would have been incorrect to use l'Hôpital's Rule a second time because evaluating the second limit no longer produced an indeterminate form.

Second, l'Hôpital's Rule says that the limit of interest of $f(x)/g(x)$ is (under the right conditions) equal to the limit of interest of $f'(x)/g'(x)$. However, it would be incorrect to say that the function $f(x)/g(x)$ is equal to the function $f'(x)/g'(x)$ for all x. For instance, in the above problem, $\sin(x)/x$ is obviously not the same as $\cos(x)/1$ for all x!

EXAMPLE
Evaluate the following limit, first shown in Section 1.3:

$$\lim_{x\to\infty} \frac{x^4+1}{2x^4-4x^3+3}$$

Solution: First notice that direct evaluation of the limit results in ∞/∞. When we have seen limits like this before, we would evaluate them as follows:

$$\lim_{x\to\infty} \frac{x^4+1}{2x^4-4x^3+3} = \lim_{x\to\infty} \frac{x^4+1}{2x^4-4x^3+3} \cdot \frac{1/x^4}{1/x^4} = \lim_{x\to\infty} \frac{1+\frac{1}{x^4}}{2-\frac{4}{x}+\frac{3}{x^4}}$$

We would then recognize that evaluating at ∞ would send the three fractions to 0, leaving the answer as $1/2$. Now let's find this limit using l'Hôpital's Rule, and we can use it because of the indeterminate form.

$$\lim_{x\to\infty} \frac{x^4+1}{2x^4-4x^3+3} = \lim_{x\to\infty} \frac{4x^3}{2\cdot 4x^3-4\cdot 3x^2}$$

Simplifying,

$$\lim_{x\to\infty} \frac{4x^3}{2\cdot 4x^3-4\cdot 3x^2} = \lim_{x\to\infty} \frac{4x^3}{8x^3-12x^2} = \lim_{x\to\infty} \frac{x}{2x-3}$$

Let's try to evaluate the transformed limit again. Unfortunately doing so once again results in ∞/∞, so we have to use l'Hôpital's Rule a second time.

$$\lim_{x\to\infty} \frac{x}{2x-3} = \lim_{x\to\infty} \frac{1}{2\cdot 1} = \frac{1}{2}$$

Thus, the original limit is equal to $1/2$.

Δ

EXAMPLE
Evaluate the following limits:

$$\lim_{x\to\infty} \frac{e^x}{x^3} \quad \text{and} \quad \lim_{x\to 1+} \frac{x^2+1}{x-1}$$

Solution: Evaluating the first limit produces ∞/∞, and so

$$\lim_{x\to\infty} \frac{e^x}{x^3} = \lim_{x\to\infty} \frac{e^x}{3x^2}$$

We still get ∞/∞, so we use l'Hôpital's Rule again:

$$\lim_{x\to\infty} \frac{e^x}{3x^2} = \lim_{x\to\infty} \frac{e^x}{6x}$$

The result is still ∞/∞, so the rule comes into play a third time:

$$\lim_{x\to\infty} \frac{e^x}{6x} = \lim_{x\to\infty} \frac{e^x}{6}$$

213

We no longer get ∞/∞. Evaluating the limit produces an infinite answer divided by 6, so

$$\lim_{x\to\infty} \frac{e^x}{6} = \infty$$

Looking at the second limit, we are approaching 1 from the right. It is tempting to use l'Hôpital's Rule right away, but remember we first need to see what happens if we evaluate right away. Approaching 1 from the right, $x^2 + 1$ approaches 2, whereas $x - 1$ approaches 0. Thus, attempting to evaluate the limit results in $2/0$, which is undefined (or positive infinity since coming from the right side, $x - 1$ was previously positive).

Thus, for the second limit, we cannot use l'Hôpital's Rule at all since the evaluation was never an indeterminate form. (Watch out for trick questions like this!) The answer is

$$\lim_{x\to 1+} \frac{x^2 + 1}{x - 1} = \infty$$

Δ

There are also limits for which we can use l'Hôpital's Rule, but only after rewriting the function. Take the following two limits as examples.

EXAMPLE
Evaluate the following limits:

$$\lim_{x\to 0+} x\ln(x) \quad \text{and} \quad \lim_{x\to -\infty} xe^x$$

Solution: These two limits require some trickery to solve. Looking at the first limit, we approach 0 from the right side, and so $\ln(x)$ is approaching negative infinity. (Note that we cannot approach 0 from the left thanks to the natural log.) Thus, evaluating would result in $0 \times -\infty$, an indeterminate form. (The negative sign doesn't matter; it's still an indeterminate form.) The strategy here is to turn the function into a fraction by creating a denominator. For instance, recognize that multiplying by x is the same as dividing by $1/x$:

$$\lim_{x\to 0+} x\ln(x) = \lim_{x\to 0+} \frac{\ln(x)}{\left(\frac{1}{x}\right)} = \lim_{x\to 0+} \frac{\ln(x)}{x^{-1}}$$

Evaluating this new form would result in $-\infty/\infty$, so now we can use l'Hôpital's Rule:

$$\lim_{x\to 0+} \frac{\ln(x)}{x^{-1}} = \lim_{x\to 0+} \frac{\left(\frac{1}{x}\right)}{-x^{-2}}$$

Simplifying,

$$\lim_{x\to 0+} \frac{\left(\frac{1}{x}\right)}{-x^{-2}} = \lim_{x\to 0+} \frac{\left(\frac{1}{x}\right)}{-\left(\frac{1}{x^2}\right)} = \lim_{x\to 0+} -\left(\frac{1}{x}\right)\cdot x^2 = \lim_{x\to 0+} -\frac{x^2}{x} = \lim_{x\to 0+} -x$$

Thus, it's clear at once that

$$\lim_{x\to 0+} -x = 0$$

Sometimes, however, we have to do some trial and error to figure out how to rewrite the fraction, as is the case with the second limit. First note that if we evaluate xe^x at negative infinity right away, the result is $-\infty \times 0$, an indeterminate form. However, l'Hôpital's Rule can only be used if the function is written as a fraction, so let's try to use the same method from the previous limit:

$$\lim_{x \to -\infty} xe^x = \lim_{x \to -\infty} \frac{e^x}{\left(\frac{1}{x}\right)} = \lim_{x \to -\infty} \frac{e^x}{x^{-1}}$$

This time evaluation results in $0/0$, so we use l'Hôpital's Rule:

$$\lim_{x \to -\infty} \frac{e^x}{x^{-1}} = \lim_{x \to -\infty} \frac{e^x}{-x^{-2}} = \lim_{x \to -\infty} \frac{e^x}{-\left(\frac{1}{x^2}\right)}$$

Evaluation still results in $0/0$, so let's use the rule again.

$$\lim_{x \to -\infty} \frac{e^x}{-x^{-2}} = \lim_{x \to -\infty} \frac{e^x}{-2x^{-3}} = \lim_{x \to -\infty} \frac{e^x}{-\left(\frac{2}{x^3}\right)}$$

Evaluation once again produced $0/0$. Not only that, the exponent degree is getting larger while e^x is staying the same, so if anything the limit is getting more complicated. Thus, our technique of dividing by $1/x$ has not helped. What if we instead took the e^x and divided by $1/e^x$, or equivalently divided by e^{-x}? Let's find out:

$$\lim_{x \to -\infty} xe^x = \lim_{x \to -\infty} \frac{x}{\left(\frac{1}{e^x}\right)} = \lim_{x \to -\infty} \frac{x}{e^{-x}}$$

Using l'Hôpital's Rule,

$$\lim_{x \to -\infty} \frac{x}{e^{-x}} = \lim_{x \to -\infty} \frac{1}{-e^{-x}}$$

Rearranging the limit,

$$\lim_{x \to -\infty} \frac{1}{-e^{-x}} = \lim_{x \to -\infty} -e^x$$

Evaluating the new limit, e^x goes to 0 as x goes to negative infinity, so we have shown that

$$\lim_{x \to -\infty} xe^x = \lim_{x \to -\infty} -e^x = 0$$

Δ

If you want to be more confident that your answer is correct, one way of checking your answer is to use your calculator to evaluate the limit at a number very close to the point of interest. For instance, consider the previous two limit problems:

$$\lim_{x \to 0+} x\ln(x) \quad \text{and} \quad \lim_{x \to -\infty} xe^x$$

For the first limit, try evaluating at $x = 0.00001$. The evaluation is $x\ln(x) \approx -0.0001151$, which is very close to the answer 0. For the second limit, since we are approaching negative infinity, try evaluating at $x = -100$. The evaluation produces $xe^x \approx -3.72 \times 10^{-42}$, which is scientific notation for an extremely small number. (To be precise, it is negative 372 but with forty-one zeros between the decimal and the 3.) Again, the answer is clearly heading toward 0. Of course, while this is a useful way of checking your work, it alone is not a proof of the limit – you actually have to go through the calculus.

We have now seen how to use l'Hôpital's Rule right away or with rewriting the function as a fraction. There is another way l'Hôpital's Rule can be used, but it requires a different approach. When dealing with certain exponential functions, sometimes the best way to evaluate the limit is to instead evaluate the natural log of the limit.

EXAMPLE
Let's evaluate

$$\lim_{x \to 0}(1 + x)^{1/x}$$

Solution: If we try to evaluate at 0, we end up with 1^∞, one of the indeterminate forms. Thus, this limit might be eligible for l'Hôpital's Rule, except we have to somehow write it as a fraction. There is no obvious way of doing this, however. Enter the natural log!

Let's define $L = \lim_{x \to 0}(1 + x)^{1/x}$, so L just represents the answer of interest. We are going to put it aside and instead evaluate the natural log of the limit, thereby finding $\ln(L)$. That means that instead of the given limit, we evaluate

$$\ln(L) = \lim_{x \to 0}\ln(1 + x)^{1/x}$$

Using properties of logs,

$$\lim_{x \to 0}\ln(1 + x)^{1/x} = \lim_{x \to 0}\frac{1}{x}\ln(1 + x) = \lim_{x \to 0}\frac{\ln(1 + x)}{x}$$

We have written this new limit in terms of a fraction. Evaluating it at 0, we get $\ln(1)/0$, which is 0/0. We are in business! Let's use l'Hôpital's Rule:

$$\lim_{x \to 0}\frac{\ln(1 + x)}{x} = \lim_{x \to 0}\frac{\left(\frac{1}{1 + x}\right)}{1}$$

Simplifying,

$$\lim_{x \to 0}\frac{\left(\frac{1}{1 + x}\right)}{1} = \lim_{x \to 0}\frac{1}{1 + x} = \frac{1}{1} = 1$$

To summarize what just happened, we did not evaluate the original limit; we instead evaluated the natural log of the limit. In other words, we want to find L, but instead we found that $\ln(L) = 1$. So how do we find L, the original limit? We exponentiate both sides with base e:

$$\ln(L) = 1 \Rightarrow e^{\ln(L)} = e^1$$
$$\Rightarrow L = e$$

Thus, we have shown that

$$\lim_{x \to 0}(1 + x)^{1/x} = e$$

Δ

Remember in Section 2.8 when we saw this limit but couldn't quite prove it at that point? We instead evaluated it at points close to 0 so you could see that the answer appeared to be e. We finally proved that limit here – but we couldn't do it earlier since at the time you did not know about l'Hôpital's Rule.

EXAMPLE
Evaluate the following limit:

$$\lim_{t \to 0+} t^t$$

Solution: First, don't worry about the change of letter; the limit still works as usual (to quote a famous English playwright, what's in a name?). Evaluating at 0 results in 0^0, an indeterminate form. Let's try the same trick of putting this limit aside and instead evaluating the natural log of the limit:

$$\lim_{t \to 0+} \ln(t^t) = \lim_{t \to 0+} t\ln(t)$$

Using the earlier trick of writing this limit as a fraction, let's try dividing by $1/t$:

$$\lim_{t \to 0+} t\ln(t) = \lim_{t \to 0+} \frac{\ln(t)}{\left(\frac{1}{t}\right)} = \lim_{t \to 0+} \frac{\ln(t)}{t^{-1}}$$

Noting that evaluating at 0 results in $-\infty/\infty$, we can now use l'Hôpital's Rule:

$$\lim_{t \to 0+} \frac{\ln(t)}{t^{-1}} = \lim_{t \to 0+} \frac{\left(\frac{1}{t}\right)}{-t^{-2}}$$

Simplifying,

$$\lim_{t \to 0+} \frac{\left(\frac{1}{t}\right)}{-t^{-2}} = \lim_{t \to 0+} \frac{\left(\frac{1}{t}\right)}{-\left(\frac{1}{t^2}\right)} = \lim_{t \to 0+} -\left(\frac{1}{t}\right) \cdot t^2 = \lim_{t \to 0+} -\frac{t^2}{t} = \lim_{t \to 0+} -t$$

Thus,

$$\lim_{t \to 0+} -t = 0$$

However, this is the result of the natural log limit, so $\ln(L) = 0$. That means that the original limit is $L = e^0 = 1$, and so we have shown that

$$\lim_{t \to 0+} t^t = 1$$

Δ

EXAMPLE
Evaluate

$$\lim_{x \to \infty} \frac{\sqrt{4x^2 + 9}}{3x + 5}$$

Solution: First, evaluating the limit at infinity results in ∞/∞, indicating that we can use l'Hôpital's Rule. Let's use it directly:

$$\lim_{x \to \infty} \frac{(4x^2 + 9)^{1/2}}{3x + 5} = \lim_{x \to \infty} \frac{\frac{1}{2}(4x^2 + 9)^{-1/2} \cdot 8x}{3} = \lim_{x \to \infty} \frac{4x}{3(4x^2 + 9)^{1/2}}$$

One again evaluation produces ∞/∞, so let's use l'Hôpital's Rule again:

$$\lim_{x\to\infty} \frac{4x}{3(4x^2+9)^{1/2}} = \lim_{x\to\infty} \frac{4}{3\cdot\frac{1}{2}(4x^2+9)^{-1/2}\cdot 8x} = \lim_{x\to\infty} \frac{(4x^2+9)^{1/2}}{3x}$$

Unfortunately, it appears that using l'Hôpital's Rule has taken us in a loop, since we ended up going from a square root on the numerator to one on the denominator and then back to one on the numerator again. Our natural log trick won't really help here since we don't have an exponent involving x. What do we do?

To get a sense of the answer, plug in a large number for the original limit, say 1000000. That evaluation results in 0.6666655556, so it appears the answer is going to be 2/3. Unfortunately, there is no obvious way of producing this.

We are going to use a very similar trick as before, where we put the limit aside and instead evaluate a transformed limit. However, instead of taking the natural log of the limit, we are going to square the limit (choosing this transformation will eliminate the square root term). Thus, let's instead evaluate

$$\lim_{x\to\infty} \frac{4x^2+9}{(3x+5)^2}$$

Using l'Hôpital's Rule (because evaluation produces ∞/∞),

$$\lim_{x\to\infty} \frac{4x^2+9}{(3x+5)^2} = \lim_{x\to\infty} \frac{8x}{2(3x+5)\cdot 3} = \lim_{x\to\infty} \frac{4x}{3(3x+5)} = \lim_{x\to\infty} \frac{4x}{9x+15}$$

We can use l'Hôpital's Rule one more time.

$$\lim_{x\to\infty} \frac{4x}{9x+15} = \lim_{x\to\infty} \frac{4}{9} = \frac{4}{9}$$

Thus, if the original limit is L, we have shown that the squared limit is $L^2 = 4/9$. That means that $L = 2/3$, or in other words the original limit is

$$\lim_{x\to\infty} \frac{\sqrt{4x^2+9}}{3x+5} = \frac{2}{3}$$

In case you were wondering why we don't consider $-2/3$ as another value for the limit, it's because we are approaching positive infinity, which means the numerator and denominator are both positive. This means that the limit is definitely going to be positive, so it has to be 2/3 and not $-2/3$.

Δ

The takeaway from the previous example is that when confronted with a limit that needs l'Hôpital's Rule but cannot be evaluated by immediate differentiation due to a rather "complicated" numerator or denominator, one approach is to apply an appropriate transformation to the limit to turn it into one that can be evaluated more easily, then at the end of the problem back-transform to arrive at the original limit's answer.

Chapter 4 – Parametric Curves and Polar Curves

In Chapter 3 we explored how to use the derivative in the context of max-min problems, with optimization and curve sketching as two possible applications. This chapter turns in a whole new direction as we learn about parametric functions and how to differentiate them, along with vector-valued functions. We also introduce polar functions and how to differentiate them. For those of you who go on to take integral calculus, some of you might instead learn this material for the first time in that class rather than in differential calculus. If that's the case, you can skip this chapter for now, but you will eventually need to learn the material here.

Section 4.1 – Parametric Curves

The first two sections of Chapter 4 deal with a new topic in this course called parametric curves. Up until now we have mostly seen functions written in terms of x and y where y is determined by a value for x, or in other words $y = f(x)$. Certainly these functions are convenient to work with, but we don't always run into situations when they can be used.

There are some functions where both y and x are determined by a third variable usually denoted as t. In other words, previously we had $y = f(x)$ where y was determined by x and x was any number in the domain. Now we turn our attention to functions where $x = f(t)$ and $y = g(t)$, so now both x and y are determined by the new variable t and t is any number in the domain. Such functions are called **parametric functions**.

DEFINITION
Suppose a function's x- and y-coordinates are both written as functions of t. This means that at time t, the coordinates are given by $(x(t), y(t))$. Such a function is called a **parametric function** or a **parametric curve**, and $x(t)$ and $y(t)$ collectively are called **parametric equations**.

ETYMOLOGY
The word parameter comes from the ancient Greek παρά (pronounced *para*) and μέτρον (pronounced *metron*), which meant "beside" and "measure," respectively.

Note that if $x(t) = t$ and $y(t)$ is any function in terms of t, then the parametric coordinates are $(t, y(t))$, which are also Cartesian coordinates. This is because here the coordinates can be written as $(x, f(x))$ or (x, y). In other words, parametric functions are an extension of Cartesian ones, and Cartesian functions are a special case of parametric ones when $x(t) = t$.

Before we go further, it would be helpful to think of some real-life situations where parametric curves would be useful.

1) An airplane leaves the Sydney airport and lands at Nadi International Airport in Fiji four hours later. The airplane's geographical coordinates at time t represent a parametric curve, where $t = 0$ represents the coordinates of the Sydney airport and $t = 4$ those of the Fiji airport.
2) You dribble a basketball while running forward. The basketball's position in the air between your hands and the floor (while moving forward) represents a parametric curve. Here $x(t)$ is the location of the ball on the court while you are moving forward, while $y(t)$ is the height of the ball off the ground at time t.
3) You launch a bowling bowl down a lane, and three seconds later it hits the pins. Here we could say that $x(t)$ is the position of the ball in the width of the lane (whether it's on the left, middle, or right

side), and $y(t)$ is the distance away from you the ball has traveled. Further, at $t = 0$ the ball is leaving your hands, and at $t = 3$ the ball has hit the pins.

These problems can be confusing at first if you are unfamiliar with them, so let's go straight to a simple example.

EXAMPLE

Let's graph the parametric curve given by $x(t) = 3t + 4$ and $y(t) = 4t - 7$ over $-3 \le t \le 3$. To warm up, let's make a table of values of $x(t)$ and $y(t)$ over the whole numbers from -3 to 3.

t	-3	-2	-1	0	1	2	3
$x(t)$	-5	-2	1	4	7	10	13
$y(t)$	-19	-15	-11	-7	-3	1	5

This table tells us that the curve starts at $(-5, -19)$ and ends at $(13, 5)$ and passes through all the other points listed above. However, what kind of curve is it – a line, a zigzagged figure, or some sort of crazy-shaped curve? As long as a function passes through the seven aforementioned points, it would be a candidate for the curve without further information.

Luckily, here we can work out the nature of the curve by solving for t in one equation and then substituting the result into the other equation:

$$x = 3t + 4 \Rightarrow t = \frac{x - 4}{3}$$

Putting this t into $y(t)$ results in

$$y = 4\left(\frac{x - 4}{3}\right) - 7 = \frac{4}{3}x - \frac{16}{3} - 7 = \frac{4}{3}x - \frac{16}{3} - \frac{21}{3}$$
$$y = \frac{4}{3}x - \frac{37}{3}$$

Our curve turns out to be a line with slope $4/3$ and y-intercept $-37/3$. This is good news since a line is easier to work with than a crazy-shaped curve! As a quick check, when $t = 2$ we had $x(t) = 10$ and therefore $y = 40/3 - 37/3 = 3/3 = 1$, matching what we obtained for $y(t)$.

However, we are not finished yet. The parametric curve is defined only from $t = -3$ to $t = 3$ including the endpoints, and so when sketching our graph, it too must encompass $-3 \le t \le 3$ and nowhere else. That means when drawing the line, we start at $(-5, -19)$ and finish at $(13, 5)$ since those are the starting and ending points. It would be incorrect to extend the whole line through the rest of the graph like we normally would do.

There is one more new thing to consider – the **direction of motion**. Noting that we start at $(-5, -19)$ and finish at $(13, 5)$, our curve moves in a "northeastern" direction, that is, from left to right and from bottom to top. We can therefore mark an arrow on the curve in the direction of motion.

The graph of this parametric function, including endpoints and motion of direction, is shown on the following graph.

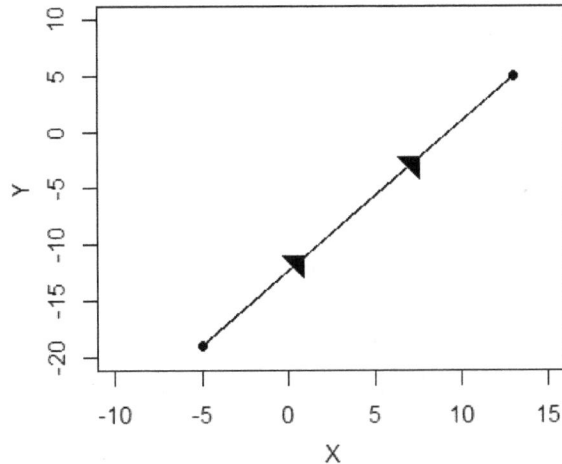

Δ

DEFINITION
A new concept for parametric curves that we haven't seen before is called **direction of motion**. When tracing a curve over time t, direction of motion tells us in which direction the curve is "traveling." It is often denoted on graphs using arrows.

MNEMONIC
Imagine a parametric curve represents the path of a roller coaster, and you are in a car on the ride. Your position on the roller coaster at time t is $(x(t), y(t))$, and you are traveling in a specific direction as t increases. There are two possible directions to take, and your car's path on the roller coaster represents the direction of motion.

We started the previous example in the simplest possible way, by picking some random values for t and computing $x(t)$ and $y(t)$. However, unless we have the TI-84 or a computer program to generate many points quickly, plotting a few points is not usually the best way to sketch a graph of a parametric curve. This is because there are loads of possible curves that could pass through the few points we sampled. One way to get around this problem is to try to solve for $x(t)$ in terms of t and then plug the result into $y(t)$. While this is not always possible or practical to do, when we can do it, it will often lead to us recognizing what sort of function we are attempting to graph.

EXAMPLE
Let's sketch the graph for the parametric curve given by $x(t) = t^2 + t$, $y(t) = 3t - 1$.

Solution: We first need to isolate t in one of the equations $x = t^2 + t$ or $y = 3t - 1$. It is easier to accomplish this with the second equation:

$$y = 3t - 1 \Rightarrow t = \frac{y+1}{3}$$

Substituting this into the first equation results in

$$x = \left(\frac{y+1}{3}\right)^2 + \frac{y+1}{3} = \frac{(y^2 + 2y + 1)}{9} + \frac{(y+1)}{3} = \frac{(y^2 + 2y + 1)}{9} + \frac{3(y+1)}{9}$$

$$= \frac{y^2 + 2y + 1 + 3y + 3}{9} = \frac{y^2 + 5y + 4}{9}$$

$$= \frac{1}{9}y^2 + \frac{5}{9}y + \frac{4}{9}$$

Thus, our parametric curve simplifies to

$$x = \frac{1}{9}y^2 + \frac{5}{9}y + \frac{4}{9}$$

You might recall from an algebra class that this is a parabola; only this one opens to the right rather than up because the x and y are flipped. Also recall that for an "ordinary" parabola $y = ax^2 + bx + c$ that opens up or down, the vertex is at $x = -b/2a$. For a parabola opening right (or left), the vertex is instead at $y = -b/2a$, and so

$$y = -\frac{b}{2a} = -\frac{(5/9)}{2(1/9)} = -\frac{5}{9} \times \frac{9}{2} = -\frac{5}{2}$$

Substituting this y-coordinate into x yields

$$x = \frac{1}{9}\left(-\frac{5}{2}\right)^2 + \frac{5}{9}\left(-\frac{5}{2}\right) + \frac{4}{9} = \frac{1}{9}\left[\left(-\frac{5}{2}\right)^2 + 5\left(-\frac{5}{2}\right) + 4\right] = \frac{1}{9}\left[\frac{25}{4} - \frac{25}{2} + 4\right]$$

$$= \frac{1}{9}\left[\frac{25}{4} - \frac{50}{4} + \frac{16}{4}\right] = \frac{1}{9}\left(-\frac{9}{4}\right) = -\frac{1}{4}$$

Thus, the parabola's vertex is at $(-1/4, -5/2)$. Next, let's pick a few more "easy" points on the curve so that we can get an idea of what the sketch looks like. Choosing $t = 0$ and $t = 1$ would be convenient, and let's choose $t = -1$ as well to get on the other side of the vertex:

$t = -1$ $x(-1) = (-1)^2 - 1 = 0$ $y(-1) = 3(-1) - 1 = -4$ $(0, -4)$
$t = \;\;0$ $x(0) = 0^2 + 0 \;\;\;\;= 0$ $y(0) = 3(0) - 1 \;\;= -1$ $(0, -1)$
$t = \;\;1$ $x(1) = 1^2 + 1 \;\;\;\;= 2$ $y(1) = 3(1) - 1 \;\;= 2$ $(2, 2)$

The sketch so far looks like this:

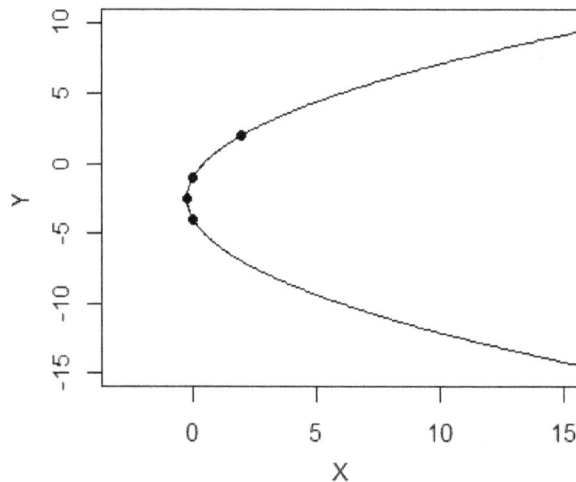

We are graphing over all values of t because no endpoints are specified. The last thing to consider is the direction of motion. If this parametric curve were a roller coaster and we were riding on it, we need to know if we are starting from the top and racing downwards before curving to the bottom right, or if we are starting from the bottom and racing upwards before curving to the top right. Luckily, it is easy to tell the direction based on comparing where we are at time $t = 0$ to $t = 1$. In that second we move from $(0, -1)$ to $(2, 2)$, which means we are moving "uphill." We can now finish sketching the graph by adding the arrows indicating the direction of motion:

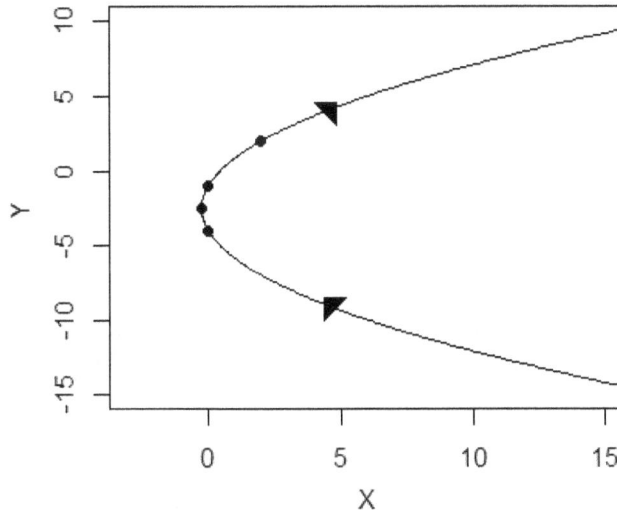

Δ

EXAMPLE
Let's now do an example where solving for t and then substituting one equation into the other is not a good idea. Sketch the graph for the parametric curve given by $x(t) = 3 \cos(t)$, $y(t) = 3 \sin(t)$ over $0 \le t \le \pi$.

Solution: If we were going to solve for t first, we would need to do so in one of the equations $x = 3 \cos(t)$ or $y = 3 \sin(t)$. Picking the first one results in $t = \arccos(x/3)$ and therefore

$$y = 3 \sin \left(\arccos \left(\frac{x}{3} \right) \right)$$

Although a computer or graphing calculator could handle this function, we have clearly made it messier than the original presentation! So what do we do? The objective is to somehow use trigonometric identities to eliminate the t, leaving x and y. Recall your uncle in every photo opportunity: $\cos^2(t) + \sin^2(t) = 1$, and observe that squaring the x and y and adding them results in

$$x^2 + y^2 = 3^2 \cos^2(t) + 3^2 \sin^2(t) = 9(\cos^2(t) + \sin^2(t))$$
$$= 9(1) = 9$$

Using this wonderfully versatile identity, our curve transforms into $x^2 + y^2 = 9$, which we immediately recognize to be a circle centered at the origin with radius 3.

Unfortunately, there's more. Not only is there direction of motion, but we also have to find what portion of the circle is actually traced. We managed to write the curve in terms of a convenient function, a circle, but due to the parametric nature of the curve, it might not necessarily sweep over the whole circle (for instance,

223

we could have a function tracing only the top half). On the other hand, it might also trace the same circle multiple times.

To figure this out, notice that $0 \leq t \leq \pi$, so the endpoints are

$$(x(0), y(0)) = (3\cos(0), 3\sin(0)) = (3 \cdot 1, 3 \cdot 0) = (3, 0)$$
$$(x(\pi), y(\pi)) = (3\cos(\pi), 3\sin(\pi)) = (3 \cdot -1, 3 \cdot 0) = (-3, 0)$$

These are the right and left sides of the circle, which means we have only traced half of the circle. The question is, do we have the top half or the bottom? To find out, let's pick a point between 0 and π and find the resulting coordinates, say $t = \pi/2$:

$$\left(x\left(\frac{\pi}{2}\right), y\left(\frac{\pi}{2}\right)\right) = \left(3\cos\left(\frac{\pi}{2}\right), 3\sin\left(\frac{\pi}{2}\right)\right) = (3 \cdot 0, 3 \cdot 1) = (0, 3)$$

The point $(0, 3)$ lies at the top of the circle, and so we have proven that the parametric curve traces the top half of the circle. As for direction of motion, note that our roller coaster starts at $(3, 0)$ and moves along the semicircle, passing through $(0, 3)$ before ending at $(-3, 0)$. That means we are moving in a counterclockwise direction. The following graph shows the complete parametric curve.

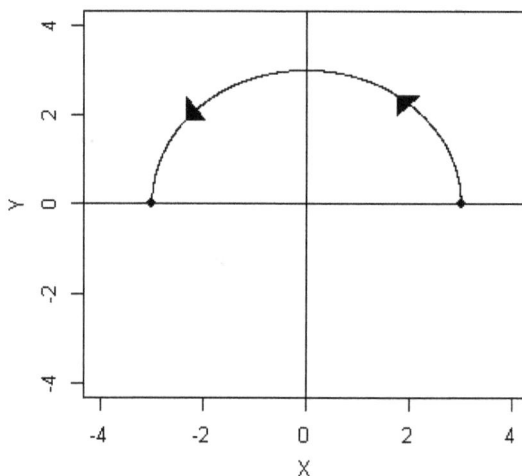

Δ

Finally, let's see how the TI-84 can help with graphing parametric functions.

TI-84 COMMAND: GRAPHING PARAMETRIC CURVES

First press $\boxed{\text{MODE}}$ and scroll down to the fourth line. The usual setting is FUNC, but now scroll right to PAR and press $\boxed{\text{ENTER}}$. Press $\boxed{\text{2nd}}$ and $\boxed{\text{MODE}}$ to go back to the home screen. Doing so changes the calculator's setting to Parametric Mode. (If you want to go back to graphing ordinary functions for other problems, return to this menu and switch back to FUNC mode.)

Now press $\boxed{\text{Y} =}$, and you can type in a function for X_{1T} and another for Y_{1T} (and more parametric curves if necessary). Note that pressing the $\boxed{\text{X, T, } \theta \text{, n}}$ button for your input variable now shows as T. Press $\boxed{\text{WINDOW}}$, and in addition to the usual plotting options you now have options for $Tmin$, $Tmax$, and $Tstep$ (sounds like a type of dance!). These are, respectively, the starting time, the ending time, and the increment you wish to use to go from start to finish.

TI-84 COMMAND: GRAPHING PARAMETRIC CURVES (CONTINUED)
Adjust your X and Y windows accordingly, and press $\boxed{\text{GRAPH}}$. You will see the parametric function traced out, and pressing $\boxed{\text{TRACE}}$ allows you to trace the curve and figure out the direction of motion.

EXAMPLE
For the previous example with the semicircle, under the $\boxed{\text{Y} =}$ menu type $X_{1T} = 3\cos(T)$ and $Y_{1T} = 3\sin(T)$. Going to $\boxed{\text{WINDOW}}$, type $Tmin = 0$ and $Tmax = \pi$, and pick something small for $Tstep$ such as $\pi/6$ (you can adjust this later). Press $\boxed{\text{GRAPH}}$, and you will see the top half of the circle traced from $(3, 0)$ to $(-3, 0)$. Pressing $\boxed{\text{TRACE}}$, you can use the left and right buttons to trace the path of the circle.

Δ

Section 4.2 – Derivatives of Parametric Curves
The previous section introduced the idea of parametric curves and how to graph them. We now turn our attention to differentiating these curves.

One way to establish a formula for the first derivative of a parametric curve is to suppose we have successfully eliminated the t variable, so now we have $y = f(x)$ for some function of x. However, remembering that both y and x were written in terms of t, the function can be written as

$$y(t) = f\big(x(t)\big)$$

Differentiating this with respect to t and remembering the Chain Rule,

$$\frac{dy}{dt} = f'\big(x(t)\big) \cdot \frac{dx}{dt}$$

Since $f(x)$ is also a function of x, that means that

$$f'\big(x(t)\big) = f'(x) = \frac{dy}{dx}$$

Substituting this into the derivative and rearranging terms,

$$\frac{dy}{dt} = \frac{dy}{dx} \cdot \frac{dx}{dt} \Rightarrow \frac{dy}{dx} = \frac{\left(\frac{dy}{dt}\right)}{\left(\frac{dx}{dt}\right)}$$

We have found the formula for the first derivative.

FIRST DERIVATIVE OF A PARAMETRIC CURVE

Define a parametric curve at time t to have x-coordinate $x = x(t)$ and y-coordinate $y = y(t)$. Assume that the derivatives $x'(t) = dx/dt$ and $y'(t) = dy/dt$ exist and that $x'(t) \neq 0$ at time t. Then the first derivative of the curve is

$$\frac{dy}{dx} = \frac{\left(\dfrac{dy}{dt}\right)}{\left(\dfrac{dx}{dt}\right)} = \frac{y'(t)}{x'(t)}$$

As with regular functions, the derivative dy/dx can be interpreted as the slope of the tangent line to the curve at time t and at the point $(x(t), y(t))$. $x'(t)$ is the rate at which the curve's x-coordinate is changing with respect to time, while $y'(t)$ is the rate at which the curve's y-coordinate is changing with respect to time.

Horizontal tangent lines occur when

$$\frac{dy}{dt} = y'(t) = 0, \quad \text{provided} \quad \frac{dx}{dt} \neq 0$$

Vertical tangent lines occur when

$$\frac{dx}{dt} = x'(t) = 0, \quad \text{provided} \quad \frac{dy}{dt} \neq 0$$

Note that if $x(t) = t$, the parametric functions reduce to Cartesian ones. In this scenario $x'(t) = 1$, and so the first derivative reduces to the familiar Cartesian one:

$$\frac{dy}{dx} = \frac{y'(t)}{1} = y'(t)$$

EXAMPLE

Returning to the first example of the previous section, find the derivative of the curve given by $x(t) = 3t + 4$ and $y(t) = 4t - 7$ over $-3 \leq t \leq 3$.

Solution: We have $x'(t) = 3$ and $y'(t) = 4$, and so

$$\frac{dy}{dx} = \frac{y'(t)}{x'(t)} = \frac{4}{3}$$

Observe that for all $-3 \leq t \leq 3$, the slope of the curve at time t is constant and is positive $4/3$. This should make sense because the slope of a line is constant everywhere. However, we can also use the derivatives to work out direction of motion for the curve. Earlier we deduced (by picking points) that the curve is traced from bottom left to top right, so let's verify that that direction is correct.

Notice that if we start at $t = -3$, the corresponding point is $(3(-3) + 4, 4(-3) - 7) = (-5, -19)$, the lower left end of the line. Next, the coordinate derivatives are both positive, which means that as t increases, $x(t)$ increases (moving to the right) and $y(t)$ increases (moving up). That means we start at $(-5, -19)$ and move to the right and upward, thereby tracing the same direction from Section 4.1.

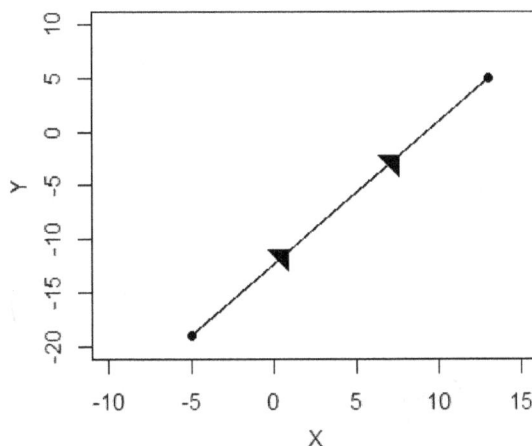

Δ

EXAMPLE

Let's once again sketch the graph for the parametric curve given by $x(t) = t^2 + t$, $y(t) = 3t - 1$, but this time find the derivative at any time t as well as any critical points. Find at what values of t the curve has negative slope and positive slope.

Solution: The coordinate derivatives are $x'(t) = 2t + 1$ and $y'(t) = 3$, which means

$$\frac{dy}{dx} = \frac{y'(t)}{x'(t)} = \frac{3}{2t + 1}$$

This derivative doesn't equal 0 anywhere, but it is undefined at one point:

$$2t + 1 = 0 \Rightarrow t = -\frac{1}{2}$$

This finding tells us that the slope of the curve at $t = -1/2$ is vertical because it is undefined. Let's find the coordinates there:

$$x\left(-\frac{1}{2}\right) = \left(-\frac{1}{2}\right)^2 + \left(-\frac{1}{2}\right) = \frac{1}{4} - \frac{1}{2} = -\frac{1}{4}$$
$$y\left(-\frac{1}{2}\right) = 3\left(-\frac{1}{2}\right) - 1 = -\frac{3}{2} - 1 = -\frac{5}{2}$$

Thus, at $t = -1/2$ the curve is at $(-1/4, -5/2)$. If this point looks familiar, that was the vertex we derived in the previous section. Next, let's find the intervals on which the function is increasing and decreasing. This works the same way it did in Chapter 3, where we pick points on either side of the critical points and put them into the derivative. Note that we do this for values of t (not values of x).

1) $\left(-\infty, -\frac{1}{2}\right)$, pick $t = -1$

$$\left.\frac{dy}{dx}\right|_{t=-1} = \frac{3}{2(-1)+1} = -3, \text{ negative}$$

2) $\left(-\frac{1}{2}, \infty\right)$, pick $t = 0$

$$\left.\frac{dy}{dx}\right|_{t=0} = \frac{3}{2(0)+1} = 3, \text{ positive}$$

227

$$\frac{dy}{dx} \qquad \xleftarrow[\quad -\frac{1}{2} \quad]{\quad - \qquad\qquad + \quad}$$

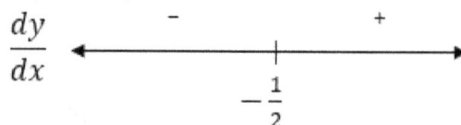

Thus, the slope of the curve is negative when $t < -1/2$ and positive when $t > -1/2$ (and the tangent line is vertical at $t = -1/2$). We earlier showed that the curve is the following parabola that opens to the right:

$$x = \frac{1}{9}y^2 + \frac{5}{9}y + \frac{4}{9}$$

Earlier we examined some chosen points to work out that the curve starts in the bottom right and traces the parabola to the vertex before going off on its merry way to the top right. Let's now show the same conclusion using the derivatives. First note that since $y'(t) = 3$ for all t, the y-coordinate is always moving upwards as time goes on. This suggests that we start at the bottom of the parabola and move up.

To further see this, note that below the vertex ($t < -1/2$) the derivative $x'(t)$ is negative, which means the x-coordinate is moving to the left. Once we pass the vertex and $t > -1/2$, $x'(t)$ is positive, which means the x-ccordinate is now moving to the right. This once again correctly describes the path on which we are moving.

Δ

EXAMPLE
Returning to the circle example, find the derivative of the parametric function given by $x(t) = 3\cos(t)$, $y(t) = 3\sin(t)$ over $0 \le t \le \pi$. Find the equation of the tangent line to the curve at $t = \pi/4$.

Solution: We showed earlier that this curve is $x^2 + y^2 = 9$, the circle centered at the origin with radius 3, except the curve only traces the top half of the circle. The derivatives are

$$x'(t) = -3\sin(t)$$
$$y'(t) = 3\cos(t)$$
$$\frac{dy}{dx} = \frac{y'(t)}{x'(t)} = \frac{3\cos(t)}{-3\sin(t)} = -\frac{\cos(t)}{\sin(t)}$$

Notice that $dy/dx = 0$ when the numerator is 0, so

$$\cos(t) = 0 \Rightarrow t = \frac{\pi}{2}, \frac{3\pi}{2}$$

However, $t = 3\pi/2$ is outside the domain, so the only time at which the slope of the curve is horizontal is $t = \pi/2$. Next, dy/dx does not exist when the denominator is 0, and that means that

$$\sin(t) = 0 \Rightarrow t = 0, \pi, 2\pi$$

We don't count $t = 2\pi$ since that gives the same location as $t = 0$, so that leaves $t = 0, \pi$. These are the times at which the slope of the curve is vertical. Let's find the corresponding points:

$$t = 0 \Rightarrow (x(t), y(t)) = (3\cos(0), 3\sin(0)) = (3, 0)$$
$$t = \frac{\pi}{2} \Rightarrow (x(t), y(t)) = \left(3\cos\left(\frac{\pi}{2}\right), 3\sin\left(\frac{\pi}{2}\right)\right) = (0, 3)$$

228

$$t = \pi \Rightarrow \big(x(t), y(t)\big) = (3\cos(\pi), 3\sin(\pi)) = (-3, 0)$$

This means that if our roller coaster starts at $t = 0$, we are at the rightmost side of the circle $(3, 0)$. Stopping at $t = \pi/2$, we are at the top $(0, 3)$, and continuing in this fashion, we end at the leftmost side $(-3, 0)$. Our journey took us in a counterclockwise path halfway around the circle. Thus, the direction of motion is counterclockwise, starting at $(3, 0)$ and tracing the upper half of the circle, ending up at $(-3, 0)$.

Next, let's find the equation of the tangent line at $t = \pi/4$. The slope is

$$\frac{dy}{dx} = -\frac{\cos(t)}{\sin(t)}\bigg|_{t=\pi/4} = -\frac{\cos\left(\frac{\pi}{4}\right)}{\sin\left(\frac{\pi}{4}\right)} = -\frac{\sqrt{2}/2}{\sqrt{2}/2} = -1$$

The point is

$$t = \frac{\pi}{4} \Rightarrow \big(x(t), y(t)\big) = \left(3\cos\left(\frac{\pi}{4}\right), 3\sin\left(\frac{\pi}{4}\right)\right) = \left(3 \times \frac{\sqrt{2}}{2}, 3 \times \frac{\sqrt{2}}{2}\right) = \left(\frac{3\sqrt{2}}{2}, \frac{3\sqrt{2}}{2}\right)$$

Thus, the tangent line is

$$y - \frac{3\sqrt{2}}{2} = -\left(x - \frac{3\sqrt{2}}{2}\right) \Rightarrow y = -x + \frac{3\sqrt{2}}{2} + \frac{3\sqrt{2}}{2}$$
$$\Rightarrow y = -x + 3\sqrt{2}$$
$$\Rightarrow y \approx -x + 4.24264$$

The following graph shows everything we have found, including direction of motion and the tangent line.

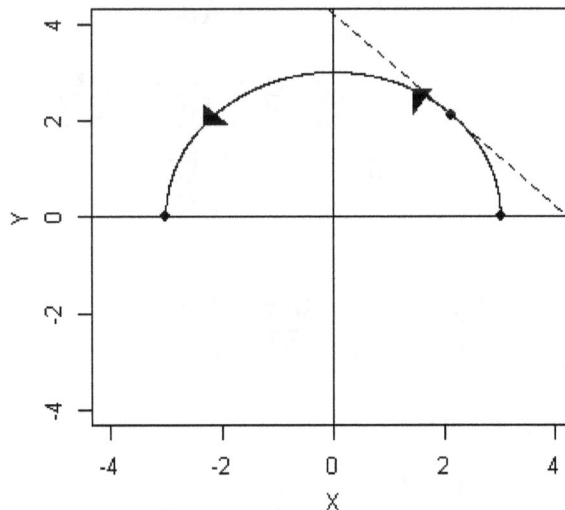

Δ

It is also possible to take the second derivative of a parametric function, although we need to be careful with the Chain Rule and notation. Recall the first line when we found the first derivative:

$$\frac{dy}{dt} = f'\big(x(t)\big) \cdot \frac{dx}{dt}$$

Differentiating both sides with respect to t (and using the Product Rule),

$$\frac{d^2y}{dt^2} = f'\big(x(t)\big) \cdot \frac{d^2x}{dt^2} + \left[f''\big(x(t)\big) \cdot \frac{dx}{dt}\right] \cdot \frac{dx}{dt}$$

To explain the second piece of the right side, the second derivative of $f'\big(x(t)\big)$ with respect to t involves finding the second derivative $f''\big(x(t)\big)$, but then you have to use the Chain Rule to multiply it by the derivative of $x(t)$ with respect to t, which is dx/dt. And don't forget to multiply that by the dx/dt that is already there, per the Product Rule.

Now let's switch derivative notation and use the following:

$$f'\big(x(t)\big) = \frac{dy}{dx} \quad \text{and} \quad f''\big(x(t)\big) = \frac{d^2y}{dx^2}$$

Putting these into the formula, we get

$$\frac{d^2y}{dt^2} = \frac{dy}{dx} \cdot \frac{d^2x}{dt^2} + \frac{d^2y}{dx^2} \cdot \frac{dx}{dt} \cdot \frac{dx}{dt}$$

The goal is to solve for the second derivative d^2y/dx^2, but first note that we can use our first derivative formula for dy/dx. (We don't usually like expressing second derivatives in terms of first derivatives.)

$$\frac{d^2y}{dt^2} = \frac{\frac{d^2x}{dt^2}\left(\frac{dy}{dt}\right)}{\left(\frac{dx}{dt}\right)} + \frac{d^2y}{dx^2} \cdot \left(\frac{dx}{dt}\right)^2$$

$$= \frac{\left(\frac{dy}{dt}\right) \cdot \frac{d^2x}{dt^2}}{\left(\frac{dx}{dt}\right)} + \frac{\frac{d^2y}{dx^2} \cdot \left(\frac{dx}{dt}\right)^2 \cdot \left(\frac{dx}{dt}\right)}{\left(\frac{dx}{dt}\right)}$$

Multiply both sides by dx/dt,

$$\frac{d^2y}{dt^2} \cdot \frac{dx}{dt} = \frac{dy}{dt} \cdot \frac{d^2x}{dt^2} + \frac{d^2y}{dx^2} \cdot \left(\frac{dx}{dt}\right)^3$$

Finally, solving for d^2y/dx^2,

$$\frac{d^2y}{dx^2} \cdot \left(\frac{dx}{dt}\right)^3 = \frac{d^2y}{dt^2} \cdot \frac{dx}{dt} - \frac{dy}{dt} \cdot \frac{d^2x}{dt^2}$$

$$\frac{d^2y}{dx^2} = \frac{\frac{dx}{dt} \cdot \frac{d^2y}{dt^2} - \frac{dy}{dt} \cdot \frac{d^2x}{dt^2}}{\left(\frac{dx}{dt}\right)^3}$$

If you prefer it in alternative notation,

$$\frac{d^2y}{dx^2} = \frac{x'(t) \cdot y''(t) - y'(t) \cdot x''(t)}{\left(x'(t)\right)^3}$$

Note that the denominator is cubed due to the derivation process and the Chain Rule. A common mistake is to square it instead, which is easy to think because of the Quotient Rule (which, by the way, we never used to get here).

SECOND DERIVATIVE OF A PARAMETRIC CURVE

Define a parametric curve at time t to have x-coordinate $x = x(t)$ and y-coordinate $y = y(t)$. Assume that the first derivatives $x'(t)$ and $y'(t)$ exist, that the second derivatives $x''(t)$ and $y''(t)$ exist, and that $x'(t) \neq 0$ at time t. Then the second derivative of the curve is

$$\frac{d^2y}{dx^2} = \frac{\frac{dx}{dt} \cdot \frac{d^2y}{dt^2} - \frac{dy}{dt} \cdot \frac{d^2x}{dt^2}}{\left(\frac{dx}{dt}\right)^3} = \frac{x'(t) \cdot y''(t) - y'(t) \cdot x''(t)}{\left(x'(t)\right)^3}$$

The second derivative indicates where the curve is concave up and concave down. It can be interpreted as the rate of change of the slope of the parametric curve with respect to x. Note that a lot of textbooks show the following as the formula for the second derivative:

$$\frac{d^2y}{dx^2} = \frac{\frac{d}{dt}\left(\frac{dy}{dx}\right)}{\frac{dx}{dt}}$$

This formula will give the same second derivative. However, I personally prefer the other formula above since you can put all the pieces in right away. Just make sure you don't confuse it with the Quotient Rule formula!

Note that if $x(t) = t$, the parametric functions reduce to Cartesian ones. In this scenario $x'(t) = 1$ and $x''(t) = 0$, and so the second derivative reduces to the familiar Cartesian one:

$$\frac{d^2y}{dx^2} = \frac{(1)y''(t) - y'(t)(0)}{(1)^3} = y''(t)$$

EXAMPLE

Returning to the parabola example, find the second derivative of the curve defined by $x(t) = t^2 + t$, $y(t) = 3t - 1$. Find where the curve is concave up and concave down.

Solution: Let's write down the first and second derivatives:

$$x'(t) = 2t + 1 \qquad y'(t) = 3$$
$$x''(t) = 2 \qquad y''(t) = 0$$

Putting these into the second derivative formula,

$$\frac{d^2y}{dx^2} = \frac{x'(t) \cdot y''(t) - y'(t) \cdot x''(t)}{(x'(t))^3} = \frac{(2t+1) \cdot 0 - 3 \cdot 2}{(2t+1)^3}$$

$$= -\frac{6}{(2t+1)^2}$$

The second derivative is never 0, but it is undefined at $t = -1/2$ like the first derivative was. Let's pick points on either side of $t = -1/2$.

1) $\left(-\infty, -\frac{1}{2}\right)$, pick $t = -1$

$$\left.\frac{d^2y}{dx^2}\right|_{t=-1} = \frac{-6}{(2(-1)+1)^3} = -\frac{6}{(-1)^3} = 6, \text{ positive}$$

2) $\left(-\frac{1}{2}, \infty\right)$, pick $t = 0$

$$\left.\frac{d^2y}{dx^2}\right|_{t=0} = \frac{-6}{(2(0)+1)^3} = -\frac{6}{1^3} = -6, \text{ negative}$$

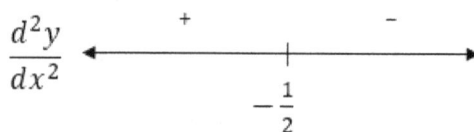

$$\frac{d^2y}{dx^2} \qquad \xleftarrow{\quad + \qquad\qquad\qquad - \quad} $$
$$-\frac{1}{2}$$

Thus, the curve is concave up when $t < -1/2$ and concave down when $t > 1/2$.

Δ

EXAMPLE

Consider the curve defined by $x(t) = e^t + t^3$ and $y(t) = \sin(t) + t$ over $0 \le t \le 2\pi$.

    A) Find the first derivative and the slope of the tangent line at $t = 0$.
    B) Find the critical points. Where is the slope of the curve horizontal and vertical?
    C) Find the intervals where the slope of the curve is positive and negative.
    D) Find the second derivative.

Solution: Here is our first example of a parametric curve where (I believe) it is impossible to solve for t explicitly to get a function in terms of just x and y. It's a jolly good thing we have now seen parametric derivatives! We get the first derivative in part A:

$$\frac{dy}{dx} = \frac{y'(t)}{x'(t)} = \frac{\cos(t) + 1}{e^t + 3t^2}$$

Evaluating at $t = 0$,

$$\left.\frac{dy}{dx}\right|_{t=0} = \frac{\cos(0) + 1}{e^0 + 3(0)^2} = \frac{1+1}{1+0} = 2$$

Going for the point,

$$x(0) = e^0 + 0^3 = 1$$
$$y(0) = \sin(0) + 0 = 0$$

The slope at $t = 0$ is 2 and the point is $(1, 0)$, so the tangent line is

$$y - 0 = 2(x - 1) \Rightarrow y = 2x - 2$$

For part B, we find the first group of critical points by setting the derivative equal to 0. Here that would be the numerator:

$$\frac{\cos(t) + 1}{e^t + 3t^2} = 0 \Rightarrow \cos(t) + 1 = 0 \Rightarrow \cos(t) = -1$$

Using our knowledge of the unit circle, we know that $t = \pi$ is the only critical point within $[0, 2\pi]$.

Next, we check if the derivative is undefined anywhere, and here that means where the denominator equals 0. Looking at $e^t + 3t^2$, we see that e^t is always positive and $3t^2$ is always positive except at $t = 0$. That means their sum is always positive and never 0, and so the derivative is never undefined (meaning the curve will never have a vertical slope).

So far we have found the time t at which there is a critical point, but what are the coordinates of the critical point? Let's find out:

$$x(\pi) = e^\pi + \pi^3$$
$$y(\pi) = \pi$$

The latter step is true because $\sin(\pi) = 0$, so the point at $t = \pi$ is $(e^\pi + \pi^3, \pi)$, or approximately $(54.14697, 3.14159)$.

We now need to find the intervals where the curve is increasing and decreasing for part C. Since the denominator of the derivative is always positive, it suffices to check the numerator $\cos(t) + 1$. However, notice that $-1 \leq \cos(t) \leq 1$ and therefore $0 \leq \cos(t) + 1 \leq 2$. That means that the curve is in fact always increasing (except at the critical point $t = \pi$, in which case it has a horizontal slope), and the curve is never decreasing. So our one critical point is neither a maximum nor a minimum!

Finally, part D asks for the second derivative. Let's write down all the derivatives we'll need.

$$x'(t) = e^t + 3t^2 \qquad y'(t) = \cos(t) + 1$$
$$x''(t) = e^t + 6t \qquad y''(t) = -\sin(t)$$

Following the formula,

$$\frac{d^2y}{dx^2} = \frac{x'(t) \cdot y''(t) - y'(t) \cdot x''(t)}{(x'(t))^3} = \frac{(e^t + 3t^2)(-\sin(t)) - (\cos(t) + 1)(e^t + 6t)}{(e^t + 3t^2)^3}$$

$$= \frac{-\sin(t)\, e^t - 3t^2 \sin(t) - e^t \cos(t) - e^t - 6t\cos(t) - 6t}{(e^t + 3t^2)^3}$$

$$= -\frac{(\sin(t)\, e^t + 3t^2 \sin(t) + e^t \cos(t) + e^t + 6t\cos(t) + 6t)}{(e^t + 3t^2)^3}$$

I won't put you through the torture of finding concavity! Lastly, here is a graph of what this parametric curve looks like. The critical point we found earlier is marked on the graph, and notice that the slope of the curve is increasing, then is horizontal, then increases again. And notice the direction of motion going uphill, seeing how we started at $(1, 0)$ and then passed through the critical point.

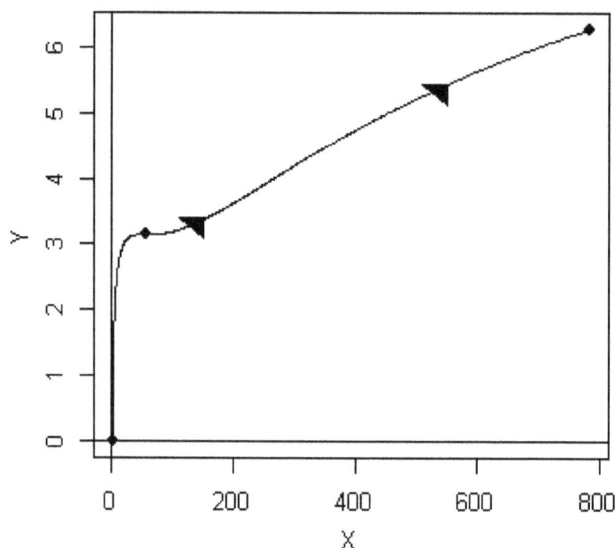

Δ

Section 4.3 – Derivatives of Vector-Valued Functions

The next topic to cover is essentially an extension of what we saw in the previous two sections with parametric functions. Previously we presented the curve as an x-coordinate function $x(t)$ and a separate y-coordinate function $y(t)$. However, we can also combine the two position functions into what is known as a **vector**.

DEFINITION

Suppose a parametric curve at time t has x-coordinate $x(t)$ and y-coordinate $y(t)$. We can write down the two functions together inside parentheses, as in

$$\left(x(t), y(t)\right)$$

When a curve is defined in this way, with both coordinate functions together inside parentheses, it is called a **vector-valued function**. When two coordinates are grouped together in this fashion, collectively it is called a **vector**.

ETYMOLOGY

The word vector comes from the Latin *vehere*, which meant "to carry" or "to transport."

For instance, the vector-valued function $\left(t^2, \sqrt{t}\right)$ for $t \geq 0$ represents the position of a particle in the x-y plane at time t. At $t = 4$, the particle is at position $(16, 2)$, which is nothing more than the classic coordinate system where the point is at $x = 16$ and $y = 2$.

We should also point out that there are several different alternative ways to denote a vector, so we'll list a few here. That way, if your main textbook uses a different notation, it will hopefully be covered below.

VECTOR-VALUED FUNCTION ALTERNATIVE NOTATION

The vector-valued function $(x(t), y(t))$ is sometimes written with pointed brackets, as in $\langle x(t), y(t) \rangle$. You may also see it written with the parametric functions stacked vertically, as in

$$\begin{pmatrix} x(t) \\ y(t) \end{pmatrix}$$

However, in terms of line spacing, this notation can get out of hand in a textbook if you have a lot of vectors appearing in the same paragraph. Another, quite different way of writing vector-valued functions uses letters i and j to represent the x and y positions, respectively, and these letters are written next to the function pieces while adding them. The vector would then be written like the following:

$$(x(t), y(t)) = (x(t))i + (y(t))j$$

Sometimes you'll see textbooks denote the i and j in bold letters or with right-pointing arrows above to indicate that we are talking about vector components (and not the imaginary number i). Thus, you might see any of the following alternative notation, all of which represent $(x(t), y(t))$:

$$\langle x(t), y(t) \rangle \qquad \begin{pmatrix} x(t) \\ y(t) \end{pmatrix} \qquad (x(t))i + (y(t))j \qquad (x(t))\boldsymbol{i} + (y(t))\boldsymbol{j} \qquad (x(t))\vec{i} + (y(t))\vec{j}$$

In this book, since we won't spend a lot of time on vector-valued functions, I'll generally write them in the form $(x(t), y(t))$.

At first glance, writing the functions this way seems like a no-brainer as we just write them together inside parentheses. However, there are important applications of vector-valued functions which we study in this section, and it goes back to what we have seen so far with physics applications: position, velocity, acceleration, and speed. Remember that the derivative of position is velocity, the derivative of velocity is acceleration, and the absolute value of velocity is speed. We now present the equivalent formulas in vector form.

DERIVATIVES OF VECTOR-VALUED FUNCTIONS

Given a parametric curve, assume that $x(t)$ and $y(t)$ are twice differentiable at time t. Then the following formulas hold:

The **position vector** at time t is $\qquad\qquad s(t) = (x(t), y(t))$.

The **velocity vector** at time t is $\qquad\qquad v(t) = (x'(t), y'(t))$.

The **acceleration vector** at time t is $\qquad\quad a(t) = (x''(t), y''(t))$.

The **speed** at time t is $\qquad\qquad\qquad \sqrt{\left(x'(t)\right)^2 + \left(y'(t)\right)^2}$.

Also, speed is said to be the **magnitude** of the velocity vector. Magnitude is the length from the origin to a given point using the distance formula, so here the distance between the origin and the point $(x(t), y(t))$ is the speed formula.

What you see above are literally two-dimensional extensions of what we saw back in Section 2.6 when we first learned about physics formulas. For instance, previously we saw that $v(t)$ was the first derivative of the position function $s(t)$. It still is now, only this time there are two functions to consider. To handle it, we just differentiate both coordinate functions separately and group them inside the same vector.

You might be wondering why the speed formula is what it is. Remember earlier we learned that speed is the absolute value of velocity, or $|v(t)|$. The two-coordinate extension is

$$\sqrt{(x'(t))^2 + (y'(t))^2}$$

One way to see why this is true is to set $y'(t) = 0$. Then the result reduces to

$$\sqrt{(x'(t))^2 + (0)^2} = \sqrt{(x'(t))^2} = |x'(t)|$$

Since $x'(t)$ is the derivative of the position function, we see that the speed vector formula reduces to the original speed formula. There is a geometric way of interpreting the speed vector, and that is to visualize the triangle formed between the origin and $\langle x'(t), y'(t)\rangle$. The length of the hypotenuse is, by the Pythagorean Theorem, equal to $\sqrt{(x'(t))^2 + (y'(t))^2}$ and therefore speed.

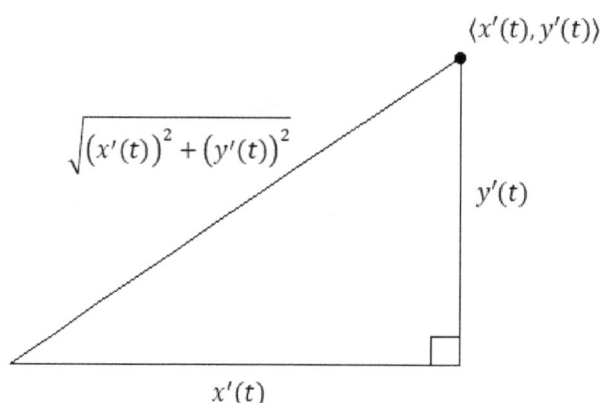

EXAMPLE
A butterfly moves in the xy-plane in such a way that its coordinates are $x(t) = t^5 - 1$ and $y(t) = 3t^4 - 2t^3$. Find the butterfly's position, velocity, and acceleration vectors and the speed, and evaluate all at $t = 1$.

Solution: First note that the position vector is

$$s(t) = (x(t), y(t)) = (t^5 - 1, 3t^4 - 2t^3)$$

The velocity vector is the first derivative of position:

$$v(t) = (x'(t), y'(t)) = (5t^4, 12t^3 - 6t^2)$$

The acceleration vector is the second derivative of position:

$$a(t) = (x''(t), y''(t)) = (20t^3, 36t^2 - 12t)$$

Evaluating all of these at $t = 1$,

$$s(1) = ((1)^5 - 1, 3(1)^4 - 2(1)^3) = (0, 1)$$
$$v(1) = (5(1)^4, 12(1)^3 - 6(1)^2) = (5, 6)$$
$$a(1) = (20(1)^3, 36(1)^2 - 12(1)) = (20, 24)$$

All of these are vectors with two components. Next, let's find the general formula for speed:

$$\text{speed}(t) = \sqrt{\left(x'(t)\right)^2 + \left(y'(t)\right)^2} = \sqrt{(5t^4)^2 + (12t^3 - 6t^2)^2}$$
$$= \sqrt{25t^8 + (6t^2)^2(2t - 1)^2} = \sqrt{25t^8 + 36t^4(4t^2 - 4t + 1)}$$
$$= \sqrt{25t^8 + 144t^6 - 144t^5 + 36t^4}$$

Thus, the speed at $t = 1$ is

$$\text{speed}(t) = \sqrt{25(1)^8 + 144(1)^6 - 144(1)^5 + 36(1)^4} = \sqrt{61}$$

The following graphs show what the position, velocity, and acceleration vectors look like for this example for $0 \leq t \leq 1$. In each graph the x-axis is $x(t)$, $x'(t)$, or $x''(t)$, and similarly for the y-axis. The direction of motion has also been indicated.

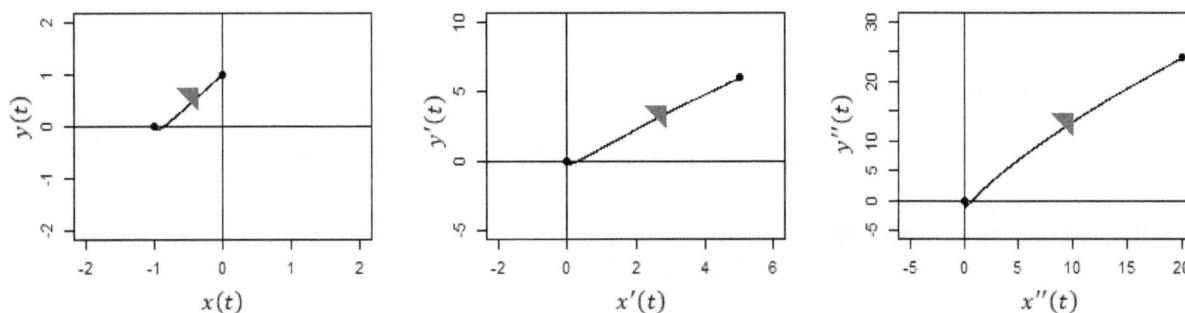

Δ

EXAMPLE

A parametric curve's position vector is represented by $x(t) = t^3$ and $y(t) = t^2 - 5t + 2$. Find the equation of the tangent line to the point $(8, -4)$, as well as the magnitude of the velocity vector at that point. Find the acceleration vector at that point as well.

Solution: First note that since we need a tangent line to a point, that means first finding the first derivative (here the velocity vector). The position vector is

$$s(t) = (t^3, t^2 - 5t + 2)$$

Notice that the point on the curve is $(8, -4)$, and yet t has not been told to us. A point on the curve comes from position, so we first need to solve for t using the parametric equations.

$$t^3 = 8 \Rightarrow t = 2$$

Just to be certain, let's solve using the y-coordinate equation as well.

$$t^2 - 5t + 2 = -4 \Rightarrow t^2 - 5t + 6 = 0 \Rightarrow (t-2)(t-3) = 0$$
$$\Rightarrow t = 2, 3$$

We get two possible answers for t, only one of which matches what we found from the x-coordinate equation. Hence, the point $(8, -4)$ occurs at $t = 2$. Armed with that information, let's find the velocity vector.

$$v(t) = (3t^2, 2t - 5)$$

Thus, $x'(t) = 3t^2$ and $y'(t) = 2t - 5$, and so

$$\frac{dy}{dx} = \frac{2t - 5}{3t^2}\bigg|_{t=2} = \frac{2(2) - 5}{3(2)^2} = -\frac{1}{12}$$

The slope of the tangent line at $t = 2$ is $-1/12$, and the point is $(8, -4)$, so the tangent line is

$$y - 4 = -\frac{1}{12}(x - 8) \Rightarrow y = -\frac{1}{12}x + \frac{8}{12} + 4 \Rightarrow y = -\frac{1}{12}x + \frac{2}{3} + \frac{12}{3}$$
$$\Rightarrow y = -\frac{1}{12}x + \frac{14}{3}$$

Next, the magnitude of the velocity vector is the speed. First note that

$$v(2) = (3(2)^2, 2(2) - 5) = \langle 12, -1 \rangle$$

Thus, speed at the point of interest is

$$\text{speed}(2) = \sqrt{(12)^2 + (-1)^2} = \sqrt{145}$$

Finally, the acceleration vector is

$$a(t) = (6t, 2)$$
$$a(2) = (6(2), 2) = (12, 2)$$

Δ

EXAMPLE
A seashell is pushed around in waves on the shore of a beach as the waves come in and recede. The seashell's position vector is defined according to the parametric equations $x(t) = \sin(2t)$ and $y(t) = \frac{1}{3}\cos(4t)$ over $0 \le t \le 2\pi$. Find at what times t and at what positions the seashell is at rest. (This problem is based on the cover photo of this textbook, which I took on the beach of Sullivan's Island in South Carolina in 2018.)

Solution: The seashell will be at rest when the velocity vector is equal to 0 for both components, or in other words when $v(t) = (0, 0)$. The velocity vector is

$$v(t) = \left(2\cos(2t), -\frac{4}{3}\sin(4t)\right)$$

We need to see if there are any points where both pieces of the vector are 0 at once. If, for instance, $x'(t) = 0$ but $y'(t) > 0$, that means the x-coordinate is not changing but the y-coordinate is increasing, so that would not count. Let's find where $x'(t) = 0$:

$$2\cos(2t) = 0 \Rightarrow \cos(2t) = 0 \Rightarrow 2t = \frac{\pi}{2}, \frac{3\pi}{2}$$
$$\Rightarrow t = \frac{\pi}{4}, \frac{3\pi}{4}$$

Now we find where $y'(t) = 0$.

$$-\frac{4}{3}\sin(4t) = 0 \Rightarrow \sin(4t) = 0 \Rightarrow 4t = 0, \pi, 2\pi$$
$$\Rightarrow t = 0, \frac{\pi}{4}, \frac{\pi}{2}$$

The only time when both $x'(t) = 0$ and $y'(t) = 0$ is at $t = \pi/4$. The corresponding position vector at that time is

$$s\left(\frac{\pi}{4}\right) = \left(\sin\left(2\left(\frac{\pi}{4}\right)\right), \frac{1}{3}\cos\left(4\left(\frac{\pi}{4}\right)\right)\right) = \left(\sin\left(\frac{\pi}{2}\right), \frac{1}{3}\cos(\pi)\right) = \left(1, \frac{1}{3}\right)$$

Thus, at $t = \pi/4$ the seashell is at rest on the beach (or in the waves), and the coordinates of the position vector where this occurs are $(1, 1/3)$.

Δ

Section 4.4 – Polar Curves

The last two sections of Chapter 4 deal with another new topic called polar curves. These are literally a special type of parametric curve defined in a specific way, but they have useful applications to mathematics. We do need to stop and introduce a new way of graphing curves that is quite different from what you are used to seeing.

Up until now we have seen graphs of functions where a point is expressed as (x, y) coordinates on the xy-plane, which translates to a point graphed by going right (or left) x units from the origin, then up (or down) y units. These are called **Cartesian coordinates**, and an example is shown below with the point $\left(2\sqrt{2}, 2\sqrt{2}\right)$.

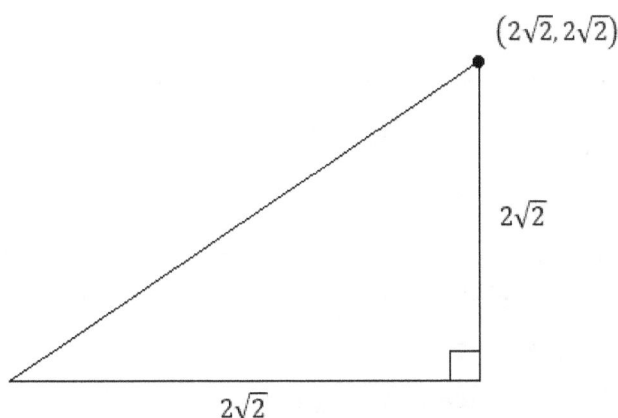

There is another way of expressing points on a graph called **polar coordinates**. Instead of saying (x, y), we write (r, θ) where r is the distance from the origin to the point and θ is the angle created going counterclockwise from the positive x-axis to the point. In the following graph, r and θ are shown, along with the original (x, y).

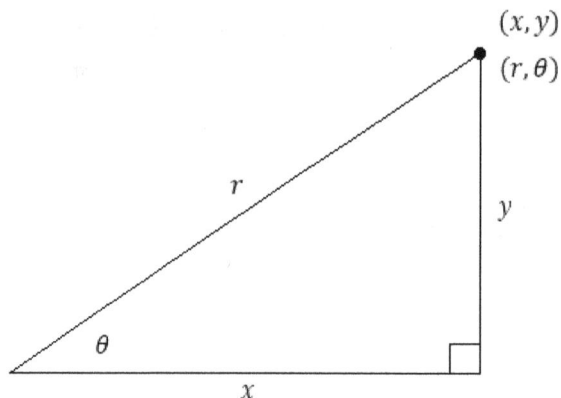

Note that r is the length of the hypotenuse of the triangle created from the origin to $\left(2\sqrt{2}, 2\sqrt{2}\right)$, and here that length is 4. Also note that the angle in this triangle between the positive x-axis and $\left(2\sqrt{2}, 2\sqrt{2}\right)$ is $\pi/4$ (we'll see in a little bit how to find these numbers). Thus, the point's Cartesian coordinates are $(x, y) = \left(2\sqrt{2}, 2\sqrt{2}\right)$, whereas the same point's polar coordinates are $(r, \theta) = (4, \pi/4)$.

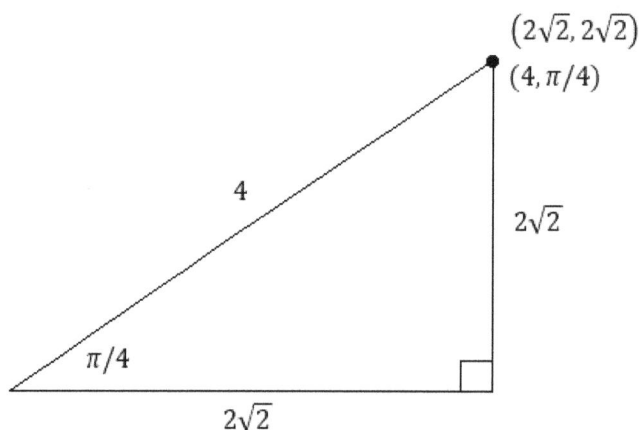

DEFINITION

Consider the point (x, y) graphed in the usual xy-plane. The **Cartesian coordinates** (sometimes called **rectangular coordinates**) are the usual ones; the point (x, y) is graphed by going right (or left) x units and then up (or down) y units.

The **polar coordinates** for the same point are represented by (r, θ). Here r is the distance from the origin to the point and θ is the angle created between the positive x-axis and the point, going in a counterclockwise direction (or anticlockwise in the United Kingdom). The origin is known as the **pole.**

ETYMOLOGY

Cartesian coordinates get their name from the French mathematician René Descartes (we saw his name earlier, the "I think, therefore I am" fellow). The word polar comes from the Latin *polus*, which meant "the end of an axis."

To be clear, in the previous example, $\left(2\sqrt{2}, 2\sqrt{2}\right)$ and $(4, \pi/4)$ in fact represent the same position in the xy-plane, as long as it is clear that the first coordinates are Cartesian and the second coordinates are polar.

This topic can be a bit confusing if you haven't seen it before, so let me give you a scenario that will hopefully help. Imagine you are standing at a specified position somewhere above the Arctic Circle (let's say northern Greenland), and your current position is base camp. Suppose the eastern direction is defined to be angle 0. You then walk 4 kilometers in the northeastern direction, which translates to the $\pi/4$ angle. Thus, your ending point as measured from base camp is found by walking 4 kilometers away and at an angle of $\pi/4$. Let's see that sketch again:

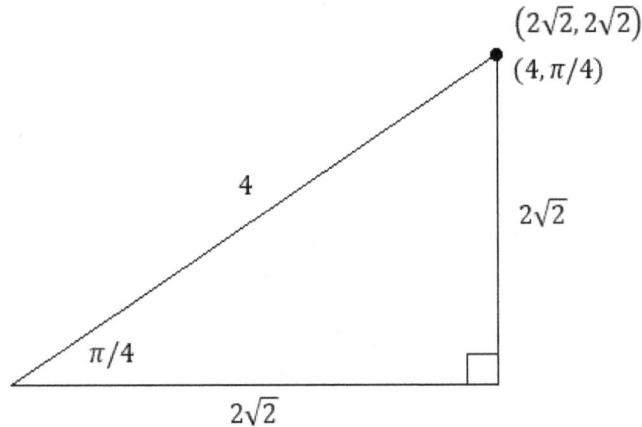

What I just described to you are polar coordinates in a real-life scenario. You walked 4 kilometers away from base camp at a $\pi/4$ angle, so the polar coordinates are $(4, \pi/4)$. However, according to the sketch, another way you could have ended up at this same new position is, starting from base camp, walking due east (right) $2\sqrt{2}$ kilometers, then walking due north (up) $2\sqrt{2}$ kilometers. This translates into Cartesian coordinates $(2\sqrt{2}, 2\sqrt{2})$.

MNEMONIC
Imagine you are standing at base camp above the Arctic Circle, and you walk away from that point at a specific angle and distance. The distance away from base camp is r, and the angle counterclockwise from the positive x-axis is θ. Why above the Arctic Circle? This is the region where polar bears live, hence polar coordinates!

An obvious question is how to convert Cartesian coordinates to polar coordinates. We can use a bit of trigonometry to figure out how. Looking at our triangle sketch, the goal is to find formulas for r and θ in terms of x and y.

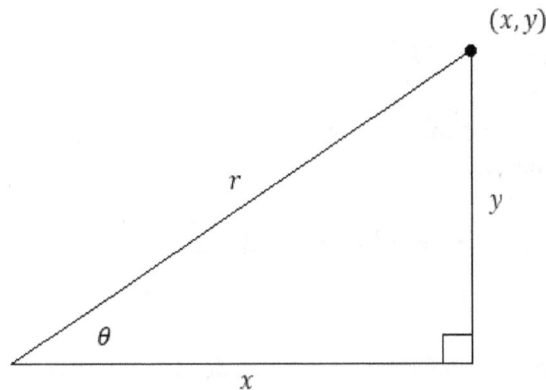

Since r is the hypotenuse of the triangle, by the Pythagorean Theorem, $r^2 = x^2 + y^2$ and therefore $r = \sqrt{x^2 + y^2}$. Usually by convention $r \geq 0$ since it's a distance from the origin, which is why we don't write the negative square root. (Some books allow r to be negative, but we won't deal with that here.) Next, note that since this is a right triangle, we know that

$$\tan(\theta) = \frac{\text{opposite}}{\text{adjacent}} = \frac{y}{x}$$

We also need to know which quadrant to aim for. The angle θ is therefore

$$\theta = \arctan\left(\frac{y}{x}\right)$$

Be careful here, however, because the arctangent function returns a value between $-\pi/2$ and $\pi/2$ (the first and fourth quadrants), and so it's possible to get an angle that does not fall in the required quadrant. If that happens, we can add π to the answer to get into the second or third quadrant. To determine whether this is needed, we need to know in which quadrant the point falls. (For instance, if x and y are both positive, we are in the first quadrant, which means $0 \le \theta \le \pi/2$. On the other hand, if x is negative and y is positive, that would be the second quadrant and therefore $\pi/2 \le \theta \le \pi$.) The following table shows what angles of θ each quadrant covers, including the equivalent negative angles.

Quadrant	X	Y	Angles	Negative Angles
1st	Positive	Positive	$0 \le \theta \le \pi/2$	$-2\pi \le \theta \le -3\pi/2$
2nd	Negative	Positive	$\pi/2 \le \theta \le \pi$	$-3\pi/2 \le \theta \le -\pi$
3rd	Negative	Negative	$\pi \le \theta \le 3\pi/2$	$-\pi \le \theta \le -\pi/2$
4th	Positive	Negative	$3\pi/2 \le \theta \le 2\pi$	$-\pi/2 \le \theta \le 0$

When writing the actual answer, usually by convention $0 \le \theta \le 2\pi$ unless stated otherwise.

CONVERTING CARTESIAN COORDINATES TO POLAR CORDINATES
Given a point in the xy-plane with Cartesian coordinates (x, y), unless stated otherwise let $r \ge 0$ and $0 \le \theta \le 2\pi$. Then the polar coordinates of the point are (r, θ) where

$$r = \sqrt{x^2 + y^2}$$
$$\theta = \begin{cases} \arctan\left(\frac{y}{x}\right), & (x, y) \text{ in 1st or 4th quadrant} \\ \arctan\left(\frac{y}{x}\right) + \pi, & (x, y) \text{ in 2nd or 3rd quadrant} \end{cases}$$

If you end up with a negative θ, you may "convert it" by adding 2π so that it falls between 0 and 2π. To state the formulas more succinctly,

$$r^2 = x^2 + y^2 \text{ and } \tan(\theta) = \frac{y}{x}$$

Going back to the earlier sketch, given Cartesian coordinates $(2\sqrt{2}, 2\sqrt{2})$ in the first quadrant,

$$r = \sqrt{\left(2\sqrt{2}\right)^2 + \left(2\sqrt{2}\right)^2} = \sqrt{4 \cdot 2 + 4 \cdot 2} = \sqrt{16} = 4$$

$$\theta = \arctan\left(\frac{2\sqrt{2}}{2\sqrt{2}}\right) = \arctan(1) = \frac{\pi}{4}$$

We can also convert polar coordinates to Cartesian coordinates using similar trigonometric results. Going back to that triangle sketch, we know from trigonometry that

$$\cos(\theta) = \frac{\text{adjacent}}{\text{hypotenuse}} = \frac{x}{r} \quad \text{and} \quad \sin(\theta) = \frac{\text{opposite}}{\text{hypotenuse}} = \frac{y}{r}$$

These lead to the conversion formulas

$$x = r\cos(\theta) \quad \text{and} \quad y = r\sin(\theta)$$

CONVERTING POLAR COORDINATES TO CARTESIAN CORDINATES
Given a point in the xy-plane with polar coordinates (r, θ), the Cartesian coordinates of the point are (x, y) where
$$x = r\cos(\theta) \quad \text{and} \quad y = r\sin(\theta)$$

EXAMPLE
Convert the Cartesian coordinates $(1, -1)$ and $(-3, 4)$ into polar coordinates.

Solution: The point $(1, -1)$ is in the fourth quadrant, so the sketch looks like this:

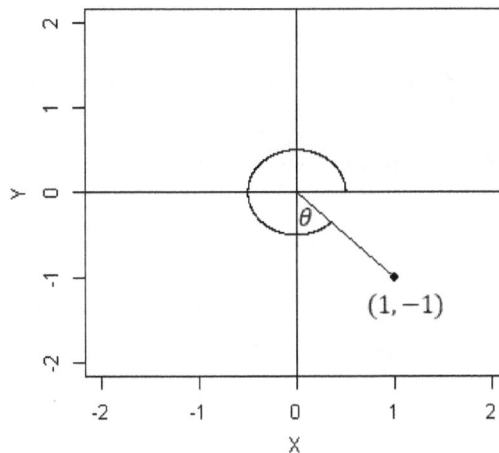

We have $r = \sqrt{(-1)^2 + 1^2} = \sqrt{2}$, and looking at the sketch, the angle θ is measured going from the positive x-axis to the r line in a counterclockwise direction. Since the point is in the fourth quadrant, that means $3\pi/2 \leq \theta \leq 2\pi$. Using the formula,

$$\tan(\theta) = \frac{y}{x} = -\frac{1}{1} = -1$$

The two angles that have a tangent equal to -1 are $\theta = 3\pi/4$ and $\theta = 7\pi/4$. Thus, the answer we are looking for is $\theta = 7\pi/4$ since that angle falls in the fourth quadrant. Had we used the calculator to compute $\arctan(-1)$, it would have given $-\pi/4$ as the answer. While this would be correct, it is more convenient to rewrite the angle to be between 0 and 2π by adding 2π, so

$$-\frac{\pi}{4} + 2\pi = -\frac{\pi}{4} + \frac{8\pi}{4} = \frac{7\pi}{4}$$

Thus, the Cartesian coordinates $(1, -1)$ correspond to the polar coordinates $\left(\sqrt{2}, 7\pi/4\right)$. Next, the sketch for $(-3, 4)$ looks like this, revealing the point to be in the second quadrant.

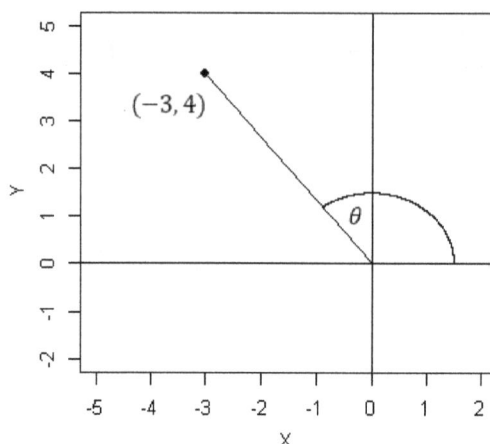

Here $r = \sqrt{(-3)^2 + 4^2} = 5$, and again θ is measured going from the positive x-axis to the r line in a counterclockwise direction. Since the point is in the second quadrant, that means $\pi/2 \le \theta \le \pi$. Using the formula,

$$\tan(\theta) = -\frac{4}{3}$$

There is no obvious angle that corresponds to this tangent value, so let's use our calculator:

$$\arctan\left(-\frac{4}{3}\right) \approx -0.92730$$

The resulting decimal answer is in the fourth quadrant (because $-\pi/2 \le -0.92730 \le 0$), so we instead find the second quadrant angle by adding π:

$$-0.92730 + \pi \approx 2.21423$$

Thus, the Cartesian coordinates $(-3, 4)$ correspond to the polar coordinates $(5, 2.21423)$.

Δ

EXAMPLE
Convert the polar coordinates $(5, 5\pi/4)$ and $(2, -\pi/3)$ into Cartesian coordinates.

Solution: Converting back to Cartesian is a little easier:

$$x = r\cos(\theta) = 5\cos\left(\frac{5\pi}{4}\right) = 5\left(-\frac{\sqrt{2}}{2}\right) = -\frac{5\sqrt{2}}{2}$$
$$y = r\sin(\theta) = 5\sin\left(\frac{5\pi}{4}\right) = 5\left(-\frac{\sqrt{2}}{2}\right) = -\frac{5\sqrt{2}}{2}$$

Thus, the polar point $(5, 5\pi/4)$ corresponds to the Cartesian point $\left(-5\sqrt{2}/2, -5\sqrt{2}/2\right)$. For the next point, we can put the numbers right away into the calculator, but it might be more convenient to convert the angle to be between 0 and 2π:

$$-\frac{\pi}{3} + 2\pi = -\frac{\pi}{3} + \frac{6\pi}{3} = \frac{5\pi}{3}$$

We therefore have

$$x = r\cos(\theta) = 2\cos\left(\frac{5\pi}{3}\right) = 2\left(\frac{1}{2}\right) = 1$$
$$y = r\sin(\theta) = 2\sin\left(\frac{5\pi}{3}\right) = 2\left(-\frac{\sqrt{3}}{2}\right) = -\sqrt{3}$$

The polar point $(2, -\pi/3)$ corresponds to the Cartesian point $\left(1, -\sqrt{3}\right)$.

Δ

We should pause here to talk about something you may have wondered about in the previous example. The polar point was at angle $\theta = -\pi/3$, but we "converted it" to $5\pi/3$ so that it was between 0 and 2π. Going counterclockwise $5\pi/3$ radians from the positive x-axis will take us to the same location as going clockwise $\pi/3$ radians from the positive x-axis. (One analogy is if you change the time on your clock from 3:00 to 5:00, you can either move the hour hand forward two hours or move it backward ten hours. Either way will end up at 5:00.)

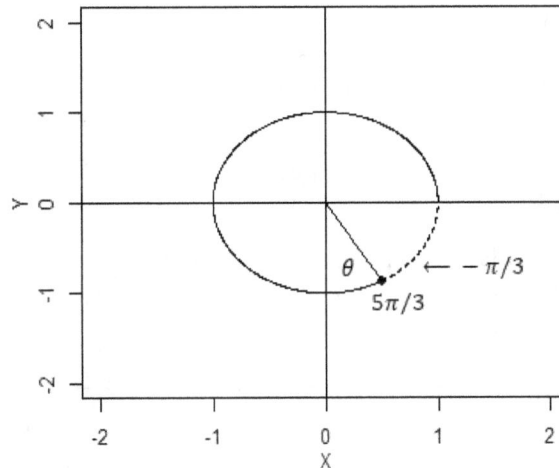

What this means is that the polar point $(2, -\pi/3)$ corresponds to the Cartesian point $\left(1, -\sqrt{3}\right)$, but so does the polar point $(2, 5\pi/3)$. By a similar argument, $(2, 11\pi/3)$ would correspond to the same Cartesian point since $5\pi/3 + 2\pi = 11\pi/3$.

Now that we have covered the basic facts about polar coordinates, the next thing to talk about is converting Cartesian functions to polar functions. This works the same way as converting individual points; you can use the formulas presented earlier.

EXAMPLE
Convert the circle $x^2 + y^2 = 16$ into polar form.

Solution: We know that $x = r\cos(\theta)$ and $y = r\sin(\theta)$, so putting those into the equation,

$$x^2 + y^2 = r^2 \cos^2(\theta) + r^2 \sin^2(\theta) = r^2(\cos^2(\theta) + \sin^2(\theta)) = r^2(1) = 16$$
$$r^2 = 16 \Rightarrow r = 4$$

Thus, $x^2 + y^2 = 16$ rewritten in polar form is $r = 4$. (By convention, we don't use the negative square root since r is the distance from the origin.)

Δ

EXAMPLE
Describe the function $\tan(\theta) = m$.

Solution: At first glance it is not obvious what sort of function this polar equation is. However, remember that $\tan(\theta) = y/x$ is one of the conversion formulas, so

$$\tan(\theta) = m \Rightarrow \frac{y}{x} = m \Rightarrow y = mx$$

Thus, $\tan(\theta) = m$ turns out to be the Cartesian equation $y = mx$, which of course is a line with slope m that passes through the origin.

Δ

EXAMPLE
Find the polar form for an ellipse centered at the origin with major axis (parallel to the x-axis) length $2a$ and minor axis length $2b$, $a \geq b > 0$.

Solution: The Cartesian equation of this ellipse is the usual one:

$$\frac{x^2}{a^2} + \frac{y^2}{b^2} = 1$$

If $a > b > 0$, then the major axis falls along the x-axis and the minor axis along the y-axis. The vertices are at $(a, 0)$ and $(-a, 0)$, and the co-vertices are at $(0, b)$ and $(0, -b)$. We are pointing this out to have points of reference to check the polar equation.

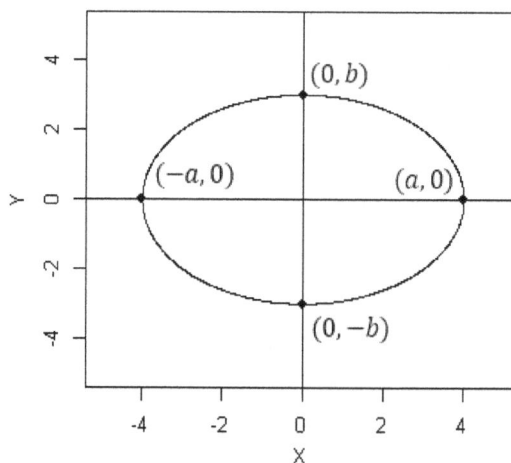

Let's use the Cartesian to polar equations $x = r\cos(\theta)$ and $y = r\sin(\theta)$:

$$\frac{x^2}{a^2} + \frac{y^2}{b^2} = 1 \Rightarrow \frac{r^2 \cos^2(\theta)}{a^2} + \frac{r^2 \sin^2(\theta)}{b^2} = 1$$

For reasons that will become clear in Section 4.5, it's desirable if possible to solve for r in terms of θ.

$$\frac{r^2 \cos^2(\theta)}{a^2} + \frac{r^2 \sin^2(\theta)}{b^2} = 1 \Rightarrow \frac{r^2 b^2\cos^2(\theta) + r^2 a^2\sin^2(\theta)}{a^2 b^2} = 1$$
$$\Rightarrow r^2 b^2\cos^2(\theta) + r^2 a^2\sin^2(\theta) = a^2 b^2$$
$$\Rightarrow r^2(b^2\cos^2(\theta) + a^2\sin^2(\theta)) = a^2 b^2$$
$$\Rightarrow r^2 = \frac{a^2 b^2}{b^2\cos^2(\theta) + a^2\sin^2(\theta)}$$
$$\Rightarrow r = \frac{ab}{\sqrt{b^2\cos^2(\theta) + a^2\sin^2(\theta)}}$$

This equation looks a little complicated, so it would be nice to feel reassured that it is correct. One vertex is at $(a, 0)$ and on the positive x-axis, so at angle $\theta = 0$. That means that evaluating r at $\theta = 0$ should give $r = a$ since this point is a units away from the origin. Let's check:

$$r(0) = \frac{ab}{\sqrt{b^2\cos^2(0) + a^2\sin^2(0)}} = \frac{ab}{\sqrt{b^2(1)^2 + a^2(0)^2}} = \frac{ab}{\sqrt{b^2}} = \frac{ab}{b} = a$$

Similarly, one co-vertex is at $(0, b)$ and on the positive y-axis, so at angle $\theta = \pi/2$. Evaluating at this angle should give $r = b$ since this point is b units away from the origin:

$$r\left(\frac{\pi}{2}\right) = \frac{ab}{\sqrt{b^2\cos^2\left(\frac{\pi}{2}\right) + a^2\sin^2\left(\frac{\pi}{2}\right)}} = \frac{ab}{\sqrt{b^2(0)^2 + a^2(1)^2}} = \frac{ab}{\sqrt{a^2}} = \frac{ab}{a} = b$$

Δ

Working with polar coordinates, certain functions appear whose graphs are very unlike those you would typically see for regular Cartesian functions. Although a Cartesian formula might exist, working in polar land is often more convenient. There are plenty of interesting and even beautiful-looking examples of polar curves, and we give three of them below. It will be good to have some practice of sketching such curves as they might not be as intuitive to graph as ordinary Cartesian functions.

EXAMPLE (CARDIOID)
Define the **cardioid** to be the polar curve

$$r = a(1 + \cos(\theta)) \ \text{ for } a > 0$$

The cardioid can actually be defined in a few different ways, but we'll stick with the above equation. The reason for the name of the function will become clear once the graph is finished. As an example of graphing one, let's take $a = 1$, so we are going to sketch $r = 1 + \cos(\theta)$. For a start, let's pick the standard points on the unit circle from 0 to π.

θ	r	r (decimal)	(r, θ)
0	$1 + 1$	2	$(2, 0)$
$\pi/6$	$1 + \sqrt{3}/2$	1.86603	$(1.86603, \pi/6)$
$\pi/4$	$1 + \sqrt{2}/2$	1.70711	$(1.70711, \pi/4)$
$\pi/3$	$1 + 1/2$	1.5	$(1.5, \pi/3)$
$\pi/2$	$1 + 0$	1	$(1, \pi/2)$
$2\pi/3$	$1 - 1/2$	0.5	$(0.5, 2\pi/3)$
$3\pi/4$	$1 - \sqrt{2}/2$	0.29289	$(0.29289, 3\pi/4)$
$5\pi/6$	$1 - \sqrt{3}/2$	0.13397	$(0.13397, 5\pi/6)$
π	$1 - 1$	0	$(0, \pi)$

The plotted points look like the following. Note that in each case the r is the length from the origin to the point, so plotting some of the points might be a little tricky. I recommend starting with the polar coordinates $(2, 0)$, $(1, \pi/2)$, and $(0, \pi)$ since those lie on the positive x-axis, positive y-axis, and negative x-axis, respectively. Those translate into the Cartesian coordinates $(2, 0)$, $(0, 1)$, and $(0, 0)$.

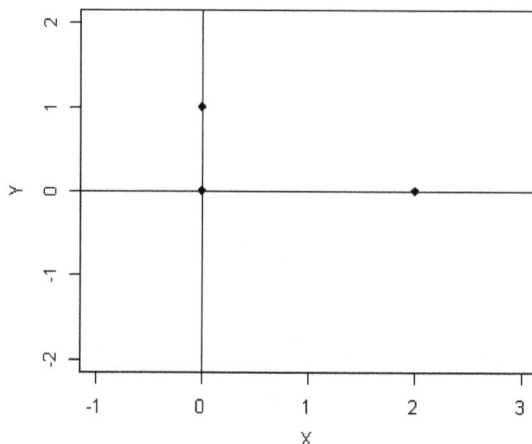

The top half of the curve looks like this when adding the sketch. Note that the curve is drawn counterclockwise from the right side to the left. (To be clear, all points in the table are polar coordinates and not Cartesian. That means that the point $(1.86603, \pi/6)$ is plotted by going out at an angle of $\pi/6$ a distance of 1.86603 units. It does not mean we go right 1.86603 units and up $\pi/6$ units.)

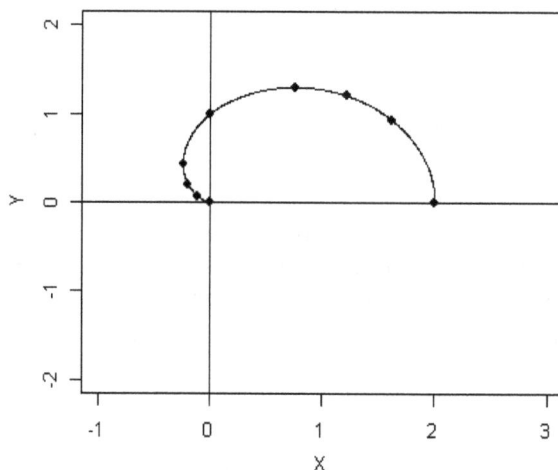

Next, we need to plot some points from π to 2π. While we could make a table like the one above and find all the calculations, one shortcut is the fact that the cosine function is symmetric in such a way that $\cos(\pi + \theta) = \cos(\pi - \theta)$ for $0 \leq \theta \leq \pi$. That means that for the next unit circle angle $\theta = 7\pi/6$, $r \approx 0.13397$, and for the next angle of $\theta = 5\pi/4$, $r \approx 0.29289$. Visually, that means the lower half of the curve is a mirror image of the top half. If you're not yet convinced about this, here is the table for the remaining values. (As a last resort, you could always compute and plot the points one at a time as with the first table.)

θ	r	r (decimal)	(r, θ)
π	$1 - 1$	0	$(0, \pi)$
$7\pi/6$	$1 - \sqrt{3}/2$	0.13397	$(0.13397, 7\pi/6)$
$5\pi/4$	$1 - \sqrt{2}/2$	0.29289	$(0.29289, 5\pi/4)$
$4\pi/3$	$1 - 1/2$	0.5	$(0.5, 4\pi/3)$
$3\pi/2$	$1 + 0$	1	$(1, 3\pi/2)$
$5\pi/3$	$1 + 1/2$	1.5	$(1.5, 5\pi/3)$
$7\pi/4$	$1 + \sqrt{2}/2$	1.70711	$(1.70711, 7\pi/4)$
$11\pi/6$	$1 + \sqrt{3}/2$	1.86603	$(1.86603, 11\pi/6)$
2π	$1 + 1$	2	$(2, 0)$

The complete graph with plotted points and fitted curve looks like this. The bottom half is indeed a mirror image of the top half.

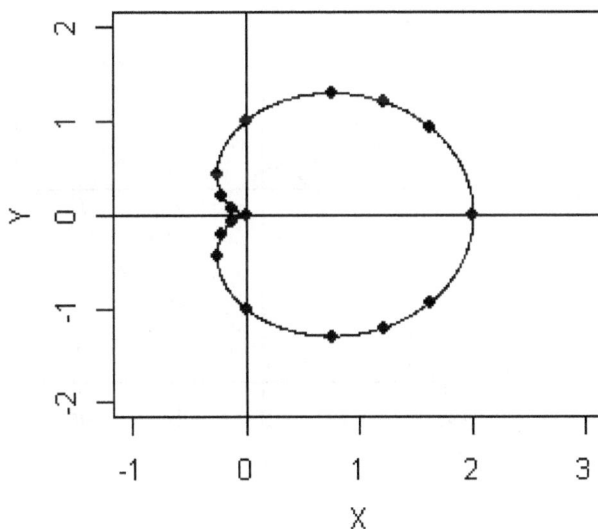

The curve is called a cardioid because it looks like a heart in appearance. The word cardioid comes from the ancient Greek καρδία (pronounced "kar-DI-a"), which meant "heart."

Δ

EXAMPLE (SPIRAL OF ARCHIMEDES)
The next example of a polar curve is called the **Spiral of Archimedes**, defined to be $r = a\theta$ for $a > 0$ and over any angles $\theta \geq 0$. To illustrate what the graph looks like, assume $a = 1$ and let's momentarily take $0 \leq \theta \leq 2\pi$. That means that five easy polar points to work with would be $(0, 0)$, $(\pi/2, \pi/2)$, (π, π), $(3\pi/2, 3\pi/2)$, and $(2\pi, 2\pi)$. These translate into the Cartesian points $(0, 0)$, $(0, \pi/2)$, $(-\pi, 0)$,

$(0, -3\pi/2)$, and $(2\pi, 0)$. This is because here the distance away from the origin is equal to the angle in radians counterclockwise from the positive x-axis. The following graph plots these points and the curve through them.

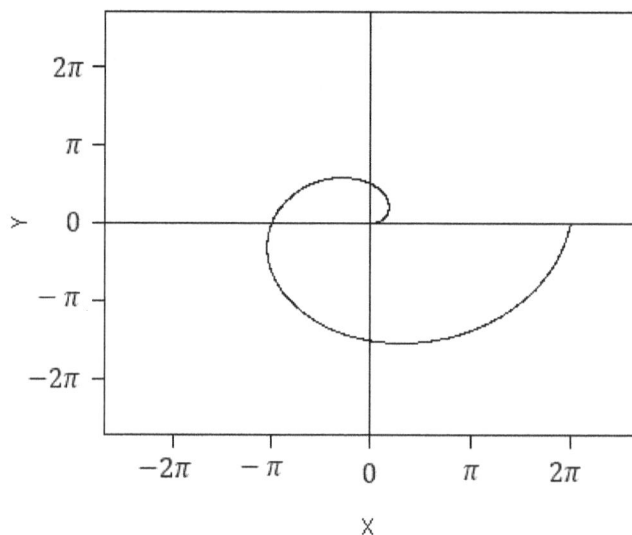

There is no reason why θ cannot be extended for the spiral. The following graph continues for $0 \le \theta \le 4\pi$, again for $a = 1$.

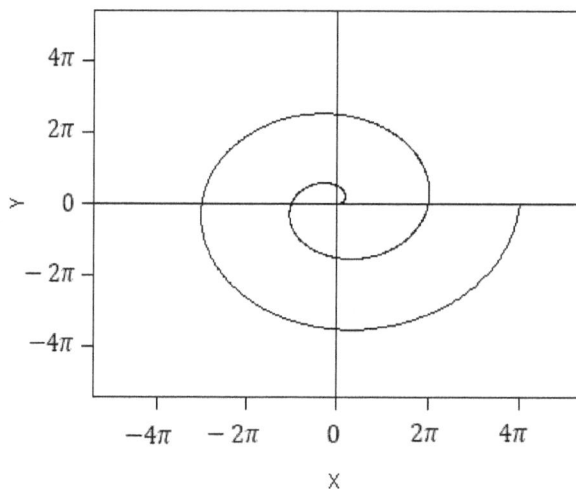

As a comparison of how the shape of the spiral changes with a, the following graph shows three spirals over $0 \le \theta \le 2\pi$ with $a = 1/2$ (solid), $a = 1$ (dashed), and $a = 3/2$ (dotted).

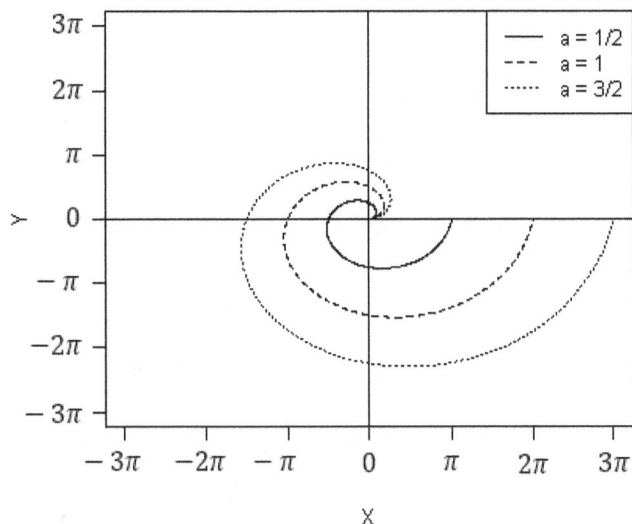

You probably recognize Archimedes' name – he was the Greek mathematician who observed that when climbing into a bathtub, the water level rose with his body in the water. You know what he did next!

Δ

EXAMPLE (FOUR-LEAVED CLOVER)

The last example we'll look at here is called a **quadrifolium**, or a **four-leaved clover**. There are several different equations to produce a shape like this, but one is $r = |\cos(2\theta)|$. Observe that at angles $\theta = 0$, $\pi/2$, π, $3\pi/2$, and 2π, $r = 1$ in each case, which corresponds to the outer tips of each "leaf" of the curve.

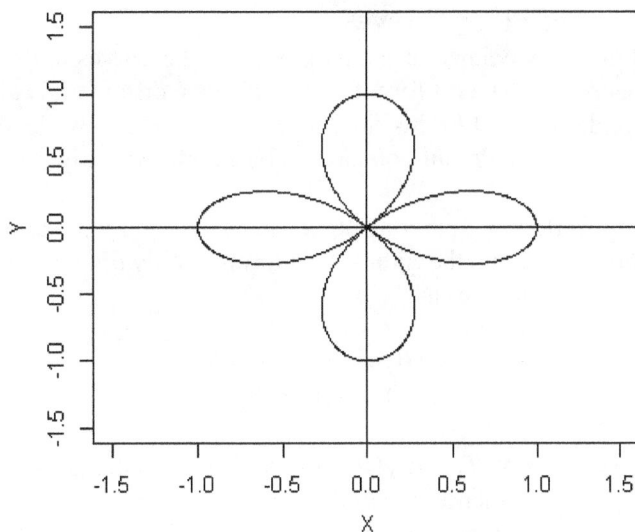

Δ

There has been a lot of new material in this section, but it was necessary for an introduction to learning about how polar functions work. The last topic to discuss is how the TI-84 can help with graphing polar functions.

TI-84 COMMAND: GRAPHING POLAR CURVES

First press MODE and scroll down to the fourth line. The usual setting is FUNC, but now scroll right to POL and press ENTER. Press 2nd and MODE to go back to the home screen. Doing so changes the calculator's setting to Polar Mode. (If you want to go back to graphing ordinary functions for other problems, return to this menu and switch back to FUNC mode.)

Now press Y =, and you can type in a function for r_1 (and more polar curves if necessary). Note that pressing the X, T, θ, n button for your input variable now shows as θ. Press WINDOW, and in addition to the usual plotting options you now have options for θmin, θmax, and $\theta step$ (sounds like another type of dance, perhaps a competitor to the $Tstep$ from parametric functions!). These are, respectively, the starting angle, the ending angle, and the increment you wish to use to go from start to finish.

Adjust your X and Y windows accordingly, and press GRAPH. You will see the polar function traced out, and pressing TRACE allows you to trace the curve and figure out the direction of motion.

EXAMPLE

For the previous example with the Archimedes spiral, under the Y = menu type $r_1 = \theta$. Going to WINDOW, type $\theta min = 0$ and $\theta max = 2\pi$, and pick something small for $\theta step$ such as $\pi/6$ (you can adjust this later). Press GRAPH, and you will see the first full revolution of the spiral traced from $(0,0)$ to the Cartesian coordinate $(2\pi, 0)$. Pressing TRACE, you can use the left and right buttons to trace the path of the spiral.

Δ

Section 4.5 – Derivatives of Polar Curves

You might be feeling a little overwhelmed at learning about polar curves since they are probably a new topic for you. However, I hope you haven't forgotten that this is a differential calculus course, and so you know what's coming next...derivatives! In this final section of Chapter 4 we learn how to find derivatives of polar curves. Doing so is not difficult, but you have to be careful with trig formulas along the way.

First recall that the polar to Cartesian equations are $x = r\cos(\theta)$ and $y = r\sin(\theta)$. If you can write the polar equation with r on the left side and the right side in terms of only θ, or in other words write $r = r(\theta)$, then you can write the Cartesian equations as

$$x(\theta) = r(\theta)\cos(\theta)$$
$$y(\theta) = r(\theta)\sin(\theta)$$

Now recognize that we have written $x(\theta)$ and $y(\theta)$ as parametric equations, only using θ instead of t, and we learned how to differentiate parametric equations earlier in Chapter 4. Thus, when written correctly, polar curves are a special case of parametric curves, in which case we can use the same differentiation techniques we used earlier. (This is why I made a point of solving for r in some equations in the previous section, to prepare us for finding derivatives.)

FIRST DERIVATIVE OF A POLAR CURVE

Define a polar curve at angle θ to have x-coordinate $x = x(\theta) = r(\theta)\cos(\theta)$ and y-coordinate $y = y(\theta) = r(\theta)\sin(\theta)$. Assume that the derivatives $dx/d\theta = x'(\theta)$ and $dy/d\theta = y'(\theta)$ exist and that $x'(\theta) \neq 0$ at angle θ. Then the first derivative of the curve is

$$\frac{dy}{dx} = \frac{\left(\frac{dy}{d\theta}\right)}{\left(\frac{dx}{d\theta}\right)} = \frac{y'(\theta)}{x'(\theta)}$$

As with regular functions, the derivative dy/dx can be interpreted as the slope of the tangent line to the curve at angle θ and at the Cartesian point $\left(x(\theta), y(\theta)\right)$. $x'(\theta)$ is the rate at which the curve's x-coordinate is changing with respect to the angle, while $y'(\theta)$ is the rate at which the curve's y-coordinate is changing with respect to the angle.

Horizontal tangent lines occur when

$$\frac{dy}{d\theta} = y'(\theta) = 0, \quad \text{provided} \quad \frac{dx}{d\theta} \neq 0$$

Vertical tangent lines occur when

$$\frac{dx}{d\theta} = x'(\theta) = 0, \quad \text{provided} \quad \frac{dy}{d\theta} \neq 0$$

Note that by using the Product Rule, $x'(\theta) = r'(\theta)\cos(\theta) - r(\theta)\sin(\theta)$ and $y'(\theta) = r'(\theta)\sin(\theta) + r(\theta)\cos(\theta)$, in which case the first derivative of a polar curve can be written as

$$\frac{dy}{dx} = \frac{y'(\theta)}{x'(\theta)} = \frac{r'(\theta)\sin(\theta) + r(\theta)\cos(\theta)}{r'(\theta)\cos(\theta) - r(\theta)\sin(\theta)}$$

However, I do not recommend that you memorize this alternative formula (unless you want to, of course). My suggestion is that you instead compute $x(\theta)$, $x'(\theta)$, $y(\theta)$, and $y'(\theta)$ on a case-by-case basis and then find $y'(\theta)/x'(\theta)$.

SECOND DERIVATIVE OF A POLAR CURVE

Define a polar curve at angle θ to have x-coordinate $x = x(\theta) = r(\theta)\cos(\theta)$ and y-coordinate $y = y(\theta) = r(\theta)\sin(\theta)$. Assume that the first derivatives $x'(\theta)$ and $y'(\theta)$ exist, that the second derivatives $x''(\theta)$ and $y''(\theta)$ exist, and that $x'(\theta) \neq 0$ at angle θ. Then the second derivative of the curve is

$$\frac{d^2y}{dx^2} = \frac{\frac{dx}{d\theta}\cdot\frac{d^2y}{d\theta^2} - \frac{dy}{d\theta}\cdot\frac{d^2x}{d\theta^2}}{\left(\frac{dx}{d\theta}\right)^3} = \frac{x'(\theta)\cdot y''(\theta) - y'(\theta)\cdot x''(\theta)}{\left(x'(\theta)\right)^3}$$

The second derivative indicates where the curve is concave up and concave down. It can be interpreted as the rate of change of the slope of the polar curve with respect to x. Note that a lot of textbooks show the following as the formula for the second derivative:

SECOND DERIVATIVE OF A POLAR CURVE (CONTINUED)

$$\frac{d^2y}{dx^2} = \frac{\frac{d}{d\theta}\left(\frac{dy}{dx}\right)}{\frac{dx}{d\theta}}$$

This formula will give the same second derivative. However, I personally prefer the other formula above since you can put all the pieces in right away. Just make sure you don't confuse it with the Quotient Rule formula!

EXAMPLE

Consider the Spiral of Archimedes again, $r = a\theta$ for $a > 0$, $r > 0$, and $0 \le \theta \le 2\pi$. Find the first derivative of the polar curve, the critical points, and the slope of the tangent line at $\theta = 2\pi/3$. Find the second derivative of the polar curve and the potential inflection points. (You'll need a calculator to find the critical and potential inflection points.)

Solution: First notice that $r(\theta) = a\theta$, so we have the following:

$$x(\theta) = a\theta \cos(\theta)$$
$$x'(\theta) = a(\cos(\theta) - \theta \sin(\theta))$$
$$x''(\theta) = a(-\sin(\theta) - \sin(\theta) - \theta \cos(\theta)) = -a(2\sin(\theta) + \theta \cos(\theta))$$
$$y(\theta) = a\theta \sin(\theta)$$
$$y'(\theta) = a(\sin(\theta) + \theta \cos(\theta))$$
$$y''(\theta) = a(\cos(\theta) + \cos(\theta) - \theta \sin(\theta)) = a(2\cos(\theta) - \theta \sin(\theta))$$

The first derivative is

$$\frac{dy}{dx} = \frac{y'(\theta)}{x'(\theta)} = \frac{a(\sin(\theta) + \theta \cos(\theta))}{a(\cos(\theta) - \theta \sin(\theta))} = \frac{\sin(\theta) + \theta \cos(\theta)}{\cos(\theta) - \theta \sin(\theta)}$$

To find where the first derivative is 0, set the numerator $\sin(\theta) + \theta \cos(\theta) = 0$. This cannot be solved by hand, so we instead need to use the TI-84 to graph this function over the window $x = 0$ to 2π. Using the zero finder on the graph, we discover that $\sin(\theta) + \theta \cos(\theta) = 0$ when $\theta = 0$, 2.0287578, and 4.9131804. These are the three angles at which the derivative is 0, or in other words where the tangent line is horizontal.

Next, to find where the first derivative is undefined, set the denominator $\cos(\theta) - \theta \sin(\theta) = 0$. This also cannot be solved by hand, so we use the TI-84's zero finder for the graph of this function. The answers are $\theta = 0.86033359$ and 3.4256185, the two angles at which the derivative is undefined, or in other words where the tangent line is vertical.

Thus, the five critical points occur at $\theta = 0$, 0.86033359 (first quadrant), 2.0287578 (second quadrant), 3.4256185 (third quadrant), and 4.9131804 (fourth quadrant). (Notice, interestingly, that the first derivative does not involve the constant a.) To find the slope of the tangent line at $\theta = 2\pi/3$, find the derivative at that angle:

$$\frac{dy}{dx}\bigg|_{\theta=\frac{2\pi}{3}} = \frac{\sin\left(\frac{2\pi}{3}\right) + \frac{2\pi}{3}\cos\left(\frac{2\pi}{3}\right)}{\cos\left(\frac{2\pi}{3}\right) - \frac{2\pi}{3}\sin\left(\frac{2\pi}{3}\right)} = \frac{\frac{\sqrt{3}}{2} + \frac{2\pi}{3}\left(-\frac{1}{2}\right)}{-\frac{1}{2} - \frac{2\pi}{3}\left(\frac{\sqrt{3}}{2}\right)}$$

$$= \dfrac{\dfrac{\sqrt{3}}{2} - \dfrac{\pi}{3}}{-\dfrac{1}{2} - \dfrac{\pi\sqrt{3}}{3}} = \dfrac{\dfrac{3\sqrt{3}}{6} - \dfrac{2\pi}{6}}{-\dfrac{3}{6} - \dfrac{2\pi\sqrt{3}}{6}} = \dfrac{3\sqrt{3} - 2\pi}{-3 - 2\pi\sqrt{3}}$$

$$= \dfrac{2\pi - 3\sqrt{3}}{2\pi\sqrt{3} + 3} \approx 0.07830$$

Next, let's find the second derivative.

$$\dfrac{d^2y}{dx^2} = \dfrac{x'(\theta) \cdot y''(\theta) - y'(\theta) \cdot x''(\theta)}{(x'(\theta))^3}$$

$$= \dfrac{a^2(\cos(\theta) - \theta\sin(\theta))(2\cos(\theta) - \theta\sin(\theta)) + a^2(\sin(\theta) + \theta\cos(\theta))(2\sin(\theta) + \theta\cos(\theta))}{(a(\cos(\theta) - \theta\sin(\theta)))^3}$$

$$= \dfrac{(\cos(\theta) - \theta\sin(\theta))(2\cos(\theta) - \theta\sin(\theta)) + (\sin(\theta) + \theta\cos(\theta))(2\sin(\theta) + \theta\cos(\theta))}{a(\cos(\theta) - \theta\sin(\theta))^3}$$

Expanding both parts of the numerator, the second derivative is

$$\dfrac{d^2y}{dx^2} = \dfrac{2\cos^2(\theta) - 3\theta\cos(\theta)\sin(\theta) + \theta^2\sin^2(\theta) + 2\sin^2(\theta) + 3\theta\cos(\theta)\sin(\theta) + \theta^2\cos^2(\theta)}{a(\cos(\theta) - \theta\sin(\theta))^3}$$

Simplifying this and using the $\cos^2(\theta) + \sin^2(\theta) = 1$ identity,

$$\dfrac{d^2y}{dx^2} = \dfrac{2\cos^2(\theta) + \theta^2\sin^2(\theta) + 2\sin^2(\theta) + \theta^2\cos^2(\theta)}{a(\cos(\theta) - \theta\sin(\theta))^3}$$

$$= \dfrac{2(\cos^2(\theta) + \sin^2(\theta)) + \theta^2(\cos^2(\theta) + \sin^2(\theta))}{a(\cos(\theta) - \theta\sin(\theta))^3}$$

$$= \dfrac{2 + \theta^2}{a(\cos(\theta) - \theta\sin(\theta))^3}$$

To find the potential inflection points, we need to see where the second derivative is 0 or undefined. The numerator is never 0 since $2 + \theta^2$ is always positive, so the only potential inflection points will occur when the derivative is undefined, or when $a(\cos(\theta) - \theta\sin(\theta))^3 = 0$. They occur when $\cos(\theta) - \theta\sin(\theta) = 0$, and we already worked out that $\theta = 0.86033359$ and 3.4256185.

The following graph shows the spiral over $0 \le \theta \le 2\pi$, taking $a = 1$ as an example. The five identified angles are plotted. Although we didn't do the first derivative test, we can see from the graph that the maximum occurs at $\theta = 2.0287578$ (2nd quadrant) and the minimum at $\theta = 4.9131804$ (4th quadrant).

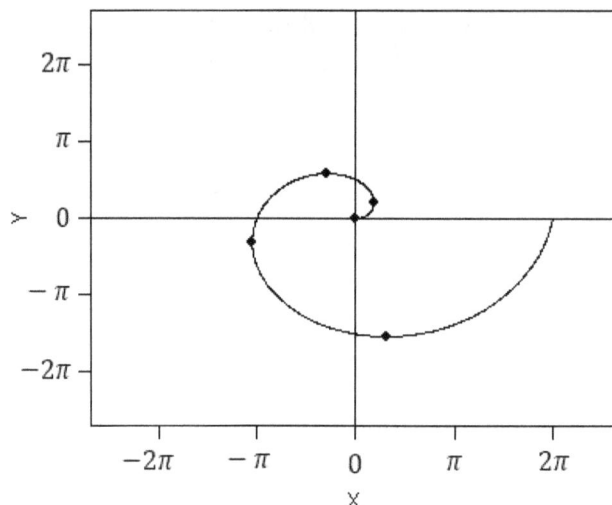

Δ

EXAMPLE

Consider the cardioid, $r = a(1 + \cos(\theta))$ for $a > 0, r > 0$, and $0 \leq \theta \leq 2\pi$. Find the first derivative of the polar curve and the critical points. Find the second derivative of the polar curve and the potential inflection points. Do not use a calculator for this problem.

Solution: First notice that $r(\theta) = a(1 + \cos(\theta))$, so we have the following:

$$x(\theta) = a(1 + \cos(\theta))\cos(\theta) = a(\cos(\theta) + \cos^2(\theta))$$
$$x'(\theta) = a(-\sin(\theta) - 2\cos(\theta)\sin(\theta)) = -a(\sin(\theta) + 2\cos(\theta)\sin(\theta))$$
$$x''(\theta) = -a(\cos(\theta) + 2\cos^2(\theta) - 2\sin^2(\theta))$$
$$y(\theta) = a(1 + \cos(\theta))\sin(\theta) = a(\sin(\theta) + \cos(\theta)\sin(\theta))$$
$$y'(\theta) = a(\cos(\theta) + \cos^2(\theta) - \sin^2(\theta))$$
$$y''(\theta) = a(-\sin(\theta) - 2\cos(\theta)\sin(\theta) - 2\cos(\theta)\sin(\theta))$$
$$= -a(\sin(\theta) + 4\cos(\theta)\sin(\theta))$$

The first derivative is

$$\frac{dy}{dx} = \frac{y'(\theta)}{x'(\theta)} = \frac{a(\cos(\theta) + \cos^2(\theta) - \sin^2(\theta))}{-a(\sin(\theta) + 2\cos(\theta)\sin(\theta))} = \frac{-(\cos(\theta) + \cos^2(\theta) - \sin^2(\theta))}{\sin(\theta) + 2\cos(\theta)\sin(\theta)}$$

Like the spiral example, the first derivative of the cardioid does not depend on the constant a. We now need to find the critical points, but doing so requires working out where the numerator and denominator are equal to 0. Doing so might not be obvious, but we can do it by hand if we use a little bit of trig trickery (or as I like to call it, "triggery," to coin a nifty word!). The goal here is to somehow factor the numerator and denominator so that we can set both equal to 0 and solve for θ. The denominator is straightforward:

$$\sin(\theta) + 2\cos(\theta)\sin(\theta) = \sin(\theta)(1 + 2\cos(\theta))$$

What's not so clear is how to factor the numerator. Noting that there are three pieces, two of which involve $\cos(\theta)$ and the third is $\sin^2(\theta)$, what we are going to do is rewrite the $\sin^2(\theta)$ in terms of $\cos(\theta)$. That's easy enough – we know that $\cos^2(\theta) + \sin^2(\theta) = 1$, and therefore $\sin^2(\theta) = 1 - \cos^2(\theta)$. The numerator rewritten is

$$-(\cos(\theta) + \cos^2(\theta) - \sin^2(\theta)) = -(\cos(\theta) + \cos^2(\theta) - (1 - \cos^2(\theta)))$$

$$= -(\cos(\theta) + \cos^2(\theta) - 1 + \cos^2(\theta))$$
$$= -(2\cos^2(\theta) + \cos(\theta) - 1)$$

We now need to factor this into the form $(* + *)(* + *)$, although it might not be obvious how to do that. If you are having trouble seeing it, temporarily write $A = \cos(\theta)$ to get $-(2A^2 + A - 1)$, and we can more easily see what to do:

$$-(2A^2 + A - 1) = -(2A - 1)(A + 1)$$

Put $A = \cos(\theta)$ back in, and we have our factored numerator:

$$= -(2A - 1)(A + 1) = -(2\cos(\theta) - 1)(\cos(\theta) + 1)$$

After all that work, the first derivative is

$$\frac{dy}{dx} = \frac{-(2\cos(\theta) - 1)(\cos(\theta) + 1)}{\sin(\theta)\,(1 + 2\cos(\theta))}$$

The first derivative is 0 when the numerator is 0, and that occurs at

$$2\cos(\theta) - 1 = 0 \Rightarrow \cos(\theta) = \frac{1}{2} \Rightarrow \theta = \frac{\pi}{3}, \frac{5\pi}{3}$$
$$\cos(\theta) + 1 = 0 \Rightarrow \cos(\theta) = -1 \Rightarrow \theta = \pi$$

The first derivative is undefined when the denominator is 0, and that occurs at

$$\sin(\theta) = 0 \Rightarrow \theta = 0, \pi, 2\pi$$
$$1 + 2\cos(\theta) = 0 \Rightarrow \cos(\theta) = -\frac{1}{2} \Rightarrow \theta = \frac{2\pi}{3}, \frac{4\pi}{3}$$

Before we go further, let's address the hippopotamus in the room (my own variation of the well-known expression!). You will note that when $\theta = \pi$, both the numerator and denominator are 0, creating an indeterminate form. The first thing that comes to mind might be l'Hôpital's Rule, which would be a useful exercise in itself, but instead let's look at the graph of this cardioid function, plotting the critical points we have so far identified (and taking $a = 1$ for the graph).

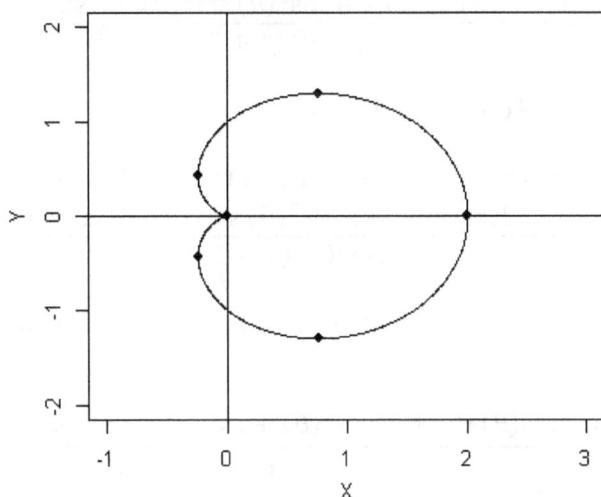

At $\theta = \pi$, the polar curve has a cusp. One of the first things you learned about derivatives in this book (Section 1.6) was that they do not exist at cusps, so we know right away that the derivative at $\theta = \pi$ does not exist. It would be incorrect to say that the derivative at $\theta = \pi$ is 0 (although it can be shown that the limits as θ approaches π from the left and right sides are both 0).

To summarize, the first derivative is 0 at $\theta = \pi/3$ and $5\pi/3$, and therefore the cardioid has horizontal tangent lines at those angles. The first derivative does not exist at $\theta = \pi$ because of a cusp there, and therefore there is no tangent line at that angle. The first derivative also does not exist at $\theta = 0, 2\pi/3, 4\pi/3$, and 2π (the same location as 0), but there are vertical tangent lines at those angles.

Next, let's find the second derivative. First recall the following from earlier:

$$x'(\theta) = -a(\sin(\theta) + 2\cos(\theta)\sin(\theta))$$
$$x''(\theta) = -a(\cos(\theta) + 2\cos^2(\theta) - 2\sin^2(\theta))$$
$$y'(\theta) = a(\cos(\theta) + \cos^2(\theta) - \sin^2(\theta))$$
$$y''(\theta) = -a(\sin(\theta) + 4\cos(\theta)\sin(\theta))$$

The second derivative is

$$\frac{d^2y}{dx^2} = \frac{x'(\theta)\cdot y''(\theta) - y'(\theta)\cdot x''(\theta)}{(x'(\theta))^3}$$

$$= \frac{\left[\begin{array}{l}-a(\sin(\theta)+2\cos(\theta)\sin(\theta))\cdot -a(\sin(\theta)+4\cos(\theta)\sin(\theta)) - \\ a(\cos(\theta)+\cos^2(\theta)-\sin^2(\theta))\cdot -a(\cos(\theta)+2\cos^2(\theta)-2\sin^2(\theta))\end{array}\right]}{(-a(\sin(\theta)+2\cos(\theta)\sin(\theta)))^3}$$

$$= \frac{\left[\begin{array}{l}a^2(\sin^2(\theta)+6\cos(\theta)\sin^2(\theta)+8\cos^2(\theta)\sin^2(\theta)) + \\ a^2(\cos^2(\theta))+3\cos^3(\theta)-3\cos(\theta)\sin^2(\theta)+2\cos^4(\theta)-4\cos^2(\theta)\sin^2(\theta)+2\sin^4(\theta)\end{array}\right]}{-a^3\sin^3(\theta)(1+2\cos(\theta))^3}$$

It's hard to believe that the second derivative can simplify, but it does quite nicely! Again, use your uncle in every photo, the identity $\cos^2(\theta) + \sin^2(\theta) = 1$. Let's first combine like terms and rearrange them (as well as factor out a^2 on the numerator).

$$\frac{d^2y}{dx^2} = \frac{a^2\left[\begin{array}{l}\sin^2(\theta)+\cos^2(\theta)+3\cos(\theta)\sin^2(\theta)+3\cos^3(\theta)+ \\ 2\cos^4(\theta)+4\cos^2(\theta)\sin^2(\theta)+2\sin^4(\theta)\end{array}\right]}{-a^3\sin^3(\theta)(1+2\cos(\theta))^3}$$

Let's now do a little factoring, and cancel out the a^2's:

$$\frac{d^2y}{dx^2} = \frac{\left[\begin{array}{l}\sin^2(\theta)+\cos^2(\theta)+3\cos(\theta)(\sin^2(\theta)+\cos^2(\theta))+ \\ 2(\cos^4(\theta)+2\cos^2(\theta)\sin^2(\theta)+\sin^4(\theta))\end{array}\right]}{-a\sin^3(\theta)(1+2\cos(\theta))^3}$$

We quickly see that the trig identity can be used twice (and the numerator can finally be written on one line!).

$$\frac{d^2y}{dx^2} = \frac{1+3\cos(\theta)(1)+2(\cos^4(\theta)+2\cos^2(\theta)\sin^2(\theta)+\sin^4(\theta))}{-a\sin^3(\theta)(1+2\cos(\theta))^3}$$

The last part of the numerator can be factored further using the identity $A^4 + 2A^2B^2 + B^4 = (A^2 + B^2)^2$. Here that would mean using $A = \cos(\theta)$ and $B = \sin(\theta)$.

$$\frac{d^2y}{dx^2} = \frac{1 + 3\cos(\theta) + 2(\sin^2(\theta) + \cos^2(\theta))^2}{-a\sin^3(\theta)(1 + 2\cos(\theta))^3}$$

Finally, the simplified second derivative is

$$\frac{d^2y}{dx^2} = \frac{1 + 3\cos(\theta) + 2(1)^2}{-a\sin^3(\theta)(1 + 2\cos(\theta))^3} = \frac{3 + 3\cos(\theta)}{-a\sin^3(\theta)(1 + 2\cos(\theta))^3}$$
$$= \frac{3(1 + \cos(\theta))}{-a\sin^3(\theta)(1 + 2\cos(\theta))^3}$$

The second derivative is 0 when the numerator is 0, and that occurs at

$$1 + \cos(\theta) = 0 \Rightarrow \cos(\theta) = -1 \Rightarrow \theta = \pi$$

The second derivative is undefined when the denominator is 0, and that occurs at

$$\sin(\theta) = 0 \Rightarrow \theta = 0, \pi, 2\pi$$
$$1 + 2\cos(\theta) = 0 \Rightarrow \cos(\theta) = -\frac{1}{2} \Rightarrow \theta = \frac{2\pi}{3}, \frac{4\pi}{3}$$

Just like with the first derivative, the second derivative has an indeterminate form at $\theta = \pi$ because direct evaluation results in 0/0. Thus, the second derivative does not exist at $\theta = \pi$, as well as at $\theta = 0, 2\pi/3$, $4\pi/3$, and 2π (the same location as 0). These are the potential inflection points. (Note that even though the second derivative doesn't exist at these points, they are still potential inflection points because the original function is defined at all of them.)

We have finally completed this massive example! Let's look at the graph again with $a = 1$, where the points are the identified critical points from the first derivative (some of which are also potential inflection points).

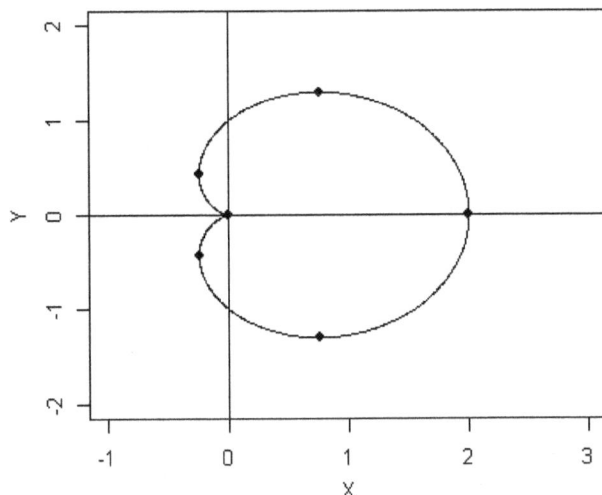

Chapter 5 – Antiderivatives and Differential Equations

This final chapter provides us with an introduction to antiderivatives, which are crucial for integral calculus. We already know how to find the derivative of a given function. Now it is time to ask ourselves, "Given a derivative $f'(x)$, what function $f(x)$ has a derivative equaling $f'(x)$?" Thus, thinking backwards will be necessary.

We first present a brief section about differentials and some of their applications. Then we discuss how to find antiderivatives, solve initial value problems and basic differential equations, and use a technique called Euler's Method that can be useful for differential equations that are too hard to solve by hand. Finally, we study some applications of antiderivatives in the sciences, especially physics.

Section 5.1 – Differentials

Suppose we fix a point (x, y) on a function $f(x)$, and we want to travel to the right, arriving at a new point (x_2, y_2). However, rather than calling the new point by these coordinates, let's simply measure it by its distance from x, the first point. Thus, our second point is

$$\left(x + \Delta x, f(x + \Delta x)\right) = (x + \Delta x, y + \Delta y)$$

Here Δx represents the change in x and Δy the change in y. (As a reminder, the triangle is the Greek letter "delta.") On a graph, we might visualize it this way:

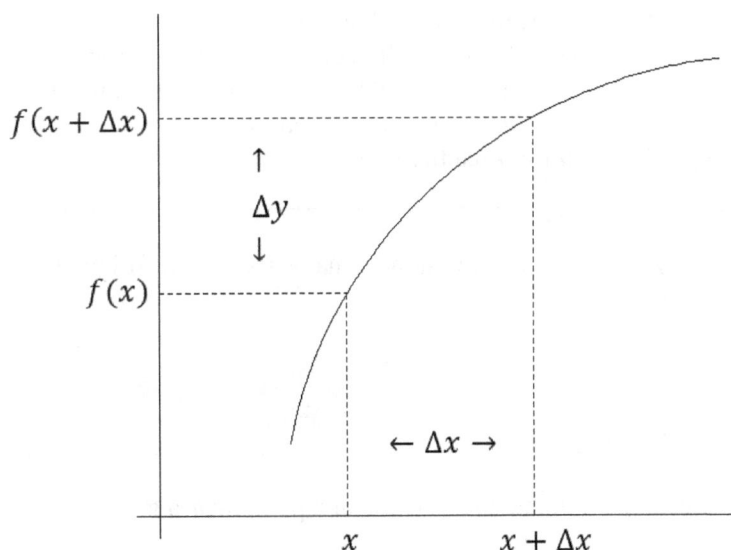

This is actually nothing new; think of it as if we are using the coordinates (x_1, y_1) and (x_2, y_2) from algebra. Only this time, we are also measuring the change in x and y.

Now imagine we want to quickly estimate the change in y another way. We first calculate the slope of $f(x)$ at the point x, getting $f'(x)$. Next, we *assume* that the slope remains the same (fixed) as x increases to $(x + \Delta x)$. Then we can get the theoretical change in y by using the fixed slope of the original change in y.

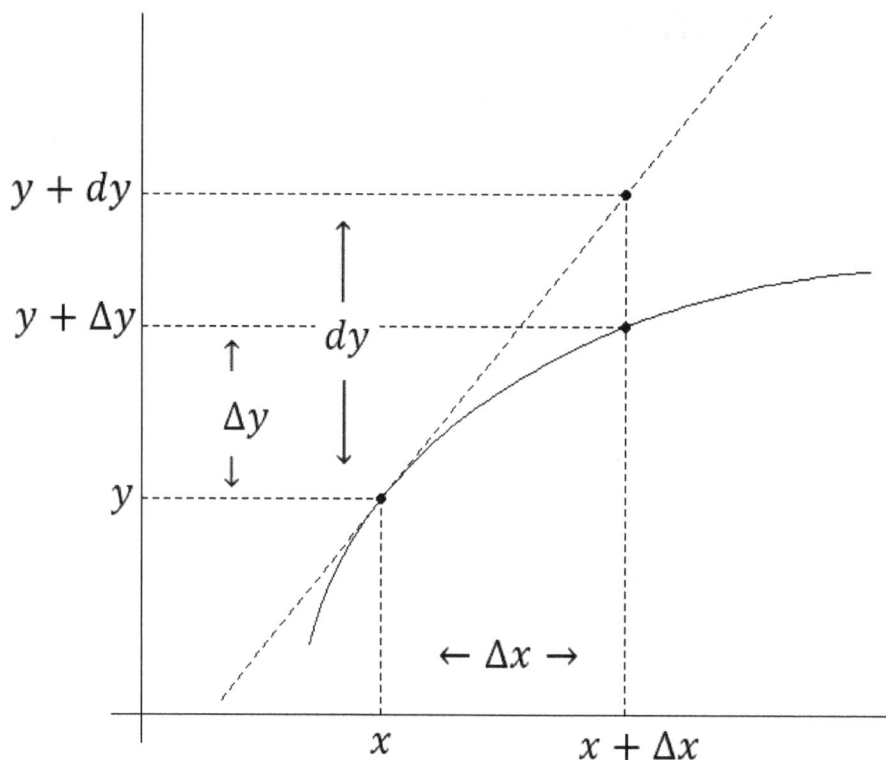

This is a little tricky to describe, practically impossible without a diagram like the one above. The value $f(x + \Delta x)$, or $(y + \Delta y)$, is the actual value of the function at that point. However, if we assume that the slope $f'(x)$ is fixed, then it will continue to change at the same rate by the time we arrive at $(x + \Delta x)$. We can then draw upon basic algebra to *estimate* what the function is at $f(x + \Delta x)$. We are interested in the hypothetical change in y, and we call this quantity dy.

DEFINITION
The hypothetical change in y, assuming that the slope remains fixed at the original point, is dy and is called a **differential**. It is written as

$$dy = f'(x)\Delta x$$

It is an approximation of Δy, so $dy \approx \Delta y$.

With this knowledge, we can approximate the function at a point *near* a given point. Here's how we do it:

$$\begin{aligned} f(x + \Delta x) &= y + \Delta y \\ &\approx y + dy \\ &= f(x) + f'(x)\Delta x \end{aligned}$$

The first step follows from the first graph. Now we substitute in what we know.

DEFINITION

We say that dy is the **linear approximation** to Δy; that is, the estimate by using the slope of the tangent line and assuming it is fixed. The formula to estimate this is

$$f(x + \Delta x) \approx f(x) + f'(x)\Delta x$$

I must stress that this is a close approximation when Δx is small (when the change is not large)! The further away we move from x, the worse our estimate.

An alternative, more user-friendly way to define a linear approximation is as follows. Suppose we start at the point a and then move to x. Then we can say that $a + \Delta x = x$, which yields $\Delta x = x - a$. The linear approximation formula to use is

$$f(x) \approx f(a) + f'(a) \cdot (x - a)$$

This might have been a confusing beginning to the chapter, for which I apologize, so let's dive straight into some examples.

EXAMPLE

Suppose $f(x) = \sqrt{x}$. Find the linear approximation formula to $f(x)$ near $a = 4$.

Solution: We need to check three things:

1) $f(a) = f(4) = \sqrt{4} = 2$
2) $f'(x) = \frac{1}{2\sqrt{x}}\Big|_{x=4} = \frac{1}{2\cdot 2} = \frac{1}{4}$
3) $(x - a) = (x - 4)$

Then the linear approximation *near* $a = 4$ is given by

$$\begin{aligned}
f(x) &\approx f(a) + f'(a) \cdot (x - a) \\
&= 2 + \frac{1}{4}(x - 4) \\
&= 2 + \frac{1}{4}x - 1 \\
&= 1 + \frac{x}{4}
\end{aligned}$$

We could use this to approximate, say, $\sqrt{5}$ (because 5 is pretty close to 4). Let $x = 5$, then the approximation tells us that

$$f(5) \approx 1 + \frac{1}{4} \cdot 5 = \frac{9}{4} = 2.25$$

The actual answer is $\sqrt{5} \approx 2.23607$, so our approximation is not too far off.

Δ

EXAMPLE

Find an estimate for the value of $e^{1/10}$.

Solution: First, if $f(x) = e^x$, then $f'(x) = e^x$. Although we certainly do not know the value of $e^{1/10}$, we do know that $e^0 = 1$, so let's take $a = 0$. Then

$$\begin{aligned} f(x) &\approx f(a) + f'(a) \cdot (x - a) \\ &= e^a + e^a \cdot (x - a) \\ &= e^0 + e^0 \cdot (x - 0) \\ &= 1 + 1 \cdot x \\ &= x + 1 \end{aligned}$$

Thus, the linear approximation is $f(x) \approx x + 1$.

Now we take $x = 1/10$, and using the approximation formula,

$$f\left(\frac{1}{10}\right) \approx \frac{1}{10} + 1 = \frac{11}{10} = 1.1$$

The actual answer is $e^{1/10} \approx 1.10517$. Not too shabby!

Δ

EXAMPLE
Let's use our last example as an application. Suppose the radius of a circle increases from 4 cm to 4.1 cm. Estimate the change in the circle's area.

Solution: This problem will use an unusual-looking technique that we have not seen before – up until now. Start by writing the area formula, then differentiating with respect to the radius:

$$A = \pi r^2$$
$$\frac{dA}{dr} = 2\pi r$$

Here comes the new step – we literally multiply both sides by the differential dr, bringing it up to the right side (yes, treating dA/dr as a fraction with a numerator and denominator).

$$dA = 2\pi r \, dr$$

This will make more sense in an integral calculus class. However, now we write down what we know: $r = 4$ and $dr = 0.1$. Then

$$\begin{aligned} dA &= 2\pi(4)(0.1) \\ &= 0.8\pi \text{ cm}^2 \\ &\approx 2.51327 \text{ cm}^2 \end{aligned}$$

The answer is that the change in the circle's area is approximately 2.51327 square centimeters. The actual change is $\Delta A = \pi(4.1)^2 - \pi(4)^2 \approx 2.54469 \text{ cm}^2$.

Δ

Section 5.2 – Antiderivatives and Slope Fields

As a motivating example, we know that given the function $f(x) = x^2$, we can quickly find the derivative: $f'(x) = 2x$. However, let's now turn the situation around, as briefly explained in the chapter introduction.

Suppose we are given the function $f(x) = 2x$. Now we ask ourselves: what has a derivative of $2x$? In this case, we can quickly answer by thinking backwards: $F(x) = x^2$ has a derivative of $2x$. However, the functions $F(x) = x^2 + 1$ and $F(x) = x^2 - 5$ also have a derivative of $2x$ because the derivative of a constant is zero.

So here's what we might answer: given $f(x) = 2x$, the **antiderivative** is $F(x) = x^2 + C$ where C is any constant.

DEFINITION
The **antiderivative** of the function $f(x)$ is another function $F(x)$ with the property that

$$F'(x) = f(x)$$

We traditionally use the capital letter $F(x)$ to denote the antiderivative of the function $f(x)$. (The same is true for other functions; for instance, $G(x)$ is the antiderivative of $g(x)$.)

Also, as we saw in the example above, when we find the antiderivative of a function, we must add "$+ C$" afterwards to denote the possibility of any constants existing.

EXAMPLE
The antiderivative of $f(x) = 3x^2$ is $F(x) = x^3 + C$. This is easily recognized by asking yourself, "What has a derivative of $3x^2$?" The answer is x^3 plus a possible constant.

Similarly, the antiderivative of $g(t) = 7x^6$ is $G(t) = x^7 + C$ because the function that has a derivative of $7x^6$ is x^7 plus a possible constant.

Δ

Since most of our problems will involve polynomials, we need to know how to quickly find their antiderivatives. We already know how to get the antiderivatives of $3x^2$ and $2x$, but now we need to examine more cases such as x^3 and $10x^4$. Let's write down an explicit formula.

We know that given $f(x) = x^n$ and any n, the derivative is $f'(x) = nx^{n-1}$ subject to certain domain constraints. However, given $f(x) = x^n$, what is the general antiderivative? Let's find a formula to use here. Previously, given $f(x) = x^n$, to get the derivative we multiplied the x by the old exponent, then deducted 1 from the exponent and arrived at $f'(x) = nx^{n-1}$.

Now we start back at $f(x) = x^n$ and think backwards. Let's first *raise* the exponent by 1 (because we previously adjusted the exponent last). Now let's *divide* by the *new* exponent $(n + 1)$. And lastly, we add a constant C at the end. We have done all the steps backwards, including division instead of multiplication. That means the antiderivative formula is

$$F(x) = \frac{1}{n + 1} x^{n+1} + C$$

This formula works for any n except for $n = -1$ because at that value we would be dividing by 0, which of course we cannot do. (We'll cover that case shortly.) In addition, you might be wondering what happens when there is a constant in front of the function, as in $f(x) = ax^n$. When taking the derivative, the constant stays in front of the function, coming along for the ride. The same is true when taking the antiderivative; the constant just stays in front of the function. In other words, if $f(x) = ax^n$, the antiderivative is

$$F(x) = \frac{a}{n+1}x^{n+1} + C$$

This is the Power Rule in reverse.

ANTIDERIVATIVE OF ax^n

If $f(x) = ax^n$ where a is any constant and $n \neq -1$, then

$$F(x) = \frac{a}{n+1}x^{n+1} + C$$

EXAMPLE

Given $f(x) = x^3$, the antiderivative is

$$F(x) = \frac{1}{3+1}x^{3+1} + C = \frac{1}{4}x^4 + C$$

Given $g(x) = 4x^7$, the antiderivative is

$$G(x) = \frac{4}{7+1}x^{7+1} = \frac{4}{8}x^8 + C$$
$$= \frac{1}{2}x^8 + C$$

Given $h(x) = 3x - 4x^2 + 8x^5$, we have

$$H(x) = \frac{3}{1+1}x^{1+1} - \frac{4}{2+1}x^{2+1} + \frac{8}{5+1}x^{5+1} + C$$
$$= \frac{3}{2}x^2 - \frac{4}{3}x^3 + \frac{8}{6}x^6 + C$$
$$= \frac{3}{2}x^2 - \frac{4}{3}x^3 + \frac{4}{3}x^6 + C$$

If you want to be assured that your answer is correct, you can always take the derivative of your answer and make sure it matches the original function. For instance, the derivative of our $H(x)$ is

$$h(x) = \frac{3}{2} \cdot 2x - \frac{4}{3} \cdot 3x^2 + \frac{4}{3} \cdot 6x^5 + 0 = 3x - 4x^2 + 8x^5$$

Δ

Notice in the previous example we took the antiderivative of $3x$. Recognize that x is the same as x^1, so $n = 1$ when finding that antiderivative.

A very easy antiderivative formula, and unfortunately one that can easily cause confusion, is the antiderivative of a constant. Suppose we need the antiderivative of $f(x) = a$, so what has a derivative of a constant a? The answer is $ax + C$. Another way to think about it is that $f(x) = a$ is the same function as $f(x) = ax^0$, in which case we can use the reverse Power Rule formula from above:

$$F(x) = \frac{a}{0+1}x^{0+1} + C = ax + C$$

ANTIDERIVATIVE OF A CONSTANT

If $f(x) = a$ where a is any constant, then

$$F(x) = ax + C$$

EXAMPLE

The antiderivative of $f(x) = -5$ is just $F(x) = -5x + C$.

Δ

You will note that when we wrote the antiderivative formula for ax^n, we mentioned that $n \neq -1$. So what happens when $n = -1$, when we need to take the antiderivative of $f(x) = ax^{-1}$? That is the same as $f(x) = a/x$, and what function has a derivative of $1/x$? The answer is the natural log! Since a is a constant in front, the function $a\ln(x) + C$ has a derivative of a/x.

ANTIDERIVATIVE OF a/x

If $f(x) = \frac{a}{x}$ where a is any constant and $x \neq 0$, then

$$F(x) = a\ln|x| + C$$

One little technicality to note is that the antiderivative requires us to write absolute value signs around the x. The reason is because we cannot take the natural log of a negative number or 0 (so of course, we assume that $x \neq 0$ for these sorts of problems as well).

EXAMPLE

The antiderivative of $f(x) = 3/x$ is

$$F(x) = 3\ln|x| + C$$

Of course, using log rules, this could also be written as

$$F(x) = \ln|x|^3 + C$$

To find the antiderivative of $g(x) = \frac{5}{4x}$, this can be a little puzzling until you realize that we can write

$$g(x) = \frac{5}{4} \cdot \frac{1}{x}$$

That means that the constant in front is $a = 5/4$, and so

$$G(x) = \frac{5}{4}\ln|x| + C$$

Δ

While we are at it, let's continue with some well-known antiderivative formulas. Remember that the derivative of e^x is itself, and when there is a constant in the exponent, as in e^{ax}, the derivative is itself multiplied by a. Going in reverse, to find the antiderivative of e^{ax}, it would be itself *divided* by a.

ANTIDERIVATIVE OF e^{ax}

If $f(x) = e^{ax}$ where $a \neq 0$ is any constant, then

$$F(x) = \frac{e^{ax}}{a} + C$$

Similarly, remember when we had $f(x) = a^x$, the derivative was $f'(x) = a^x \ln(a)$, provided $a > 0$. So the derivative was the original function multiplied by $\ln(a)$. Going in reverse, the antiderivative of $f(x) = a^x$ would be itself *divided* by $\ln(a)$.

ANTIDERIVATIVE OF a^x

If $f(x) = a^x$ where $a > 0$, then

$$F(x) = \frac{a^x}{\ln(a)} + C$$

EXAMPLE

Find the antiderivative of $h(r) = 1 + 2e^{-r} + 4^r$.

Solution: Using the formulas we've learned so far,

$$H(r) = r + \frac{2e^{-r}}{-1} + \frac{4^r}{\ln(4)} + C = r - 2e^{-r} + \frac{4^r}{\ln(4)} + C$$

Be careful with signs here since in the exponential function the constant is -1, so dividing by -1 is the same as dividing by 1 and then negating the sign in front.

Δ

The next two formulas may be a little tougher because it is easy to get the negative signs mixed up. You can probably guess what they are – the sine and cosine functions! Just to review, if $f(x) = \sin(ax)$, the derivative is $f'(x) = a\cos(ax)$, and if $g(x) = \cos(ax)$, the derivative is $g'(x) = -a\sin(ax)$.

To antidifferentiate $\sin(ax)$, ask yourself what has a derivative of $\sin(ax)$. We know it's going to involve the cosine function and that it will also involve dividing by a rather than multiplying. But what about the sign in front? Let's see what we have so far:

$$\text{The derivative of } \frac{\cos(ax)}{a} \text{ is } \frac{-a\sin(ax)}{a} = -\sin(ax)$$

This is almost finished, except we ended up with $-\sin(ax)$ when we wanted $\sin(ax)$. That means that we still need a negative sign in front of the cosine function, as in the following:

The derivative of $\dfrac{-\cos(ax)}{a}$ is $\dfrac{--a\sin(ax)}{a} = \sin(ax)$

We have therefore shown that the antiderivative of $f(x) = \sin(ax)$ is

$$F(x) = -\frac{\cos(ax)}{a} + C$$

Similarly, given $g(x) = \cos(ax)$, what has a derivative equal to this? It's going to involve the sine function and dividing by a, but what about the sign? Let's look at what we have:

The derivative of $\dfrac{\sin(ax)}{a}$ is $\dfrac{a\cos(ax)}{a} = \cos(ax)$

This time we got lucky since the derivative of the sine function is the cosine function with the same sign.

ANTIDERIVATIVES OF SINE AND COSINE

If $f(x) = \sin(ax)$ where $a \neq 0$ is any constant, the antiderivative is

$$F(x) = -\frac{\cos(ax)}{a} + C$$

Given $g(x) = \cos(ax)$, the antiderivative is

$$G(x) = \frac{\sin(ax)}{a} + C$$

Be very careful with these formulas as it is easy to get confused with which sign to use. Remember, if you are in doubt about your answer, simply differentiate it and see if it matches the original function.

EXAMPLE
Suppose $f(x) = 2\cos(3x) - \sin(-4x)$. The antiderivative of the first piece is

$$\frac{2\sin(3x)}{3}$$

The 2 is a constant in front, so it just stays with us. To find the antiderivative of the second piece, we need to be extremely careful with the signs. The negative sign in front of the sine function is a -1 constant in front, and so the constant inside the sine is $a = -4$. Using the formula, the antiderivative is

$$-1 \cdot \frac{-\cos(ax)}{a} = -1 \cdot \frac{-\cos(-4x)}{-4} = -\frac{\cos(-4x)}{4}$$

There are three negative signs that ultimately appear in front of the cosine, and three negatives make a negative. Thus, the full antiderivative is

$$F(x) = \frac{2\sin(3x)}{3} - \frac{\cos(-4x)}{4} + C$$

Δ

EXAMPLE

Find the antiderivative of $f(x) = 2\sin(x)\cos(x)$.

Solution: This looks hard because we do not yet know any techniques to find the antiderivative of a product of functions. However, look carefully and you will see that this is really a well-known trig formula:

$$f(x) = 2\sin(x)\cos(x) = \sin(2x)$$

Then $F(x) = -\frac{1}{2}\cos(2x) + C$.

Δ

EXAMPLE

Let's find the antiderivative of $f(x) = 3\cos^2(2x) + 3\sin^2(2x)$.

Solution: Once again we are confronted with some trig functions that don't quite fit the formulas we've learned. However, let's first try simplifying $f(x)$:

$$f(x) = 3(\cos^2(2x) + \sin^2(2x)) = 3 \cdot 1 = 3$$

That was easy! The antiderivative is then $F(x) = 3x + C$. (You simply can't escape that trig identity, can you?)

Δ

The moral of the previous two examples is that if you need to find the antiderivative of a function that is not a formula you recognize, see if the function can somehow be manipulated into one that is simpler. Let's do one more example of an antiderivative.

EXAMPLE

Find the antiderivative of $h(x) = \frac{5}{1+x^2}$.

Solution: Again, we have a function that clearly does not match anything we have seen so far in this section. However, take a closer look:

$$h(x) = 5 \cdot \left(\frac{1}{1+x^2}\right)$$

Do you recognize $1/(1 + x^2)$ to be the derivative of anything? It is in fact the derivative of the arctangent function back in Section 2.9, so

$$H(x) = 5\arctan(x) + C$$

Δ

The other topic to discuss in this section is slope fields. When we find the antiderivative $F(x)$ of a function $f(x)$, we need to write $+C$ to allow for possible constants. Of course, that C could be any constant. That means if we need to sketch the graph of the antiderivative $F(x)$, the curve could be in multiple locations depending on the choice of C.

For instance, suppose $f(x) = 2x$, then the antiderivative is $F(x) = x^2 + C$. This is a parabola with y-intercept $(0, C)$, but C could be any value. That means that a graph of the antiderivative could look like x^2,

$x^2 + 1$, $x^2 + 5$, $x^2 - 2$, etc., all of which involve different values of C and therefore different locations on the graph. A slope field is a graph of several possible choices of $F(x)$, each of which involves different choices for C.

DEFINITION
Given a function $f(x)$ and its antiderivative $F(x)$, a **slope field** is a graph of $F(x)$ with several different values of C. That means there are several different curves on the same graph, each of which has a different C.

Going back to $f(x) = 2x$ and $F(x) = x^2 + C$, the following slope field shows the graph of $F(x)$ for whole number values of C between -10 and 10 (although not all of them are visible on this graph).

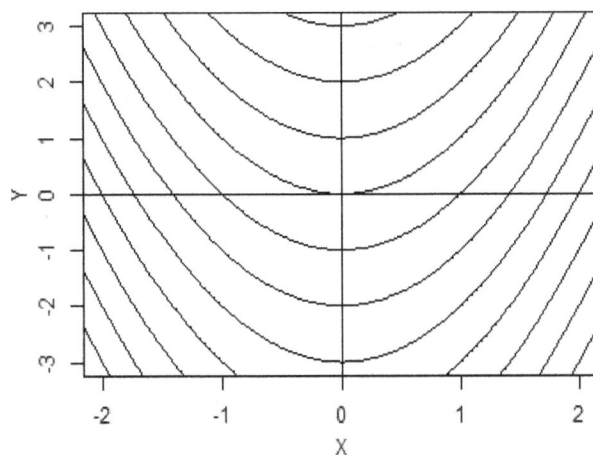

When drawing these on paper, it suffices to sketch just a few curves rather than many. However, a computer can of course include as many as you like, in which case the slope field would look something like this (looks a little like a fingerprint!):

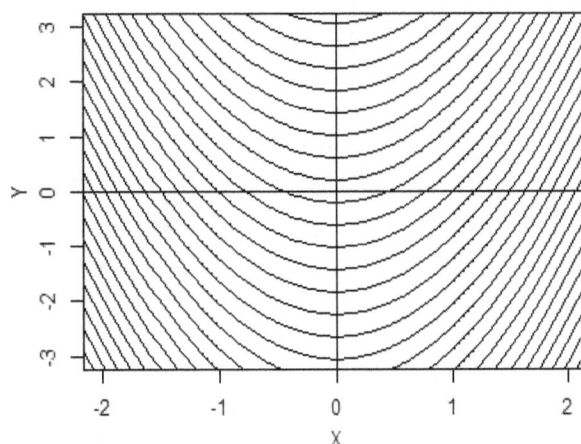

EXAMPLE

Sketch the slope field for the antiderivative of $f(x) = \frac{2}{x}$ for $x > 0$.

Solution: The antiderivative is

$$F(x) = 2\ln|x| + C$$

The following slope field plots $F(x)$ for whole number values of C between -10 and 10 (although not all of them are visible on this graph).

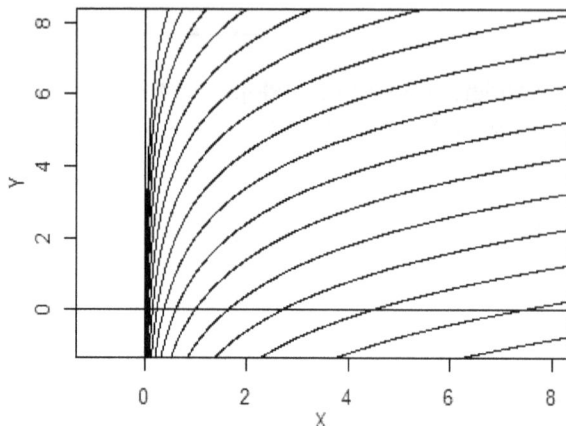

Δ

EXAMPLE

Here is a slope field for an antiderivative $F(x)$. What would be a likely original function $f(x)$?

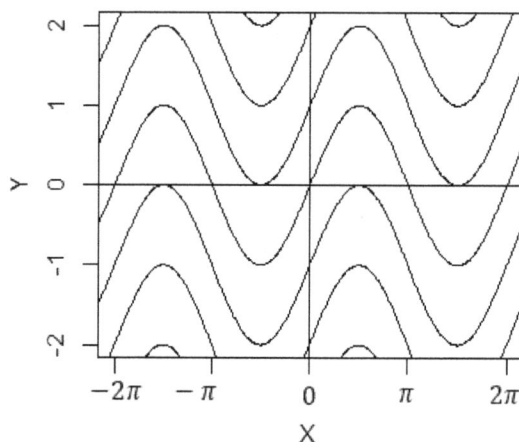

Solution: The function is clearly some sort of "wave," which suggests either the sine or cosine functions. To work out which one is the antiderivative, let's look at the same slope field but only one of the curves, the one passing through the origin.

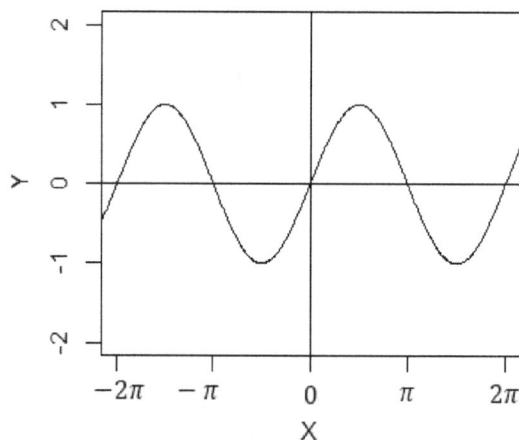

Since the curve passes through $(0, 0)$ and then increases to a height of 1 before falling to a height of -1 and then repeating this path, the curve must be $\sin(x)$. (If you are having trouble understanding this, go back to Chapter 0 and look carefully at the graphs of $\sin(x)$ and $\cos(x)$. Thus, the antiderivative is likely $F(x) = \sin(x) + C$, in which case the original function would be $f(x) = \cos(x)$.

Δ

The last thing to introduce to you in this section is a new notation that will appear in integral calculus. We avoided using it earlier, but now it is needed for the topics in the rest of this chapter.

NOTATION

Suppose the antiderivative of $f(x)$ is $F(x) + C$. Then we can write

$$\int f(x)dx = F(x) + C$$

This expression is read as "the **integral** of $f(x)$ with respect to x is equal to $F(x)$ plus a constant C." It is another way of saying and writing "the antiderivative of $f(x)$ is equal to $F(x) + C$."

The curly S-shape in front of the expression is the integral symbol. The reason we write dx in the integral expression will be explained in integral calculus, but for now just know that it denotes the variable that is being integrated. An analogy is that when we find the derivative dy/dx, it is the derivative of y with respect to x. So the expression $\int f(x)dx$ is the integral of $f(x)$ with respect to x.

ETYMOLOGY

The word **integral** derives from the Latin *integralis*, which meant "integral" or "complete."

EXAMPLE

We know that if $f(x) = x^3$, then the antiderivative is $F(x) = \frac{1}{4}x^4 + C$. Writing this in integral notation,

$$\int x^3 dx = \frac{1}{4}x^4 + C$$

If $g(x) = e^{3x}$, then the antiderivative is $G(x) = \frac{1}{3}e^{3x} + C$, so in integral notation we have

$$\int e^{3x} dx = \frac{1}{3}e^{3x} + C$$

The integral of $h(x) = \cos(x)$ would be

$$\int \cos(x)\, dx = \sin(x) + C$$

Δ

Section 5.3 – Initial Value Problems and Differential Equations

In the first part of this section we discuss initial value problems. Here is the basis of the problem: you are given a function $f(x)$ whose antiderivative $F(x)$ passes through a given point. With that information, you can actually find the value of the constant C, meaning that there is only one antiderivative instead of infinitely many, each with different constants. We work through some examples, but the general process involves the following steps.

METHOD FOR SOLVING INITIAL VALUE PROBLEMS

The following is a general process for solving initial value problems. Given a function $f(x)$ whose antiderivative $F(x)$ passes through a given point (a, b), we perform the following steps:

Step 1: Find the antiderivative $F(x) + C$.
Step 2: Substitute the given point (a, b) into the antiderivative, as in $F(a) + C = b$.
Step 3: Solve for the constant C.
Step 4: Write down the answer, the complete antiderivative with the unique constant.

EXAMPLE

Solve the initial value problem $\frac{dy}{dx} = 2x + 1$ and $y(0) = 3$.

Solution: We first find the general antiderivative (and let's use the new integral notation):

$$y = \int (2x + 1)\, dx = x^2 + x + C$$

Right now there are many possible values for the constant C, as reflected if we drew a slope field. However, we are also given that $y(0) = 3$, so the point $(0, 3)$ lies on the original curve. We substitute these values of x and y into the antiderivative:

$$y = x^2 + x + C$$
$$3 = (0)^2 + (0) + C$$
$$3 = C$$

The solution is therefore $y = x^2 + x + 3$.

Δ

EXAMPLE

Solve the initial value problem $\frac{dy}{dx} = \sqrt{x}$ with $y(9) = 0$.

Solution: Let's first write $\frac{dy}{dx} = \sqrt{x} = x^{1/2}$, which we can work with more easily. The general solution is

$$= \int x^{1/2} dx = \frac{1}{\left(\frac{1}{2} + 1\right)} x^{(1/2)+1} + C = \frac{1}{(3/2)} x^{3/2} + C = \frac{2}{3} x^{3/2} + C$$

We know that $(0, 9)$ lies on this curve, so

$$y = \frac{2}{3} e^{3/2} + C \Rightarrow 9 = \frac{2}{3}(0)^{3/2} + C$$
$$\Rightarrow C = 9$$

The solution is thus $y = \frac{2}{3} x^{3/2} + 9$.

Δ

EXAMPLE

To solve $\frac{dy}{dx} = 3e^{2x}$ and $y(0) = 7$, we first have

$$y = \int 3e^{2x}\,dx = \frac{3}{2}e^{2x} + C$$

Once we know that $(0, 7)$ lies on the curve, then

$$y = \frac{3}{2}e^{2x} + C \Rightarrow 7 = \frac{3}{2}e^0 + C \Rightarrow 7 = \frac{3}{2} + C$$

$$\Rightarrow C = \frac{11}{2}$$

This provides the solution

$$y = \frac{3}{2}e^{2x} + \frac{11}{2}$$

Δ

The above examples were straightforward in that the left side of the equation was dy/dx and the right side was in terms of just x. However, there are some problems where the x terms and y terms are mixed together, in which case we have to somehow separate them before an antiderivative can be computed. If a point (x, y) is given, then these are still initial value problems. We are going to switch names and call them differential equations.

DEFINITION

A **differential equation** is an equation involving both an unknown function and the derivative of that unknown function. Sometimes the two variables are mixed together, in which case we have to separate them using a technique called **separation of variables**.

To be clear, a differential equation is also an initial value problem when the point on the antiderivative is given. If no initial point was given, then solving the differential equation will result in the antiderivative with $+C$ without the ability to find C, in which case the differential equation is not an initial value problem.

We now need to tackle some problems where the variables are mixed together. These can get quite complicated, but fortunately an introductory calculus class will usually focus on simple scenarios. To understand separation of variables, we need to do some problems.

EXAMPLE

Solve the differential equation $\frac{dy}{dx} = 2y$ given that $y(1) = 1$ falls on the original function.

Solution: What makes this problem different from the previous ones is that the right side involves y and not x. We can still do separation of variables, but doing so requires us to get the y terms on the left side and x terms on the right side. Remember in Section 5.1, there was an example where we split up the derivative fraction into two pieces? We are going to do the same thing here, treating dy and dx as the numerator and denominator of a fraction.

$$\frac{dy}{dx} = 2y \Rightarrow dy = 2y\,dx$$

$$\Rightarrow \frac{1}{y}dy = 2dx$$

Now what happens is we integrate both sides of the equation, the left side with respect to y and the right side with respect to x. We can do this using the antiderivative formulas we've learned.

$$\int \frac{1}{y}dy = \int 2dx \Rightarrow \ln|y| + C_1 = 2x + C_2$$

Since there are two integrals, there are two constants to add, C_1 and C_2. We can combine them together into one constant C:

$$\ln|y| = 2x + C$$

Given that $(1, 1)$ falls on the curve, we can find C:

$$\ln|1| = 2(1) + C \Rightarrow 0 = 2 + C$$
$$\Rightarrow C = -2$$

Thus, our equation is

$$\ln|y| = 2x - 2$$

It is customary to solve for y whenever possible, so the original equation is

$$y = e^{2x-2}$$

Δ

EXAMPLE

Solve the differential equation $\frac{dy}{dx} = \frac{4y}{x}$ if $y(1) = e$ falls on the curve.

Solution: Once again we need to separate the variables before finding the antiderivatives. Fortunately this is not too difficult:

$$\frac{dy}{dx} = \frac{4y}{x} \Rightarrow xdy = 4ydx$$
$$\Rightarrow \frac{1}{y}dy = \frac{4}{x}dx$$

Now we integrate both sides:

$$\int \frac{1}{y}dy = \int \frac{4}{x}dx \Rightarrow \ln|y| + C_1 = 4\ln|x| + C_2$$

Combining the constants into one constant C, the equation so far is

$$\ln|y| = 4\ln|x| + C$$

Given that $(1, e)$ falls on the curve, we find C:

$$\ln|e| = 4\ln|1| + C \Rightarrow 1 = 0 + C$$
$$\Rightarrow C = 1$$

The function is now

$$\ln|y| = 4\ln|x| + 1$$

Let's solve for y, but also taking advantage of some log rules.

$$\ln|y| = \ln|x|^4 + 1 \Rightarrow y = e^{\ln|x|^4+1}$$
$$\Rightarrow y = e^{\ln|x|^4} \cdot e^1$$
$$\Rightarrow y = ex^4$$

Note that we no longer need to write absolute values around x since raising it to the fourth power makes the result positive anyway.

Δ

EXAMPLE

Solve the differential equation $\frac{d^2y}{dx^2} = 2 - 6x$ given $y'(0) = 3$ and $y(1) = 4$.

Solution: This example presents to us the second derivative and two initial values. The goal is still the same, to get to the original function, but this time we have to recover the first derivative and then use that answer to get the unknown function. Fortunately separation of variables does not apply here, so we can just find the antiderivative:

$$\frac{d^2y}{dx^2} = 2 - 6x \Rightarrow \frac{dy}{dx} = 2x - \frac{6x^2}{2} + C_1$$
$$\Rightarrow \frac{dy}{dx} = 2x - 3x^2 + C_1$$

We know from $y'(0) = 3$ that the point $(0, 3)$ lies on the first derivative, which means

$$3 = 2(0) - 3(0)^2 + C_1 \Rightarrow C_1 = 3$$

The complete first derivative is

$$\frac{dy}{dx} = 2x - 3x^2 + 3$$

Now we antidifferentiate again:

$$y = \frac{2x^2}{2} - \frac{3x^3}{3} + 3x + C_2 \Rightarrow y = x^2 - x^3 + 3x + C_2$$

We wrote the constants as C_1 and C_2 to indicate that they are possibly different numbers. Next, $y(1) = 4$ tells us that $(1, 4)$ is on the original function, so

$$4 = (1)^2 - (1)^3 + 3(1) + C_2 \Rightarrow 4 = 3 + C_2$$
$$\Rightarrow C_2 = 1$$

The original function is $y = x^2 - x^3 + 3x + 1$.

Δ

Section 5.4 – Euler's Method

While the techniques we saw in the previous section are useful for solving some differential equations, there are other differential equations that are difficult or impossible to solve by hand. Such equations often appear in various science problems, especially chemistry and physics. When we encounter such a problem, it is important to know how to solve them using numerical techniques. One such technique, and the only one we'll see here, is called Euler's Method, popularized by the Swiss mathematician Leonhard Euler (the same fellow who gave us the number e).

There are more advanced methods of solving differential equations, but those are best left for a college level class (we won't go into those here). This section discusses how to use Euler's Method for problems that are not obvious to solve by hand. It's another of those topics that is more easily understood by working examples, but first I'll show you the steps to use this algorithm.

Given a differential equation y' and an initial point (x_0, y_0) on the original function, the goal is to estimate the y-coordinate on the original function for another given point. That is, given another x-coordinate x_n, we want to find the corresponding y-coordinate y_n. If we could find the original function using separation of variables, then finding this y_n value would be easy, so the presumption here is that numerical methods are needed.

First we will be moving from x_0 to x_n in h steps, or in other words with a step size of h. That means there are $n = (x_n - x_0)/h$ total steps taken to do this. For instance, to go from 2 to 4 with a step size of 0.5 means our x-coordinates will be at 2, 2.5, 3, 3.5, and 4, a total of four steps, so we would write $x_0 = 2$ and $x_4 = 4$.

It will also be convenient to write the differential equation $y' = f(x, y)$ to allow for the possibility that the derivative is in terms of both x and y. We now present Euler's Method written out as a step-by-step algorithm.

EULER'S METHOD
Given a differential equation $y' = f(x, y)$ and an initial point (x_0, y_0) on the original function, we want to find y_n for an x-coordinate of interest x_n. We also need to go from x_0 to x_n with a step size of h.

Step 1: Decide how many steps are needed to go from x_0 to x_n; this number is $n = (x_n - x_0)/h$.
Step 2: The x values for the table are x_0, x_1, and so on through x_n.
Step 3: Given the initial point (x_0, y_0), evaluate the derivative $f(x_0, y_0)$.

Step 4: Given x_1, compute $y_1 \approx y_0 + hf(x_0, y_0)$.
Step 5: Given the estimated point (x_1, y_1), evaluate the derivative $f(x_1, y_1)$.
Step 6: Given x_2, compute $y_2 \approx y_1 + hf(x_1, y_1)$.
Step 7: Given the estimated point (x_2, y_2), evaluate the derivative $f(x_2, y_2)$.
Step 8: Repeat in this fashion until you arrive at $y_n \approx y_{n-1} + hf(x_{n-1}, y_{n-1})$.

I should stress once again that these estimates are just that, estimates (that's why we use the $\approx$ symbol rather than =). They will not be the exact answer, but with a small enough step size, they will hopefully be close. Generally speaking, the smaller the step size, the more accurate the estimate, but such problems become more cumbersome to work on paper when there are lots of steps (that's what computers are for!).

To see briefly why these formulas work, remember that a derivative y' can be estimated locally as the slope of a secant line between two points (x_0, y_0) and (x_1, y_1):

$$y' \approx \frac{y_1 - y_0}{x_1 - x_0}$$

Since $x_1 - x_0$ is, by definition, the step size h, we can substitute that in and rearrange the equation:

$$y' \approx \frac{y_1 - y_0}{h} \Rightarrow hy' \approx y_1 - y_0 \Rightarrow y_1 \approx y_0 + hy'$$

Switching to the other notation $y' = f(x, y)$, we get $y_1 \approx y_0 + hf(x_0, y_0)$. Next, to move from (x_1, y_1) to (x_2, y_2), we would go through the same process but end up with $y_2 \approx y_1 + hf(x_1, y_1)$. Continuing in this way, the last step would be $y_n \approx y_{n-1} + hf(x_{n-1}, y_{n-1})$.

If you didn't understand this explanation, no need to worry – what's more important is knowing how to do problems involving Euler's Method, so let's go right to those.

EXAMPLE
Given the differential equation $y' = 3y - 1$ and $y(0) = 1$, estimate $y(1)$ using $h = 0.25$ as the step size.

Solution: The initial value provided is $(0, 1)$, so $x_0 = 0$ and $y_0 = 1$. We want to find the y-coordinate at $x = 1$, and with a step size of $h = 0.25$, that means four steps will be necessary. This is because to go from 0 to 1 means starting at $x_0 = 0$ and passing through $x_1 = 0.25$, $x_2 = 0.50$, and $x_3 = 0.75$ before finishing at $x_4 = 1$.

In addition, our derivative is defined as $f(x, y) = 3y - 1$ (so it does not involve x). Thus, our table starts out looking like this:

Step	x	y	f(x,y)
0	0	1	
1	0.25		
2	0.50		
3	0.75		
4	1		

Now we carefully sweep through the table down the rows. The first job is to get $f(x_0, y_0) = 3y_0 - 1$, which is $f(x_0, y_0) = 3(1) - 1 = 2$.

Step	x	y	f(x,y)
0	0	1	3(1)-1=2
1	0.25		
2	0.50		
3	0.75		
4	1		

On the next row, we need to compute $y_1 \approx y_0 + 0.25f(x_0, y_0)$. That gives us $y_1 \approx 1 + 0.25(2) = 1.5$. The next step is to find $f(x_1, y_1) = 3y_1 - 1 = 3(1.5) - 1 = 3.5$.

Step	x	y	f(x,y)
0	0	1	3(1)-1=2
1	0.25	1+0.25(2)=1.5	3(1.5)-1=3.5
2	0.50		
3	0.75		
4	1		

Moving to the $n = 2$ row, we have to compute $y_2 \approx y_1 + hf(x_1, y_1) = 1.5 + 0.25(3.5) = 2.375$. This in turn leads to $f(x_2, y_2) = 3y_2 - 1 = 3(2.375) - 1 = 6.125$.

Step	x	y	f(x,y)
0	0	1	3(1)-1=2
1	0.25	1+0.25(2)=1.5	3(1.5)-1=3.5
2	0.50	1.5+0.25(3.5)=2.375	3(2.375)-1=6.125
3	0.75		
4	1		

Next, the third row calculation is $y_3 \approx y_2 + hf(x_2, y_2) = 2.375 + 0.25(6.125) = 3.906$, and so the derivative is $f(x_3, y_3) = 3y_3 - 1 = 3(3.906) - 1 = 10.718$.

Step	x	y	f(x,y)
0	0	1	3(1)-1=2
1	0.25	1+0.25(2)=1.5	3(1.5)-1=3.5
2	0.50	1.5+0.25(3.5)=2.375	3(2.375)-1=6.125
3	0.75	2.375+0.25(6.125)=3.906	3(3.906)-1=10.718
4	1		

One more row to go! We have $y_4 \approx y_3 + hf(x_3, y_3) = 3.906 + 0.25(10.718) = 6.586$, which tells us that when $x_4 = 1$, the corresponding y-coordinate y_4 is estimated to be 6.586. That is the answer we are looking for – in other words, $y(1) \approx 6.586$. The completed table is below (and notice we don't need to write anything in the lower right cell).

Step	x	y	f(x,y)
0	0	1	3(1)-1=2
1	0.25	1+0.25(2)=1.5	3(1.5)-1=3.5
2	0.50	1.5+0.25(3.5)=2.375	3(2.375)-1=6.125
3	0.75	2.375+0.25(6.125)=3.906	3(3.906)-1=10.718
4	1	3.906+0.25(10.718)=6.586	

Δ

That's a fully worked out example of Euler's Method! Let's do a couple more to get the hang of how they work.

EXAMPLE
Given the differential equation $y' = y$ and $y(1) = 4$, estimate $y(2)$ using $h = 0.2$ as the step size.

Solution: First, here we actually can find the true answer since this differential equation can be solved explicitly as follows:

$$\frac{dy}{dx} = y \Rightarrow \int \frac{dy}{y} = \int dx \Rightarrow \ln|y| = x + C \Rightarrow y = e^{x+C} \Rightarrow y = Ke^x$$

Here $K = e^C$. Substituting $x = 1$ and $y = 4$,

$$4 = Ke^1 \Rightarrow C = \frac{4}{e}$$

The antiderivative is therefore

$$y = \frac{4}{e}e^x = 4e^{x-1}$$

Finally, the answer is $y(2) = 4e^{2-1} = 4e \approx 10.87312731$. This is the answer we get when solving the differential equation explicitly, but now we will estimate it using Euler's Method to see how close we get. The initial value provided is $(1, 4)$, so $x_0 = 1$ and $y_0 = 4$. We want to find the y-coordinate at $x = 2$, and with a step size of $h = 0.2$, that means five steps will be necessary. This is because to go from 1 to 2 means starting at $x_0 = 1$ and passing through $x_1 = 1.2$, $x_2 = 1.4$, $x_3 = 1.6$ and $x_4 = 1.8$ before finishing at $x_5 = 2$. Lastly, the derivative is $f(x, y) = y$, which once again does not involve the x-coordinate. Our table starts out like this:

Step	x	y	f(x,y)
0	1	4	
1	1.2		
2	1.4		
3	1.6		
4	1.8		
5	2		

First we find $f(x_0, y_0) = y_0 = 4$.

Step	x	y	f(x,y)
0	1	4	4
1	1.2		
2	1.4		
3	1.6		
4	1.8		
5	2		

On the next row, we need to compute $y_1 \approx y_0 + 0.2f(x_0, y_0)$. That gives us $y_1 \approx 4 + 0.2(4) = 4.8$. The next step is to find $f(x_1, y_1) = y_1 = 4.8$.

Step	x	y	f(x,y)
0	1	4	4
1	1.2	4+0.2(4)=4.8	4.8
2	1.4		
3	1.6		
4	1.8		
5	2		

The remaining rows work the same way:

$$y_2 \approx y_1 + 0.2f(x_1, y_1) = 4.8 + 0.2(4.8) = 5.76 \qquad f(x_2, y_2) = y_2 = 5.76$$
$$y_3 \approx y_2 + 0.2f(x_2, y_2) = 5.76 + 0.2(5.76) = 6.912 \qquad f(x_3, y_3) = y_3 = 6.912$$
$$y_4 \approx y_3 + 0.2f(x_3, y_3) = 6.912 + 0.2(6.912) = 8.294 \qquad f(x_4, y_4) = y_4 = 5.76$$
$$y_5 \approx y_4 + 0.2f(x_4, y_4) = 8.294 + 0.2(8.294) = 9.953$$

We have arrived at the answer, which is $y_5 \approx 9.953$, or $y(2) \approx 9.953$. Although this is somewhat different from the true answer of 10.87312731, it's not too bad for an estimate. (It can be shown that if we use a smaller step size, we'll arrive at a better estimate. For instance, here it can be shown that if $h = 0.1$, then Euler's Method gives $y(2) \approx 10.37497$, and if $h = 0.05$, then the estimate is $y(2) \approx 10.61319$.) Here is the completed table:

Step	x	y	f(x,y)
0	1	4	4
1	1.2	4+0.2(4)=4.8	4.8
2	1.4	4.8+0.2(4.8)=5.76	5.76
3	1.6	5.76+0.2(5.76)=6.912	6.912
4	1.8	6.912+0.2(6.912)=8.294	8.294
5	2	8.294+0.2(8.294)=9.953	

Δ

EXAMPLE

Here's one more example. Given the differential equation $g'(u) = u[4 - g(u)]$ and $g(0) = 8$, estimate $g(1)$ using $h = 0.5$ as the step size.

Solution: This is another differential equation that cannot be solved with techniques we've seen, so Euler's Method will be useful once again. First, because there is alternative notation here, I would suggest temporarily changing it to use x and y notation so that we can more easily see how to use our algorithm. Rewriting it results in

$$y' = x(4 - y)$$

This means that $x_0 = 0$, $y_0 = 8$, $h = 0.5$, and $f(x, y) = x(4 - y)$. This is also our first example where the derivative involves both x and y, but it still works the same way.

We want to find the y-coordinate at $x = 1$, and with a step size of $h = 0.5$, that means two steps will be necessary. This is because to go from 0 to 1 means starting at $x_0 = 0$ and passing through $x_1 = 0.5$ before finishing at $x_2 = 1$. Our table starts out like this:

Step	x	y	f(x,y)
0	0	8	
1	0.5		
2	1		

First we find $f(x_0, y_0) = x_0(4 - y_0) = 0(4 - 8) = 0$.

Step	x	y	f(x,y)
0	0	8	0(4-8)=0
1	0.5		
2	1		

On the next row, we need to compute $y_1 \approx y_0 + 0.5f(x_0, y_0)$. That would be $y_1 \approx 8 + 0.5(0) = 8$, which in turn gives $f(x_1, y_1) = x_1(4 - y_1) = 0.5(4 - 8) = -2$.

Step	x	y	f(x,y)
0	0	8	0(4-8)=0
1	0.5	8+0.5(0)=8	0.5(4-8)=-2
2	1		

The last calculation is

$$y_2 \approx y_1 + 0.5f(x_1, y_1) = 8 + 0.5(-2) = 7$$

This means $y_2 \approx 7$, and switching back to the original notation, $g(1) \approx 7$.

Step	x	y	f(x,y)
0	0	8	0(4-8)=0
1	0.5	8+0.5(0)=8	0.5(4-8)=-2
2	1	8+0.5(-2)=7	

Δ

Section 5.5 – Newton's Law of Cooling and Other Applications

This section explores a few examples where differential equations appear in the sciences. They come into play with applications to physics, but that deserves its own section (the next one).

For the first scientific application of differential equations, let's turn to our good friend Sir Isaac Newton. He noted that the rate at which an object's temperature drops is proportional to the difference in temperature of the object and the temperature of the surrounding environment. In mathematical terms, the rate at which the object's temperature T changes with respect to time t is the derivative dT/dt. The difference in the object's temperature (T) and the surrounding temperature (T_S) is represented as $T - T_S$ (we assume that the object is warmer than the surrounding environment and therefore cools over time). Finally, when we say the derivative is proportional to this difference, that means there is a constant k so that

$$\frac{dT}{dt} = -k(T - T_S)$$

The negative sign is needed because we are studying when the temperature is dropping (decreasing). Next, recalling that Δ represents a difference, we can write $\Delta T = T - T_S$ to represent the difference in temperature between the object and the surroundings at time t. In a similar way, $\Delta T_0 = T_0 - T_S$ is the difference in the object's initial temperature T_0 (at $t = 0$) and the surroundings.

In these problems we assume that the temperature of the surrounding environment, T_S, is constant, and another way to say that with differentials is that $dT_S = 0$ (no change). That means that we can write

$$dT = dT - dT_S = d(T - T_S) = d(\Delta T)$$

Thus, the derivative formula above is rewritten as

$$\frac{d(\Delta T)}{dt} = -k\Delta T$$

Now let's rearrange terms:

$$\frac{1}{\Delta T} \cdot d(\Delta T) = -kdt$$

We are now in a position to integrate both sides, the left side with respect to ΔT.

$$\int \frac{1}{\Delta T} \cdot d(\Delta T) = \int -kdt \Rightarrow \ln|\Delta T| + C_1 = -kt + C_2$$
$$\Rightarrow \ln|\Delta T| = -kt + C$$

Substituting in $\Delta T = T - T_S$,

$$\ln|T - T_S| = -kt + C$$

We know an initial value on this curve: at time $t = 0$, the temperature is T_0. Substituting this in,

$$\ln|T_0 - T_S| = -k(0) + C \Rightarrow C = \ln|T_0 - T_S|$$

Now we solve for T, the temperature of the object at time t.

$$\ln|T - T_S| = -kt + \ln|T_0 - T_S| \Rightarrow e^{\ln|T - T_S|} = e^{-kt + \ln|T_0 - T_S|}$$
$$\Rightarrow T - T_S = e^{-kt}e^{\ln|T_0 - T_S|}$$
$$\Rightarrow T - T_S = (T_0 - T_S)e^{-kt}$$
$$\Rightarrow T = T_S + (T_0 - T_S)e^{-kt}$$

We have just derived Newton's Law of Cooling, which tells us what the temperature T of an object will be at time t if the surrounding environment's temperature is T_S and the object's initial temperature at time $t = 0$ is T_0.

NEWTON'S LAW OF COOLING
Suppose that as time goes by the temperature of an object cools due to the temperature of the surrounding environment (denoted as T_S). The initial temperature of the object (at $t = 0$) is T_0. Then the temperature T of the object at time t is given by

$$T = T_S + (T_0 - T_S)e^{-kt}$$

Here k is a constant that affects the rate at which the temperature of the object cools.

If you didn't understand the above derivation, don't worry – just be familiar with the formula and how to use it, as in the next two examples.

EXAMPLE

A bowl of soup that is initially 100°F is placed on an outside table where the outside temperature is 45°F. After 10 minutes, the temperature of the soup is 80°F. After how many more minutes will the temperature of the soup be 60°F?

Solution: First, the surrounding temperature is $T_S = 45$ and the initial temperature of the soup is $T_0 = 100$, so Newton's Law of Cooling says that after t minutes, the soup's temperature is

$$T = 45 + (100 - 45)e^{-kt} \Rightarrow T = 45 + 55e^{-kt}$$

Next, we are told that after $t = 10$ minutes the soup's temperature is $T = 80$. Using this information, we can solve for k.

$$80 = 45 + 55e^{-10k} \Rightarrow 35 = 55e^{-10k} \Rightarrow \frac{7}{11} = e^{-10k}$$
$$\Rightarrow \ln\left(\frac{7}{11}\right) = -10k$$
$$\Rightarrow k = -\frac{1}{10}\ln\left(\frac{7}{11}\right)$$

It would be nice to have a simplified formula despite a messy looking answer for k. Let's work on that by first deriving $-kt$ and then e^{-kt}.

$$k = -\frac{1}{10}\ln\left(\frac{7}{11}\right) \Rightarrow -kt = \frac{t}{10}\ln\left(\frac{7}{11}\right) = \ln\left(\frac{7}{11}\right)^{t/10}$$

Next,

$$e^{-kt} = e^{\ln(7/11)^{t/10}} = \left(\frac{7}{11}\right)^{t/10}$$

Thus, e^{-kt} simplifies to a slightly cleaner form. Our cooling formula in terms of elapsed minutes is therefore

$$T = 45 + 55\left(\frac{7}{11}\right)^{t/10}$$

Finally, remember we needed to know at what time t the temperature of the soup was 60°F, or $T = 60$. That means we need to solve

$$60 = 45 + 55\left(\frac{7}{11}\right)^{t/10} \Rightarrow 15 = 55\left(\frac{7}{11}\right)^{t/10} \Rightarrow$$
$$\Rightarrow \ln\left(\frac{3}{11}\right) = \frac{t}{10}\ln\left(\frac{7}{11}\right)$$
$$\Rightarrow t = \frac{10\ln(3/11)}{\ln(7/11)} = \frac{10(\ln(3) - \ln(11))}{\ln(7) - \ln(11)}$$
$$t \approx 28.74614 \text{ minutes}$$

To be clear, 10 minutes after the soup has been brought outside, its temperature has cooled to 80°F, and 28.7 minutes after the soup has been brought outside, its temperature is 60°F. The original question was after how many *more* minutes the temperature cools from 80°F to 60°F, and so the answer is $28.7 - 10 = 18.7$ minutes.

Δ

EXAMPLE
You boil an egg to 90°C and then submerse it in cold water. After 10 minutes the egg has cooled to 40°C, and after 10 more minutes the egg's temperature is 20°C. Find the temperature of the water in which the egg was placed. Assume the water temperature remains constant.

Solution: This problem is a bit scrambled (I couldn't resist an egg pun!) The initial egg temperature is $T_0 = 90$, at $t = 10$ the egg's temperature is $T = 40$, and at $t = 20$ the egg's temperature is $T = 20$. (The 20 minutes comes from the first 10 minutes plus 10 more minutes.) The goal is to solve for T_S, the temperature of the surrounding medium (in this case, the cold water). Let's look at the two equations we can set up.

$$40 = T_S + (90 - T_S)e^{-10k}$$
$$20 = T_S + (90 - T_S)e^{-20k}$$

The trick is to solve for e^{-10k} in the first equation and then substitute the result into the second equation.

$$40 = T_S + (90 - T_S)e^{-10k} \Rightarrow e^{-10k} = \frac{40 - T_S}{90 - T_S}$$

Now recognize that e^{-20k} is equal to $\left(e^{-10k}\right)^2$, and so we can put the previous expression into the second equation.

$$20 = T_S + (90 - T_S)\left(\frac{40 - T_S}{90 - T_S}\right)^2$$
$$20 = T_S + \frac{(40 - T_S)^2}{90 - T_S}$$

We need to solve for T_S, and to do that we need to rearrange terms.

$$20 - T_S = \frac{(40 - T_S)^2}{90 - T_S} \Rightarrow (20 - T_S)(90 - T_S) = (40 - T_S)^2$$

Next, we need to expand both sides of the equation and simplify.

$$1800 - 110T_S + T_S^2 = 1600 - 80T_S + T_S^2$$
$$200 = 30T_S$$
$$T_S = 15$$

After all that work (which was mostly creative algebra), we discover that the temperature of the cold water in which the egg was submerged is 15°C.

Δ

Another application to sciences such as chemistry is exponential decay, especially concerning the half-life of a substance, element, or particle. To set this up, exponential decay says that the decline of a population is proportional to the amount present. If y represents the amount present, then the rate at which the population declines can be represented by

$$\frac{dy}{dt} = -ky$$

Rearranging terms and integrating, we get

$$dy = -kydt \Rightarrow \int \frac{1}{y} dy = \int -kdt$$
$$\Rightarrow \ln|y| + C_1 = -kt + C_2$$
$$\Rightarrow \ln|y| = -kt + C$$
$$\Rightarrow y = e^{-kt+C} = e^{-kt}e^C$$
$$\Rightarrow y = Pe^{-kt}$$

The P represents another constant equal to e^C. To solve exponential decay problems, we also need to know a point on the curve. For instance, $y(0) = P$ represents the original population size at time $t = 0$.

EXPONENTIAL DECAY

Suppose that as time goes by the size of a population (this could be for chemical elements, bacteria, substances, even animals in some cases) gets smaller exponentially. If the initial population size at time t is P, then the size of the population y at time t is given by

$$y = Pe^{-kt}$$

Here k is a constant that affects the rate at which the population declines. Note the negative sign in the exponent, which indicates a decline. If you remove the negative sign, the function would represent a growth in the population.

EXAMPLE (APPLICATION TO CHEMISTRY)

In a healthy adult, caffeine generally has a half-life of 5 hours on average. (In reality this figure varies per adult, but for simplicity let's assume it's 5 hours.) If you consume 400 mg of caffeine in one sitting, find a formula for how much caffeine remains in your system after t hours. How much caffeine is in your body after 8 hours? How long will it take to have 50 mg remaining in your body?

Solution: If you drink $P = 400$ mg of caffeine, 5 hours later half of it (200 mg) is still in your body. That means $y(5) = 200$, so we use this information to solve for k:

$$200 = 400e^{-5k} \Rightarrow \frac{1}{2} = e^{-5k} \Rightarrow \ln\left(\frac{1}{2}\right) = -5k$$
$$\Rightarrow k = -\frac{1}{5}\ln\left(\frac{1}{2}\right)$$

Using a similar technique we used for Newton's Law of Cooling, we next get an expression for $-kt$ and then e^{-kt}.

$$-kt = \frac{t}{5}\ln\left(\frac{1}{2}\right) = \ln\left(\frac{1}{2}\right)^{t/5}$$

This means that

$$e^{-kt} = e^{\ln(1/2)^{t/5}} = \left(\frac{1}{2}\right)^{t/5}$$

Thus, our half-life formula is

$$y = 400\left(\frac{1}{2}\right)^{t/5}$$

After 8 hours, the amount of caffeine left in your body is

$$y = 400 \left(\frac{1}{2}\right)^{8/5} \approx 131.95079 \text{ mg}$$

When 50 mg of caffeine remain in your body, we need to solve for t.

$$50 = 400 \left(\frac{1}{2}\right)^{t/5} \Rightarrow \frac{1}{8} = \left(\frac{1}{2}\right)^{t/5} \Rightarrow 8 = 2^{t/5}$$

$$\Rightarrow \ln(8) = \frac{t}{5}\ln(2)$$

$$\Rightarrow t = \frac{5\ln(8)}{\ln(2)} = \frac{5\ln(2^3)}{\ln(2)} = 5 \cdot \frac{3\ln(2)}{\ln(2)} = 15$$

Thus, 50 mg remain in your body after 15 hours.

Δ

You might occasionally see word problems asking you to set up a differential equation based on some given information. Let's do an example of that.

EXAMPLE (APPLICATION TO ECOLOGY)
In a certain area, suppose the growth of the population of House Sparrows (*Passer domesticus*) is proportional to the square root of the number present. Find the formula (in terms of a constant k) for the number of House Sparrows present at time t months given that there were nine at $t = 0$.

Solution: If y represents the number of House Sparrows after t months, then the rate at which the population grows with respect to time is dy/dt. This rate is proportional to the square root of the number present, which is $\sqrt{y} = y^{1/2}$, so there is a positive constant k such that

$$\frac{dy}{dt} = ky^{1/2}$$

There is no negative sign here, indicating that the rate is a growth rather than a decline. Rearranging the equation and integrating,

$$y^{-1/2} dy = kdt \Rightarrow \int y^{-1/2} dy = \int kdt$$

$$\Rightarrow \frac{y^{1/2}}{\left(\frac{1}{2}\right)} + C_1 = kt + C_2$$

$$\Rightarrow 2\sqrt{y} = kt + C$$

Next, at $t = 0$ there were $y = 9$ House Sparrows, and so

$$2\sqrt{9} = k(0) + C \Rightarrow C = 6$$

Without further information given, the formula for the number of House Sparrows after t months is, for some constant k,

$$2\sqrt{y} = kt + 6 \Rightarrow \sqrt{y} = \frac{kt + 6}{2}$$

$$\Rightarrow y = \left(\frac{kt + 6}{2}\right)^2$$

We can't find k unless another observation is provided, such as the number present after $t = 1$ month. However, this is the general differential equation for this population.

$$\Delta$$

There is one more topic that is sometimes taught in calculus classes called the logistic growth model. However, deriving it requires an integration technique that you won't see until further in integral calculus, so we won't cover it here. You will instead see it in my next book!

Section 5.6 – Antiderivatives and Physics

We now revisit some concepts in physics that were first introduced in Section 2.6. An object or particle is assumed to be moving around in space, so at any given time it has a specific position. The derivative of position is velocity, and the derivative of velocity is acceleration. Now armed with the knowledge of how antiderivatives work, we can say that the antiderivative of acceleration is velocity, and the antiderivative of velocity is position. If we are given acceleration and a specific velocity and position at a given time, then the situation becomes an initial value problem that allows us to solve for the position function.

Recall the following definitions and their interconnections from Section 2.6.

DEFINITION

If $s(t)$ describes the position of the object at time t, then $v(t)$ describes the rate at which position is changing at time t. In other words, the derivative of position with respect to time is velocity:

$$v(t) = s'(t) = \frac{d}{dt}\big(s(t)\big)$$

Similarly, $a(t)$ describes the rate at which velocity is changing at time t. In other words, the derivative of velocity with respect to time is acceleration:

$$a(t) = v'(t) = \frac{d}{dt}\big(v(t)\big)$$

This means that the second derivative of position with respect to time squared is acceleration:

$$a(t) = s''(t) = s^{(2)}(t)$$

When we first learned about position, velocity, and acceleration, this was the only way we could study them since all we knew about at the time were derivatives. Now, having introduced antiderivatives, we can go a little further.

DEFINITION

If $s(t)$, $v(t)$, and $a(t)$ are as defined earlier, then they are also connected as antiderivatives and integrals as follows. The antiderivative of $a(t)$ is $v(t)$, and the antiderivative of $v(t)$ is $s(t)$. Using integral notation,

$$v(t) = \int a(t)dt \qquad s(t) = \int v(t)dt$$

You might be wondering why we haven't written $+C$ for $v(t)$ and $s(t)$ after taking the antiderivatives. That is because the moving object has specific formulas that will be defined in the problem for at least one of the position, velocity, and acceleration, so when taking antiderivatives, you will introduce the $+C$ there (and often we can find what C is with enough information). The formulas above are just general formulas, so let's go straight to an example.

EXAMPLE

Suppose a marble starts moving at the point $s(0) = 0$ with an initial velocity of $v(0) = -10$. Let $a(t) = 3t - 1$ be its acceleration with time. Find the position function of the marble.

Solution: This is an initial value problem. Let's first write down what we know:

$$a(t) = 3t - 1 \qquad v(0) = -10 \qquad s(0) = 0$$

These data come from the fact that we are starting at the beginning (time $t = 0$). Now let's solve:

$$v(t) = \int a(t)dt = \int (3t - 1)dt = \frac{3}{2}t^2 - t + C_1$$

As before, we write C_1 because we will be using another, possibly different constant when we integrate velocity. This is a simple way of distinguishing the two. Now we use the fact that $v(0) = -10$:

$$v(0) = \frac{3}{2}(0)^2 - (0) + C_1 = -10$$
$$C_1 = -10$$

And so the velocity equation is $v(t) = \frac{3}{2}t^2 - t - 10$. Now we integrate this to get the position.

$$s(t) = \int v(t)dt = \int \left(\frac{3}{2}t^2 - t - 10\right)dt$$
$$= \frac{3}{2} \times \frac{1}{3}t^3 - \frac{1}{2}t^2 - 10t + C_2$$
$$= \frac{1}{2}t^3 - \frac{1}{2}t^2 - 10t + C_2$$

Now we use the fact that $s(0) = 0$:

$$s(0) = \frac{1}{2}(0)^3 - \frac{1}{2}(0)^2 - 10(0) + C_2 = 0$$
$$C_2 = 0$$

Thus, the equation of the position function is

$$s(t) = \frac{1}{2}t^3 - \frac{1}{2}t^2 - 10t$$

Δ

EXAMPLE

Here is a more general example that ends up deriving some commonly used formulas in physics. Let's assume constant acceleration at any moment, so $a(t) = a$. Let's also assume that the particle is initially at position s_0 and velocity v_0. (We call these "s-naught" and "v-naught" – this notation is used to denote initial qualities.) Thus,

$$a(t) = a \qquad v(0) = v_0 \qquad s(0) = s_0$$

Find the formulas for velocity and position.

Solution: We antidifferentiate (or integrate) to get

$$v(t) = \int a\, dt = at + C_1$$

Using the fact that $v(0) = v_0$,

$$v(0) = a(0) + C_1 = v_0$$
$$C_1 = v_0$$

This means that the formula for velocity is

$$v(t) = at + v_0$$

Now we get the position function:

$$s(t) = \int (at + v_0)\, dt = \frac{1}{2}at^2 + v_0 t + C_2$$

Using the fact that $s_0 = s(0)$, we finally arrive at

$$s(0) = \frac{1}{2}a(0)^2 + v_0(0) + C_2 = s_0$$
$$C_2 = s_0$$

The position function is therefore

$$s(t) = \frac{1}{2}at^2 + v_0 t + s_0$$

All these formulas assume that acceleration is constant! If acceleration is not constant, these formulas cannot be used.

Δ

Let's recap these formulas once again, especially because if you ever take a physics class, you will certainly see them there.

POSITION AND VELOCITY WITH CONSTANT ACCELERATION

Suppose a particle travels with *constant* acceleration a, initial velocity v_0, and initial position s_0. Then the following formulas are true:

$$s(t) = \frac{1}{2}at^2 + v_0t + s_0$$
$$v(t) = at + v_0$$

Let's turn to one final topic. Suppose now that our particle travels vertically before falling back to Earth. Now gravity plays a role in determining acceleration, velocity, and position. In physics, we denote gravity by the letter g, the gravitational constant, where

$$a = -g = -32 \text{ ft/s}^2 = -9.8 \text{ m/s}^2$$

Gravity is the acceleration in this case, and we make it negative because it is pulling the object downwards towards Earth. The units are "feet per second squared," or if you use the metric system, "meters per second squared." Of course, this acceleration is constant, so we can use the formulas we just derived to account for this new force. (If you remember a couple of examples in Section 2.6 that involved falling objects, they ended up having acceleration equal to -32 ft/s^2. I mentioned at the time that that was not coincidence, and now you see why. Again, in the metric system, it's instead -9.8 m/s^2.)

POSITION AND VELOCITY WITH FALLING OBJECTS

Suppose a particle is subject to a downward acceleration; that is, it begins falling back to Earth. Then $a = -g = -32 \text{ ft/s}^2$, and neglecting air resistance (a phrase that appears quite a bit in physics), the position and velocity are

$$s(t) = -\frac{1}{2}gt^2 + v_0t + s_0 \qquad v(t) = -gt + v_0$$

Since $g = 32 \text{ ft/s}^2$, we may simplify these:

$$s(t) = -16t^2 + v_0t + s_0 \qquad v(t) = -32t + v_0$$

In the metric system $g = 9.8 \text{ m/s}^2$, in which case

$$s(t) = -4.9t^2 + v_0t + s_0 \qquad v(t) = -9.8t + v_0$$

EXAMPLE

Suppose you toss a ball vertically into the air from the ground with an initial velocity of 80 feet per second. Neglecting air resistance, calculate

    A) How high the ball rises.
    B) How long it takes the ball to reach its maximum height.
    C) At what time the ball hits the ground.

<u>Solution</u>: We have constant acceleration of $a = -g$ in this situation. The initial velocity is 80 feet per second, and the initial position on the ground is 0 feet (since you have not yet thrown the ball). Noting that the units are in feet,

$$a = -g = -32 \text{ ft/s}^2 \qquad v(0) = 80 \text{ ft/s} \qquad s(0) = 0 \text{ ft}$$

This gives us the following formulas:

$$s(t) = -16t^2 + v_0 t + s_0$$
$$= -16t^2 + 80t$$
$$v(t) = -32t + v_0$$
$$= -32t + 80$$

Part A asks us to find the highest spot on the position function, or in other words where its derivative achieves a maximum value. Let's look at the velocity function and set it equal to zero:

$$v(t) = -32 + 80 = 0 \Rightarrow 32t = 80$$
$$\Rightarrow t = \frac{5}{2} = 2.5$$

We have also just answered part B. The ball achieves its maximum height after 2.5 seconds. Then

$$\left(\frac{5}{2}\right) = -16\left(\frac{5}{2}\right)^2 + 80\left(\frac{5}{2}\right) = -100 + 200 = 100 \text{ ft}$$

The ball reaches a maximum height of 100 feet. Lastly, part C asks when the ball hits the ground. Since the ground is at 0 feet, we can simply set the position function equal to zero and solve for t.

$$-16t^2 + 80t = 0 \Rightarrow -16t(t - 5) = 0$$
$$\Rightarrow t(t - 5) = 0$$
$$\Rightarrow t = 0, 5$$

However, $t = 0$ was the initial time, so all we are concerned with is $t = 5$ since that is when the ball hits the ground. Thus, our answers are:

A) The ball reaches a maximum height of 100 feet.
B) The ball reaches its maximum height at 2.5 seconds.
C) The ball hits the ground after 5 seconds.

Δ

EXAMPLE
You throw a tennis ball out of a window 12 meters above the ground with an initial upward velocity of 10 meters per second. Neglecting air resistance, find the ball's maximum height and at what time it hits the ground.

Solution: The starting position is $s_0 = 12$ while the starting velocity is $v_0 = 10$, so the position using the metric system is
$$s(t) = -4.9t^2 + 10t + 12$$

Finding the velocity and setting it equal to 0 results in

$$v(t) = -9.8t + 10 = 0 \Rightarrow 9.8t = 10$$
$$\Rightarrow t = \frac{50}{49} \approx 1.02041$$

The tennis ball reaches its maximum height at $t = 50/49$ seconds, and let's now find that height.

$$s\left(\frac{50}{49}\right) = -4.9\left(\frac{50}{49}\right)^2 + 10\left(\frac{50}{49}\right) + 12 \approx 17.10204 \text{ m}$$

Next, let's find where the ball hits the ground, which means where the position is 0.

$$s(t) = -4.9t^2 + 10t + 12 = 0$$
$$t = \frac{-(10) \pm \sqrt{10^2 - 4(-9.8)(12)}}{2(-4.9)} \approx -1.41664, 3.45745$$

However, we don't need the negative answer since time cannot be negative here. Thus, the tennis ball hits the ground after 3.45745 seconds.

Δ

Epilogue

As if having a Chapter 0 wasn't enough, this math book also has an epilogue!

Congratulations – you have reached the end of my differential calculus notes! It was certainly a lot of material, but I really hope you found my book interesting, useful, and user friendly. I want to thank you for taking the time to buy and read my book, and I welcome any feedback you have about it. Wherever you go in life, I hope the material you learned here helps you pass any exams and other requirements necessary for you to achieve your dreams.

Thank you for allowing me to guide you through this course, and I hope you stick around for integral calculus!

Epilogue

Appendices
The following appendices present content that will be useful for various aspects of differential calculus.

Appendix A – The Unit Circle

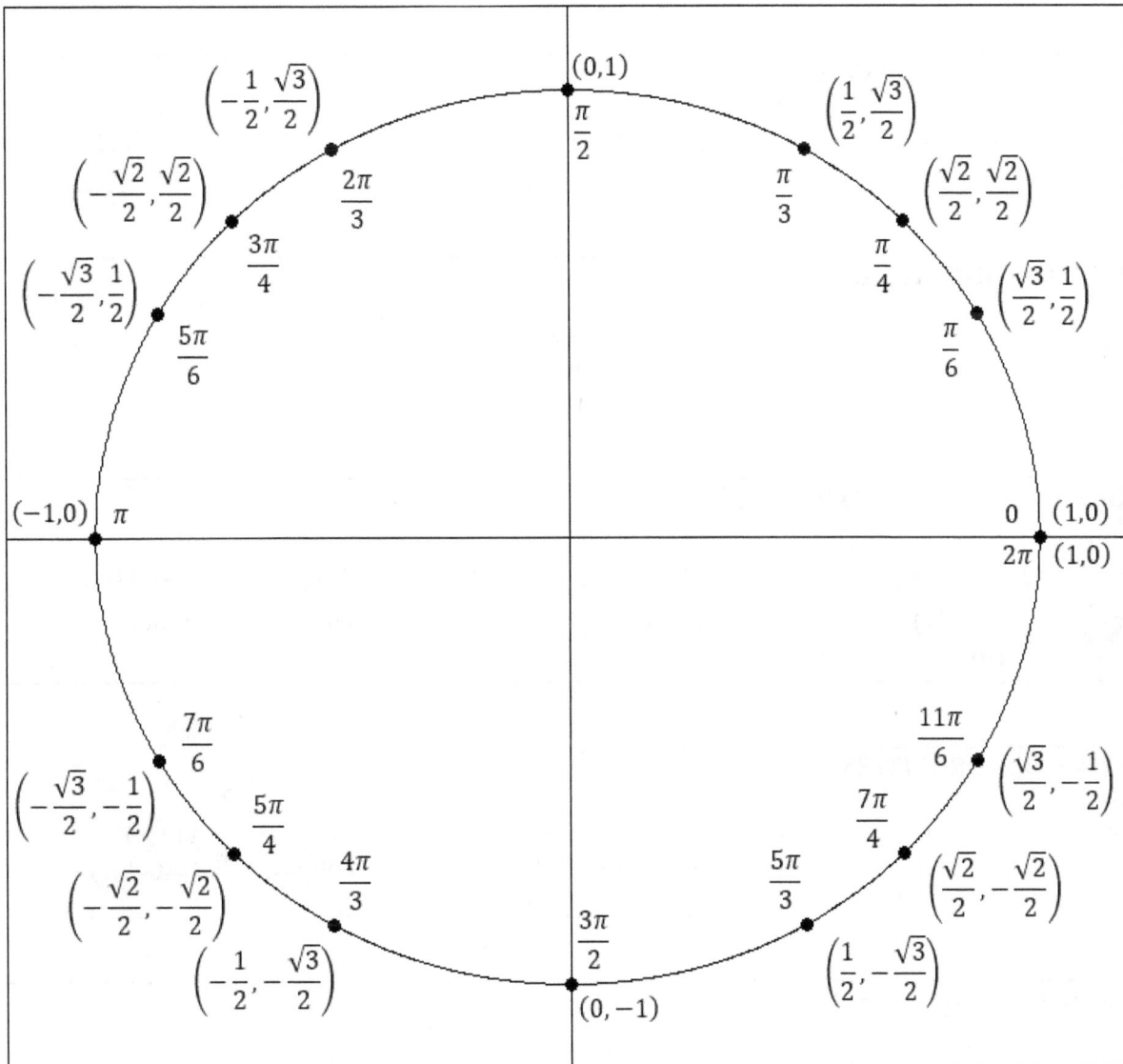

Appendix B – Trigonometric Identities

RECIPROCAL IDENTITIES

$$\sin(x) = \frac{1}{\csc(x)} \qquad \cos(x) = \frac{1}{\sec(x)} \qquad \tan(x) = \frac{1}{\cot(x)}$$

$$\csc(x) = \frac{1}{\sin(x)} \qquad \sec(x) = \frac{1}{\cos(x)} \qquad \cot(x) = \frac{1}{\tan(x)}$$

PYTHAGOREAN IDENTITIES

$$\sin^2(x) + \cos^2(x) = 1 \qquad 1 + \tan^2(x) = \sec^2(x) \qquad 1 + \cot^2(x) = \csc^2(x)$$

QUOTIENT IDENTITIES

$$\tan(x) = \frac{\sin(x)}{\cos(x)} \qquad \cot(x) = \frac{\cos(x)}{\sin(x)}$$

CO-FUNCTION IDENTITIES

$$\sin\left(\frac{\pi}{2} - x\right) = \cos(x) \qquad \cos\left(\frac{\pi}{2} - x\right) = \sin(x) \qquad \tan\left(\frac{\pi}{2} - x\right) = \cot(x)$$

$$\csc\left(\frac{\pi}{2} - x\right) = \sec(x) \qquad \sec\left(\frac{\pi}{2} - x\right) = \csc(x) \qquad \cot\left(\frac{\pi}{2} - x\right) = \tan(x)$$

EVEN-ODD IDENTITIES

$$\sin(-x) = -\sin(x) \qquad \cos(-x) = \cos(x) \qquad \tan(-x) = -\tan(x)$$

$$\csc(-x) = -\csc(x) \qquad \sec(-x) = \sec(x) \qquad \cot(-x) = -\cot(x)$$

SUM-DIFFERENCE FORMULAS

$$\sin(a + b) = \sin(a)\cos(b) + \cos(a)\sin(b) \qquad \tan(a + b) = \frac{\tan(a) + \tan(b)}{1 - \tan(a)\tan(b)}$$

$$\sin(a - b) = \sin(a)\cos(b) - \cos(a)\sin(b) \qquad \tan(a - b) = \frac{\tan(a) - \tan(b)}{1 + \tan(a)\tan(b)}$$

$$\cos(a + b) = \cos(a)\cos(b) - \sin(a)\sin(b)$$

$$\cos(a - b) = \cos(a)\cos(b) + \sin(a)\sin(b)$$

DOUBLE-ANGLE FORMULAS

$\cos(2x) = \cos^2(x) - \sin^2(x)$

$\cos(2x) = 2\cos^2(x) - 1$

$\cos(2x) = 1 - 2\sin^2(x)$

$\sin(2x) = 2\sin(x)\cos(x)$

$\tan(2x) = \frac{2\tan(x)}{1 - \tan^2(x)}$

HALF-ANGLE FORMULAS

$\sin^2(x) = \frac{1 - \cos(2x)}{2}$ $\qquad$ $\cos^2(x) = \frac{1 + \cos(2x)}{2}$ $\qquad$ $\tan^2(x) = \frac{1 - \cos(2x)}{1 + \cos(2x)}$

SUM-TO-PRODUCT FORMULAS

$\sin(a) + \sin(b) = 2\sin\left(\frac{a+b}{2}\right)\cos\left(\frac{a-b}{2}\right)$ $\qquad$ $\sin(a) - \sin(b) = 2\cos\left(\frac{a+b}{2}\right)\sin\left(\frac{a-b}{2}\right)$

$\cos(a) + \cos(b) = 2\cos\left(\frac{a+b}{2}\right)\cos\left(\frac{a-b}{2}\right)$ $\qquad$ $\cos(a) - \cos(b) = -2\sin\left(\frac{a+b}{2}\right)\sin\left(\frac{a-b}{2}\right)$

PRODUCT-TO-SUM FORMULAS

$\sin(a)\sin(b) = \frac{1}{2}[\cos(a-b) - \cos(a+b)]$ $\qquad$ $\cos(a)\cos(b) = \frac{1}{2}[\cos(a-b) + \cos(a+b)]$

$\sin(a)\cos(b) = \frac{1}{2}[\sin(a+b) + \sin(a-b)]$ $\qquad$ $\cos(a)\sin(b) = \frac{1}{2}[\sin(a+b) - \sin(a-b)]$

HYPERBOLIC FUNCTION IDENTITIES

$\sinh(x) = \frac{e^x - e^{-x}}{2}$ $\qquad$ $\cosh(x) = \frac{e^x + e^{-x}}{2}$ $\qquad$ $\tanh(x) = \frac{\sinh(x)}{\cosh(x)}$

$\operatorname{csch}(x) = \frac{1}{\sinh(x)}$ $\qquad$ $\operatorname{sech}(x) = \frac{1}{\cosh(x)}$ $\qquad$ $\coth(x) = \frac{1}{\tanh(x)}$

Appendix C – Derivative Formulas

GENERAL DERIVATIVE FORMULAS

$$f'(x) = \lim_{h \to 0} \frac{f(x+h)-f(x)}{h}$$

$$\frac{d}{dx}(c) = 0$$

$$\frac{d}{dx}(cf(x)) = cf'(x)$$

$$\frac{d}{dx}(f(x) \pm g(x)) = f'(x) \pm g'(x)$$

$$(f^{-1})'(x) = \frac{1}{f'(f^{-1}(x))}$$

$$\frac{d}{dx}(f(x)g(x)) = f(x)g'(x) + f'(x)g(x)$$

$$\frac{d}{dx}\left(\frac{1}{f(x)}\right) = -\frac{f'(x)}{(f(x))^2}$$

$$\frac{d}{dx}\left(\frac{f(x)}{g(x)}\right) = \frac{g(x)f'(x) - f(x)g'(x)}{(g(x))^2}$$

$$\frac{d}{dx}\left(f(g(x))\right) = f'(g(x))g'(x)$$

DERIVATIVES OF POLYNOMIAL, EXPONENTIAL, AND LOG FUNCTIONS

$$\frac{d}{dx}(x^n) = nx^{n-1}$$

$$\frac{d}{dx}(\ln(x)) = \frac{1}{x}$$

$$\frac{d}{dx}(e^x) = e^x$$

$$\frac{d}{dx}(\log_b(x)) = \frac{1}{x\ln(b)}$$

$$\frac{d}{dx}(a^x) = a^x \ln(a)$$

DERIVATIVES OF TRIG FUNCTIONS

$$\frac{d}{dx}(\sin(x)) = \cos(x)$$

$$\frac{d}{dx}(\cot(x)) = -\csc^2(x)$$

$$\frac{d}{dx}(\cos(x)) = -\sin(x)$$

$$\frac{d}{dx}(\sec(x)) = \sec(x)\tan(x)$$

$$\frac{d}{dx}(\tan(x)) = \sec^2(x)$$

$$\frac{d}{dx}(\csc(x)) = -\csc(x)\cot(x)$$

DERIVATIVES OF INVERSE TRIG FUNCTIONS

$$\frac{d}{dx}(\arcsin(x)) = \frac{1}{\sqrt{1-x^2}} \quad \text{for } -1 < x < 1$$

$$\frac{d}{dx}(\arctan(x)) = \frac{1}{1+x^2} \quad \text{for } -\infty < x < \infty$$

$$\frac{d}{dx}(\text{arcsec}(x)) = \frac{1}{|x|\sqrt{x^2-1}} \quad \text{for } |x| > 1$$

$$\frac{d}{dx}(\arccos(x)) = -\frac{1}{\sqrt{1-x^2}} \quad \text{for } -1 < x < 1$$

$$\frac{d}{dx}(\text{arccot}(x)) = -\frac{1}{1+x^2} \quad \text{for } -\infty < x < \infty$$

$$\frac{d}{dx}(\text{arccsc}(x)) = -\frac{1}{|x|\sqrt{x^2-1}} \quad \text{for } |x| > 1$$

DERIVATIVES OF HYPERBOLIC FUNCTIONS

$$\frac{d}{dx}(\sinh(x)) = \cosh(x)$$

$$\frac{d}{dx}(\coth(x)) = -\text{csch}^2(x)$$

$$\frac{d}{dx}(\cosh(x)) = \sinh(x)$$

$$\frac{d}{dx}(\text{sech}(x)) = -\text{sech}(x)\tanh(x)$$

$$\frac{d}{dx}(\tanh(x)) = \text{sech}^2(x)$$

$$\frac{d}{dx}(\text{csch}(x)) = -\text{csch}(x)\coth(x)$$

DERIVATIVES OF INVERSE HYPERBOLIC FUNCTIONS

$\frac{d}{dx}(\text{arcsinh}(x)) = \frac{1}{\sqrt{1+x^2}}$ for $-\infty < x < \infty$ $\frac{d}{dx}(\text{arccosh}(x)) = \frac{1}{\sqrt{x^2-1}}$ for $1 < x < \infty$

$\frac{d}{dx}(\text{arctanh}(x)) = \frac{1}{1-x^2}$ for $-1 < x < 1$ $\frac{d}{dx}(\text{arccoth}(x)) = \frac{1}{1-x^2}$ for $|x| > 1$

$\frac{d}{dx}(\text{arcsech}(x)) = -\frac{1}{x\sqrt{1-x^2}}$ for $0 < x < 1$ $\frac{d}{dx}(\text{arccsch}(x)) = -\frac{1}{|x|\sqrt{1+x^2}}$ for $x \neq 0$

Appendix D – Antiderivative Formulas

There are plenty of additional antiderivative formulas, but the ones below are what were presented in Chapter 5. For more formulas, I'll see you in integral calculus!

COMMON ANTIDERIVATIVES / INTEGRALS

$\int a\,dx = ax + C$ $\int ax^n dx = \frac{ax^{n+1}}{n+1} + C, n \neq -1$ $\int \frac{a}{x}\,dx = a\ln|x| + C$

$\int e^{ax} dx = \frac{e^{ax}}{a} + C$ $\int \sin(ax)\,dx = -\frac{\cos(ax)}{a} + C$ $\int \cos(ax)\,dx = \frac{\sin(ax)}{a} + C$

Appendix E – Physics, Parametric, and Polar Formulas

PHYSICS FORMULAS

Position $= s(t)$

Velocity $= v(t)$ $\qquad v(t) = s'(t)$

Acceleration $= a(t)$ $\qquad a(t) = v'(t) = s''(t)$

Speed $= |v(t)|$

$s(t) = \int v(t)dt$

$v(t) = \int a(t)dt$

VECTOR-VALUED FUNCTIONS

Position Vector $= s(t) = \langle x(t), y(t)\rangle$ $\qquad$ Acceleration Vector $= a(t) = \langle x''(t), y''(t)\rangle$

Velocity Vector $= v(t) = \langle x'(t), y'(t)\rangle$ $\qquad$ Speed $= \sqrt{\left(x'(t)\right)^2 + \left(y'(t)\right)^2}$

PARAMETRIC FUNCTIONS

Define a parametric curve to have x-coordinate $x(t)$ and y-coordinate $y(t)$.

$$\frac{dy}{dx} = \frac{y'(t)}{x'(t)} \qquad\qquad \frac{d^2y}{dx^2} = \frac{\frac{d}{dt}\left(\frac{dy}{dx}\right)}{\frac{dx}{dt}} = \frac{x'(t)\cdot y''(t) - y'(t)\cdot x''(t)}{\left(x'(t)\right)^3}$$

POLAR FUNCTIONS

Cartesian to Polar Coordinates

$r = \sqrt{x^2 + y^2}$

$\tan(\theta) = \frac{y}{x}$

Polar to Cartesian Coordinates

$x = r\cos(\theta)$

$y = r\sin(\theta)$

Define a polar curve at angle θ to have x-coordinate $x(\theta) = r(\theta)\cos(\theta)$ and y-coordinate $y(\theta) = r(\theta)\sin(\theta)$.

$$\frac{dy}{dx} = \frac{y'(\theta)}{x'(\theta)} = \frac{r'(\theta)\sin(\theta) + r(\theta)\cos(\theta)}{r'(\theta)\cos(\theta) - r(\theta)\sin(\theta)} \qquad \frac{d^2y}{dx^2} = \frac{\frac{d}{d\theta}\left(\frac{dy}{dx}\right)}{\frac{dx}{d\theta}} = \frac{x'(\theta)\cdot y''(\theta) - y'(\theta)\cdot x''(\theta)}{\left(x'(\theta)\right)^3}$$

Appendix F – Various Algebra and Geometry Formulas

FORMULAS INVOLVING TRIANGLES

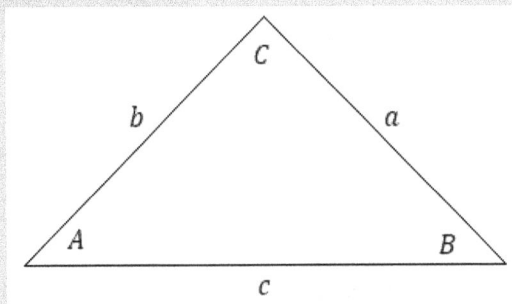

LAW OF SINES

$$\frac{\sin(A)}{a} = \frac{\sin(B)}{b} = \frac{\sin(C)}{c}$$
$$\frac{a}{\sin(A)} = \frac{b}{\sin(B)} = \frac{c}{\sin(C)}$$

LAW OF COSINES

$$a^2 = b^2 + c^2 - 2bc\cos(A)$$
$$b^2 = a^2 + c^2 - 2ac\cos(B)$$
$$c^2 = a^2 + b^2 - 2ab\cos(C)$$

PYTHAGOREAN THEOREM

$a^2 = b^2 + c^2$ where a is hypotenuse

AREA OF A TRIANGLE

$$\text{Area} = \frac{1}{2}ab\sin(C)$$
$$\text{Area} = \frac{1}{2}ac\sin(B)$$
$$\text{Area} = \frac{1}{2}bc\sin(A)$$

HERON'S FORMULA

$$\text{Area} = \sqrt{s(s-a)(s-b)(s-c)} \text{ with } s = \frac{a+b+c}{2}$$

DISTANCE FORMULA

$$d = \sqrt{(x_2 - x_1)^2 + (y_2 - y_1)^2}$$

MIDPOINT FORMULA

$$\left(\frac{x_1+x_2}{2}, \frac{y_1+y_2}{2}\right)$$

PROPERTIES OF NATURAL LOGS

$$\ln(ab) = \ln(a) + \ln(b)$$
$$\ln\left(\frac{a}{b}\right) = \ln(a) - \ln(b)$$

$$\ln(a^k) = k\ln(a)$$
$$\ln\left(\frac{1}{a}\right) = -\ln(a)$$

$$\ln(1) = 0$$
$$\ln(e) = 1$$

PROPERTIES OF EXPONENTIALS

$$a^{k+l} = a^k a^l$$
$$\left(a^k\right)^l = \left(a^l\right)^k = a^{kl}$$

$$a^{-k} = \frac{1}{a^k}$$
$$(ab)^k = a^k b^k$$

BINOMIAL EXPANSION

$n! = n(n-1)(n-2)\cdots 3\cdot 2\cdot 1$

$\binom{n}{k} = \frac{n!}{(n-k)!k!}$

$(a+b)^n = \binom{n}{0}a^n b^0 + \binom{n}{1}a^{n-1}b^1 + \binom{n}{2}a^{n-2}b^2 + \cdots + \binom{n}{n-1}a^1 b^{n-1} + \binom{n}{n}a^0 b^n$

2-D OBJECTS

SQUARE
Area $= s^2$

PARALLELOGRAM
Area $= lw$

TRIANGLE
Area $= \frac{1}{2}bh$

CIRCLE
Area $= \pi r^2$
Circumference $= 2\pi r$

RECTANGLE
Area $= lw$

3-D OBJECTS

CUBE
Surface Area $= 6s^2$
Volume $= s^3$

SPHERE
Surface Area $= 4\pi r^2$
Volume $= \frac{4}{3}\pi r^3$

RECTANGULAR PRISM
S. Area $= 2lw + 2lh + 2wh$
Volume $= lwh$

CYLINDER (RIGHT)
Surface Area $= 2\pi r^2 + 2\pi rh$
Volume $= \pi r^2 h$

CONE (RIGHT)
Surface Area $= \pi r^2 + \pi rs$ where s is slant height
Volume $= \frac{1}{3}\pi r^2 h$

Appendix G – TI-84 Commands

The following boxes are repeats of what was shown earlier in this book.

CONVERTING DECIMALS TO FRACTIONS

Suppose you have a decimal answer on your screen and wish to turn it into a fraction if possible. Calculus problems usually prefer exact answers rather than decimal answers when possible, unless it's an answer that can only be found using a calculator or computer and not by hand.

With a decimal answer already on the screen, press MATH and under the first menu (MATH), select Option 1: ▷ Frac. Press ENTER, and if possible, the calculator will convert the answer to a fraction.

π AND e

To type π on the home screen, press 2nd and ^ . To type e, press 2nd and ÷ , but if you want to compute e raised to a specific exponent (such as e^x), press 2nd and LN .

RADIAN MODE

To make sure your calculator is in **radian mode**, press MODE and scroll to the third line that says RADIAN and DEGREE. If RADIAN is already highlighted, you are all set. If DEGREE is highlighted, move the cursor over RADIAN and press ENTER. You can then leave the MODE menu by pressing 2nd and MODE, which is the QUIT command. (In the unlikely event you need to do a problem in **degree mode**, do the same instructions but select DEGREE instead.)

GRAPHING FUNCTIONS

To graph a function, press Y = and type the function next to the first line, $\backslash Y_1 =$. If you have more functions to type, enter them on the subsequent lines. Now press GRAPH, and the function will appear on the graph.

If you need to adjust the viewing window, press WINDOW and enter the values you think are best. Then press GRAPH, and the function will be drawn using the new window dimensions.

$$Xmin = \text{lower bound for the } x \text{ values appearing on the graph}$$
$$Xmax = \text{upper bound for the } x \text{ values appearing on the graph}$$
$$Xscl = \text{axis increment for the } x \text{ values}$$
$$Ymin = \text{lower bound for the } y \text{ values appearing on the graph}$$
$$Ymax = \text{upper bound for the } y \text{ values appearing on the graph}$$
$$Yscl = \text{axis increment for the } y \text{ values}$$

To clarify, if $Xscl = 1$, that means that the "tick marks" on the x-axis are spaced apart by 1 unit each (for instance, going from 0 to 1 to 2 and so on through 10). If $Xscl = \pi/4$, then the tick marks would appear at $0, \pi/4, \pi/2, 3\pi/4, \pi$, etc., and similarly for $Yscl$.

If you want to reset the window to the automatic convention without manually typing in those numbers, press ZOOM and choose Option 6: $ZStandard$. Doing so will automatically graph the function over $-10 \leq x \leq 10$ and $-10 \leq y \leq 10$, with both axis increments equal to 1.

FINDING ROOTS OF A FUNCTION

To find an x-value at which a function $f(x) = 0$, first press $\boxed{Y =}$ and type the function next to Y_1. Adjust the window as necessary, and press $\boxed{GRAPH}$. If the window is appropriate, you will see the function and the general area at which it crosses the x-axix.

Next, press $\boxed{2nd}$ and $\boxed{TRACE}$ to go to the CALC menu. Select Option 2: $zero$, and you'll return to the graph. The calculator says "Left Bound?", so type a guess and press $\boxed{ENTER}$. The calculator then says "Right Bound?", so type a guess and press $\boxed{ENTER}$ again. Finally, the calculator says "Guess?", so type an x-value that looks to be close to the root and press $\boxed{ENTER}$. The calculator then shows you the approximate x-coordinate of the root.

FINDING INTERSECTION POINTS OF TWO FUNCTIONS

To find the x-values at which two functions $f(x)$ and $g(x)$ intersect, first press $\boxed{Y =}$ and type the two functions next to Y_1 and Y_2. Adjust the window as necessary, and press $\boxed{GRAPH}$. If the window is appropriate, you will see the two functions and the general area at which they intersect.

Next, press $\boxed{2nd}$ and $\boxed{TRACE}$ to go to the CALC menu. Select Option 5: $intersect$, and you'll return to the graph. The calculator says "First curve?", and press $\boxed{ENTER}$. The calculator then says "Second curve?", and press $\boxed{ENTER}$ again. Finally, the calculator says "Guess?", so type an x-value that looks to be close to the intersection point and press $\boxed{ENTER}$. The calculator then shows you the approximate (x, y) coordinates.

FINDING DERIVATIVES AT SPECIFIC POINTS

To find the slope of the tangent line at a specific point $x = a$ on the function $f(x)$, press $MATH$ and choose Option 8: $nDeriv($. Type the following:

$$nDeriv(f(x), x, a)$$

In other words, you type the function in terms of x followed by a comma, then type x and a comma, and finally type the point a of interest.

GRAPHING PARAMETRIC CURVES

First press $\boxed{MODE}$ and scroll down to the fourth line. The usual setting is FUNC, but now scroll right to PAR and press $\boxed{ENTER}$. Press $\boxed{2nd}$ and $\boxed{MODE}$ to go back to the home screen. Doing so changes the calculator's setting to Parametric Mode. (If you want to go back to graphing ordinary functions for other problems, return to this menu and switch back to FUNC mode.)

Now press $\boxed{Y =}$, and you can type in a function for X_{1T} and another for Y_{1T} (and more parametric curves if necessary). Note that pressing the $\boxed{X, T, \theta, n}$ button for your input variable now shows as T. Press $\boxed{WINDOW}$, and in addition to the usual plotting options you now have options for $Tmin$, $Tmax$, and $Tstep$. These are, respectively, the starting time, the ending time, and the increment you wish to use to go from start to finish.

Adjust your X and Y windows accordingly, and press $\boxed{GRAPH}$. You will see the parametric function traced out, and pressing $\boxed{TRACE}$ allows you to trace the curve and figure out the direction of motion.

GRAPHING POLAR CURVES

First press MODE and scroll down to the fourth line. The usual setting is FUNC, but now scroll right to POL and press ENTER. Press 2nd and MODE to go back to the home screen. Doing so changes the calculator's setting to Polar Mode. (If you want to go back to graphing ordinary functions for other problems, return to this menu and switch back to FUNC mode.)

Now press Y =, and you can type in a function for r_1 (and more polar curves if necessary). Note that pressing the X, T, θ, n button for your input variable now shows as θ. Press WINDOW, and in addition to the usual plotting options you now have options for θmin, θmax, and $\theta step$. These are, respectively, the starting angle, the ending angle, and the increment you wish to use to go from start to finish.

Adjust your X and Y windows accordingly, and press GRAPH. You will see the polar function traced out, and pressing TRACE allows you to trace the curve and figure out the direction of motion.

Appendix H – The Greek Alphabet

Just like the English alphabet, the Greek alphabet has uppercase and lowercase letters. The following table shows the 24 letters as uppercase and lowercase, along with how to pronounce them in English. Note that lowercase "sigma" has two different forms: σ is most commonly used in mathematics as a symbol. When writing in Greek, if "sigma" appears at the end of a word, the ς form is used instead.

Uppercase	Lowercase	English	Pronunciation
A	α	Alpha	AL-fa
B	β	Beta	BAY-ta
Γ	γ	Gamma	GAM-ma
Δ	δ	Delta	DEL-ta
E	ε	Epsilon	EP-si-lon
Z	ζ	Zeta	ZAY-ta or ZEE-ta
H	η	Eta	ZT-ta or EE-ta
Θ	θ	Theta	THAY-ta or THEE-ta
I	ι	Iota	EYE-o-ta
K	κ	Kappa	KAP-pa
Λ	λ	Lambda	LAMB-da
M	μ	Mu	MYOO
N	ν	Nu	NYOO
Ξ	ξ	Xi	ZAI or KSAI
O	o	Omicron	OM-ay-cron or oh-MY-cron
Π	π	Pi	PIE
P	ρ	Rho	ROW
Σ	σ or ς	Sigma	SIG-ma
T	τ	Tau	TAU
Υ	υ	Upsilon	OOPS-i-lon
Φ	ϕ	Phi	FAI
X	χ	Chi	KAI
Ψ	ψ	Psi	PSAI or SIGH
Ω	ω	Omega	Oh-MEG-a or OH-meg-a